TSUBASA

18

CLAMP

TRANSLATED AND ADAPTED BY
William Flanagan

LETTERED BY
Dana Hayward

BALLANTINE BOOKS • NEW YORK

A Del Rey Manga/Kodansha Trade Paperback Original

Tsubasa, volume 18 copyright © 2007 by CLAMP
English translation copyright © 2008 by CLAMP

Published in the United States by Del Rey Books, an imprint of The Random House Publishing Group, a division of Random House, Inc., New York.

DEL REY is a registered trademark and the Del Rey colophon is a trademark of Random House, Inc.

Publication rights arranged through Kodansha Ltd.

First published in Japan in 2007 by Kodansha Ltd., Tokyo

ISBN 978-0-345-50409-8

Printed in the United States of America

www.delreymanga.com

9 8 7 6 5 4 3 2

Translator/Adapter—William Flanagan
Lettering—Dana Hayward

Contents

Tsubasa crosses over with *xxxHOLiC*. Although it isn't necessary to read *xxxHOLiC* to understand the events in *Tsubasa*, you'll get to see the same events from different perspectives if you read both series!

Honorifics Explained

Throughout the Del Rey Manga books, you will find Japanese honorifics left intact in the translations. For those not familiar with how the Japanese use honorifics and, more important, how they differ from American honorifics, we present this brief overview.

Politeness has always been a critical facet of Japanese culture. Ever since the feudal era, when Japan was a highly stratified society, use of honorifics—which can be defined as polite speech that indicates relationship or status—has played an essential role in the Japanese language. When you address someone in Japanese, an honorific usually takes the form of a suffix attached to one's name (example: "Asuna-san"), is used as a title at the end of one's name, or appears in place of the name itself (example: "Negi-sensei," or simply "Sensei!").

Honorifics can be expressions of respect or endearment. In the context of manga and anime, honorifics give insight into the nature of the relationship between characters. Many English translations leave out these important honorifics and therefore distort the feel of the original Japanese. Because Japanese honorifics contain nuances that English honorifics lack, it is our policy at Del Rey not to translate them. Here, instead, is a guide to some of the honorifics you may encounter in Del Rey Manga.

-san: This is the most common honorific and is equivalent to Mr., Miss, Ms., or Mrs. It is the all-purpose honorific and can be used in any situation where politeness is required.

-sama: This is one level higher than "-san" and is used to confer great respect.

-dono: This comes from the word "tono," which means "lord." It is an even higher level than "-sama" and confers utmost respect.

-kun: This suffix is used at the end of boys' names to express familiarity or endearment. It is also sometimes used by men among friends, or when addressing someone younger or of a lower station.

-chan: This is used to express endearment, mostly toward girls. It is also used for little boys, pets, and even among lovers. It gives a sense of childish cuteness.

Bozu: This is an informal way to refer to a boy, similar to the English terms "kid" and "squirt."

Sempai/Senpai: This title suggests that the addressee is one's senior in a group or organization. It is most often used in a school setting, where underclassmen refer to their upperclassmen as "sempai." It can also be used in the workplace, such as when a newer employee addresses an employee who has seniority in the company.

Kohai: This is the opposite of "sempai" and is used toward underclassmen in school or newcomers in the workplace. It connotes that the addressee is of a lower station.

Sensei: Literally meaning "one who has come before," this title is used for teachers, doctors, or masters of any profession or art.

-[blank]: This is usually forgotten in these lists, but it is perhaps the most significant difference between Japanese and English. The lack of honorific means that the speaker has permission to address the person in a very intimate way. Usually, only family, spouses, or very close friends have this kind of permission. Known as *yobisute*, it can be gratifying when someone who has earned the intimacy starts to call one by one's name without an honorific. But when that intimacy hasn't been earned, it can be very insulting.

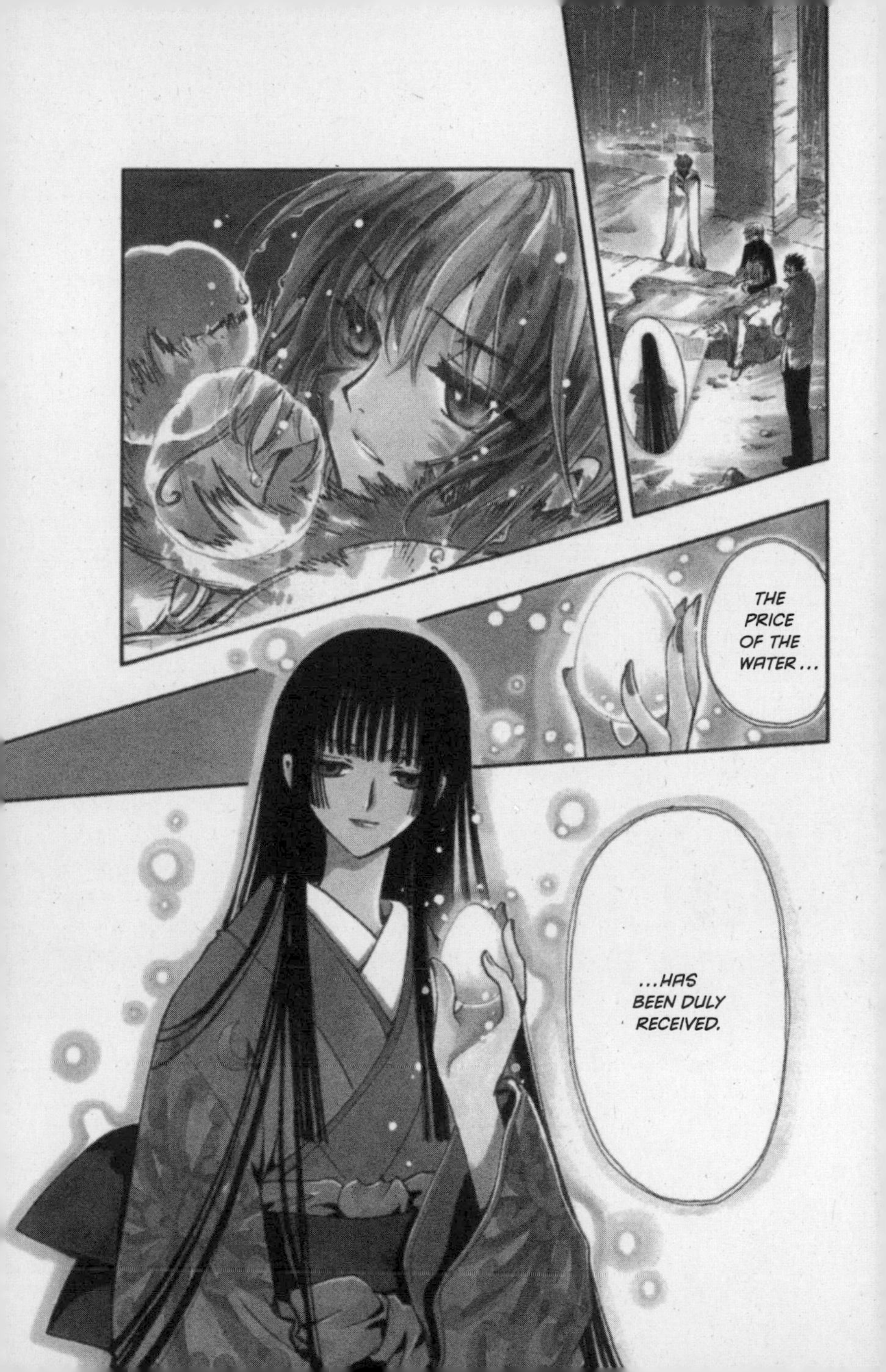
THE PRICE OF THE WATER...
...HAS BEEN DULY RECEIVED.

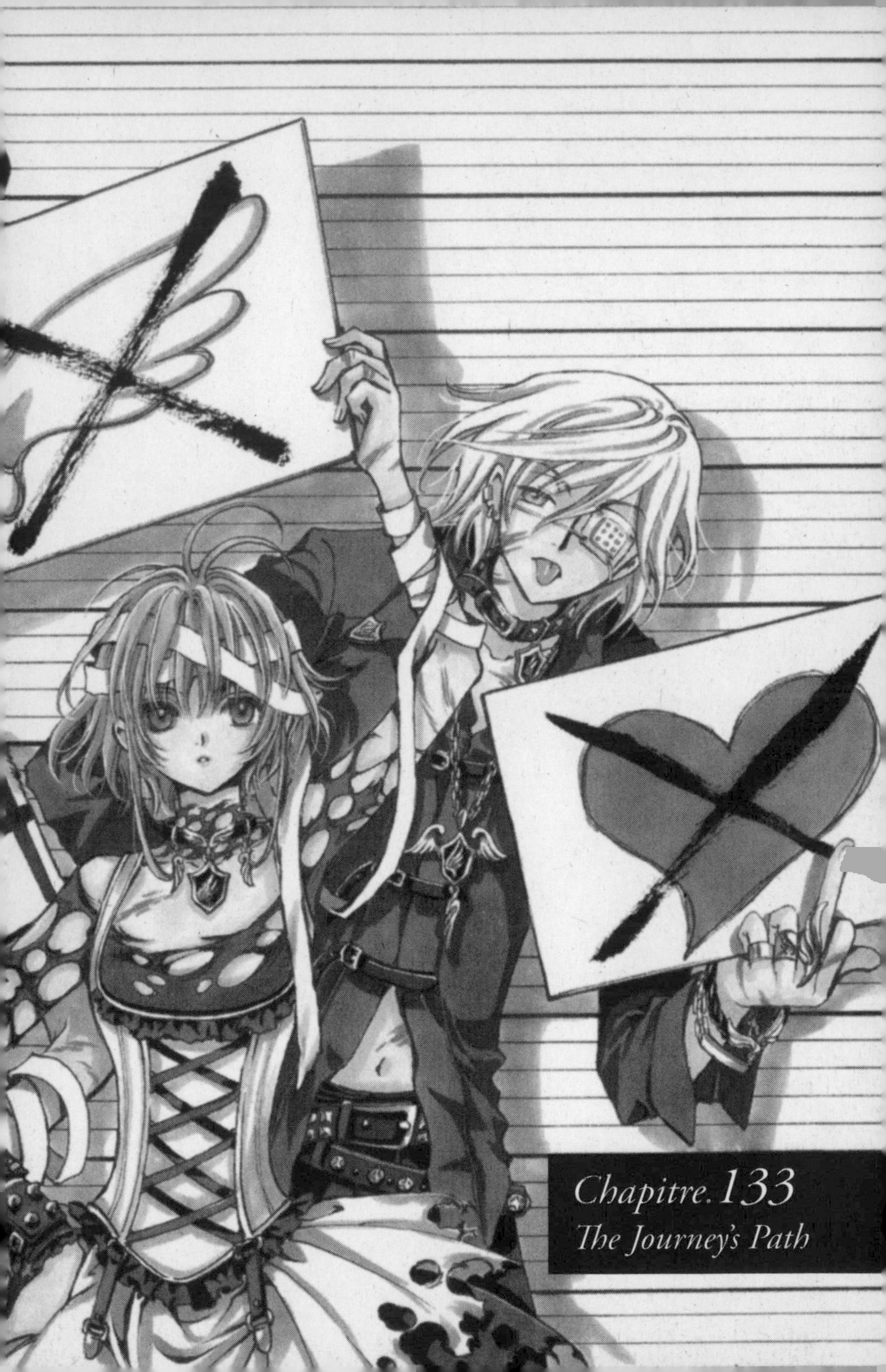
Chapitre.133
The Journey's Path

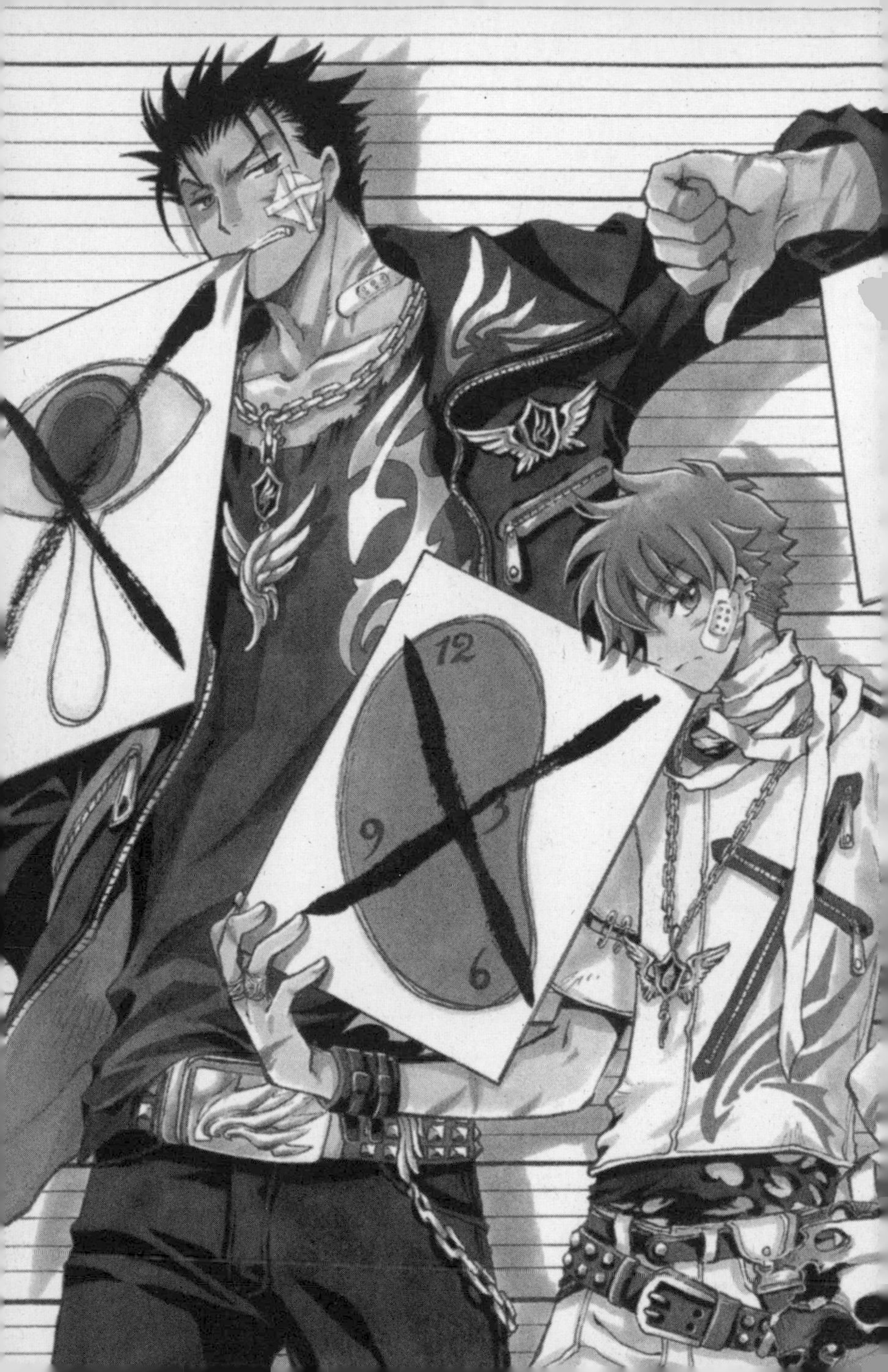

ツバサ
RESERVoir CHRoNiCLE

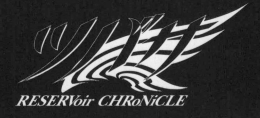

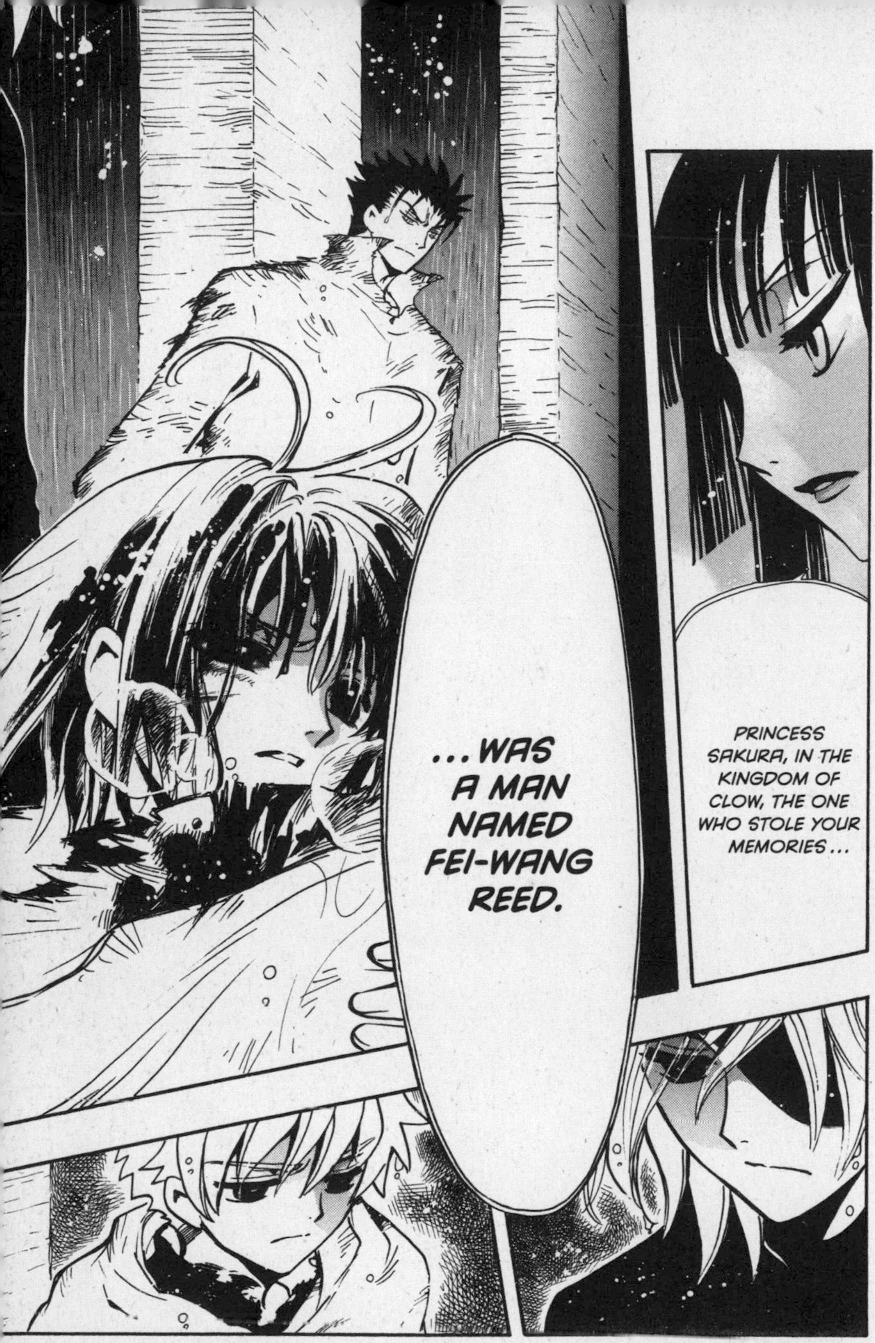
PRINCESS SAKURA, IN THE KINGDOM OF CLOW, THE ONE WHO STOLE YOUR MEMORIES...
...WAS A MAN NAMED FEI-WANG REED.

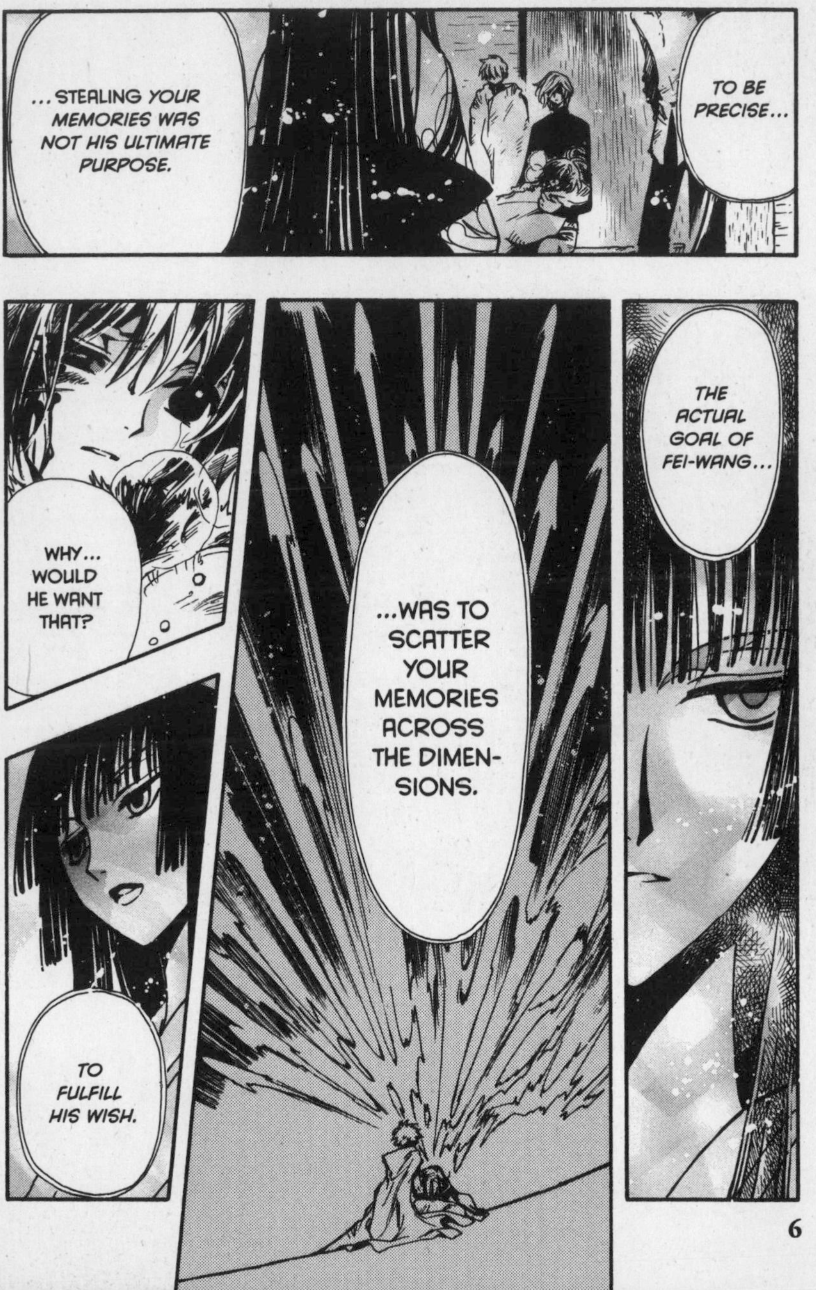
TO BE PRECISE...
...STEALING YOUR MEMORIES WAS NOT HIS ULTIMATE PURPOSE.
THE ACTUAL GOAL OF FEI-WANG...
...WAS TO SCATTER YOUR MEMORIES ACROSS THE DIMENSIONS.
WHY... WOULD HE WANT THAT?
TO FULFILL HIS WISH.

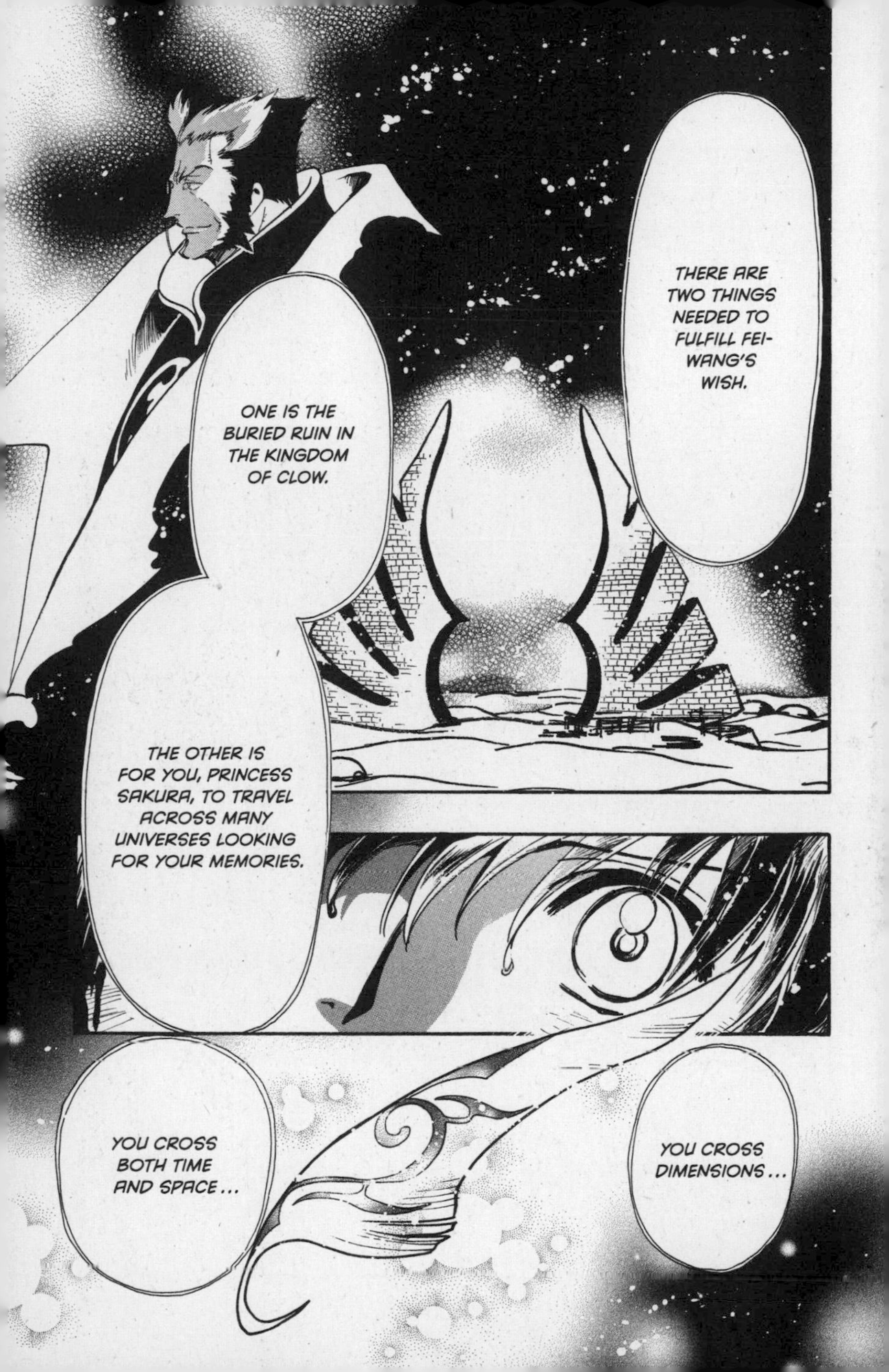
THERE ARE TWO THINGS NEEDED TO FULFILL FEI-WANG'S WISH.
ONE IS THE BURIED RUIN IN THE KINGDOM OF CLOW.
THE OTHER IS FOR YOU, PRINCESS SAKURA, TO TRAVEL ACROSS MANY UNIVERSES LOOKING FOR YOUR MEMORIES.
YOU CROSS DIMENSIONS...
YOU CROSS BOTH TIME AND SPACE...

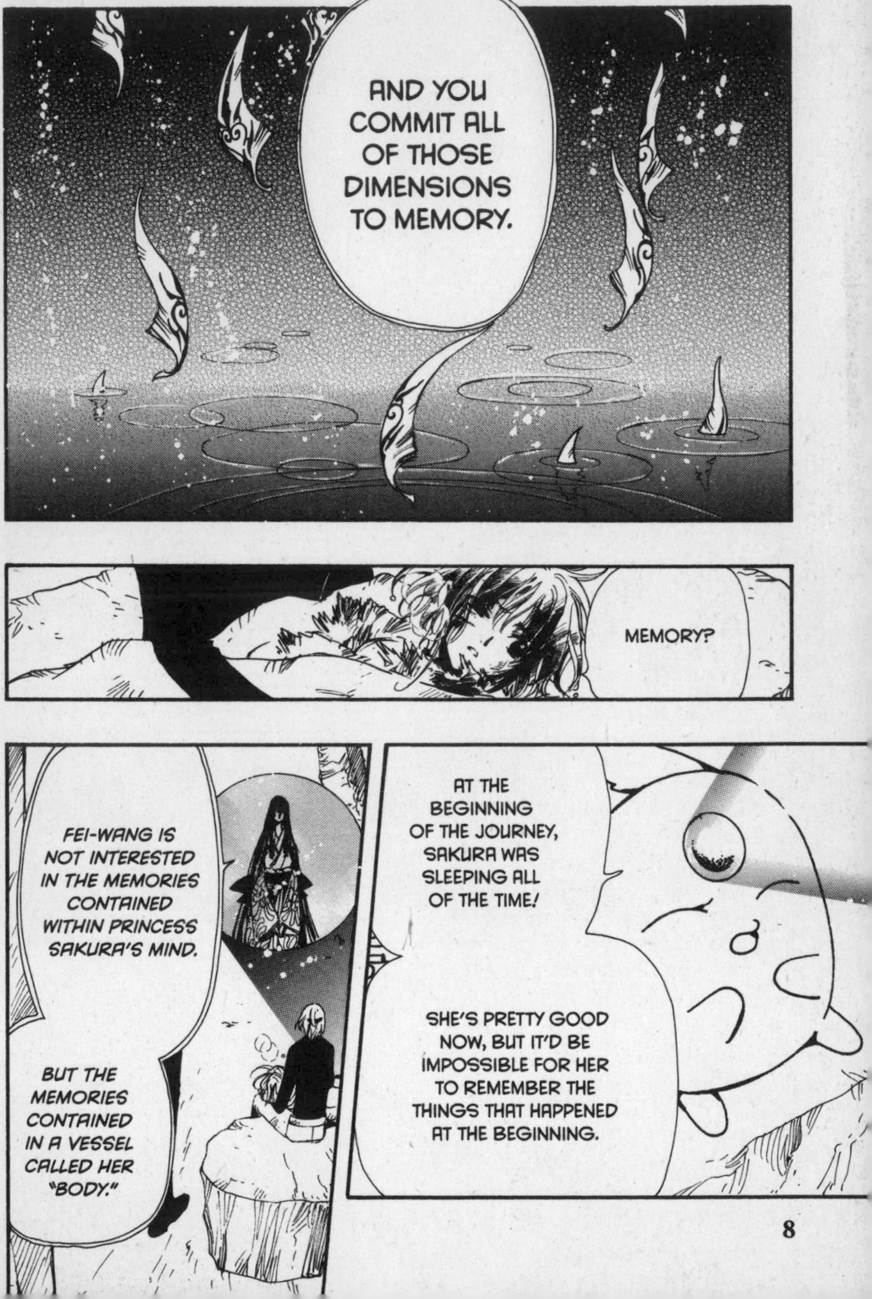
AND YOU COMMIT ALL OF THOSE DIMENSIONS TO MEMORY.
MEMORY?
AT THE BEGINNING OF THE JOURNEY, SAKURA WAS SLEEPING ALL OF THE TIME!
SHE'S PRETTY GOOD NOW, BUT IT'D BE IMPOSSIBLE FOR HER TO REMEMBER THE THINGS THAT HAPPENED AT THE BEGINNING.
FEI-WANG IS NOT INTERESTED IN THE MEMORIES CONTAINED WITHIN PRINCESS SAKURA'S MIND.
BUT THE MEMORIES CONTAINED IN A VESSEL CALLED HER "BODY."

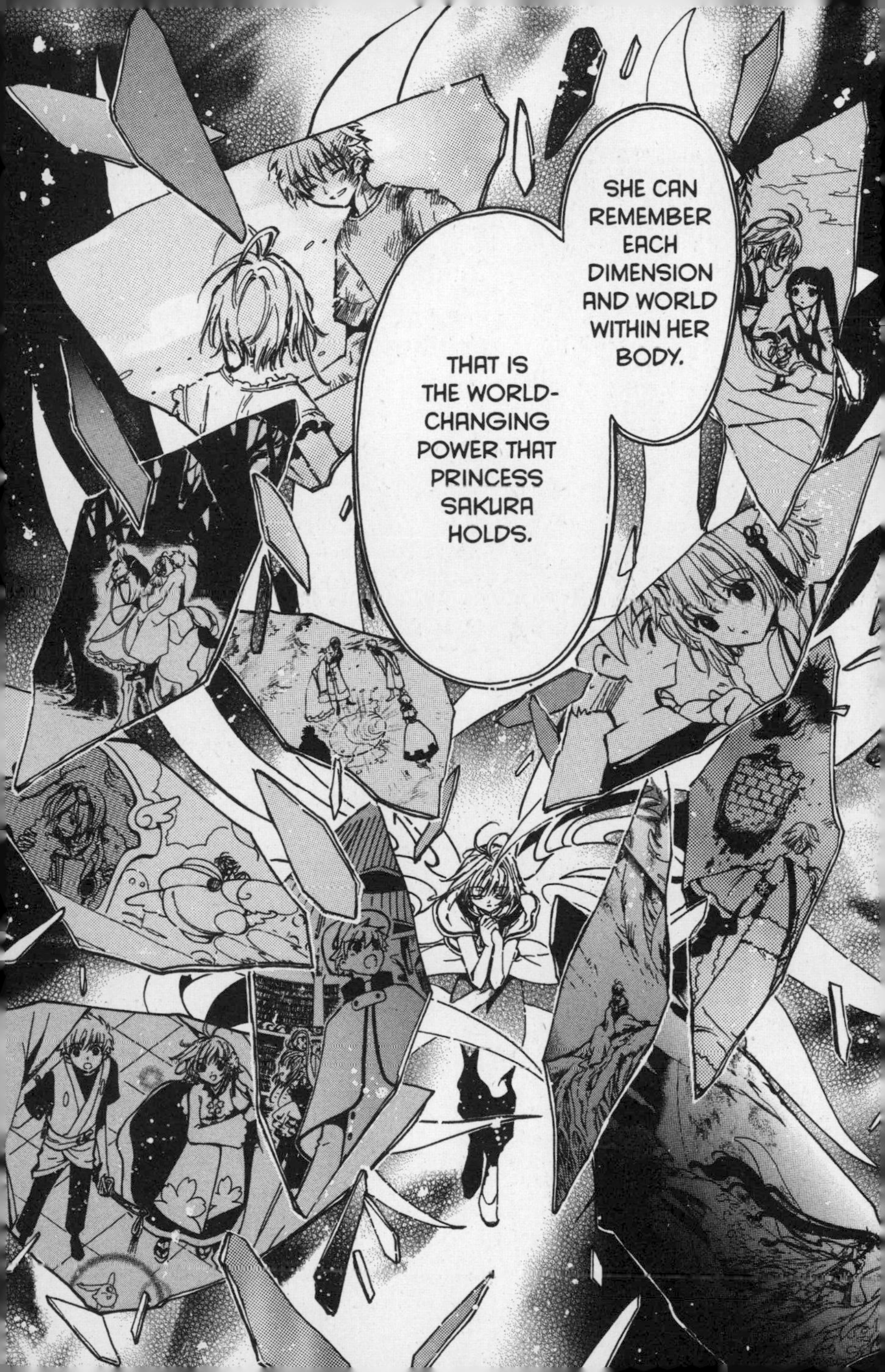
SHE CAN REMEMBER EACH DIMENSION AND WORLD WITHIN HER BODY.
THAT IS THE WORLD-CHANGING POWER THAT PRINCESS SAKURA HOLDS.

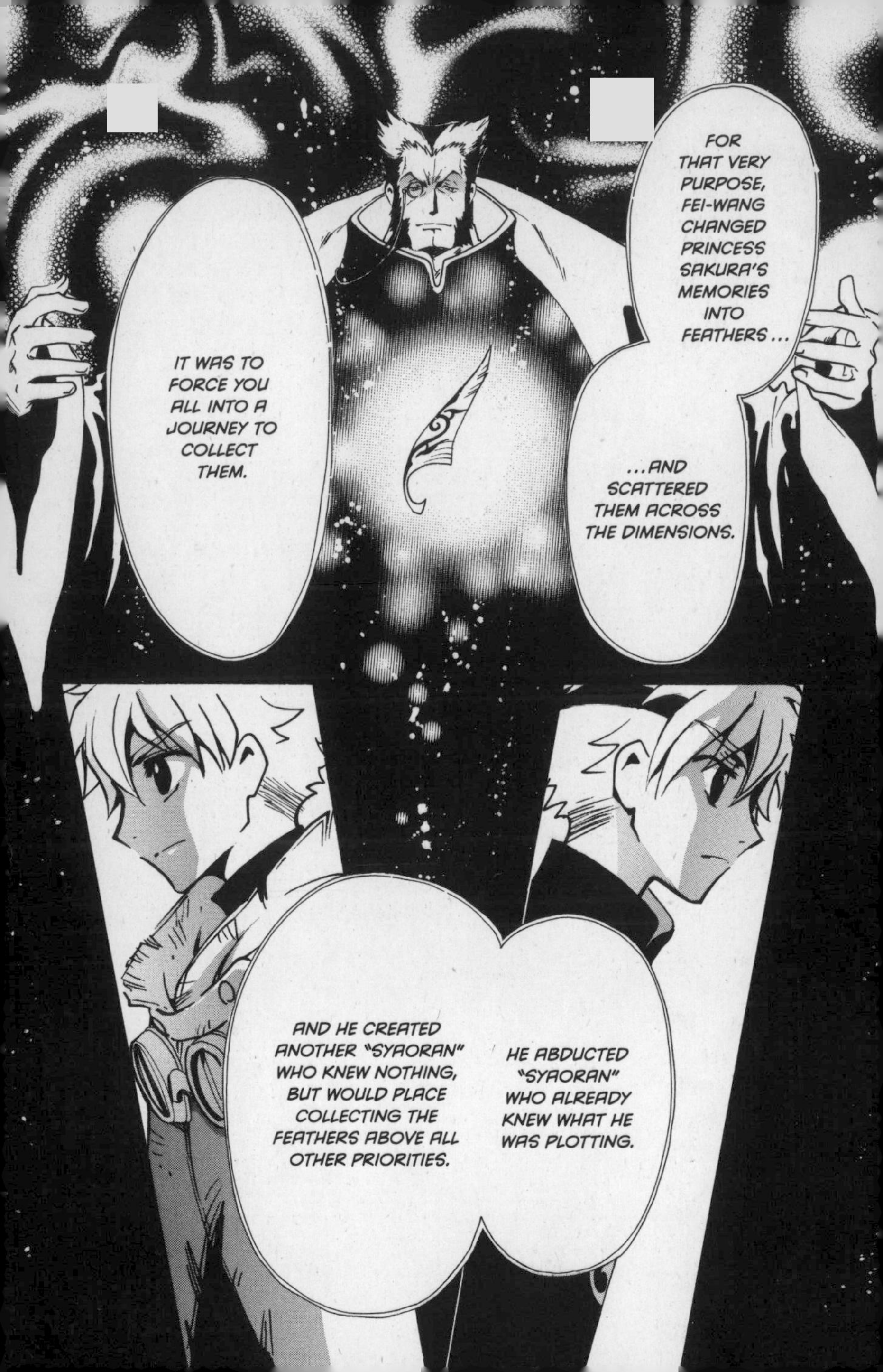
FOR THAT VERY PURPOSE, FEI-WANG CHANGED PRINCESS SAKURA'S MEMORIES INTO FEATHERS...
...AND SCATTERED THEM ACROSS THE DIMENSIONS.
IT WAS TO FORCE YOU ALL INTO A JOURNEY TO COLLECT THEM.
HE ABDUCTED "SYAORAN" WHO ALREADY KNEW WHAT HE WAS PLOTTING.
AND HE CREATED ANOTHER "SYAORAN" WHO KNEW NOTHING, BUT WOULD PLACE COLLECTING THE FEATHERS ABOVE ALL OTHER PRIORITIES.

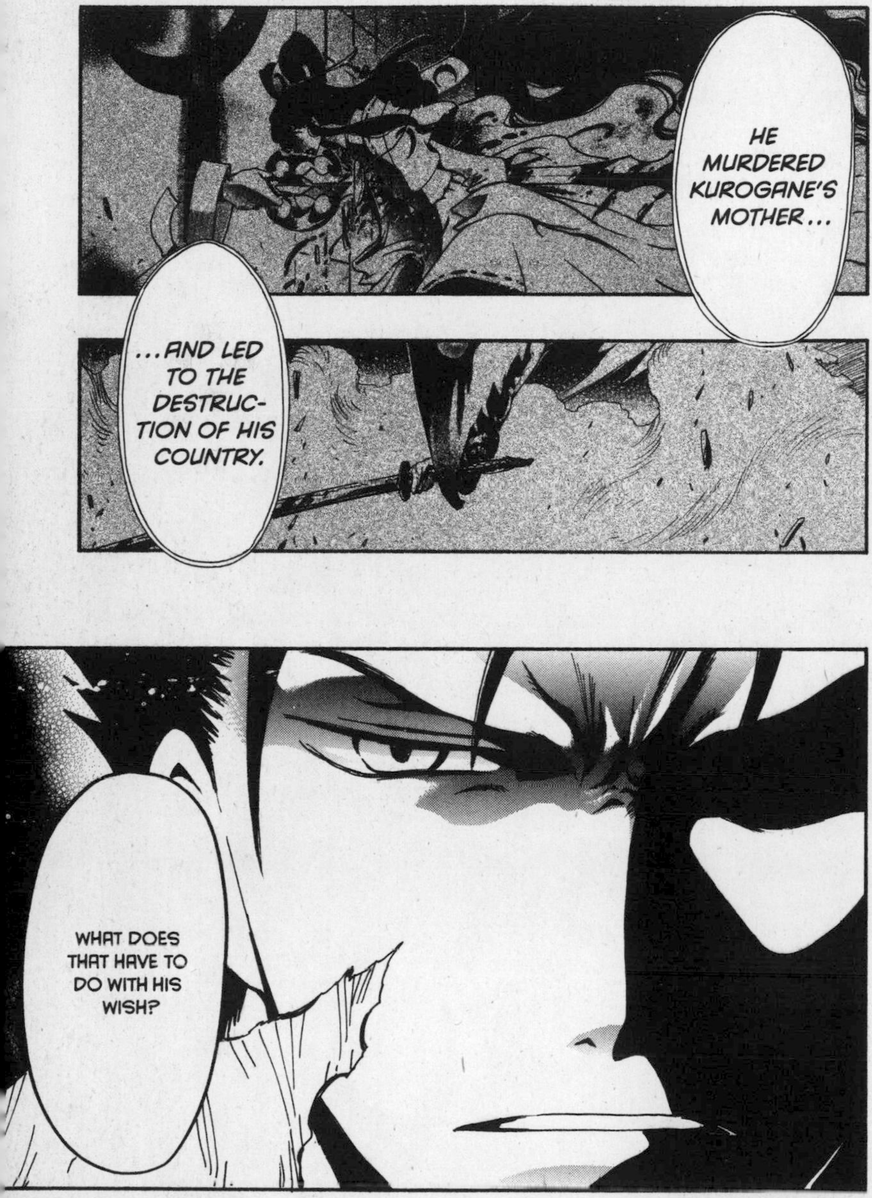
HE MURDERED KUROGANE'S MOTHER...
...AND LED TO THE DESTRUCTION OF HIS COUNTRY.
WHAT DOES THAT HAVE TO DO WITH HIS WISH?

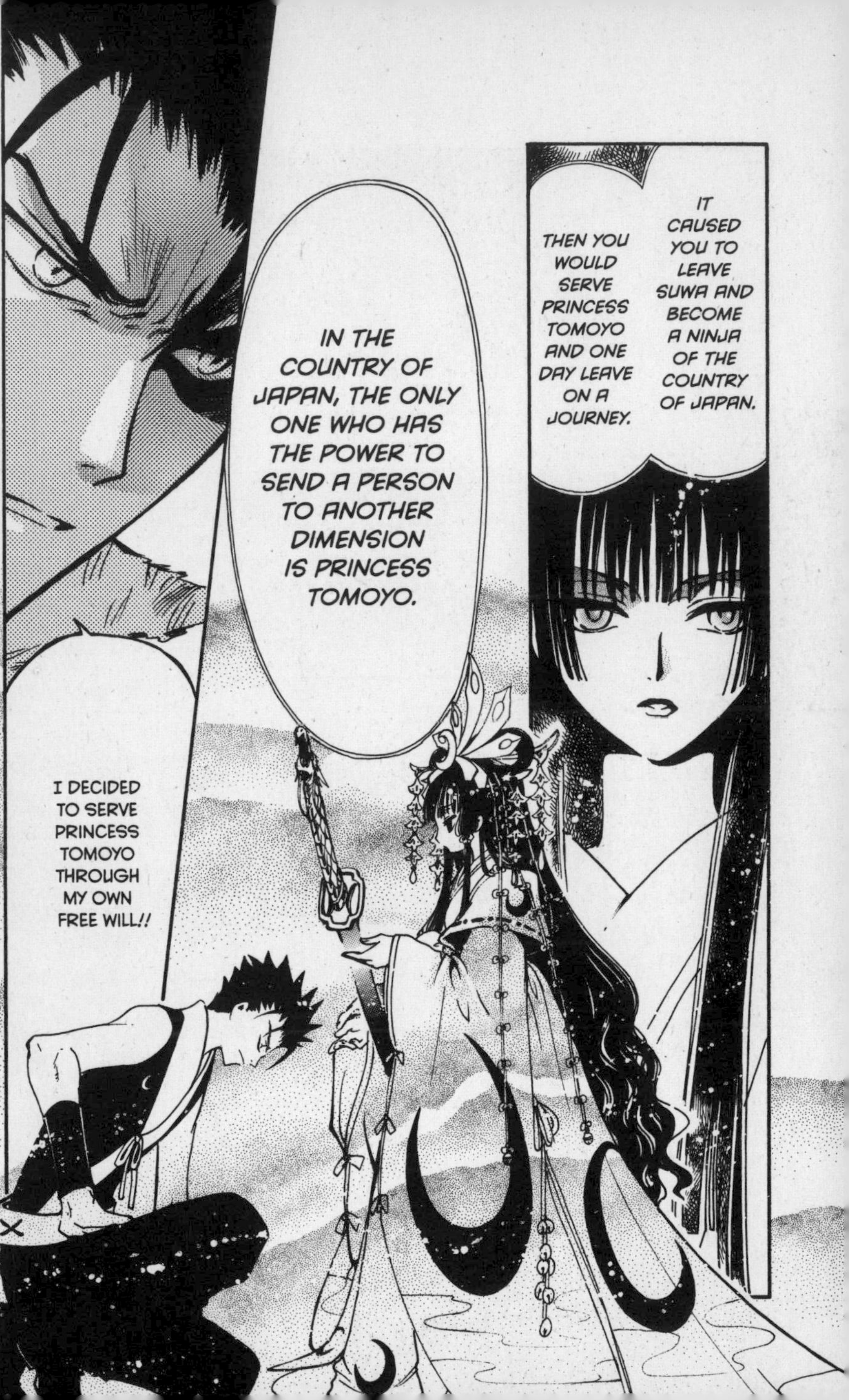
IT CAUSED YOU TO LEAVE SUWA AND BECOME A NINJA OF THE COUNTRY OF JAPAN.
THEN YOU WOULD SERVE PRINCESS TOMOYO AND ONE DAY LEAVE ON A JOURNEY.
IN THE COUNTRY OF JAPAN, THE ONLY ONE WHO HAS THE POWER TO SEND A PERSON TO ANOTHER DIMENSION IS PRINCESS TOMOYO.
I DECIDED TO SERVE PRINCESS TOMOYO THROUGH MY OWN FREE WILL!!

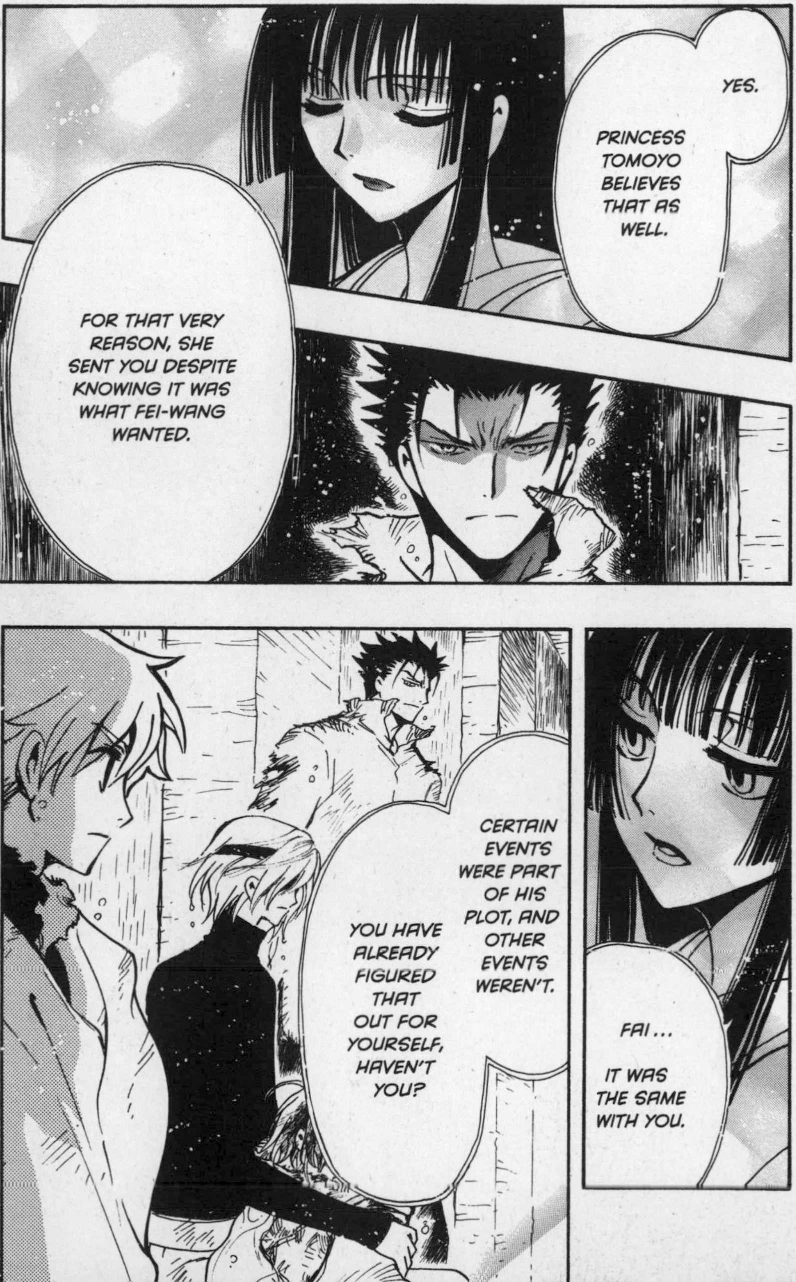
YES.
PRINCESS TOMOYO BELIEVES THAT AS WELL.
FOR THAT VERY REASON, SHE SENT YOU DESPITE KNOWING IT WAS WHAT FEI-WANG WANTED.
FAI... IT WAS THE SAME WITH YOU.
CERTAIN EVENTS WERE PART OF HIS PLOT, AND OTHER EVENTS WEREN'T.
YOU HAVE ALREADY FIGURED THAT OUT FOR YOURSELF, HAVEN'T YOU?

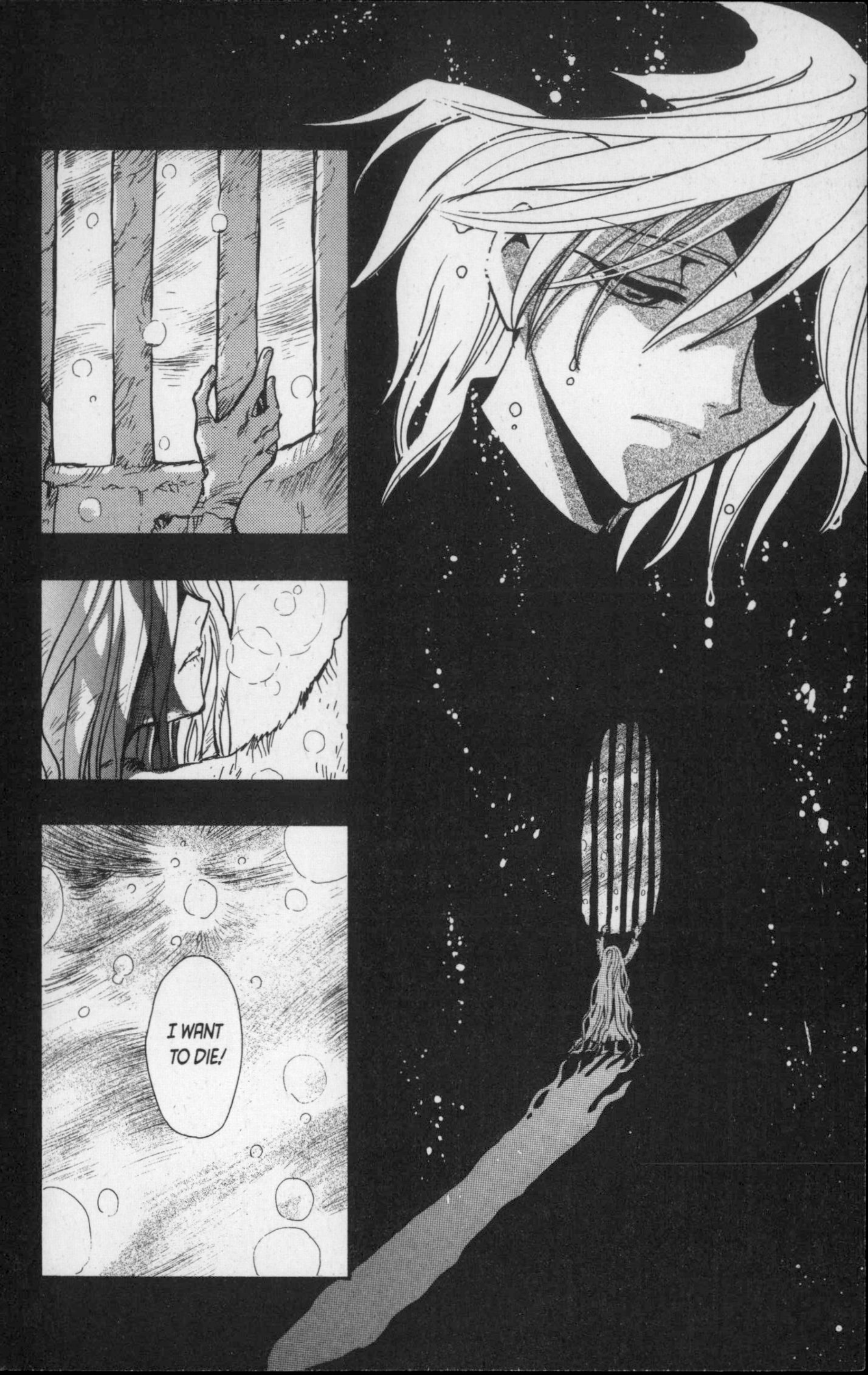
I WANT TO DIE!

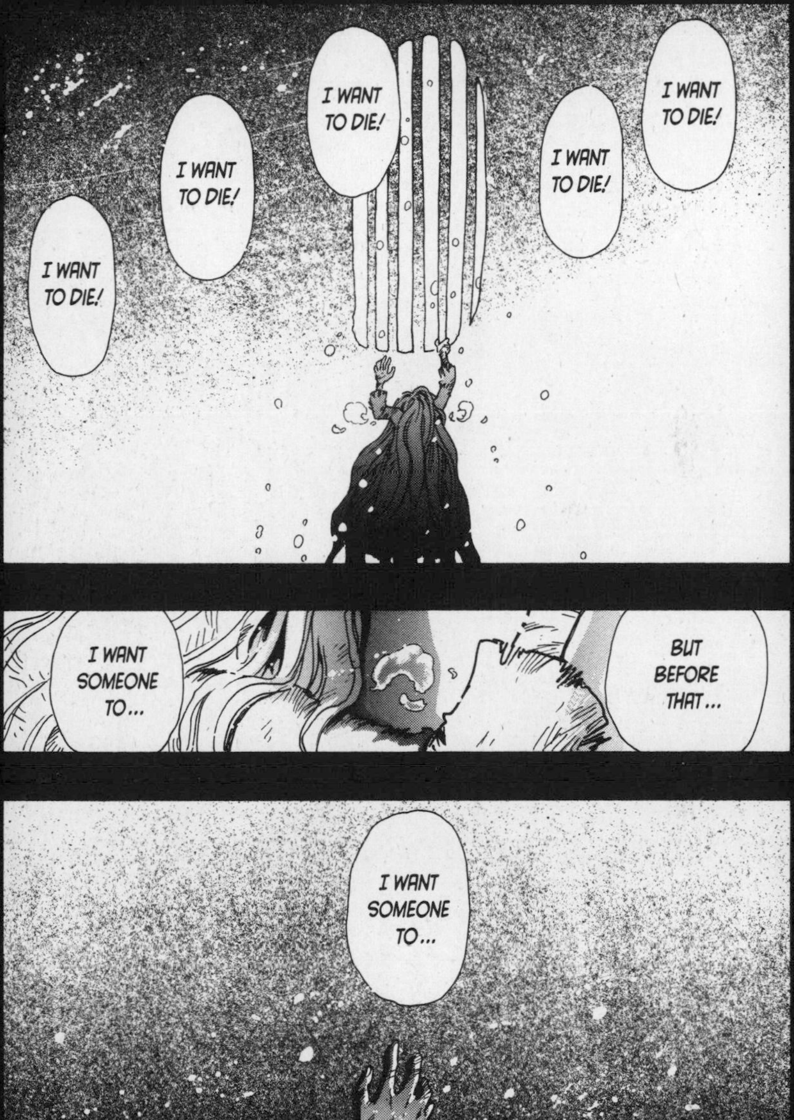
I WANT TO DIE!
I WANT TO DIE!
I WANT TO DIE!
I WANT TO DIE!
I WANT TO DIE!
BUT BEFORE THAT...
I WANT SOMEONE TO...
I WANT SOMEONE TO...

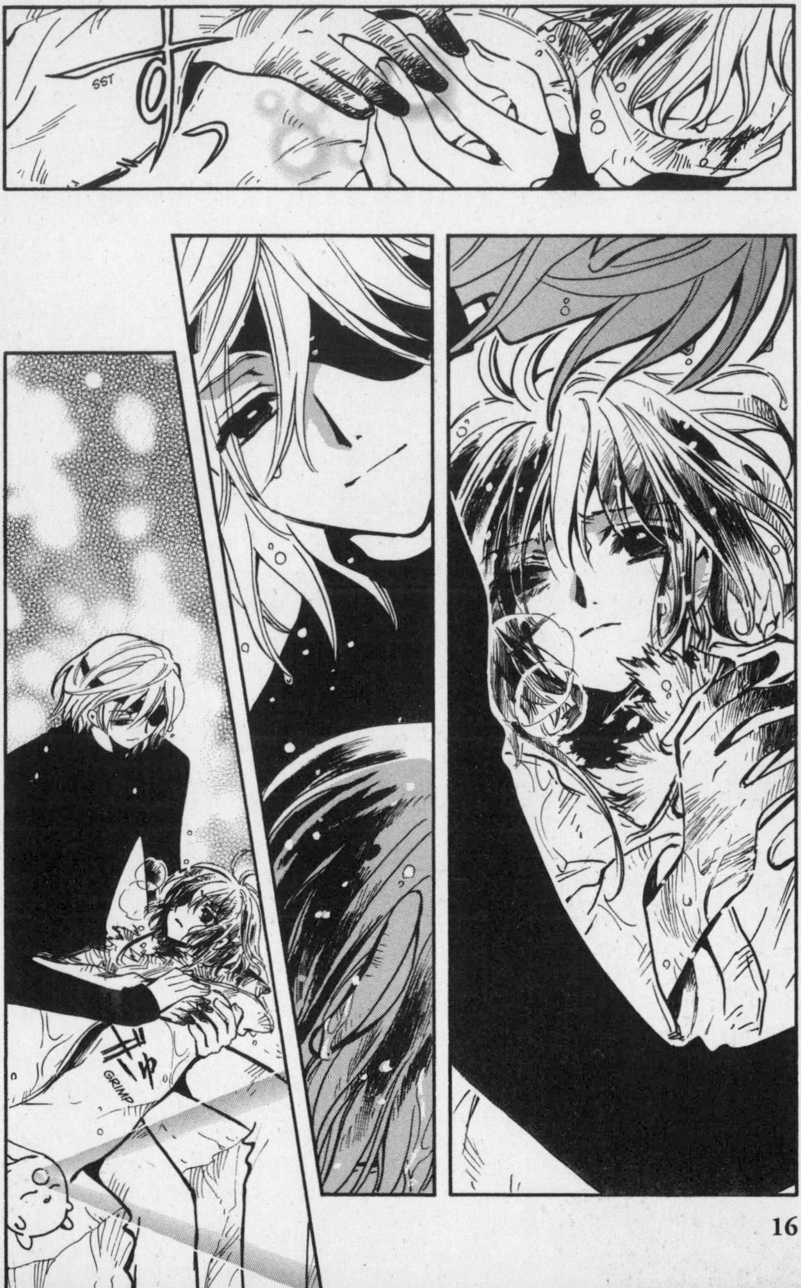
SST
GRIMP

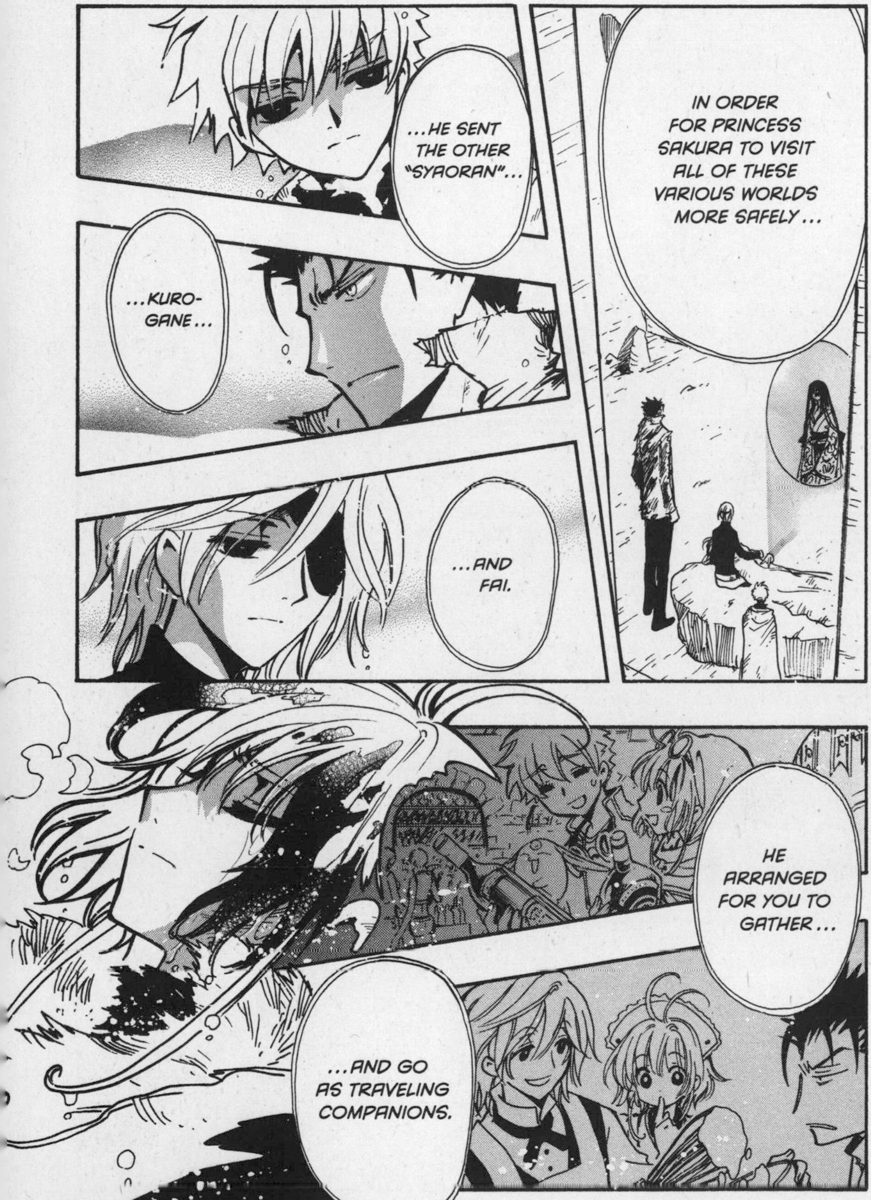
IN ORDER FOR PRINCESS SAKURA TO VISIT ALL OF THESE VARIOUS WORLDS MORE SAFELY...
...HE SENT THE OTHER "SYAORAN"...
...KURO-GANE...
...AND FAI.
HE ARRANGED FOR YOU TO GATHER...
...AND GO AS TRAVELING COMPANIONS.

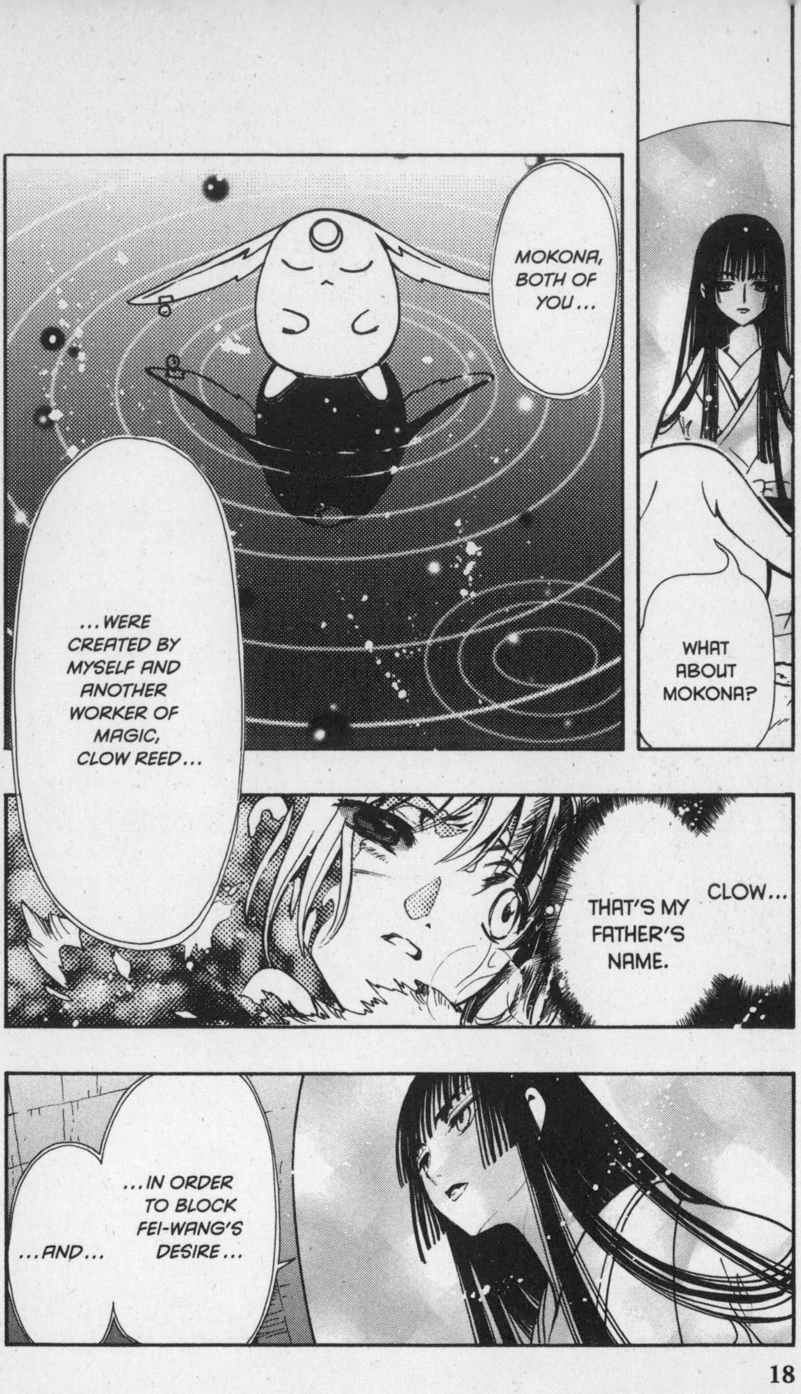
WHAT ABOUT MOKONA?
MOKONA, BOTH OF YOU...
...WERE CREATED BY MYSELF AND ANOTHER WORKER OF MAGIC, CLOW REED...
CLOW...
THAT'S MY FATHER'S NAME.
...IN ORDER TO BLOCK FEI-WANG'S DESIRE...
...AND...

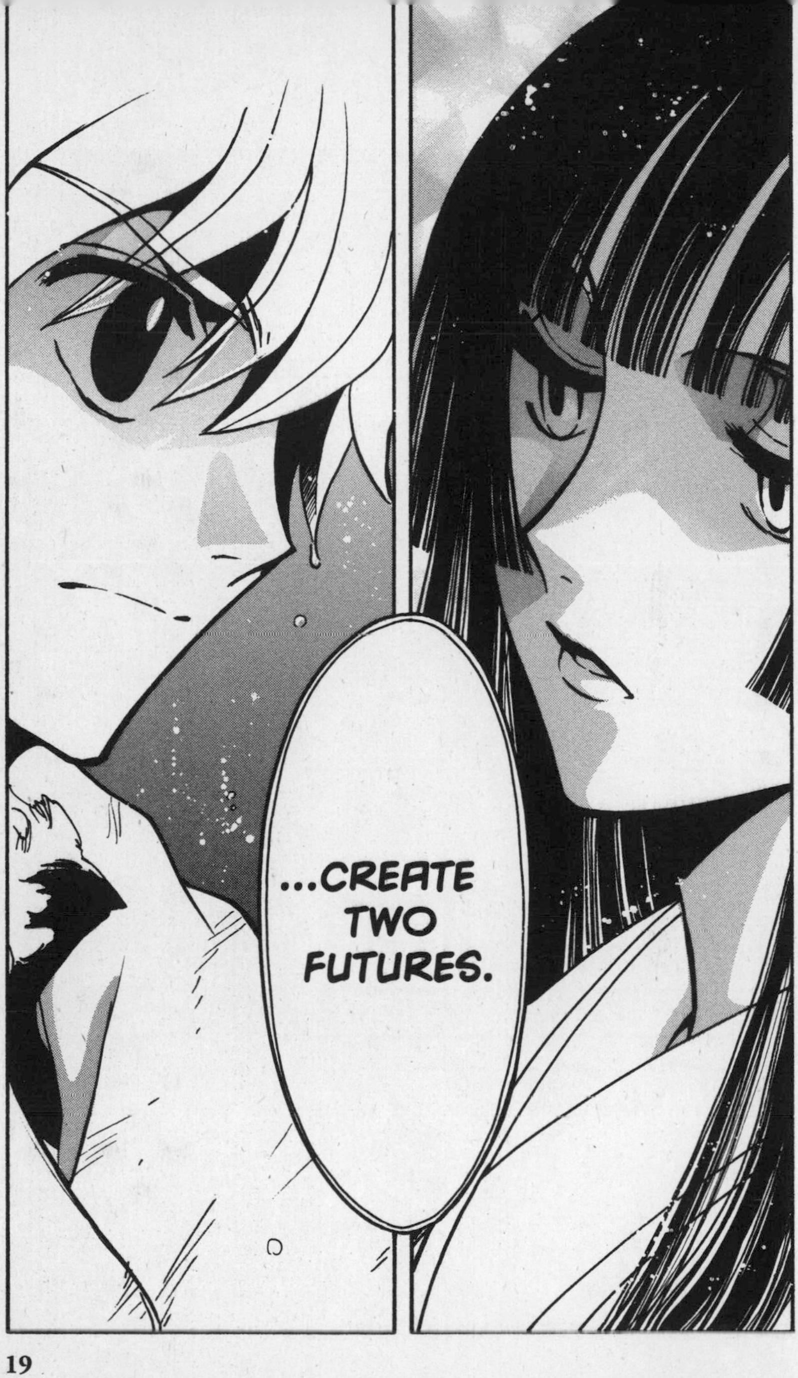
...CREATE TWO FUTURES.

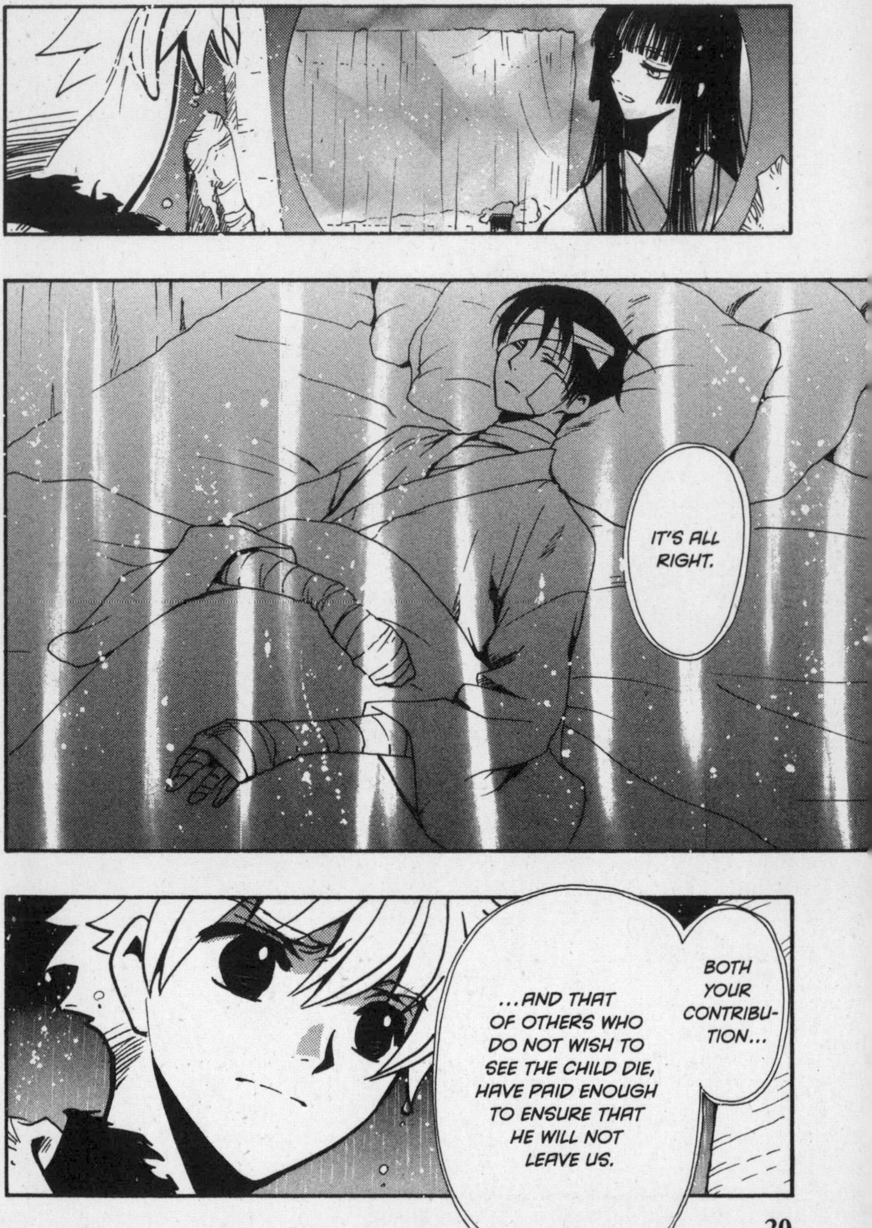
IT'S ALL RIGHT.
BOTH YOUR CONTRIBUTION...
...AND THAT OF OTHERS WHO DO NOT WISH TO SEE THE CHILD DIE, HAVE PAID ENOUGH TO ENSURE THAT HE WILL NOT LEAVE US.

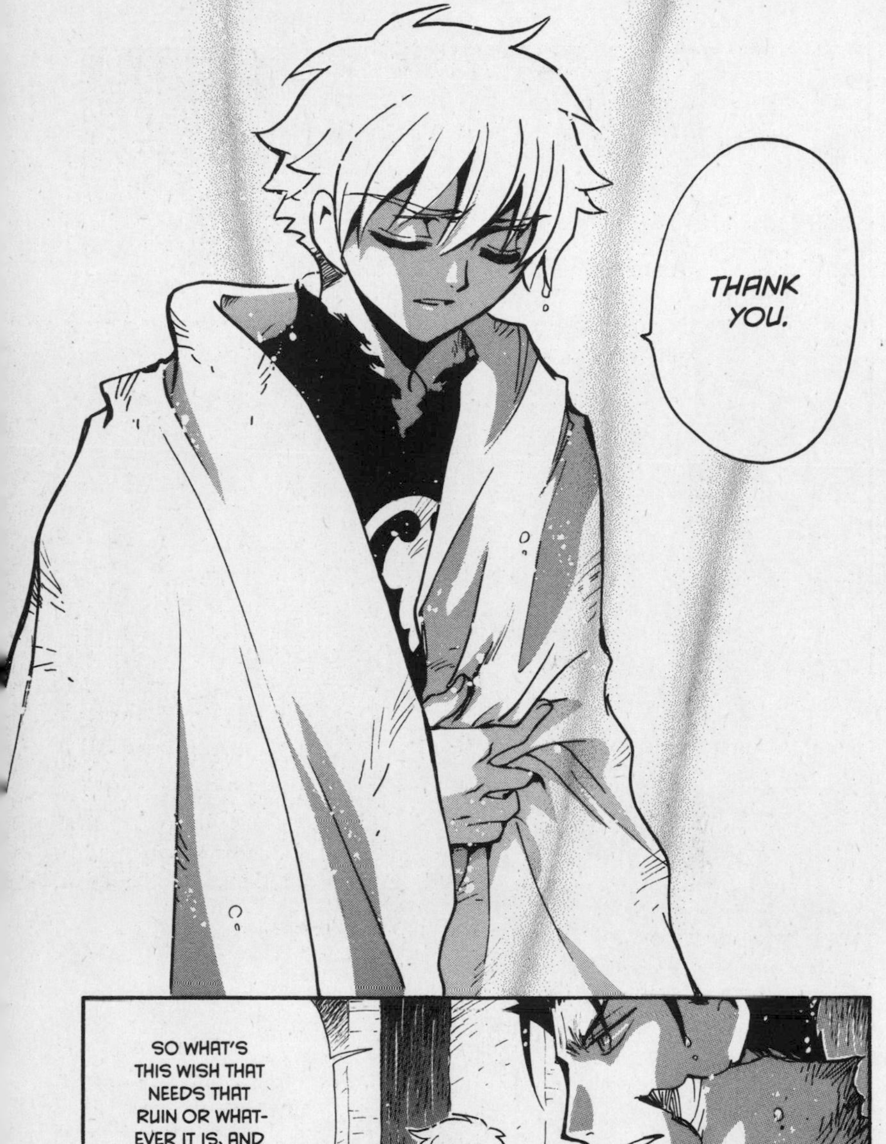
THANK YOU.
SO WHAT'S THIS WISH THAT NEEDS THAT RUIN OR WHATEVER IT IS, AND THE PRINCESS'S MEMORIES?

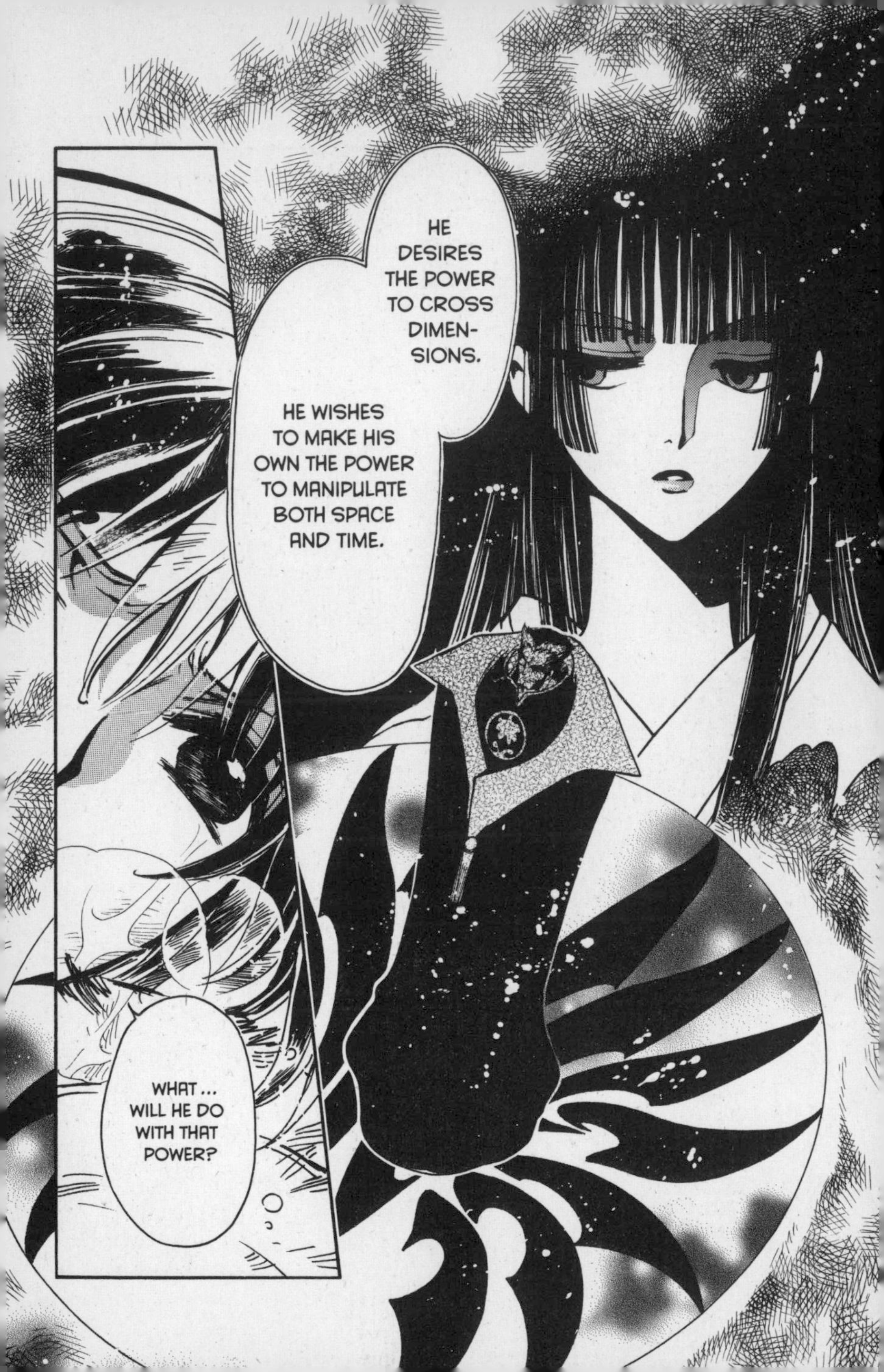
HE DESIRES THE POWER TO CROSS DIMEN- SIONS.
HE WISHES TO MAKE HIS OWN THE POWER TO MANIPULATE BOTH SPACE AND TIME.
WHAT ... WILL HE DO WITH THAT POWER?

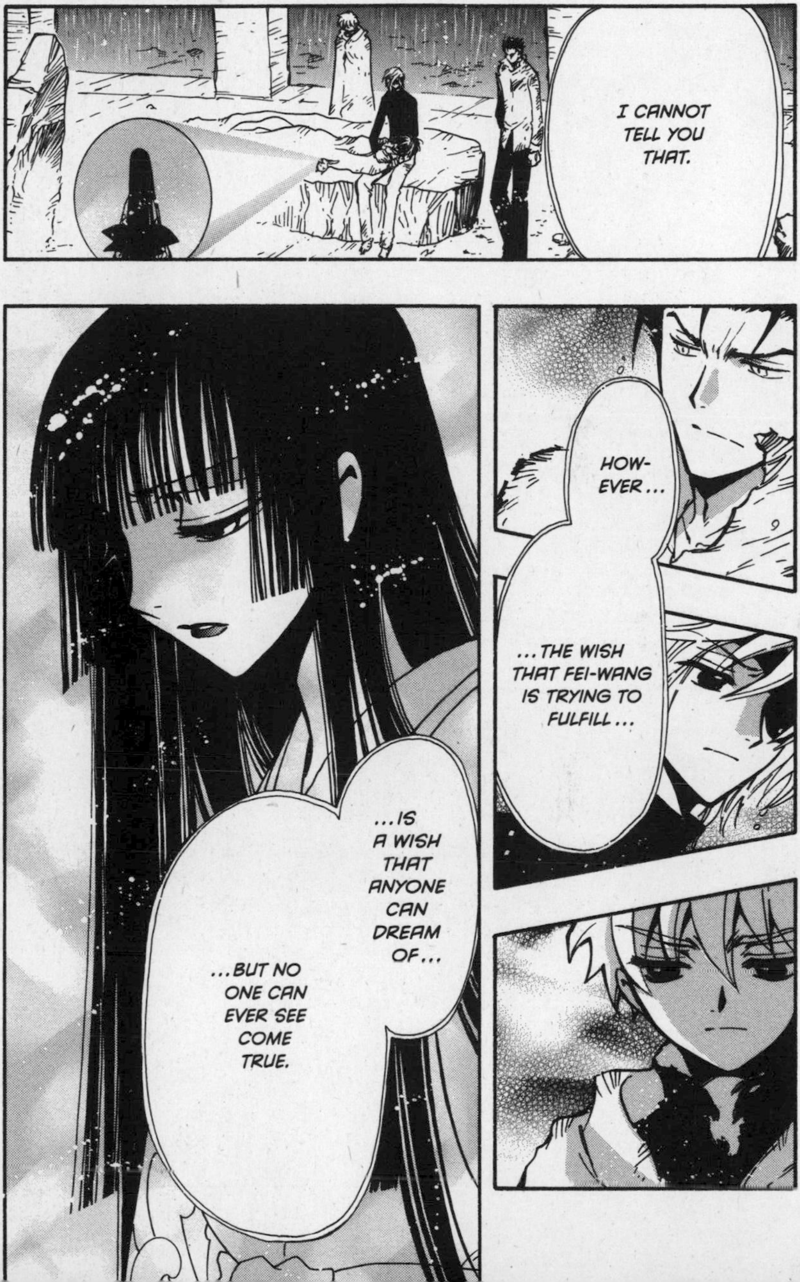
I CANNOT TELL YOU THAT.
HOW-EVER...
...THE WISH THAT FEI-WANG IS TRYING TO FULFILL...
...IS A WISH THAT ANYONE CAN DREAM OF...
...BUT NO ONE CAN EVER SEE COME TRUE.

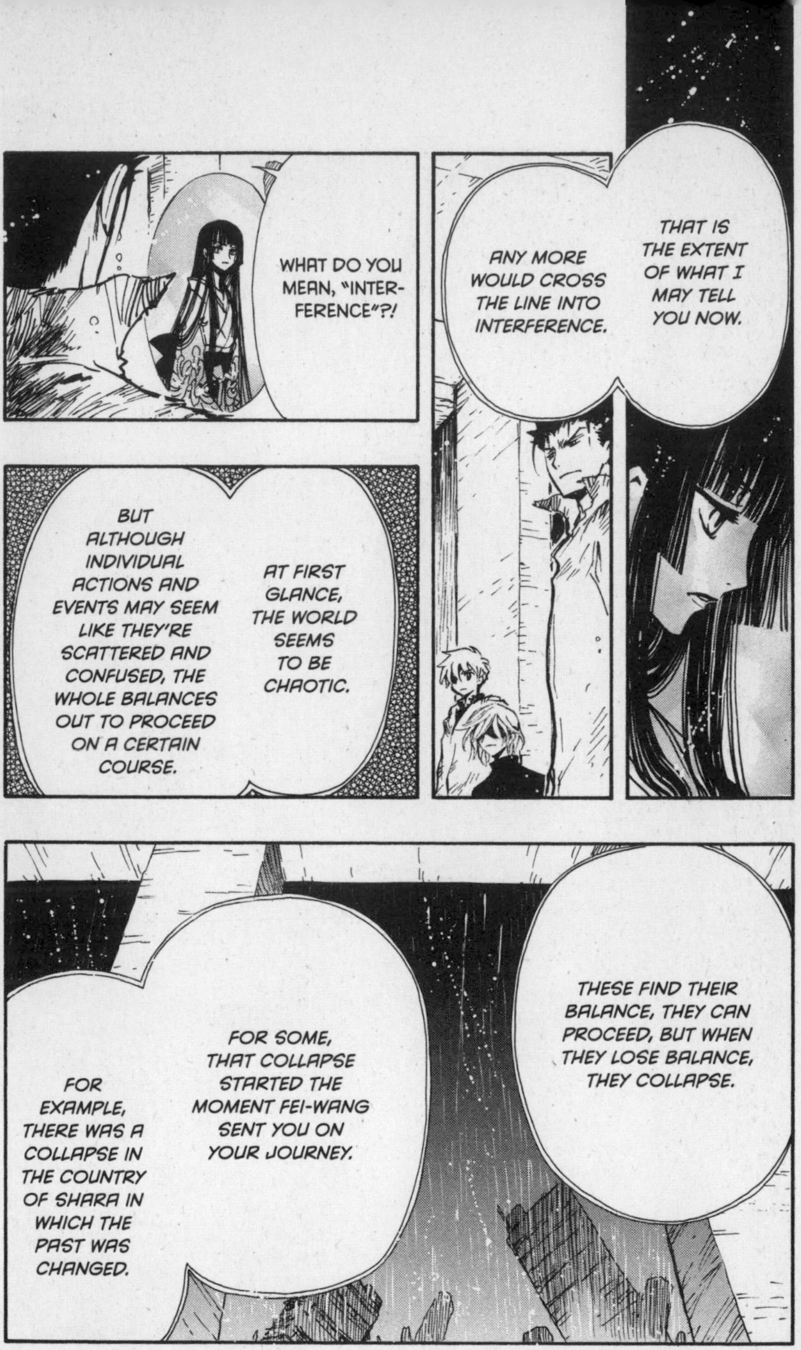
THAT IS THE EXTENT OF WHAT I MAY TELL YOU NOW.
ANY MORE WOULD CROSS THE LINE INTO INTERFERENCE.
WHAT DO YOU MEAN, "INTERFERENCE"?!
AT FIRST GLANCE, THE WORLD SEEMS TO BE CHAOTIC.
BUT ALTHOUGH INDIVIDUAL ACTIONS AND EVENTS MAY SEEM LIKE THEY'RE SCATTERED AND CONFUSED, THE WHOLE BALANCES OUT TO PROCEED ON A CERTAIN COURSE.
THESE FIND THEIR BALANCE, THEY CAN PROCEED, BUT WHEN THEY LOSE BALANCE, THEY COLLAPSE.
FOR SOME, THAT COLLAPSE STARTED THE MOMENT FEI-WANG SENT YOU ON YOUR JOURNEY.
FOR EXAMPLE, THERE WAS A COLLAPSE IN THE COUNTRY OF SHARA IN WHICH THE PAST WAS CHANGED.

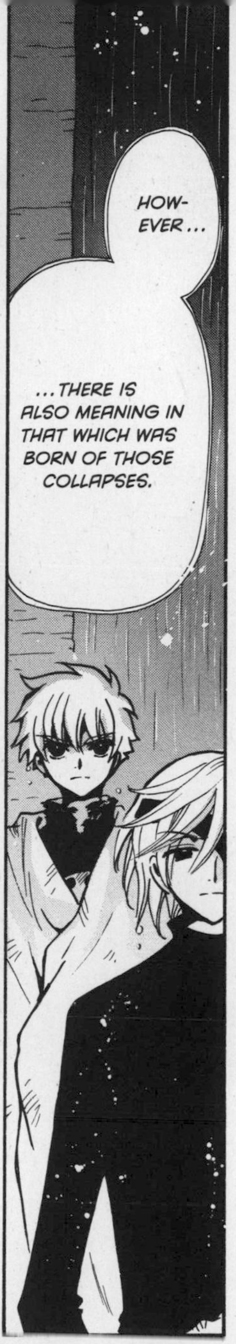
HOW-EVER...
...THERE IS ALSO MEANING IN THAT WHICH WAS BORN OF THOSE COLLAPSES.
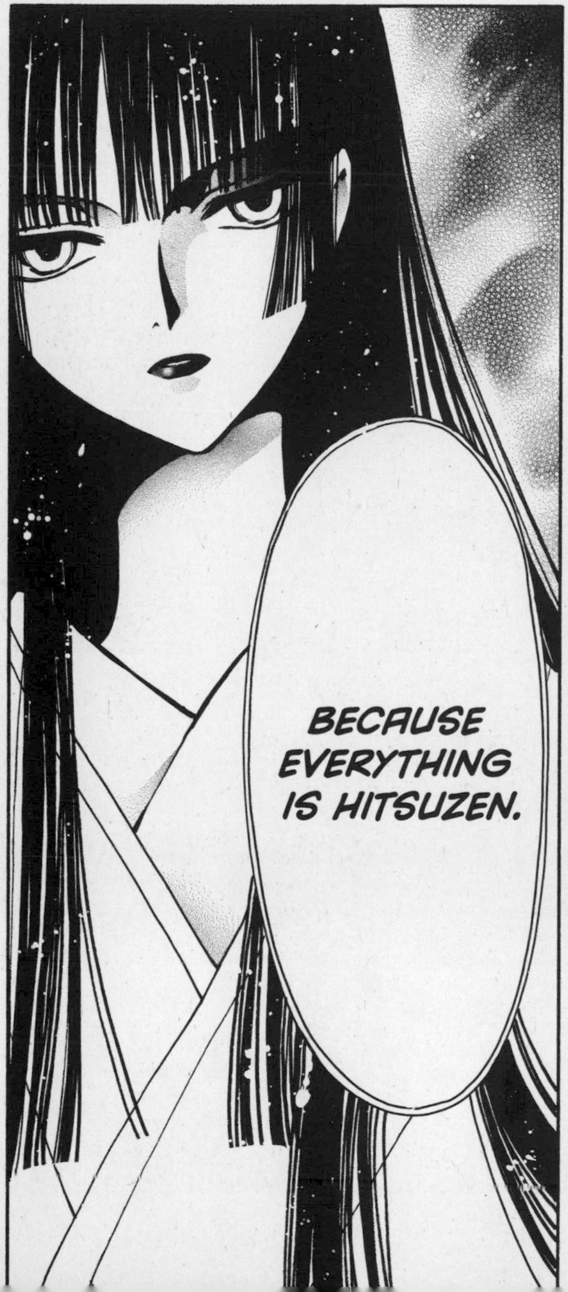
BECAUSE EVERYTHING IS HITSUZEN.

ツバサ

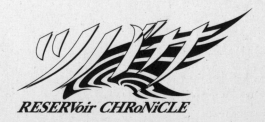

RESERVoir CHRoNiCLE

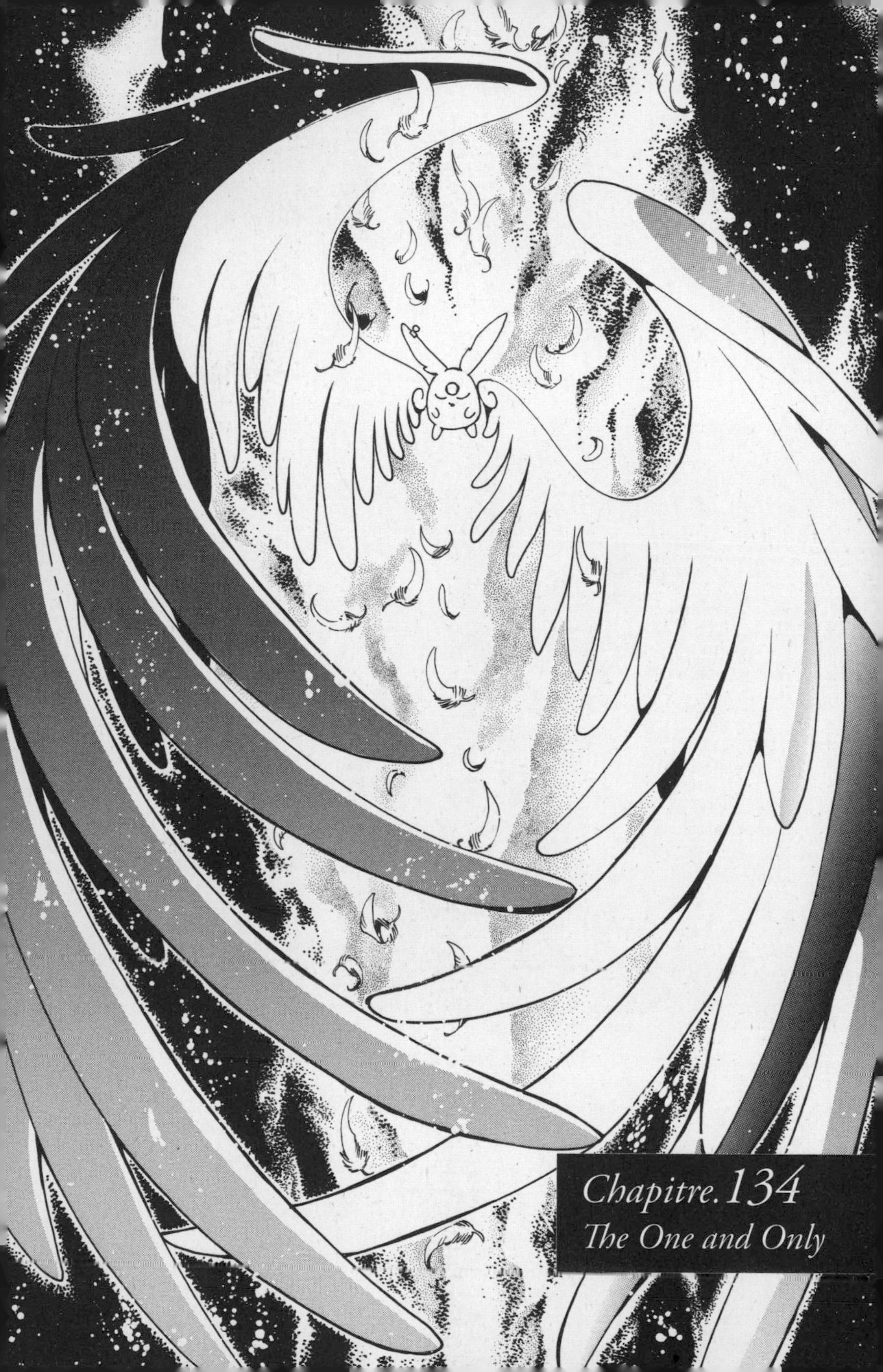

Chapitre.134
The One and Only

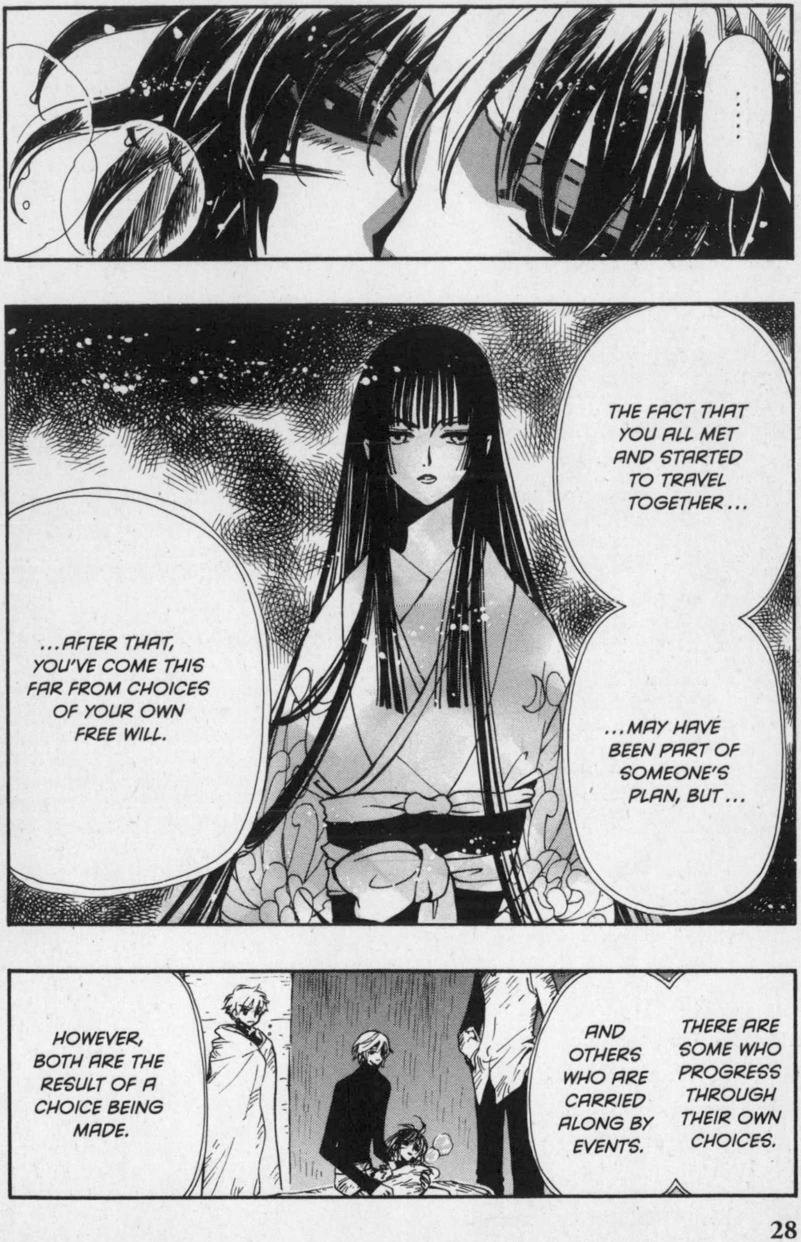
......
THE FACT THAT YOU ALL MET AND STARTED TO TRAVEL TOGETHER...
...MAY HAVE BEEN PART OF SOMEONE'S PLAN, BUT...
...AFTER THAT, YOU'VE COME THIS FAR FROM CHOICES OF YOUR OWN FREE WILL.
THERE ARE SOME WHO PROGRESS THROUGH THEIR OWN CHOICES.
AND OTHERS WHO ARE CARRIED ALONG BY EVENTS.
HOWEVER, BOTH ARE THE RESULT OF A CHOICE BEING MADE.

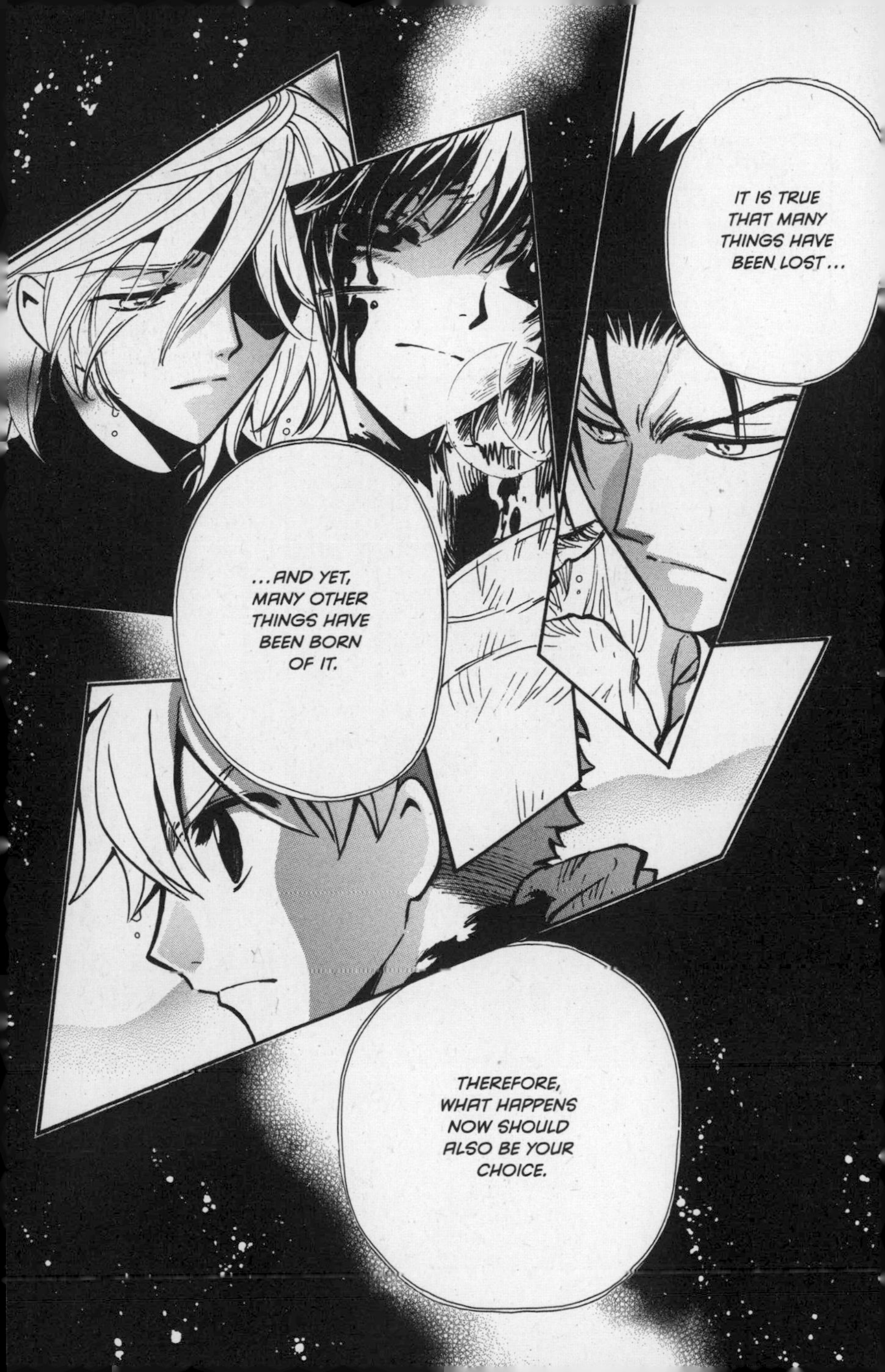
IT IS TRUE THAT MANY THINGS HAVE BEEN LOST...
...AND YET, MANY OTHER THINGS HAVE BEEN BORN OF IT.
THEREFORE, WHAT HAPPENS NOW SHOULD ALSO BE YOUR CHOICE.

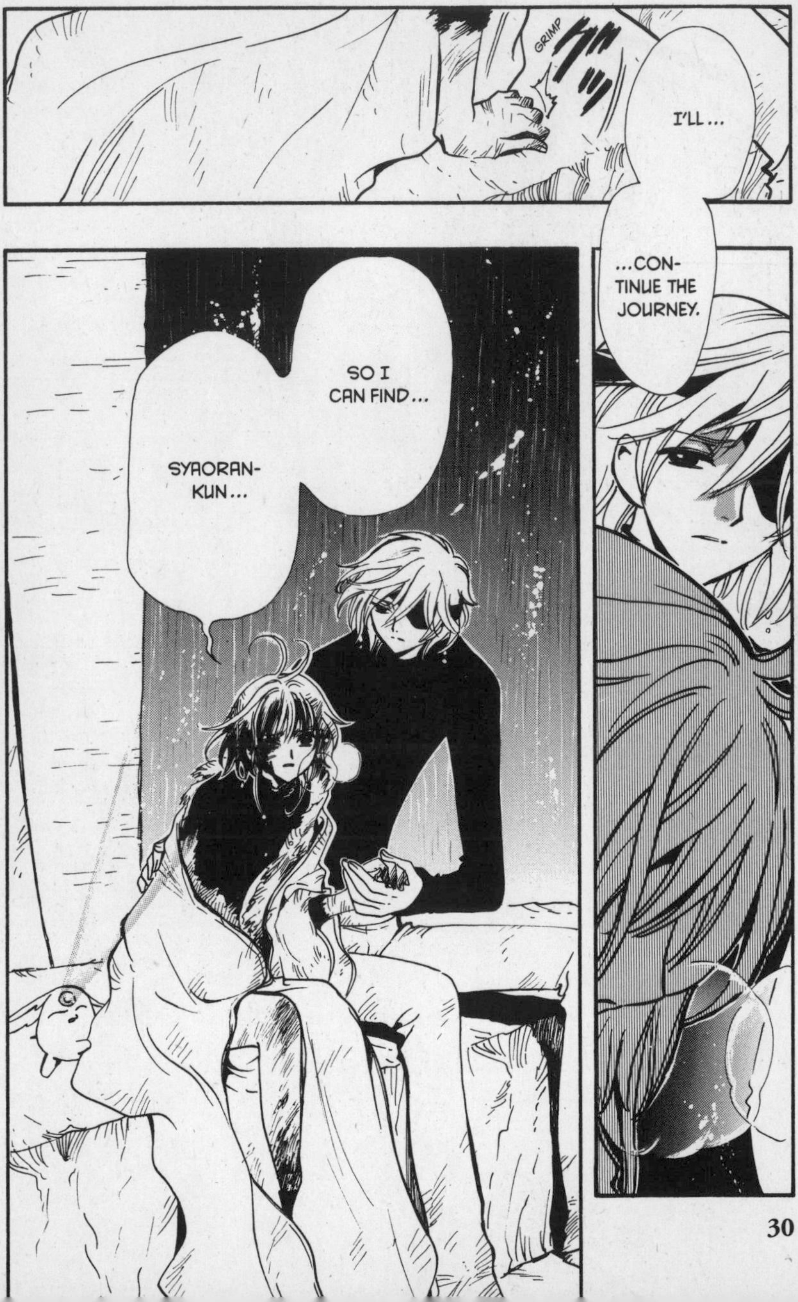
GRIMP
I'LL...
...CON-TINUE THE JOURNEY.
SO I CAN FIND...
SYAORAN-KUN...

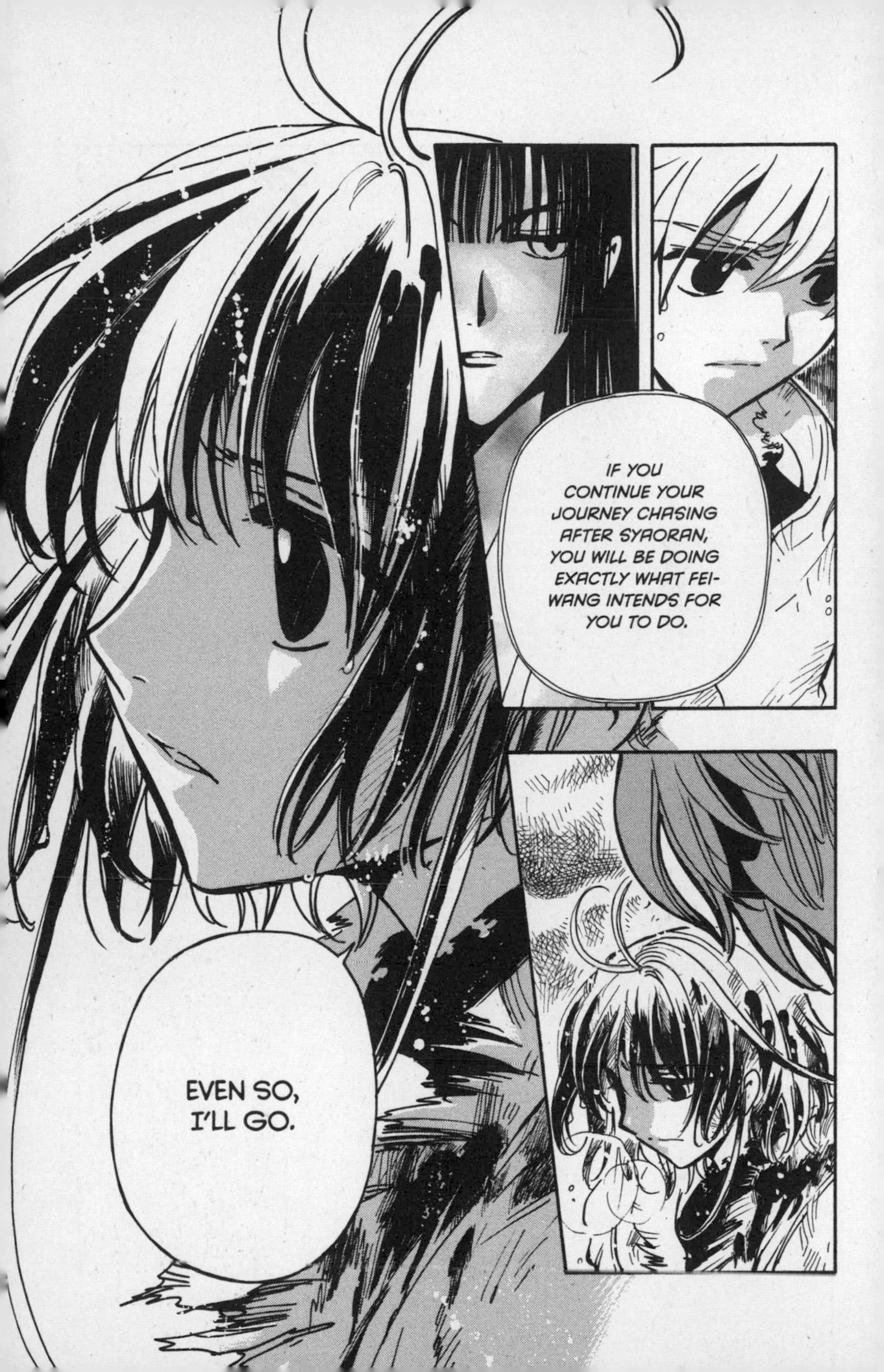
IF YOU CONTINUE YOUR JOURNEY CHASING AFTER SYAORAN, YOU WILL BE DOING EXACTLY WHAT FEI-WANG INTENDS FOR YOU TO DO.
EVEN SO, I'LL GO.

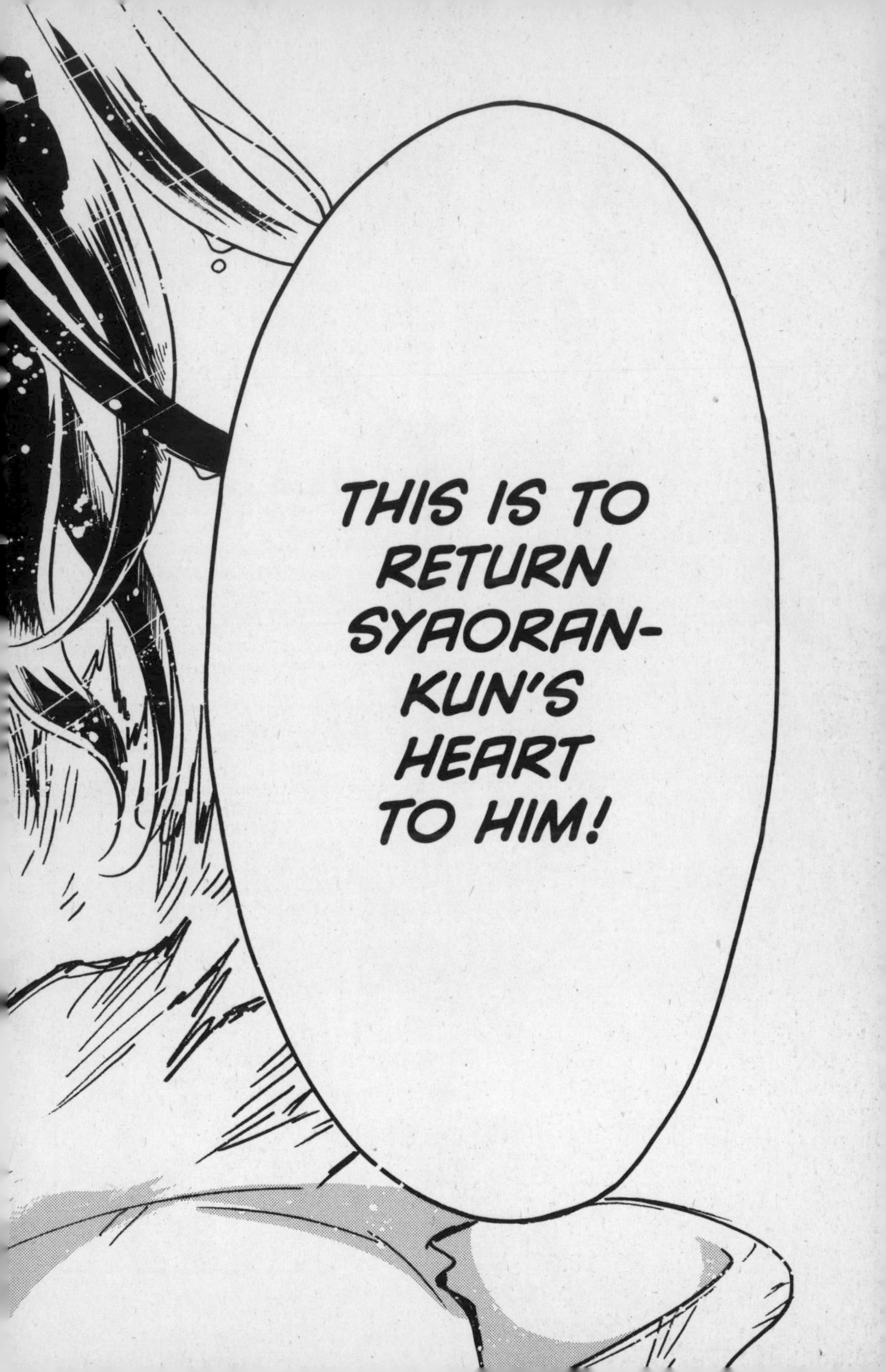
THIS IS TO RETURN SYAORAN-KUN'S HEART TO HIM!

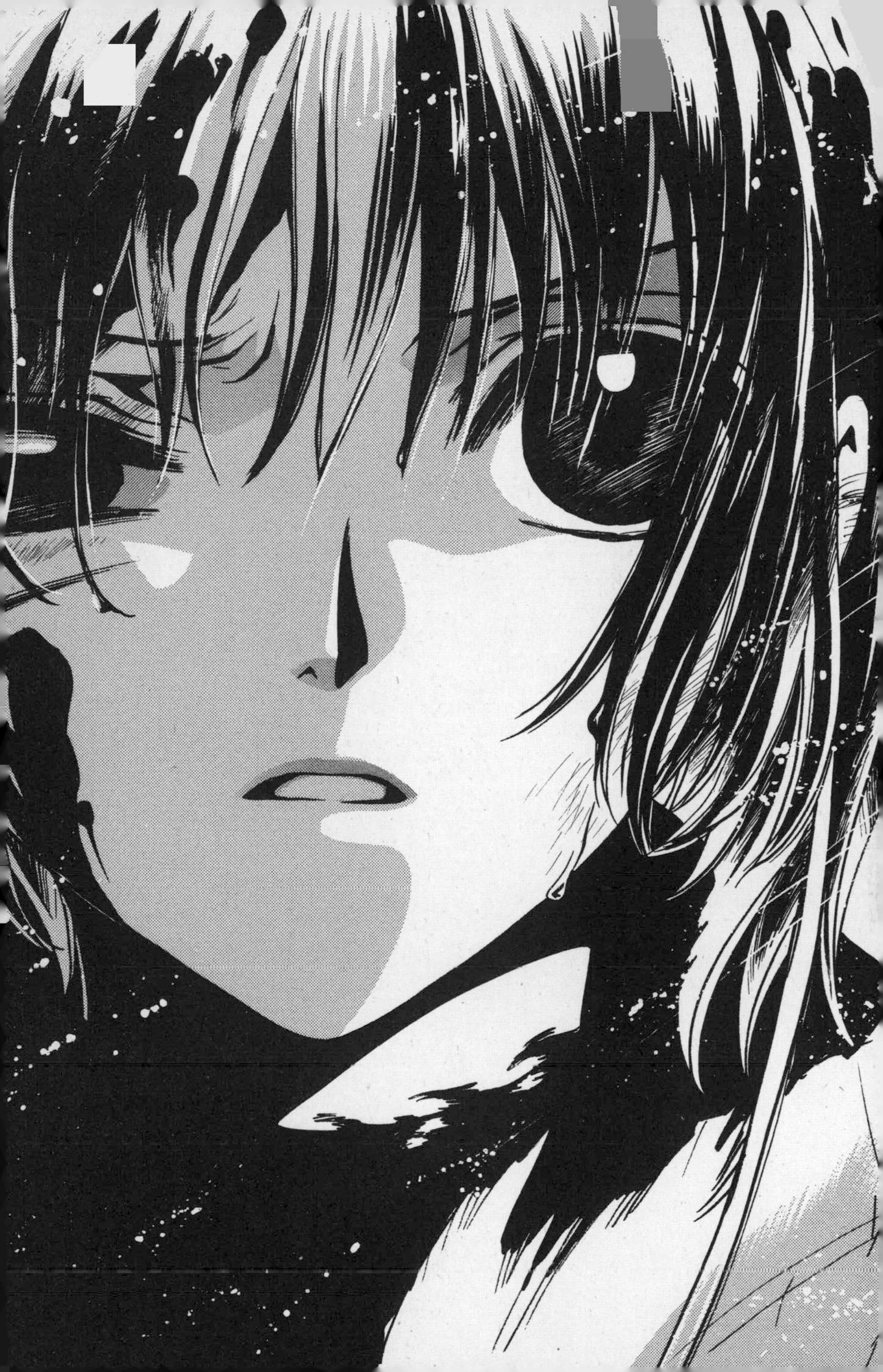

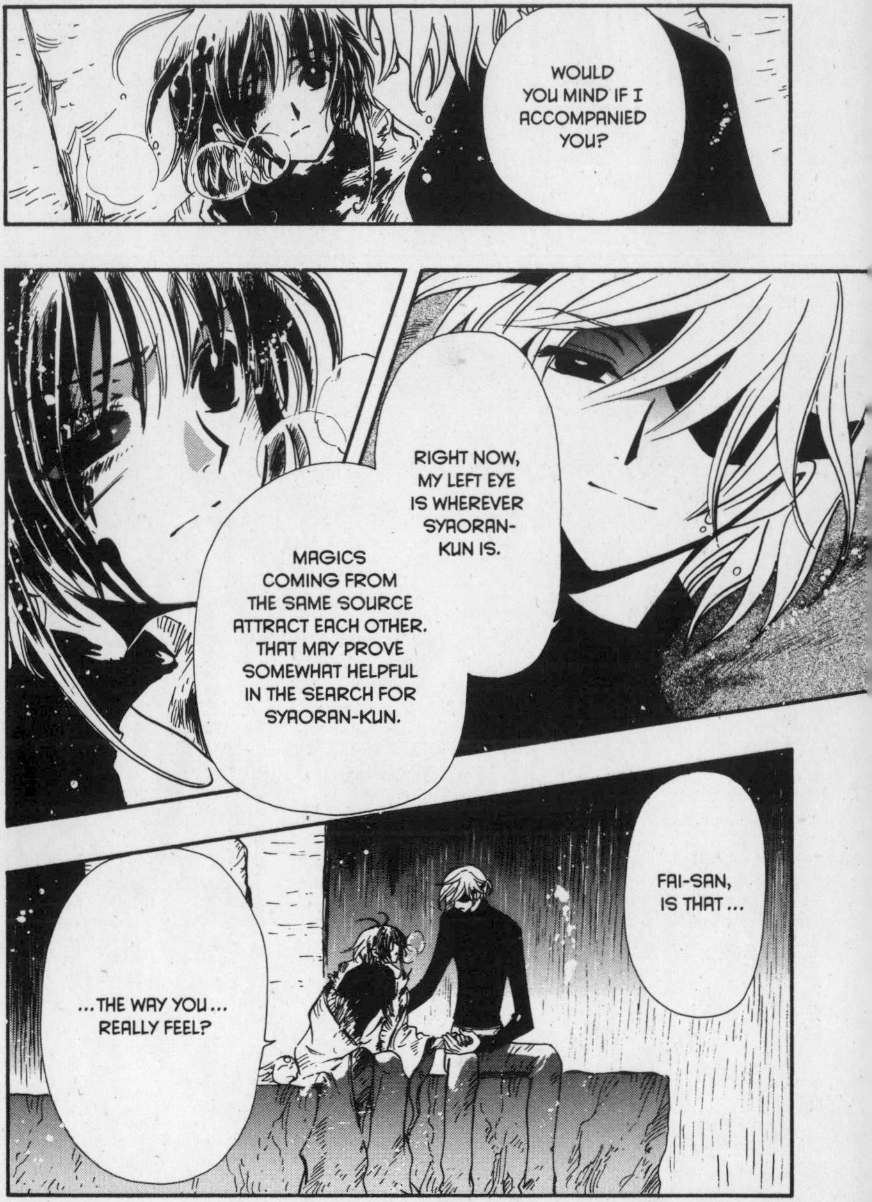
WOULD YOU MIND IF I ACCOMPANIED YOU?
RIGHT NOW, MY LEFT EYE IS WHEREVER SYAORAN-KUN IS.
MAGICS COMING FROM THE SAME SOURCE ATTRACT EACH OTHER. THAT MAY PROVE SOMEWHAT HELPFUL IN THE SEARCH FOR SYAORAN-KUN.
FAI-SAN, IS THAT...
...THE WAY YOU... REALLY FEEL?

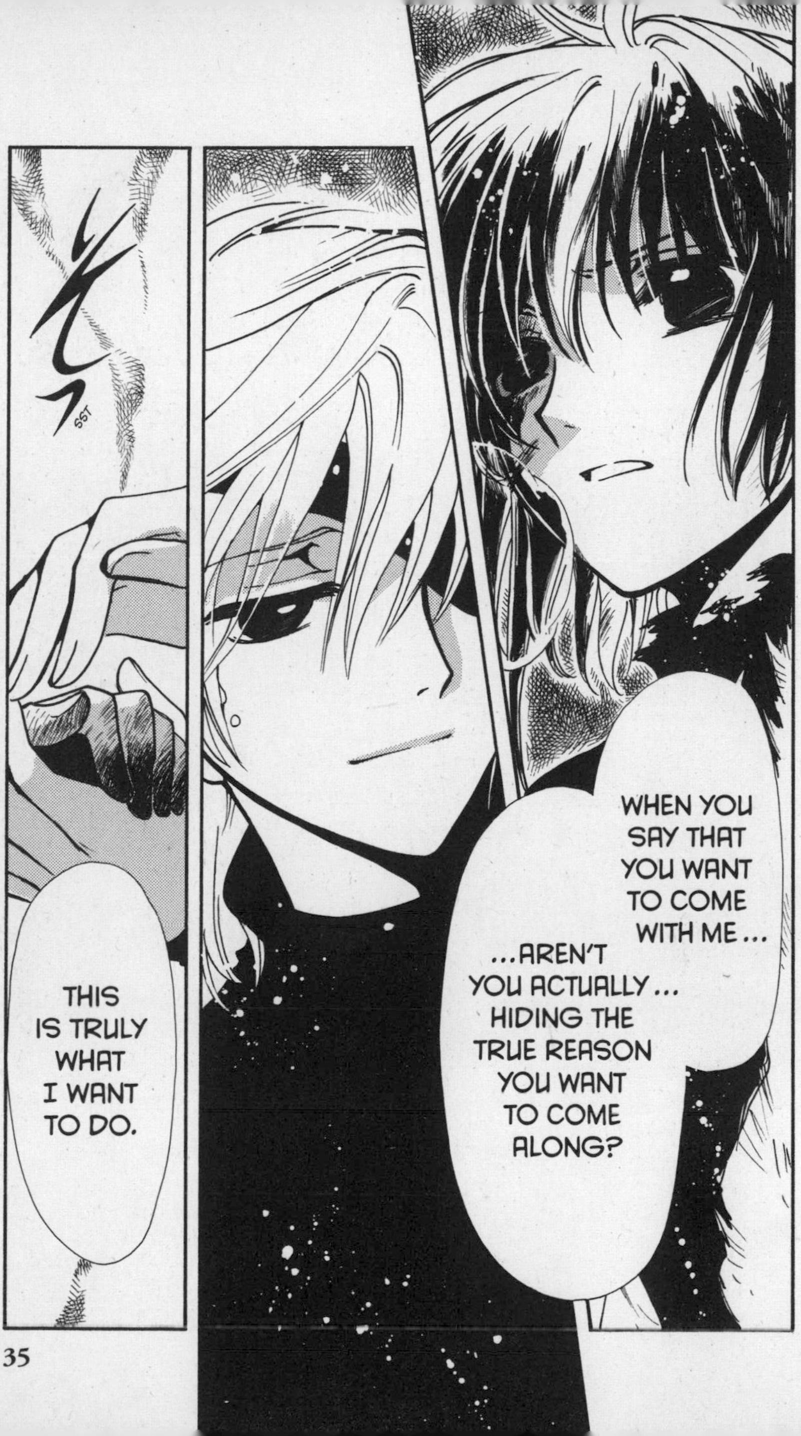
WHEN YOU SAY THAT YOU WANT TO COME WITH ME...
...AREN'T YOU ACTUALLY... HIDING THE TRUE REASON YOU WANT TO COME ALONG?
SST
THIS IS TRULY WHAT I WANT TO DO.

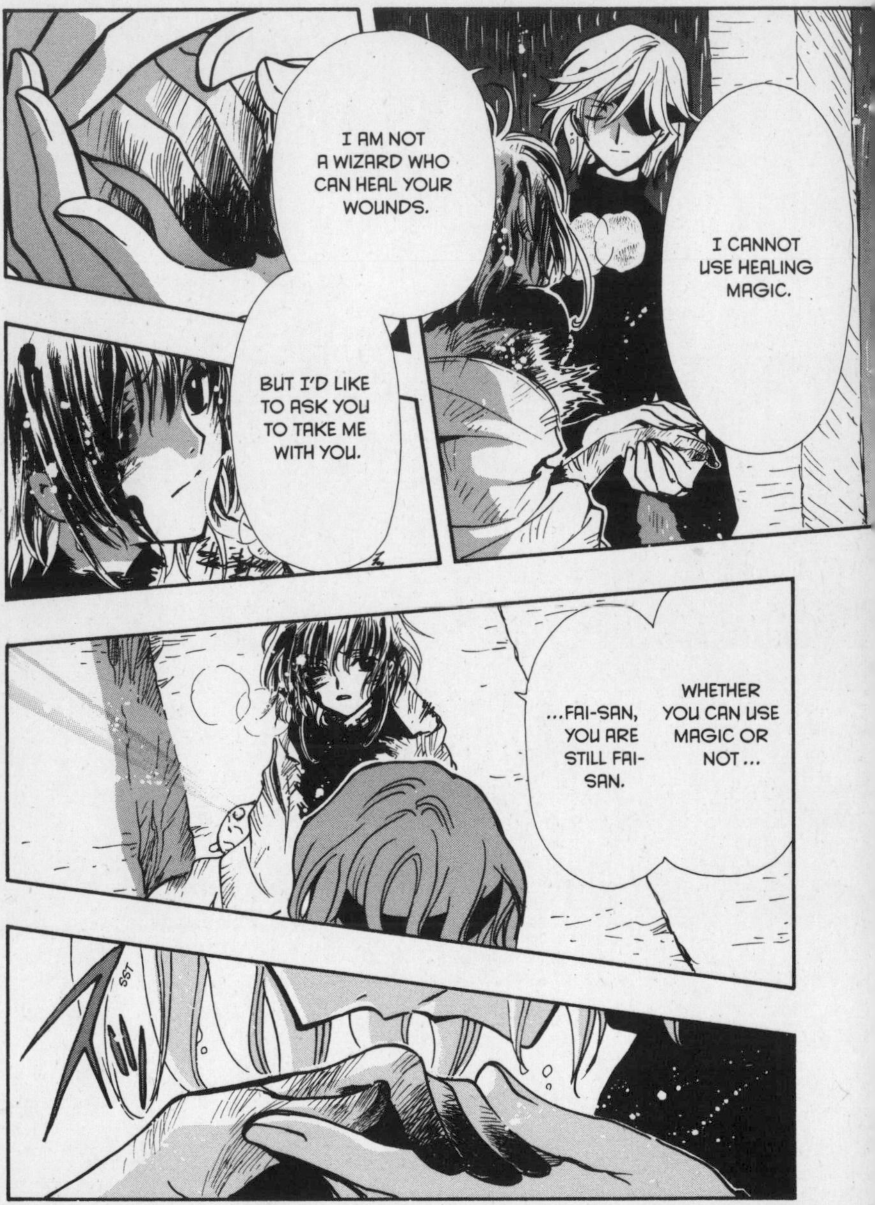
I CANNOT USE HEALING MAGIC.
I AM NOT A WIZARD WHO CAN HEAL YOUR WOUNDS.
BUT I'D LIKE TO ASK YOU TO TAKE ME WITH YOU.
WHETHER YOU CAN USE MAGIC OR NOT...
...FAI-SAN, YOU ARE STILL FAI-SAN.
SST

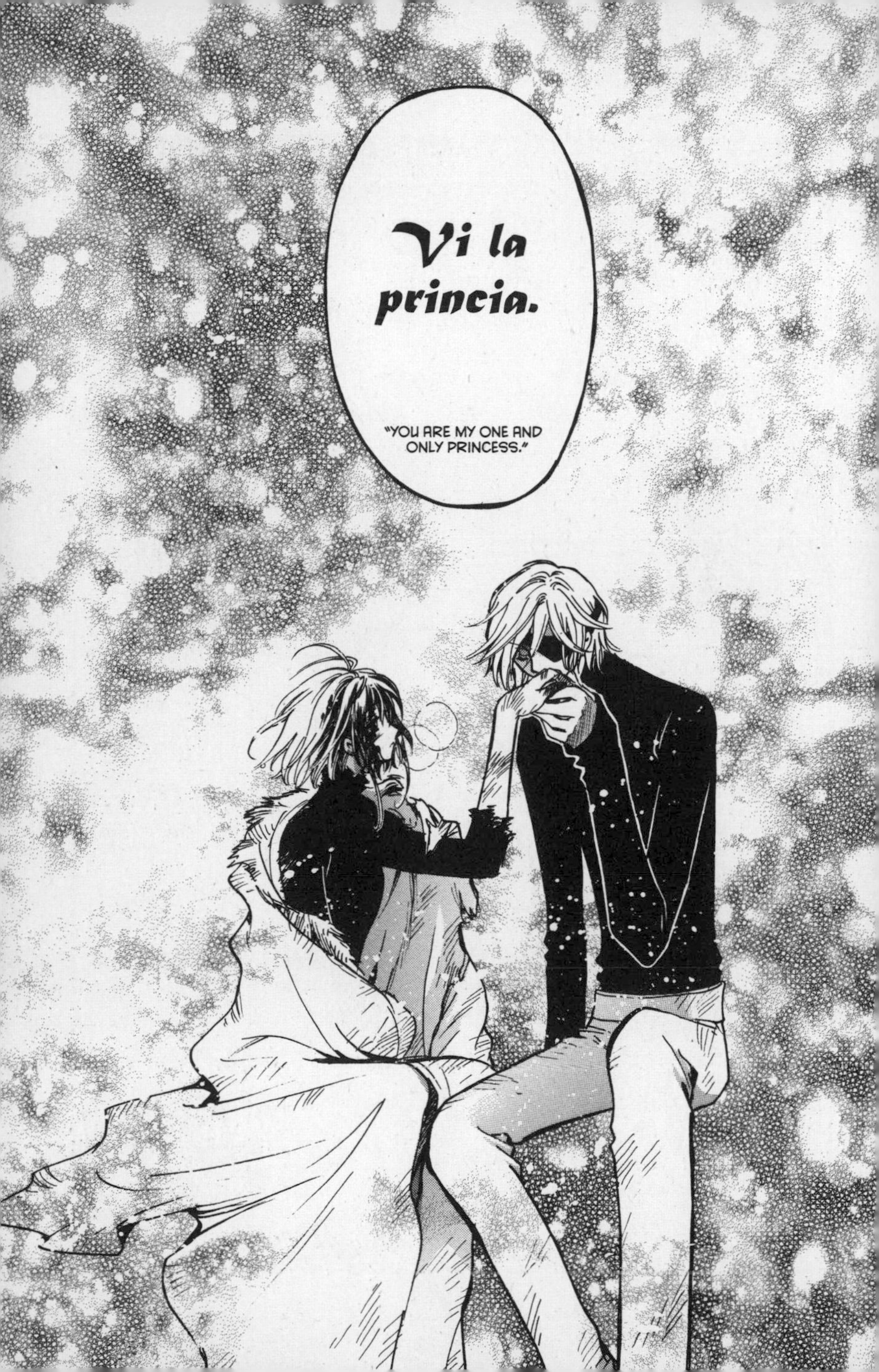
Vi la princia.
"YOU ARE MY ONE AND ONLY PRINCESS."

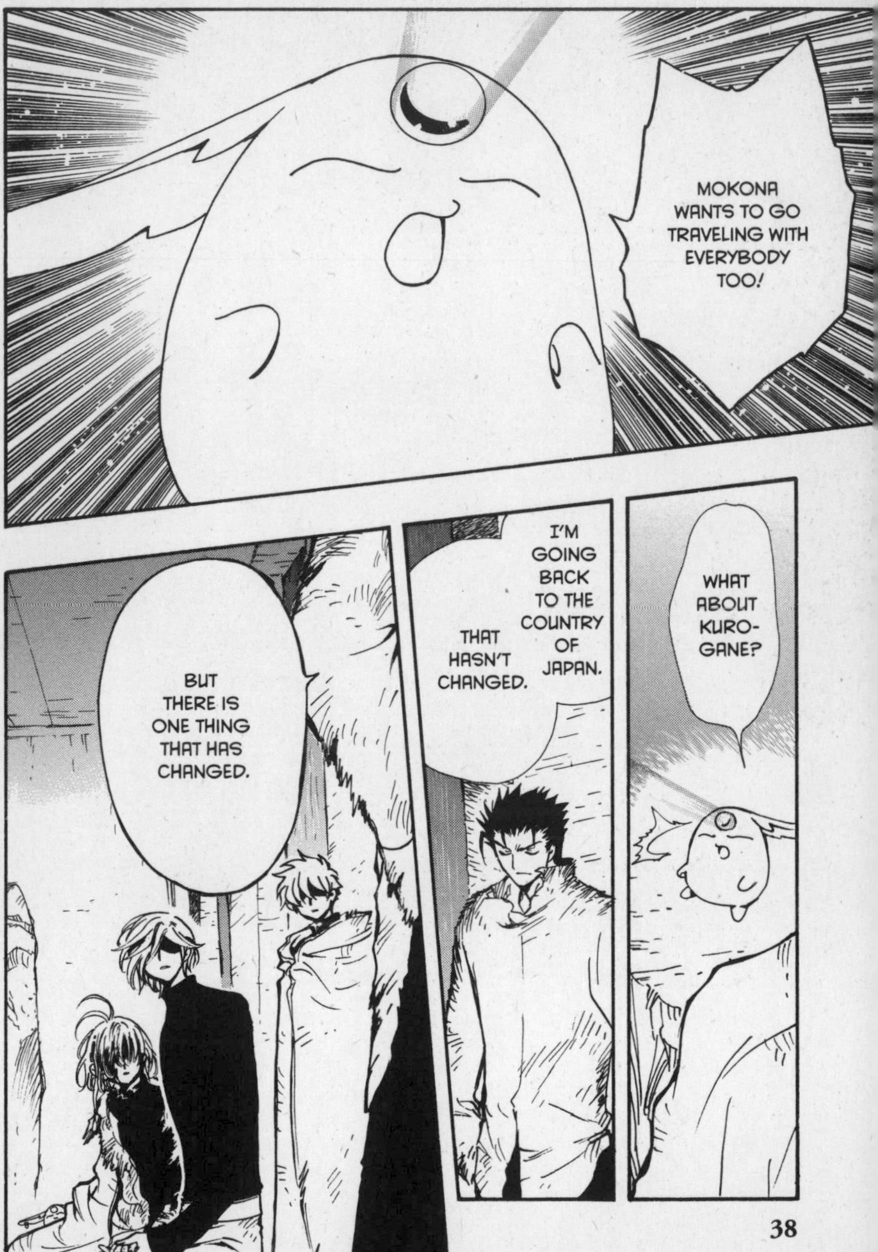
MOKONA WANTS TO GO TRAVELING WITH EVERYBODY TOO!
WHAT ABOUT KURO-GANE?
I'M GOING BACK TO THE COUNTRY OF JAPAN.
THAT HASN'T CHANGED.
BUT THERE IS ONE THING THAT HAS CHANGED.

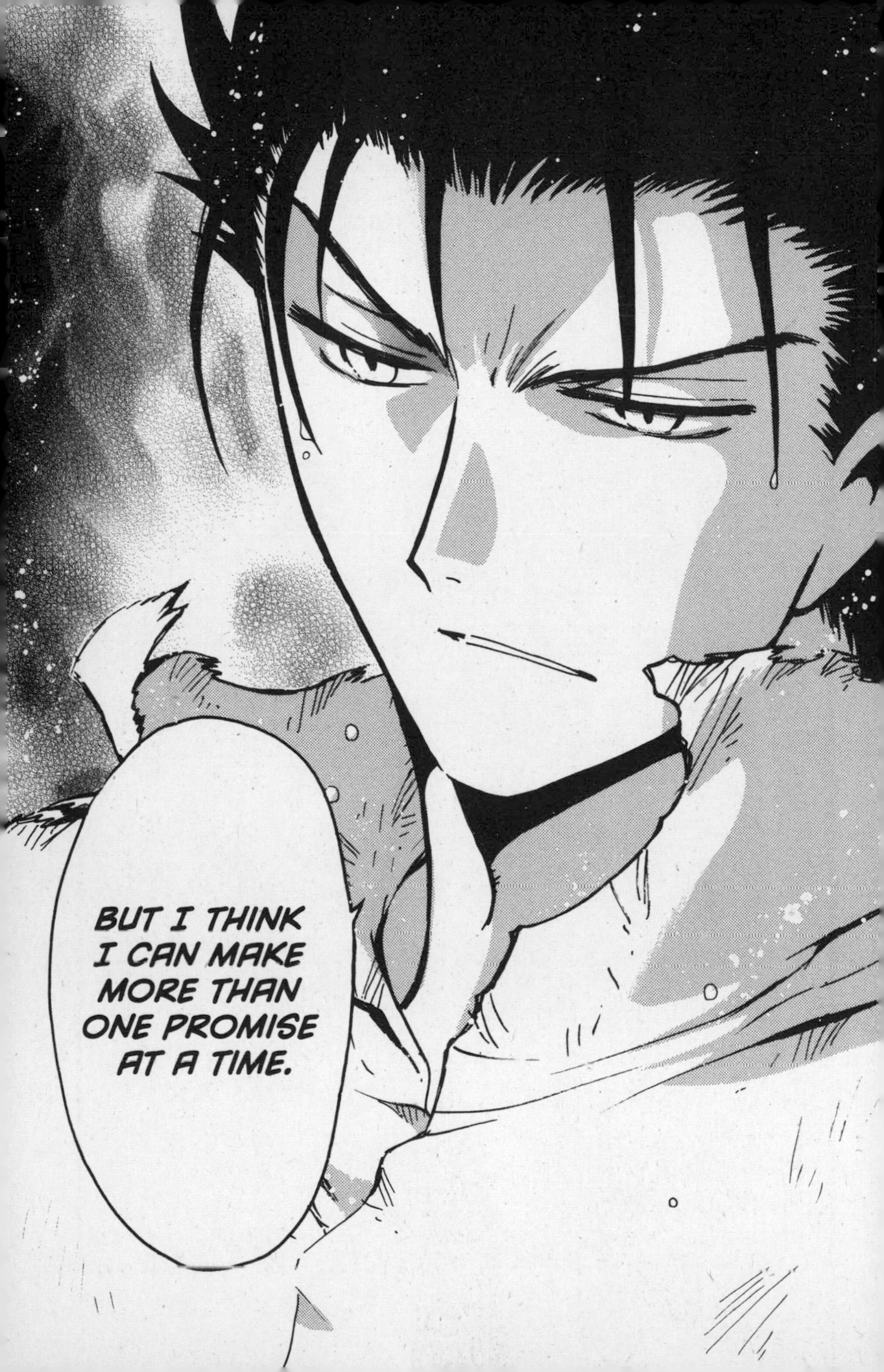
BUT I THINK I CAN MAKE MORE THAN ONE PROMISE AT A TIME.

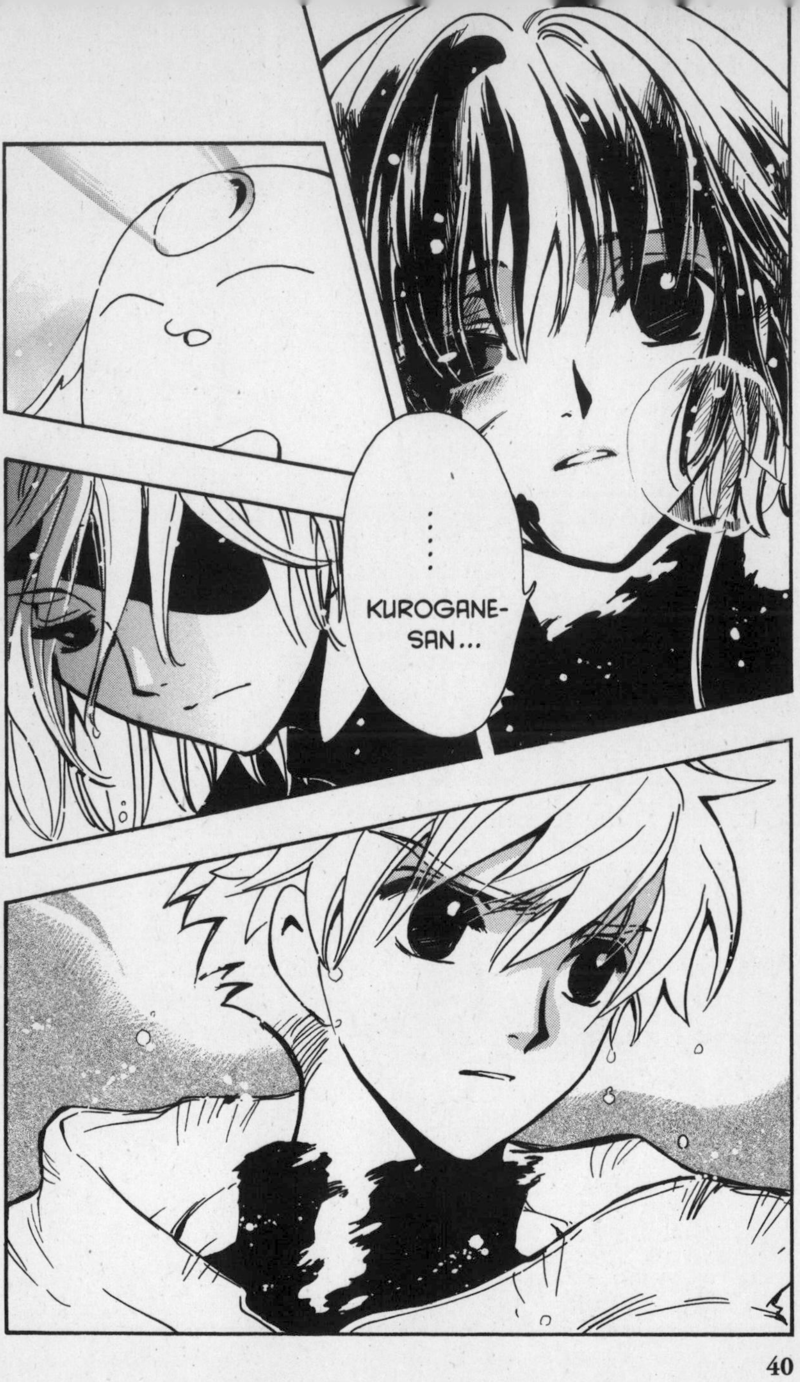
......
KUROGANE-
SAN...

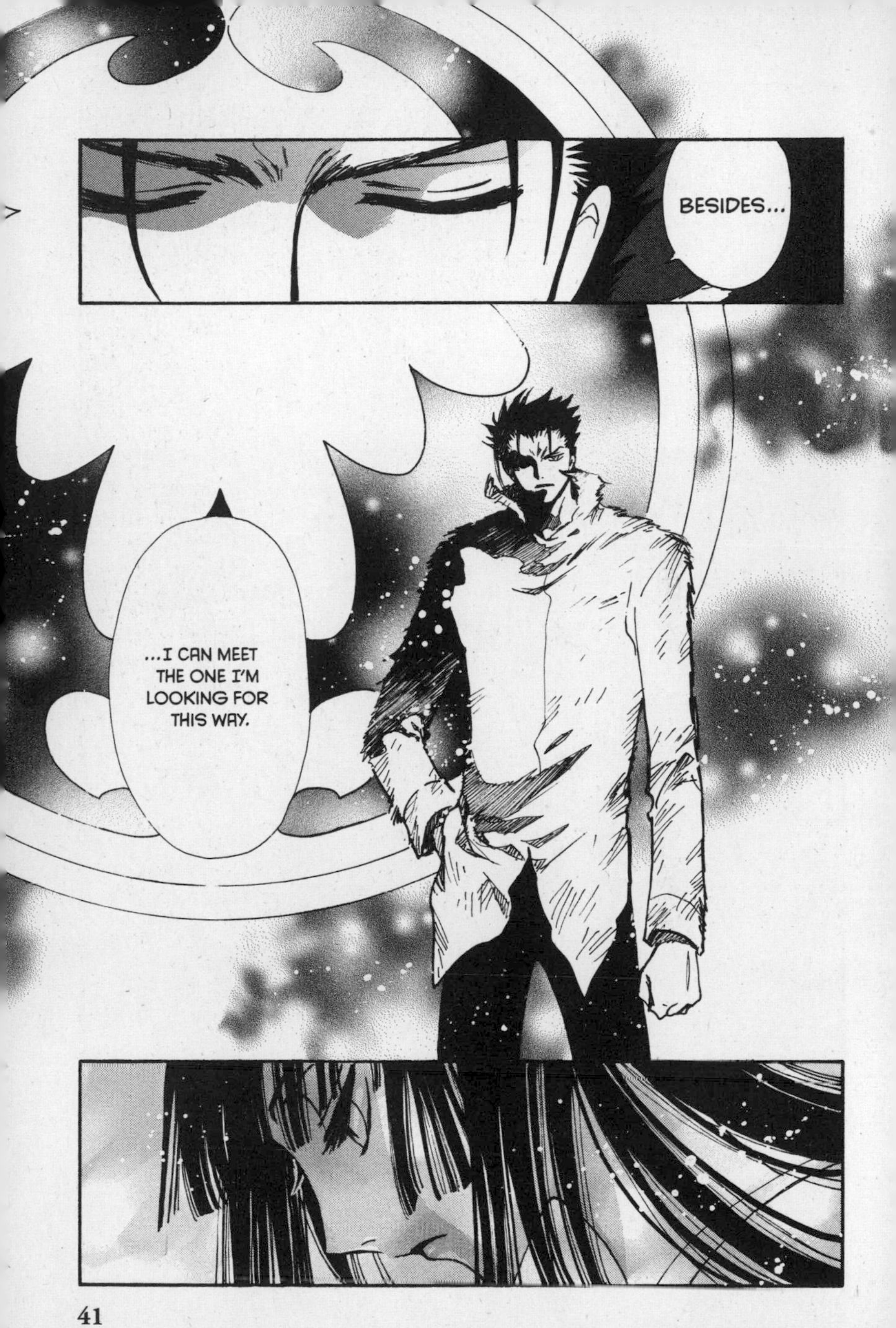
BESIDES...
...I CAN MEET THE ONE I'M LOOKING FOR THIS WAY.

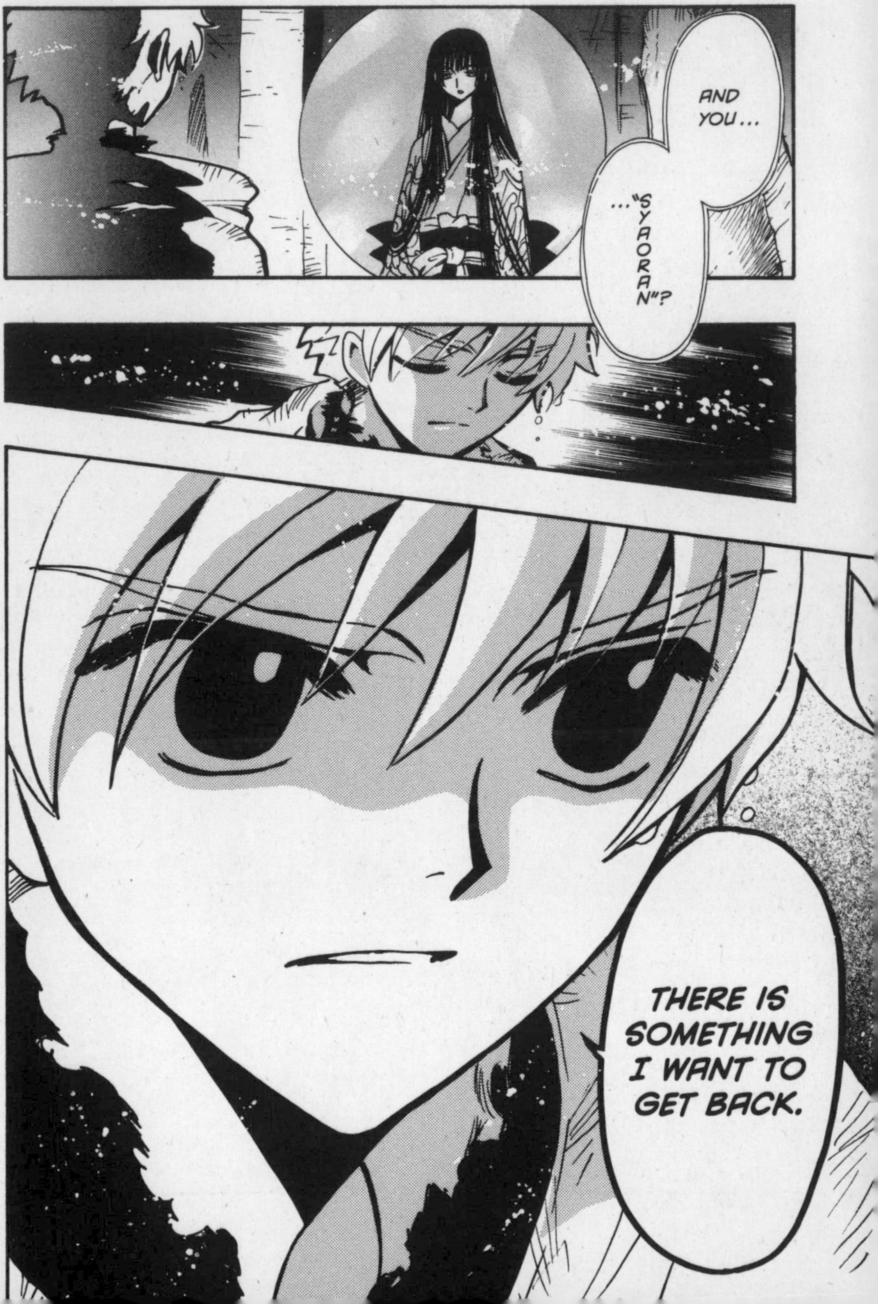
AND YOU...
..."SYAORAN"?
THERE IS SOMETHING I WANT TO GET BACK.

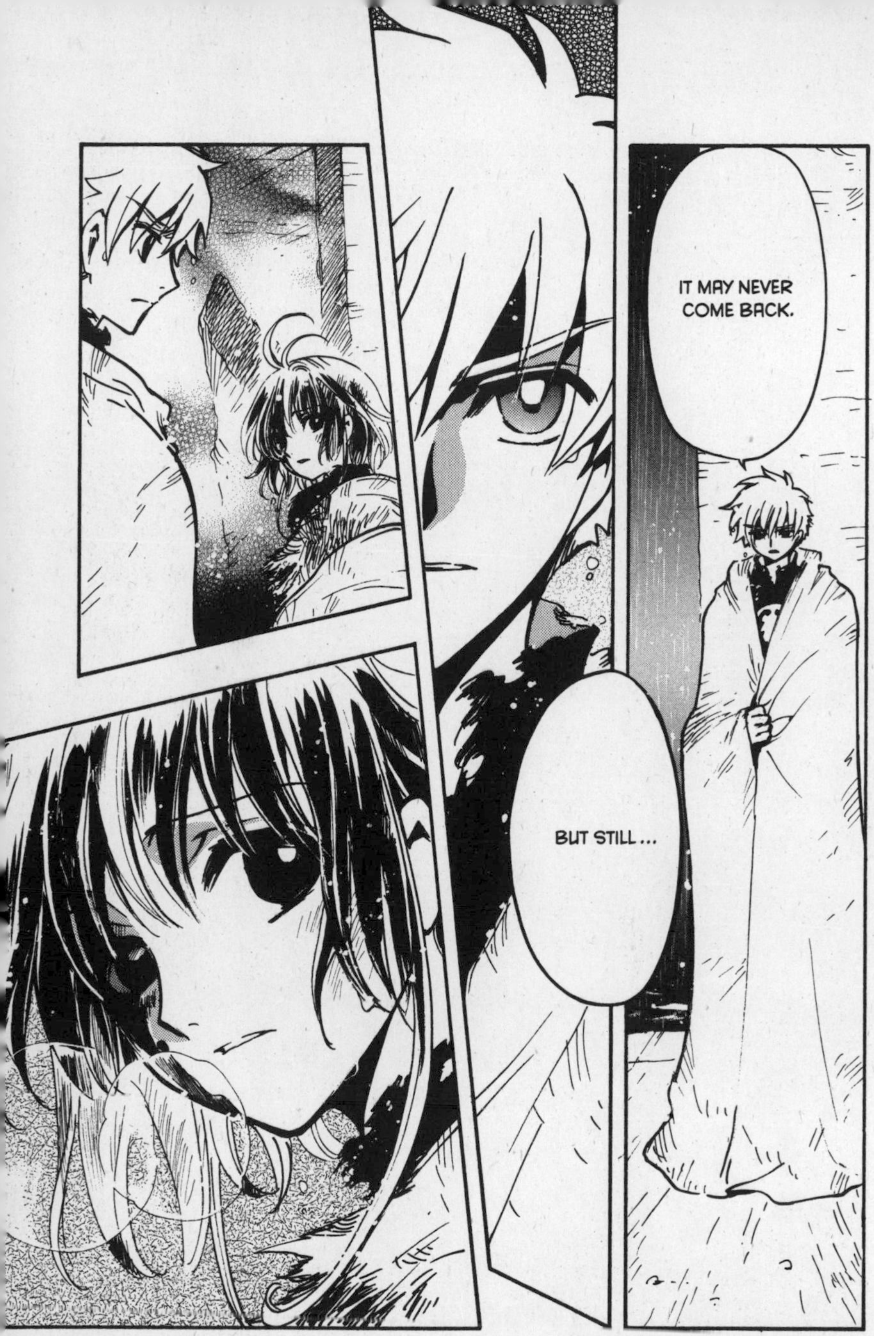
IT MAY NEVER COME BACK.
BUT STILL...

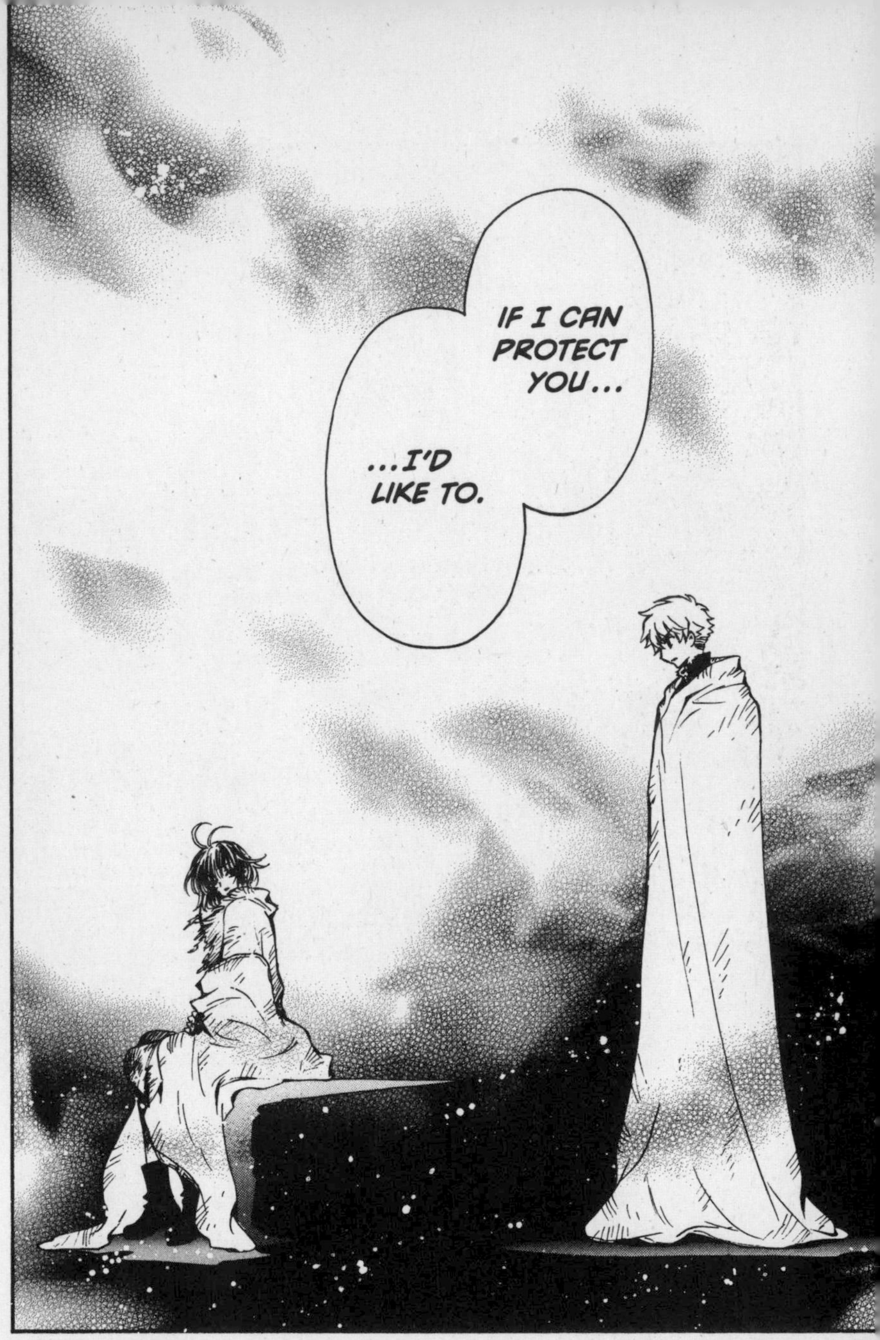
IF I CAN PROTECT YOU...
...I'D LIKE TO.

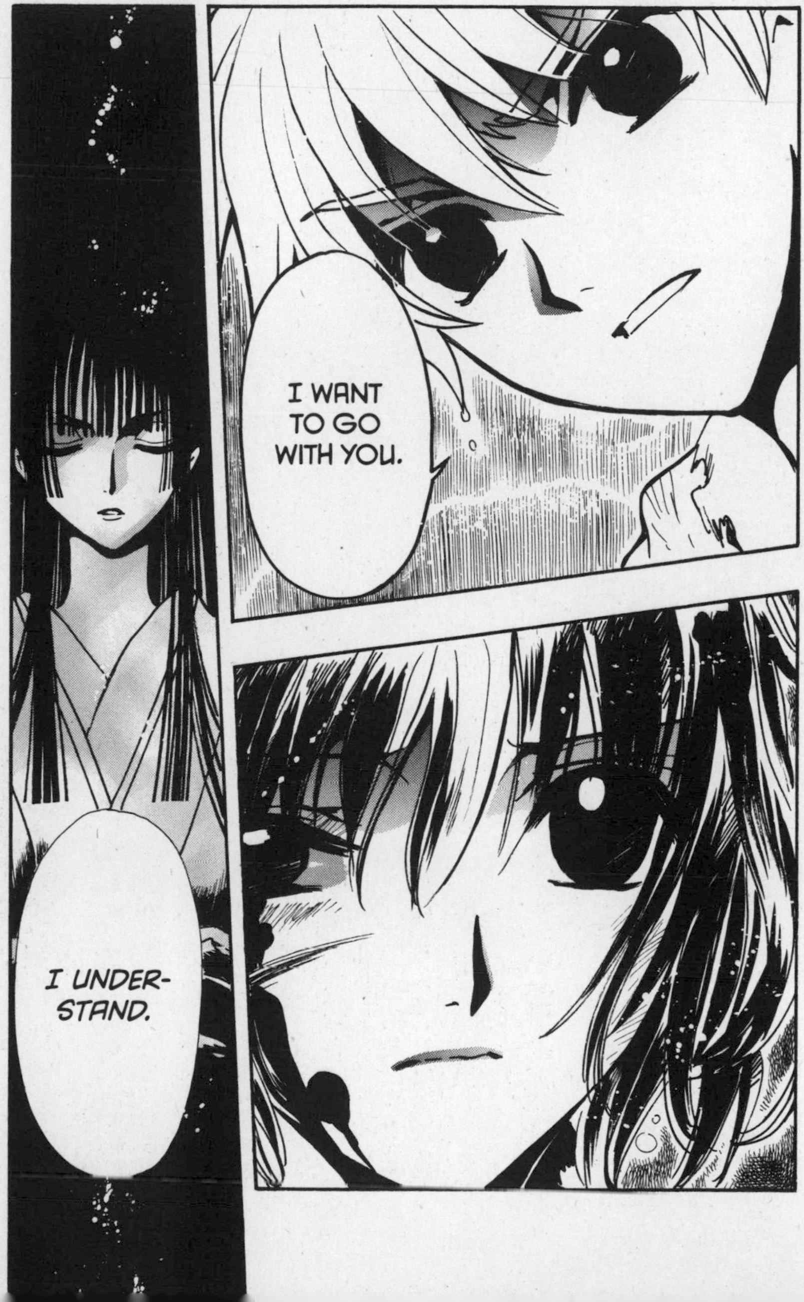
I WANT TO GO WITH YOU.
I UNDER-STAND.

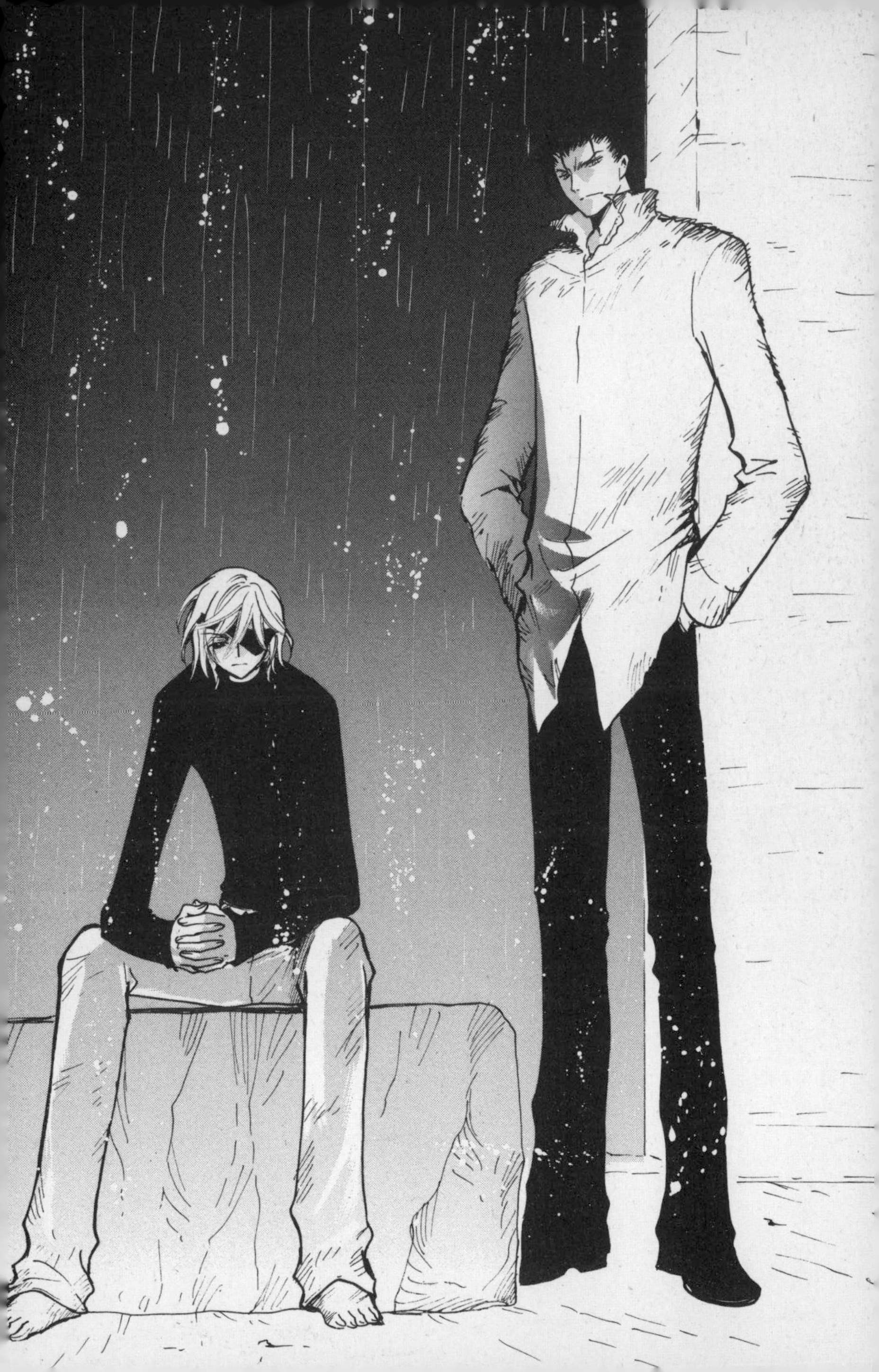

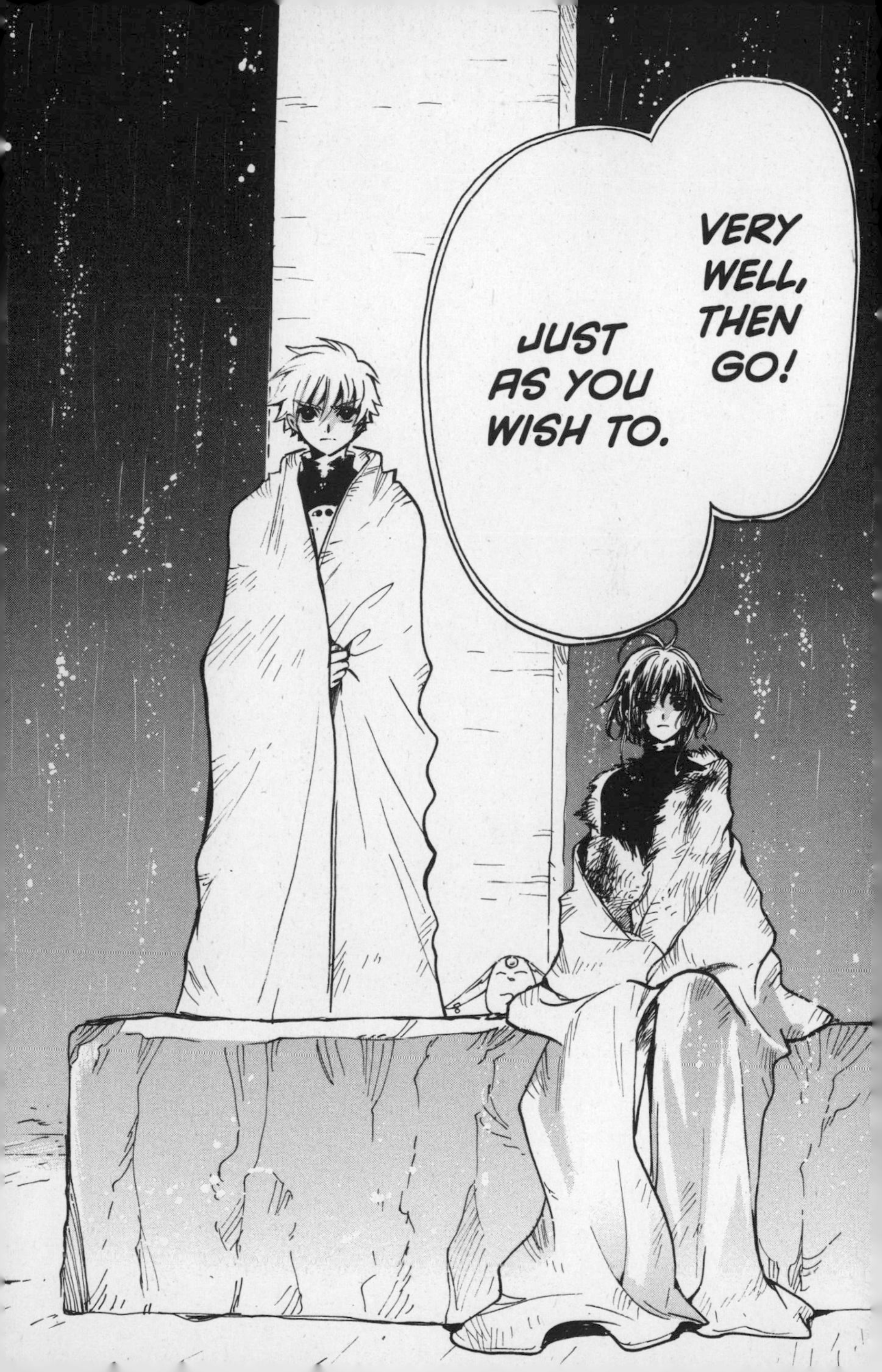
VERY WELL, THEN GO!
JUST AS YOU WISH TO.

ツバサ

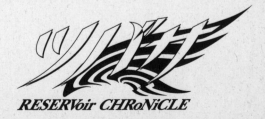

RESERVoir CHRoNiCLE

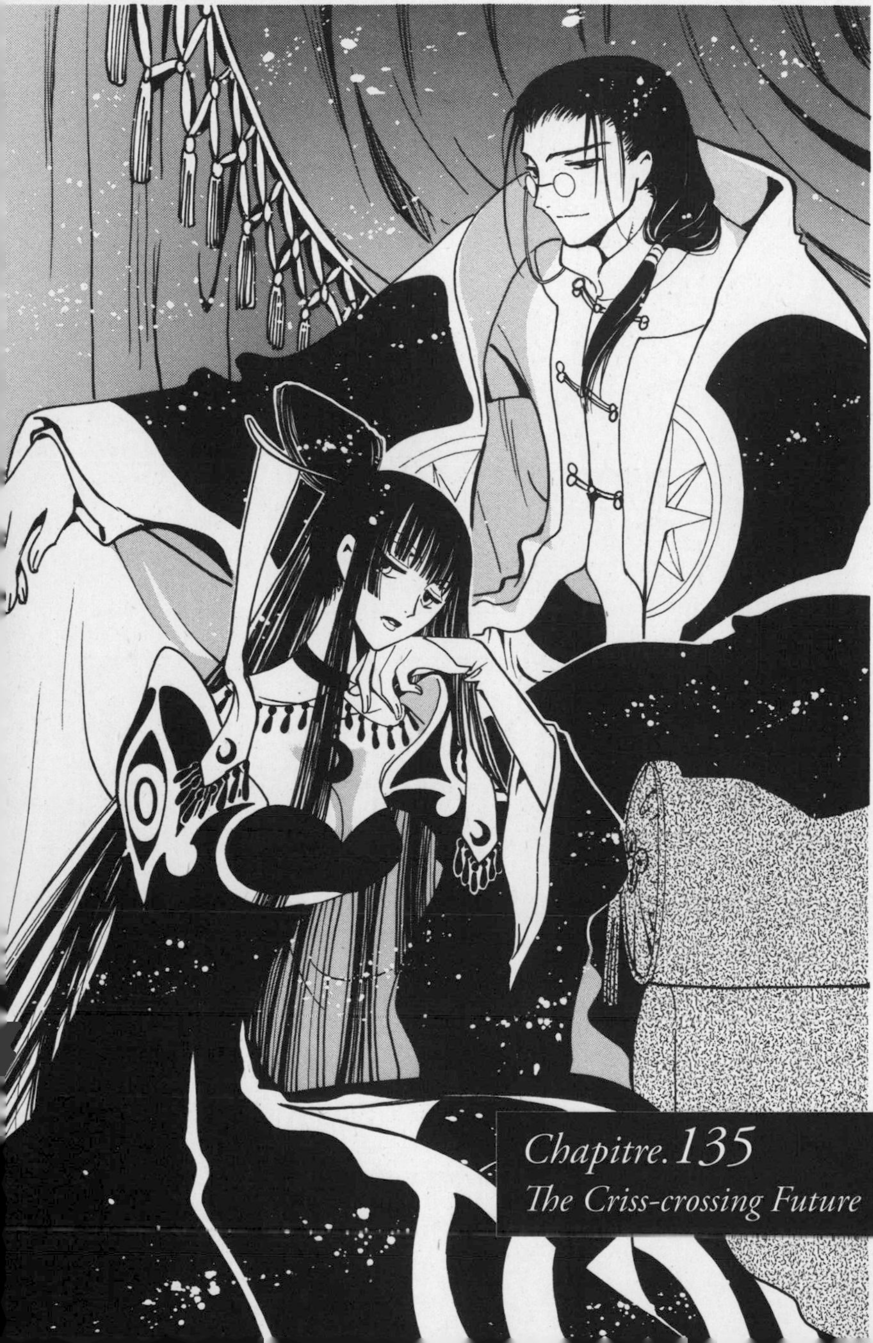

Chapitre. 135
The Criss-crossing Future

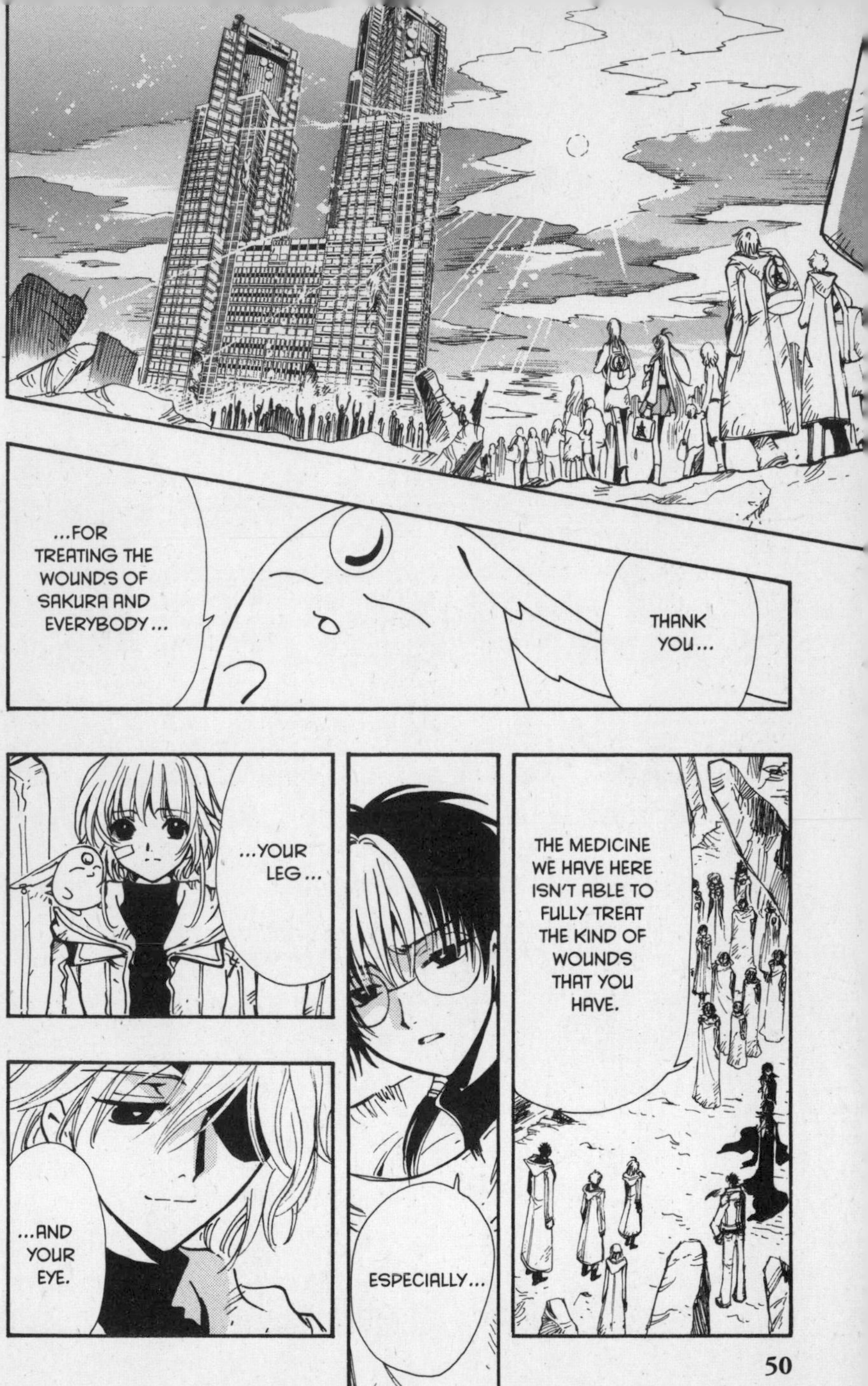

THANK YOU...
...FOR TREATING THE WOUNDS OF SAKURA AND EVERYBODY...
THE MEDICINE WE HAVE HERE ISN'T ABLE TO FULLY TREAT THE KIND OF WOUNDS THAT YOU HAVE.
ESPECIALLY...
...YOUR LEG...
...AND YOUR EYE.

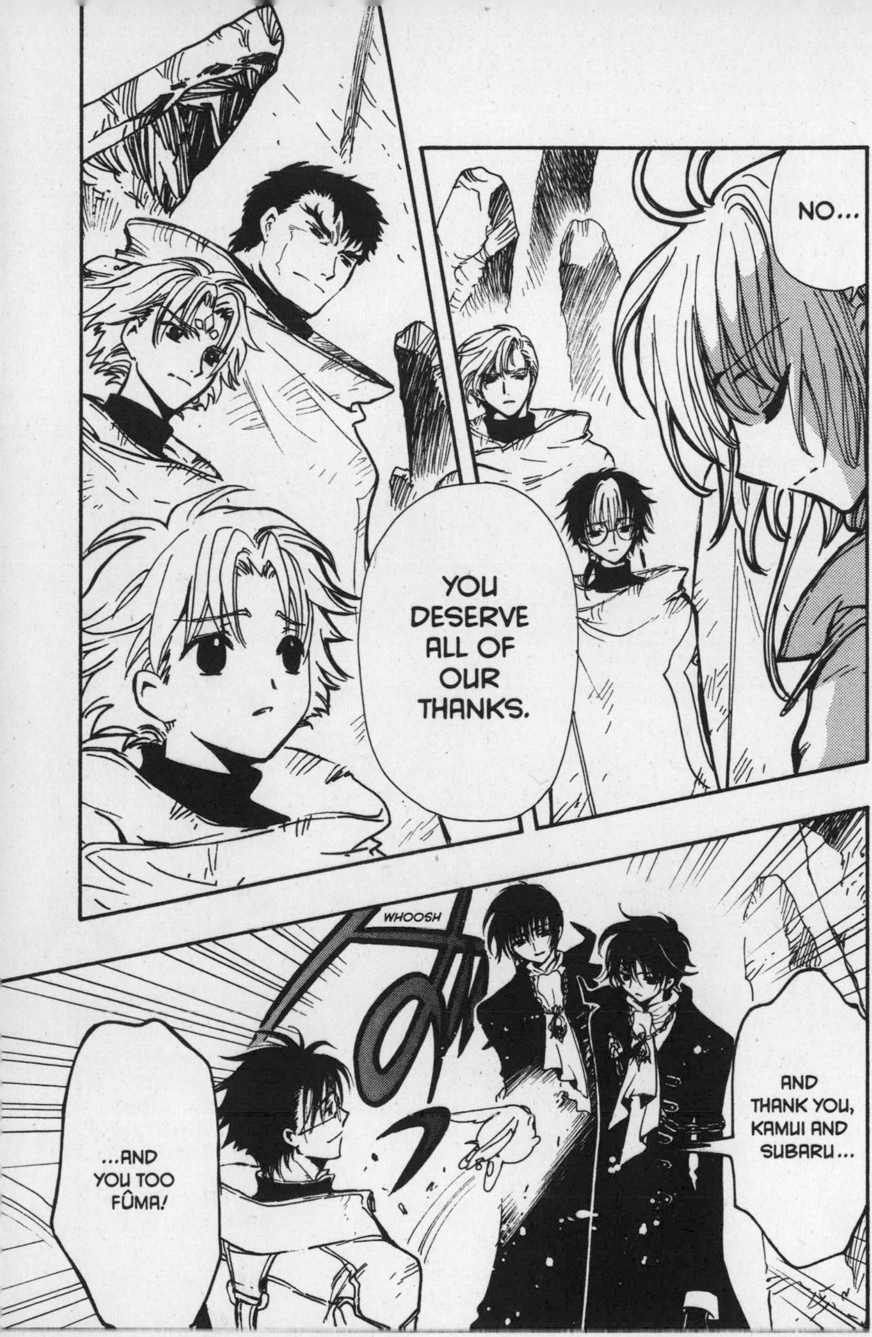
NO...
YOU DESERVE ALL OF OUR THANKS.
WHOOSH
AND THANK YOU, KAMUI AND SUBARU...
...AND YOU TOO FÛMA!

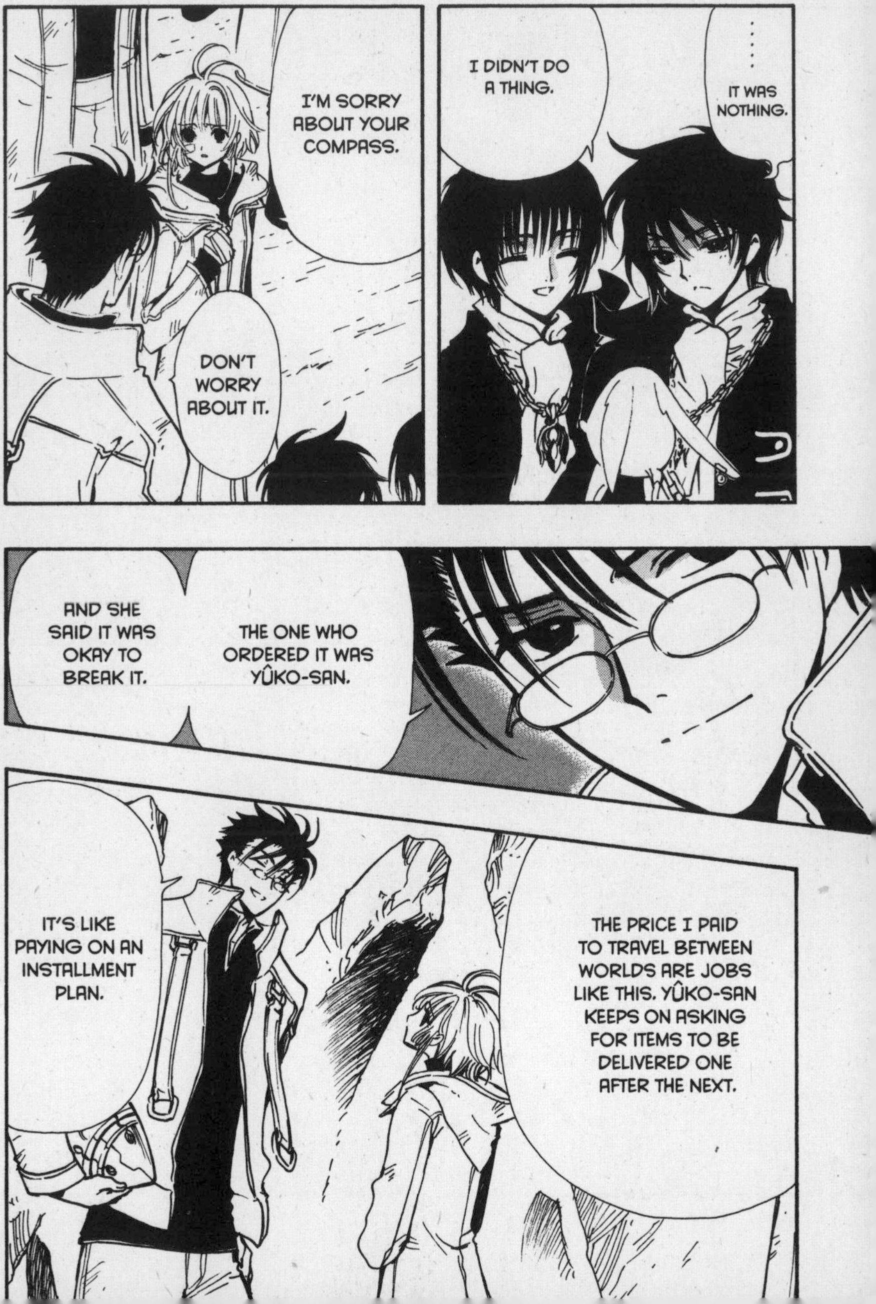
......
IT WAS NOTHING.
I DIDN'T DO A THING.
I'M SORRY ABOUT YOUR COMPASS.
DON'T WORRY ABOUT IT.
THE ONE WHO ORDERED IT WAS YÛKO-SAN.
AND SHE SAID IT WAS OKAY TO BREAK IT.
THE PRICE I PAID TO TRAVEL BETWEEN WORLDS ARE JOBS LIKE THIS. YÛKO-SAN KEEPS ON ASKING FOR ITEMS TO BE DELIVERED ONE AFTER THE NEXT.
IT'S LIKE PAYING ON AN INSTALLMENT PLAN.

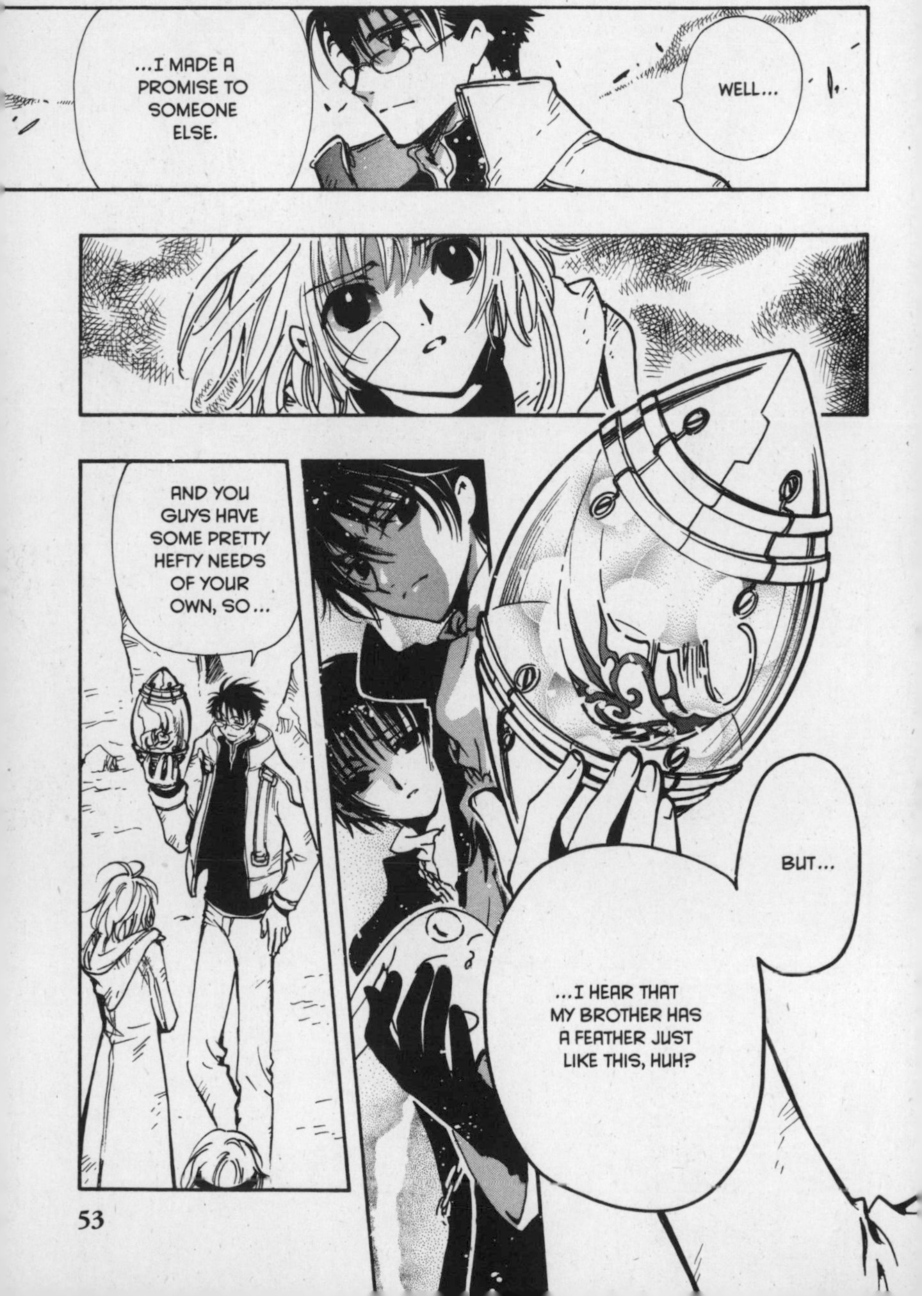
WELL...
...I MADE A PROMISE TO SOMEONE ELSE.
AND YOU GUYS HAVE SOME PRETTY HEFTY NEEDS OF YOUR OWN, SO...
BUT...
...I HEAR THAT MY BROTHER HAS A FEATHER JUST LIKE THIS, HUH?

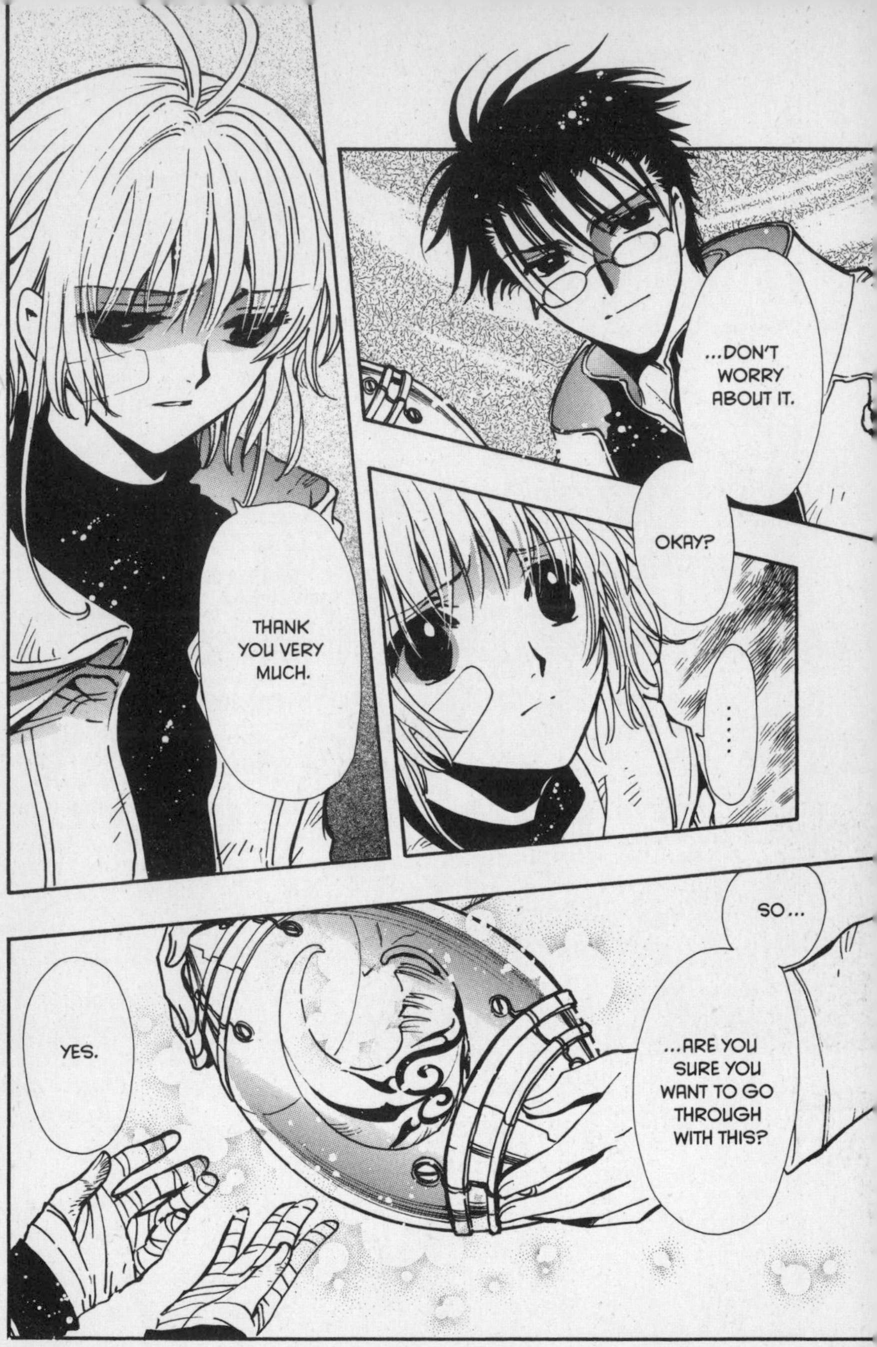
...DON'T WORRY ABOUT IT.
OKAY?
......
THANK YOU VERY MUCH.
SO...
...ARE YOU SURE YOU WANT TO GO THROUGH WITH THIS?
YES.

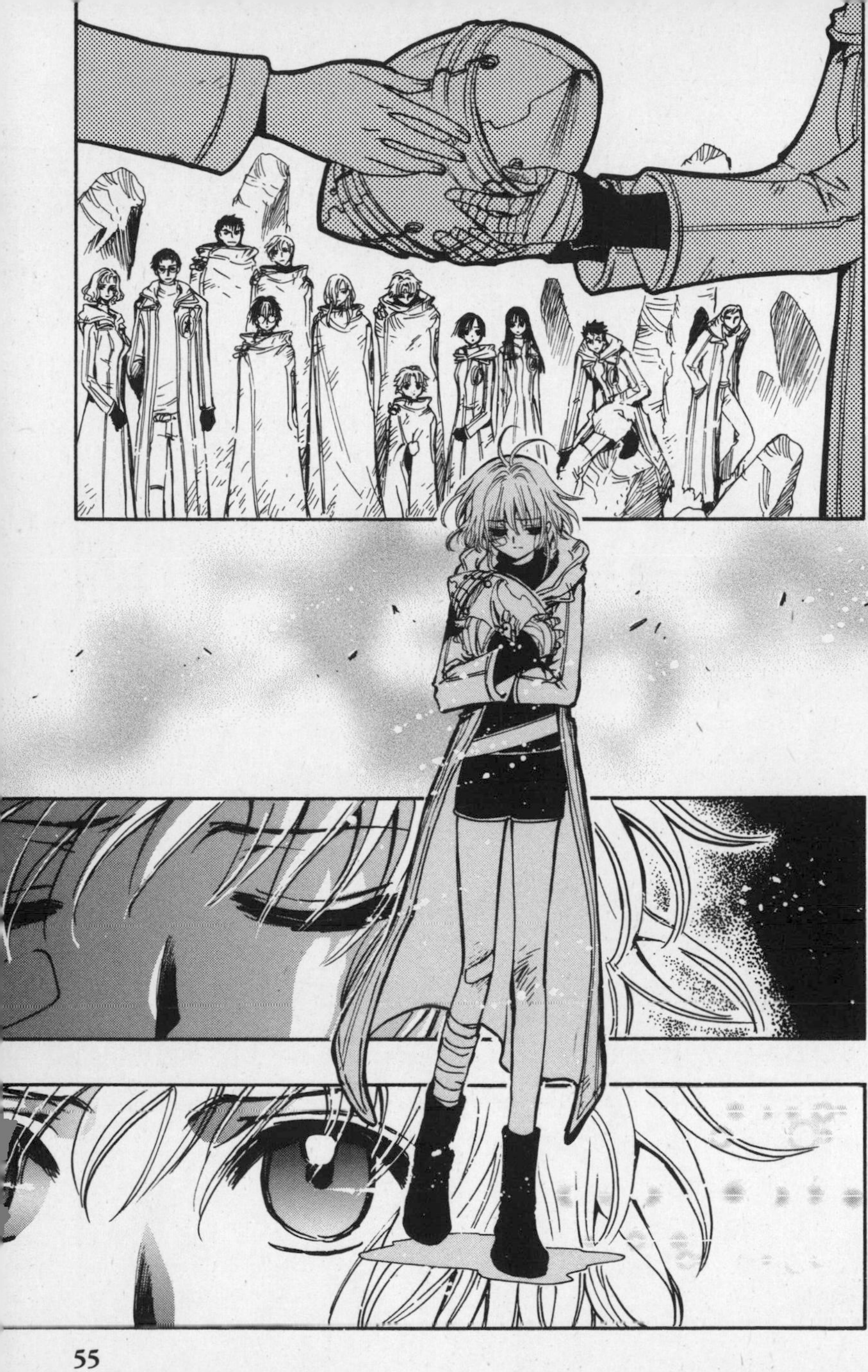

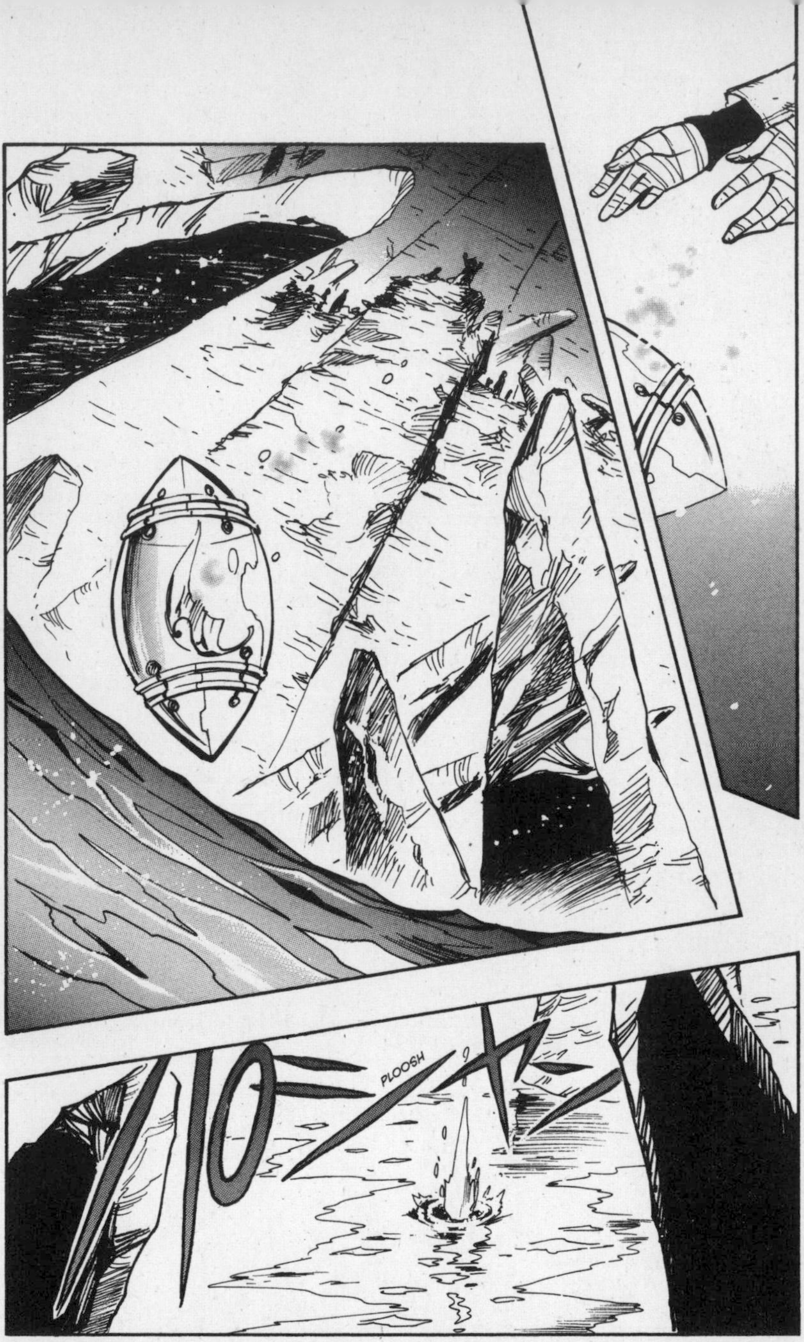
PLOOSH

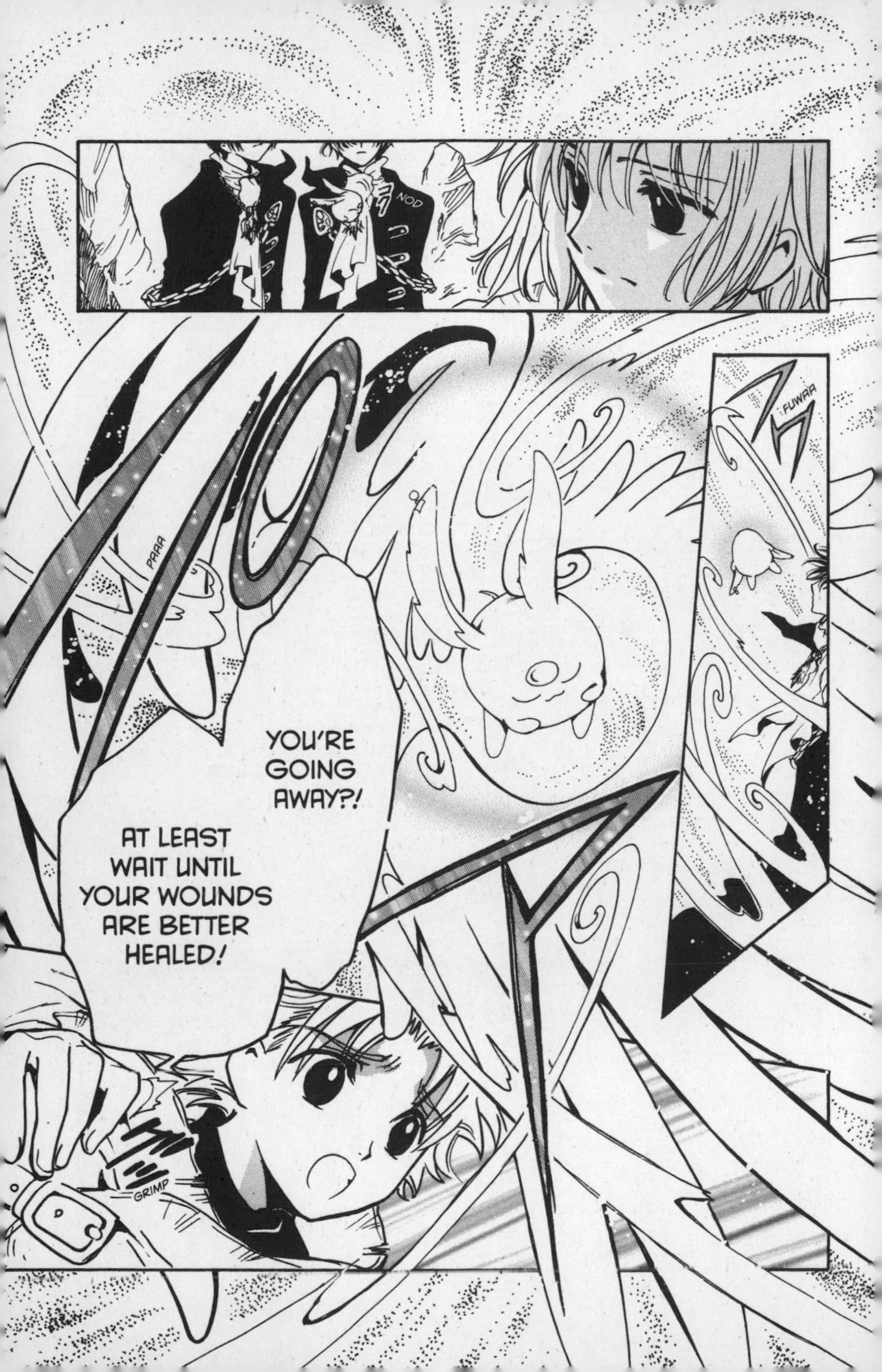
NOD
FUWAA
PAAA
YOU'RE GOING AWAY?!
AT LEAST WAIT UNTIL YOUR WOUNDS ARE BETTER HEALED!
GRIMP

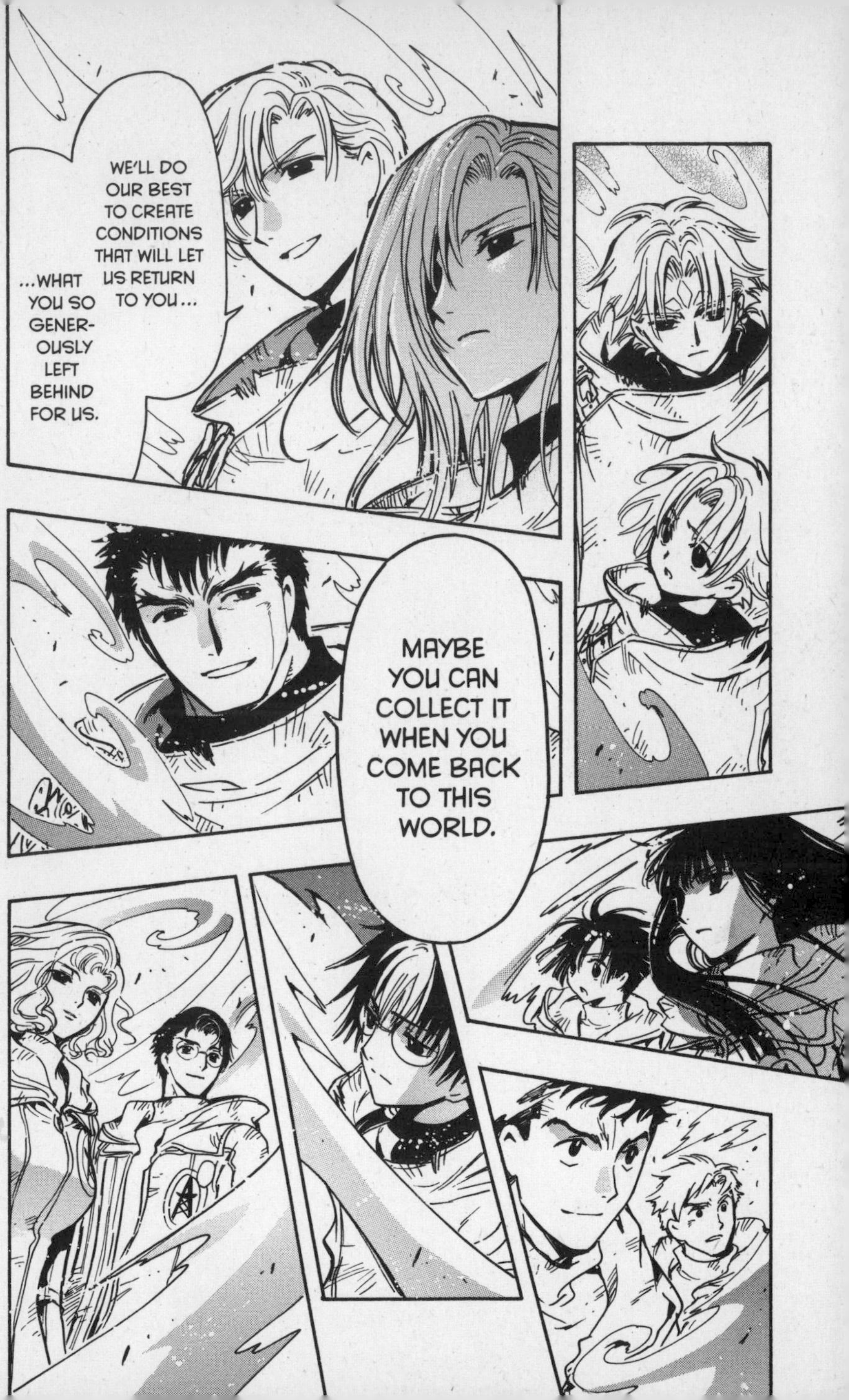
WE'LL DO OUR BEST TO CREATE CONDITIONS THAT WILL LET US RETURN TO YOU...
...WHAT YOU SO GENER-OUSLY LEFT BEHIND FOR US.
MAYBE YOU CAN COLLECT IT WHEN YOU COME BACK TO THIS WORLD.

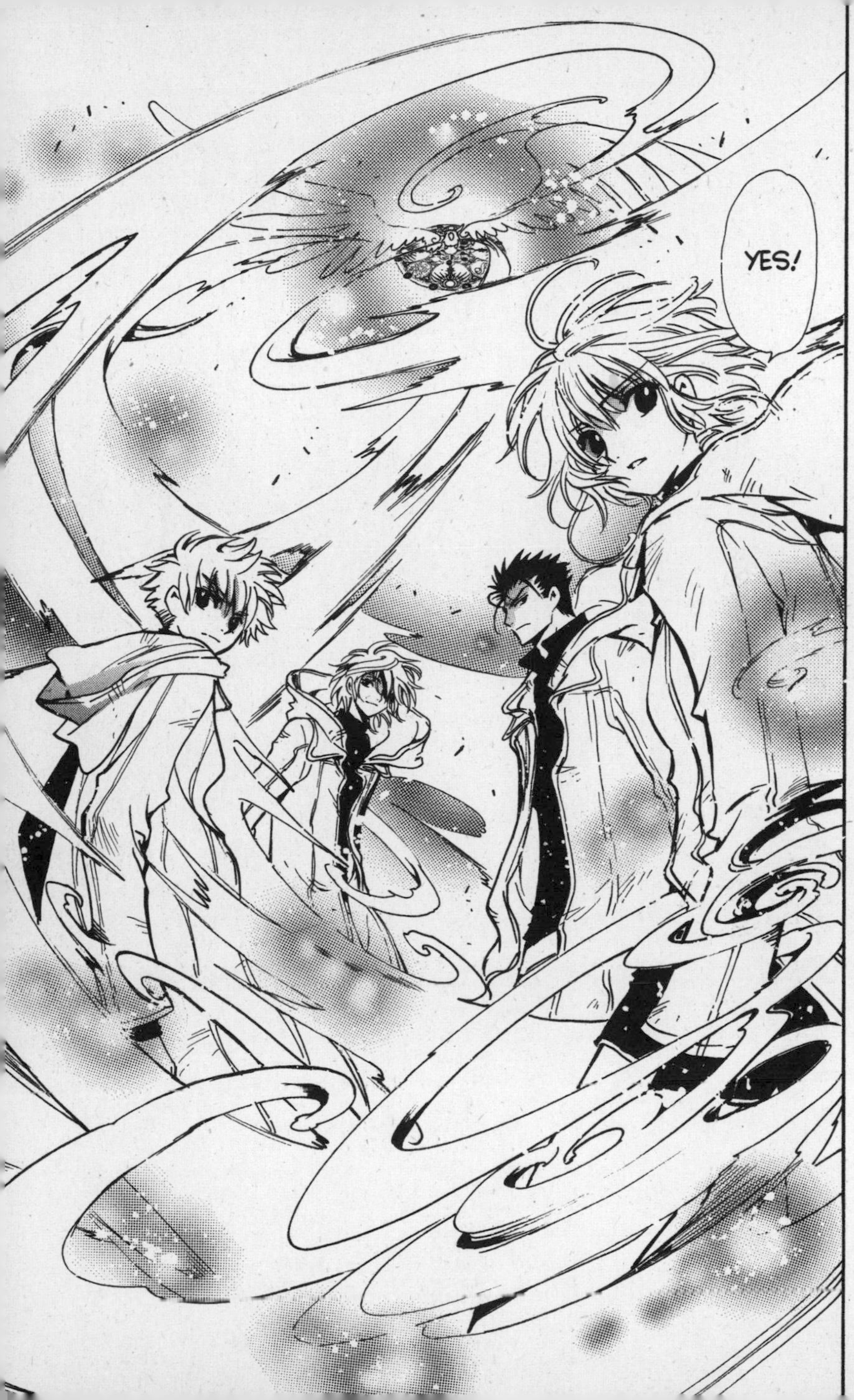
YES!

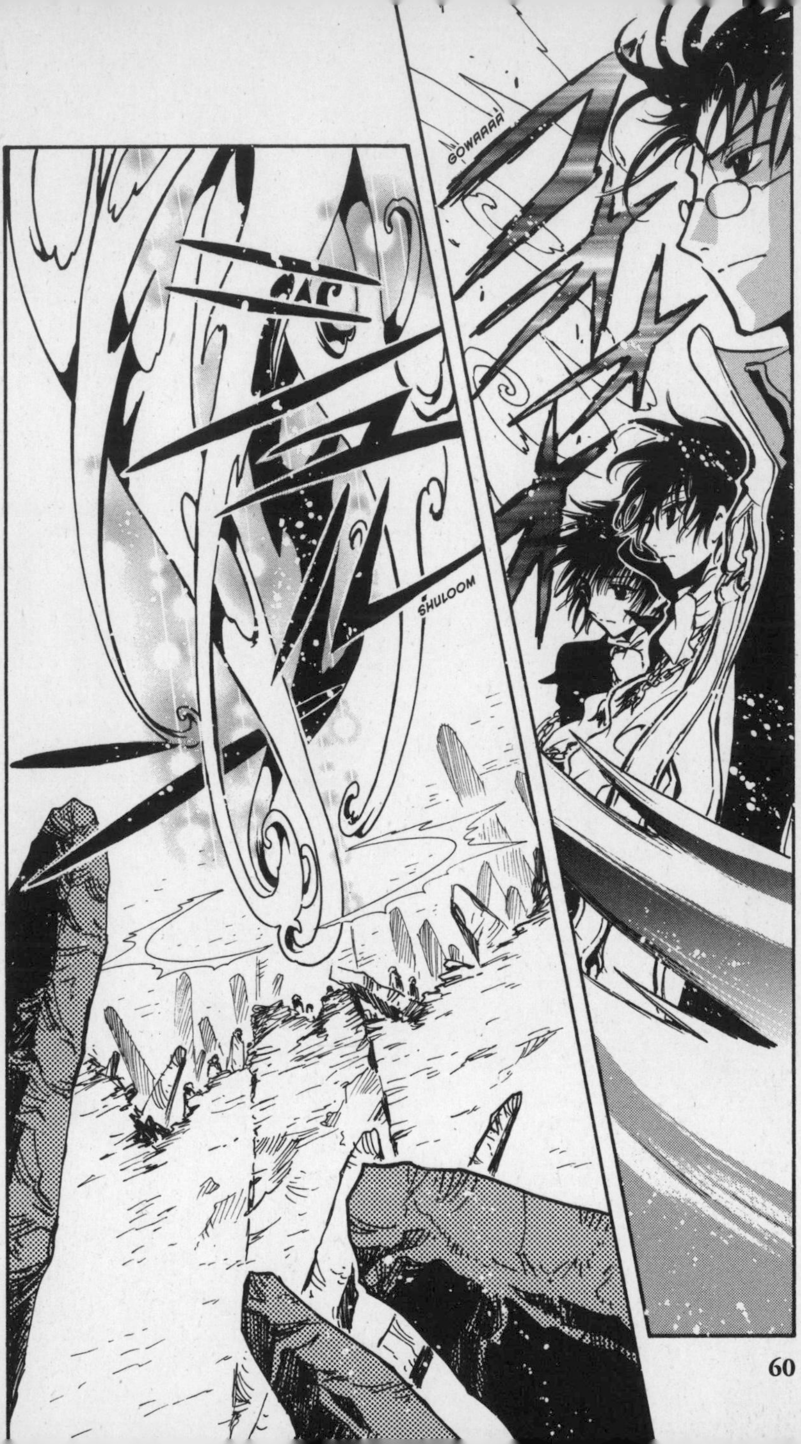
GOWAAAA
SHULOOM

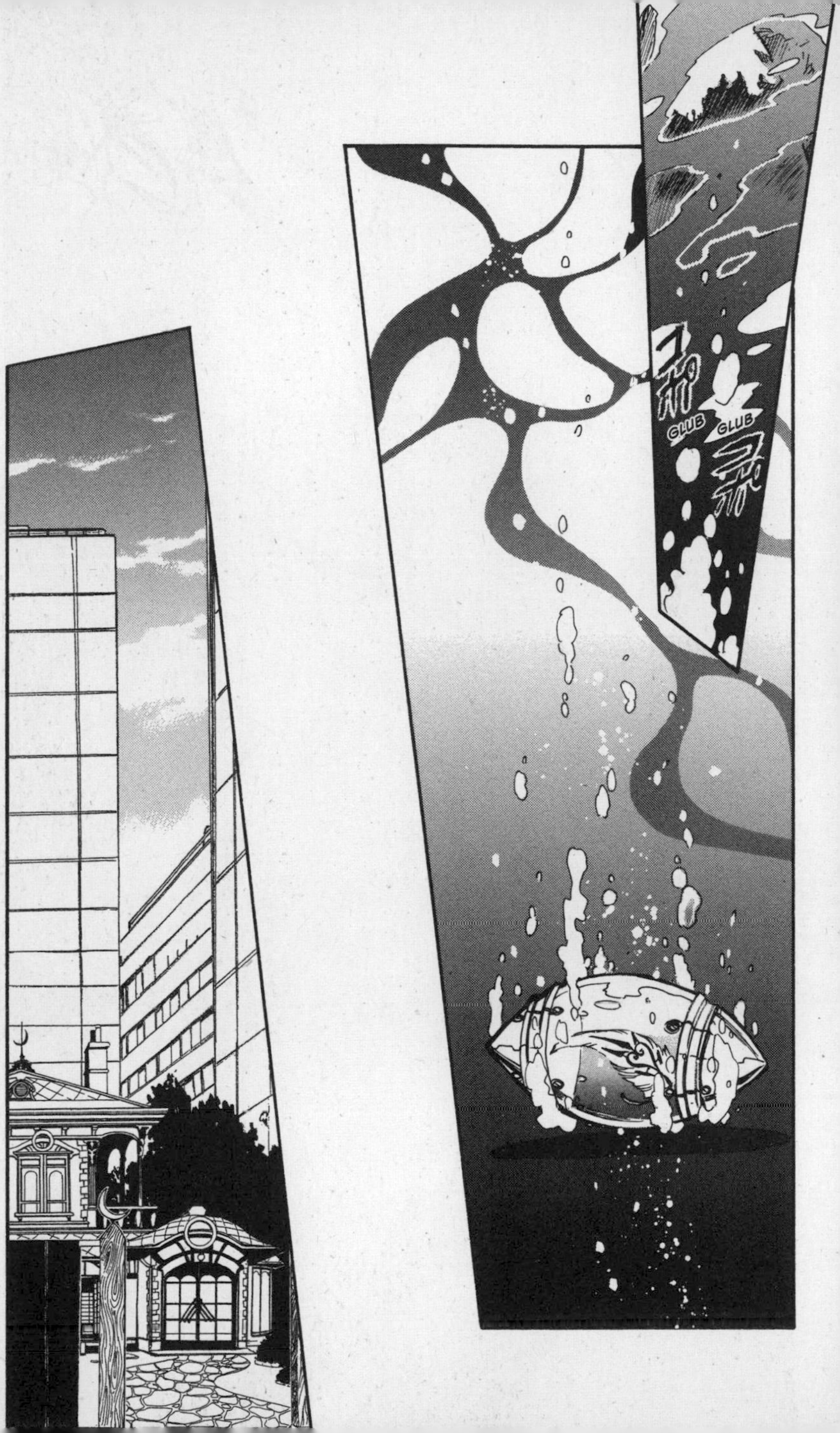
GLUB
GLUB

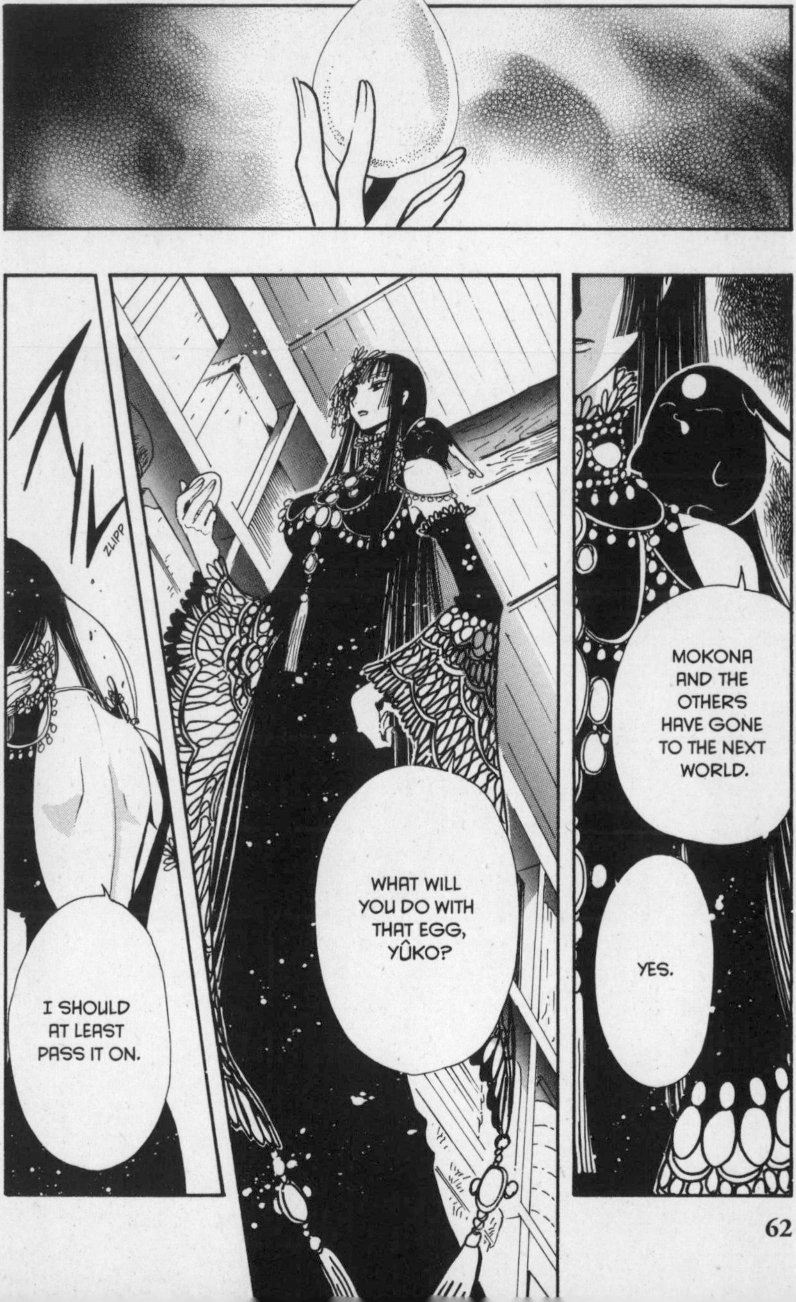
MOKONA AND THE OTHERS HAVE GONE TO THE NEXT WORLD.
YES.
WHAT WILL YOU DO WITH THAT EGG, YÛKO?
ZLIPP
I SHOULD AT LEAST PASS IT ON.

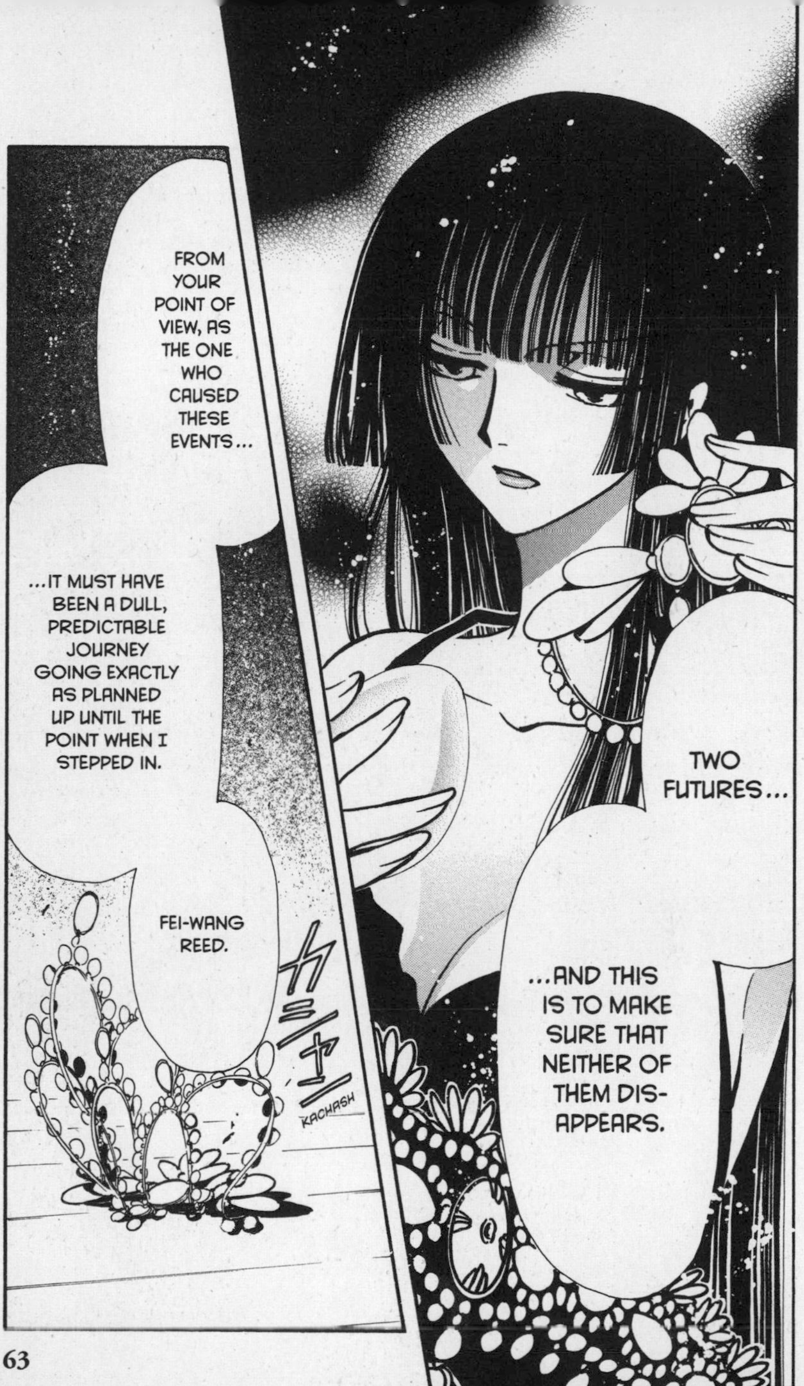
TWO FUTURES...
...AND THIS IS TO MAKE SURE THAT NEITHER OF THEM DIS-APPEARS.
FROM YOUR POINT OF VIEW, AS THE ONE WHO CAUSED THESE EVENTS...
...IT MUST HAVE BEEN A DULL, PREDICTABLE JOURNEY GOING EXACTLY AS PLANNED UP UNTIL THE POINT WHEN I STEPPED IN.
FEI-WANG REED.
KACHASH

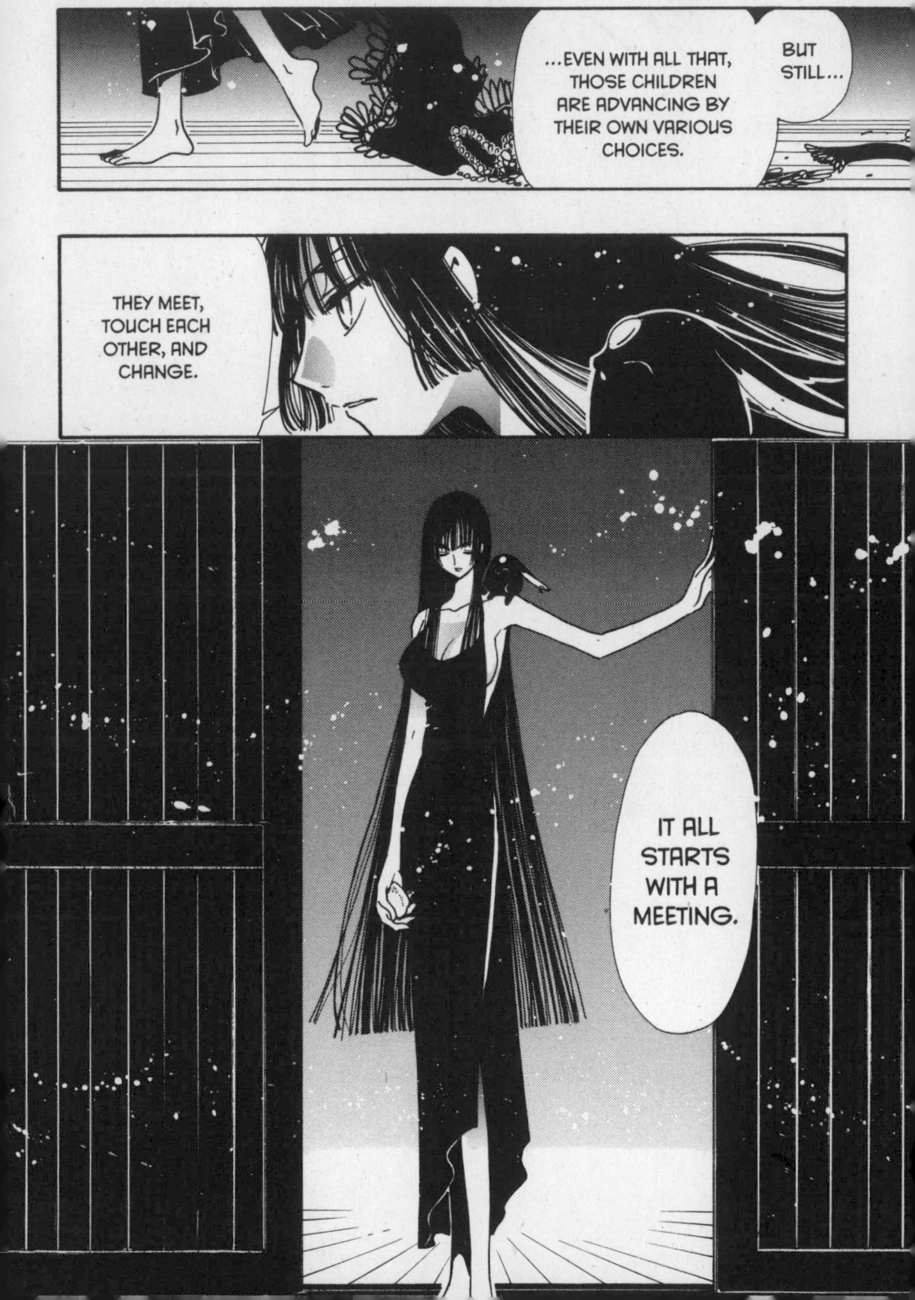
BUT STILL...
...EVEN WITH ALL THAT, THOSE CHILDREN ARE ADVANCING BY THEIR OWN VARIOUS CHOICES.
THEY MEET, TOUCH EACH OTHER, AND CHANGE.
IT ALL STARTS WITH A MEETING.

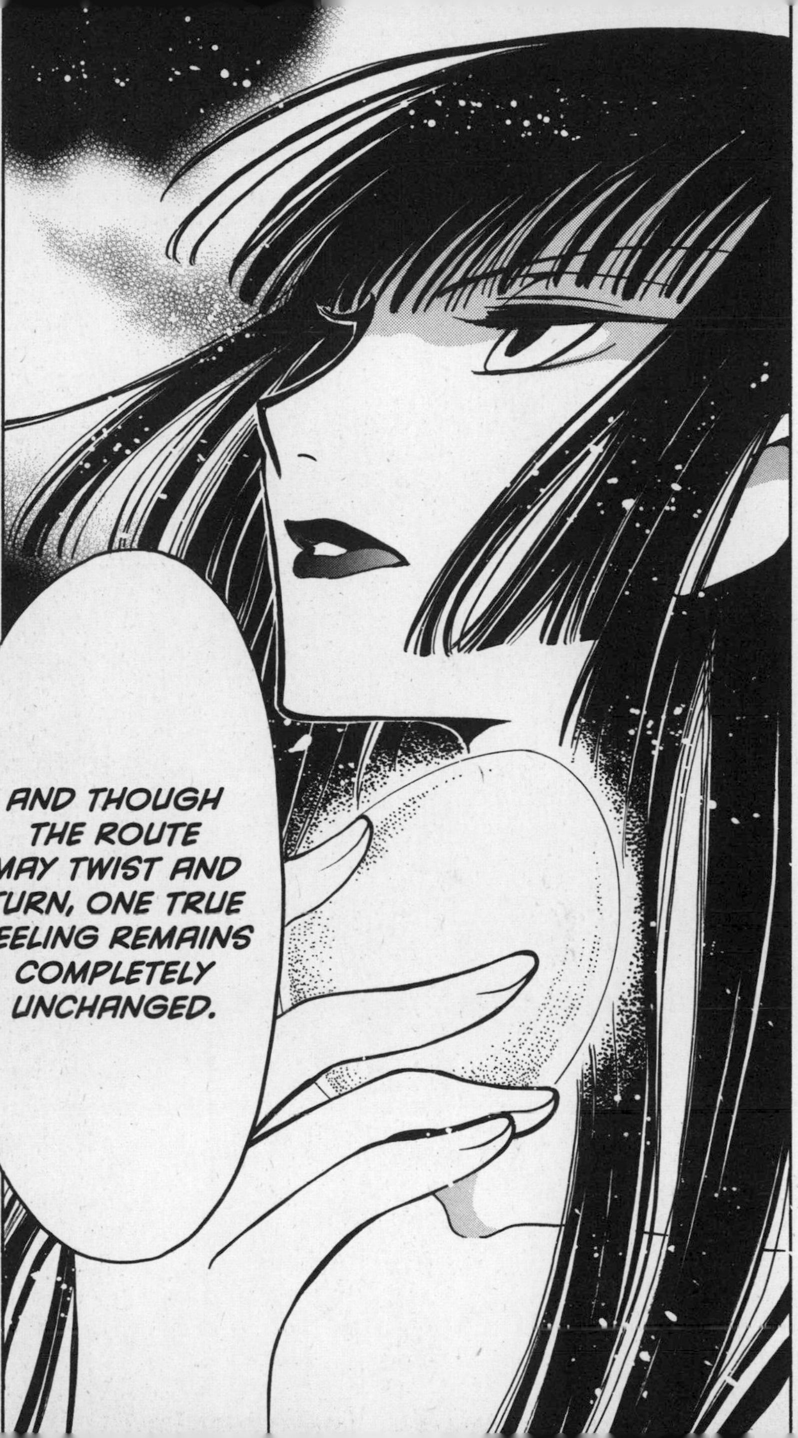
AND THOUGH THE ROUTE MAY TWIST AND TURN, ONE TRUE FEELING REMAINS COMPLETELY UNCHANGED.

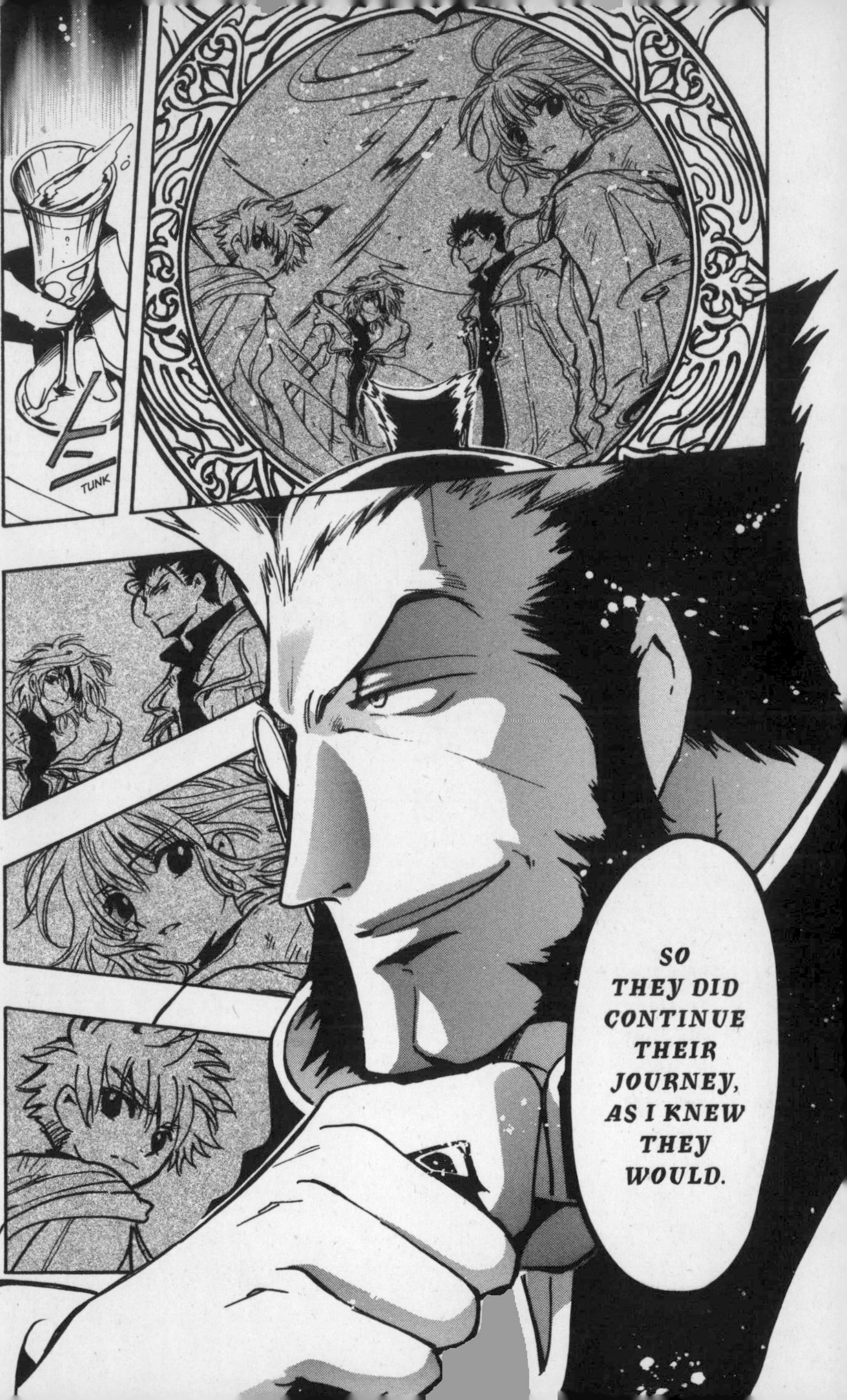
TUNK
SO THEY DID CONTINUE THEIR JOURNEY, AS I KNEW THEY WOULD.

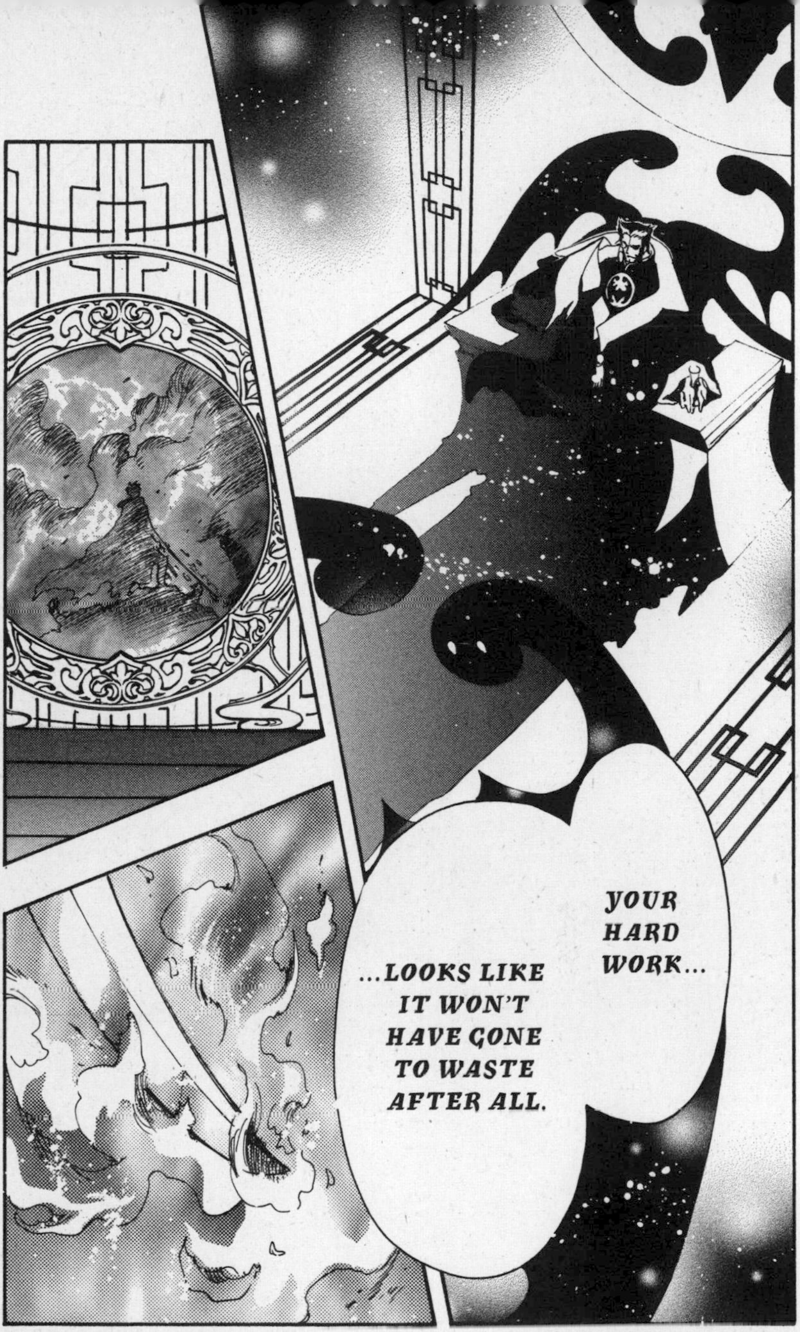
YOUR HARD WORK...
...LOOKS LIKE IT WON'T HAVE GONE TO WASTE AFTER ALL.

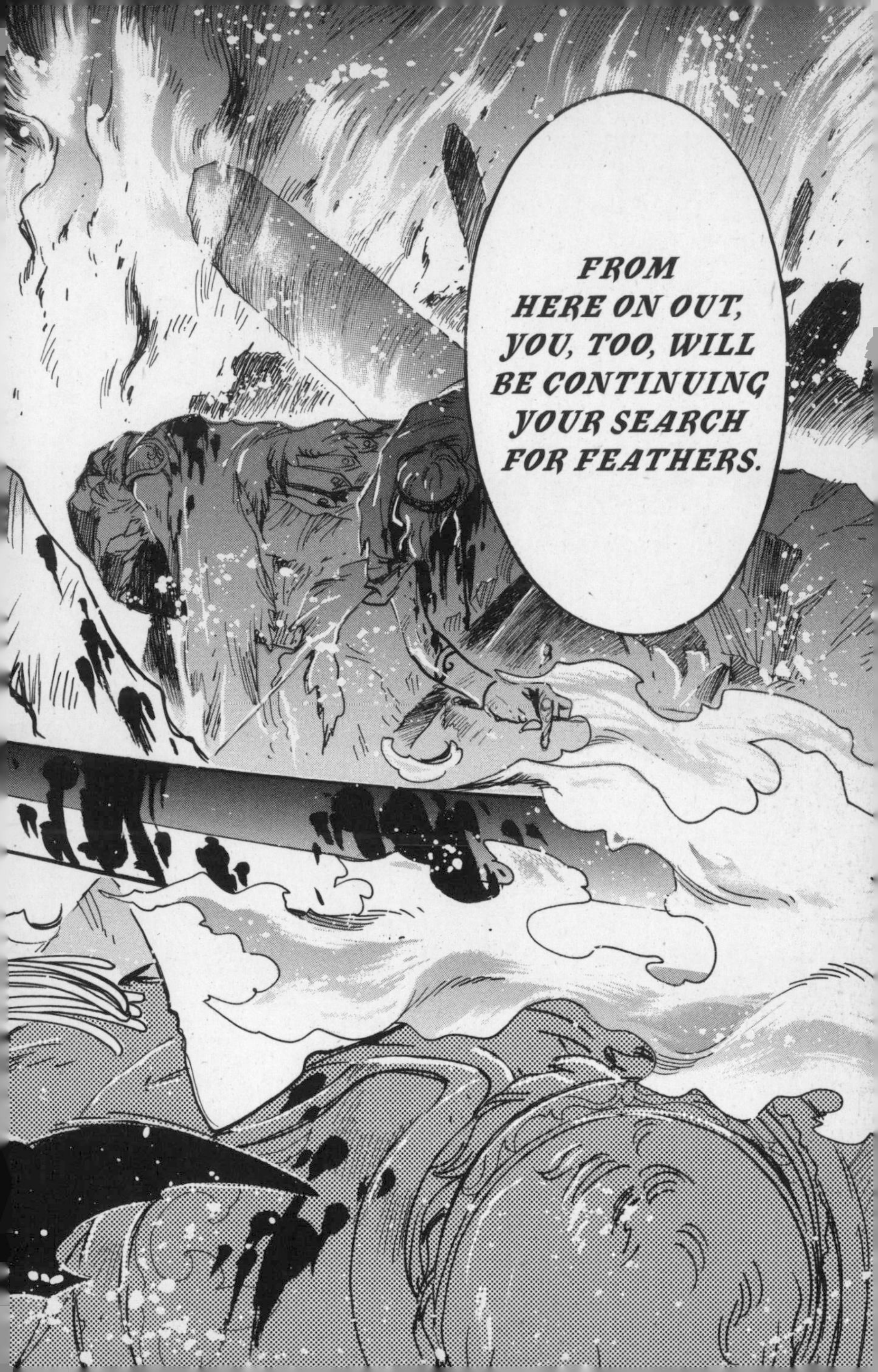
FROM HERE ON OUT, YOU, TOO, WILL BE CONTINUING YOUR SEARCH FOR FEATHERS.

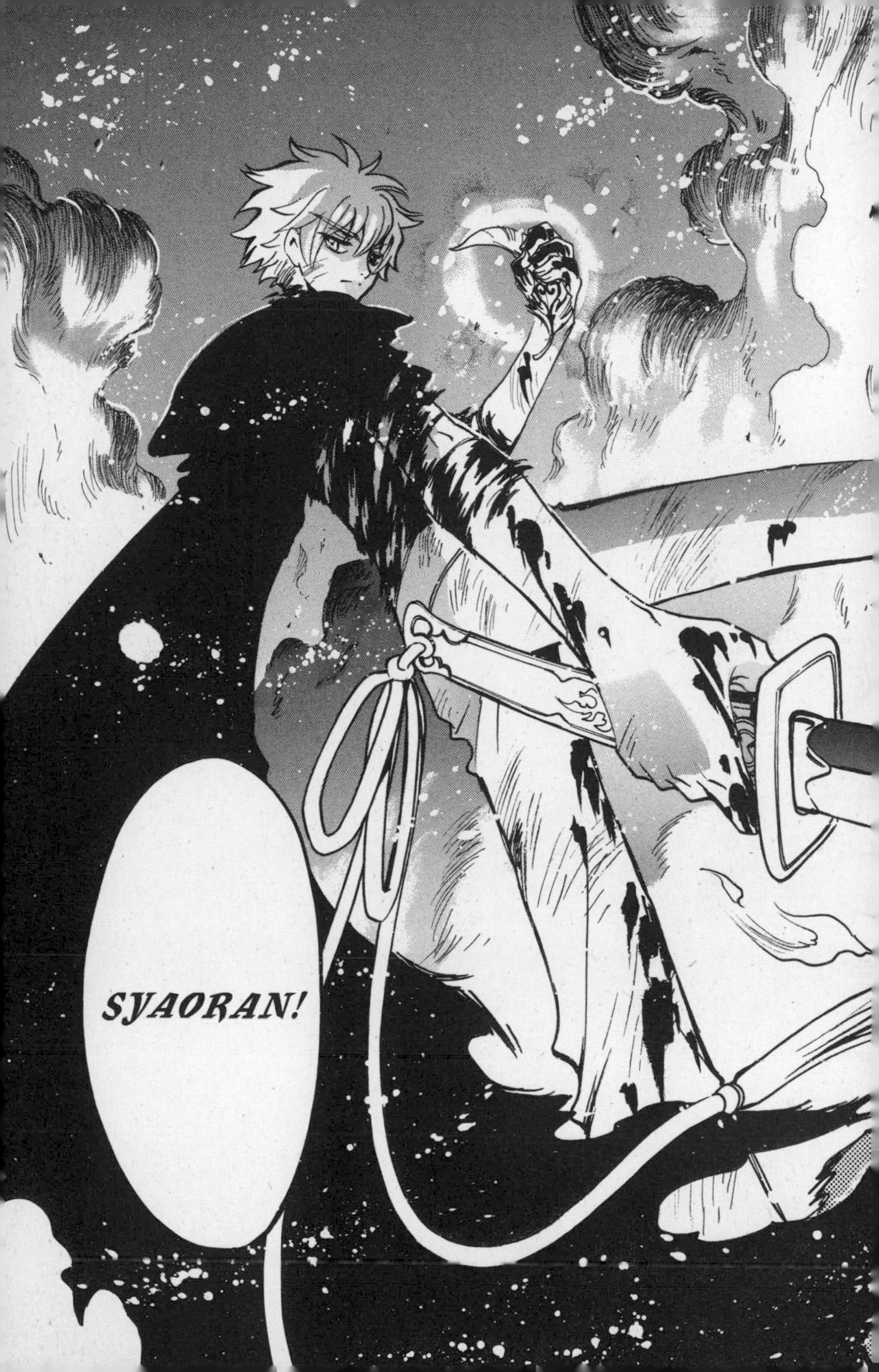
SYAORAN!

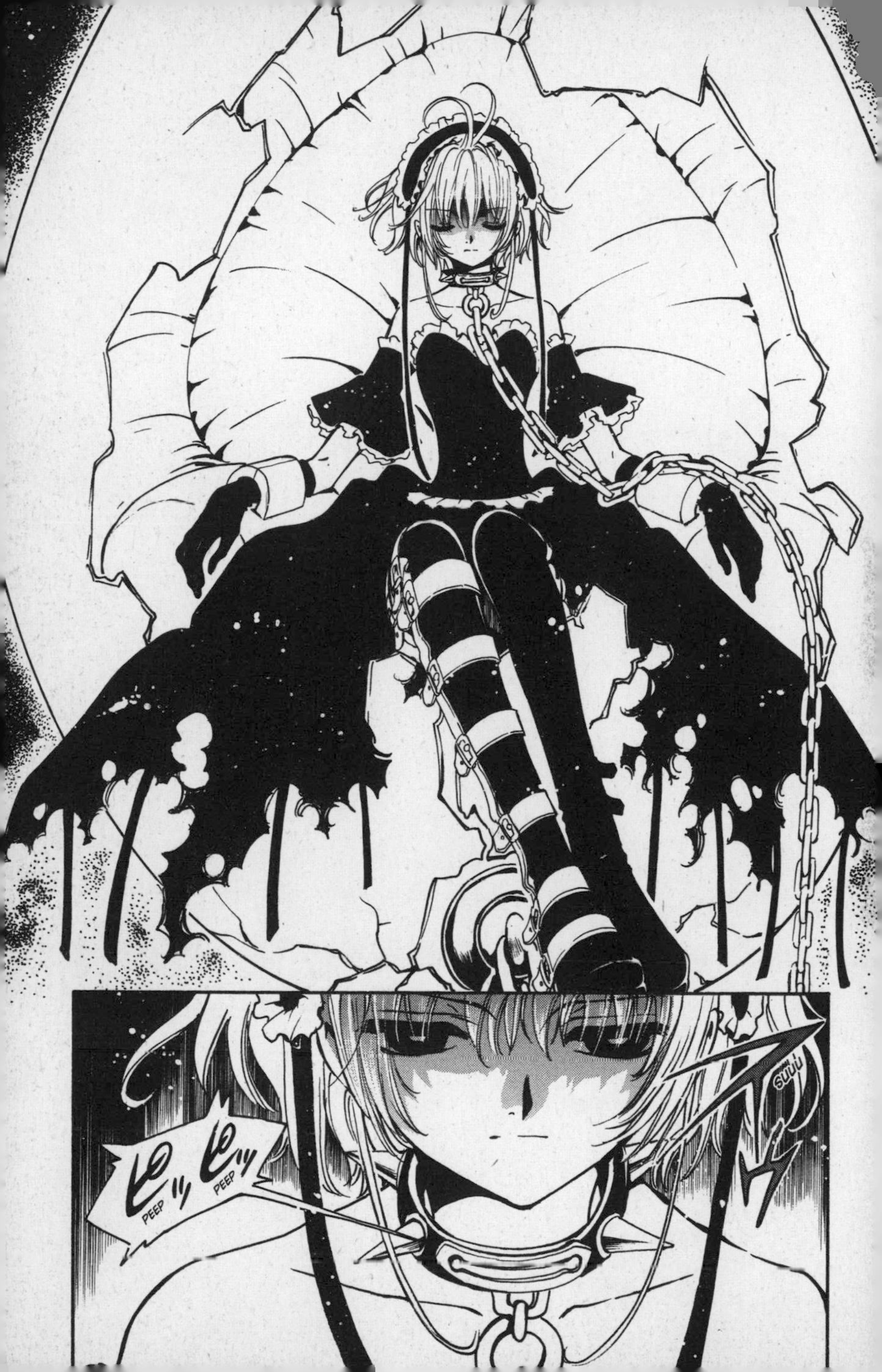
SUUU
PEEP PEEP

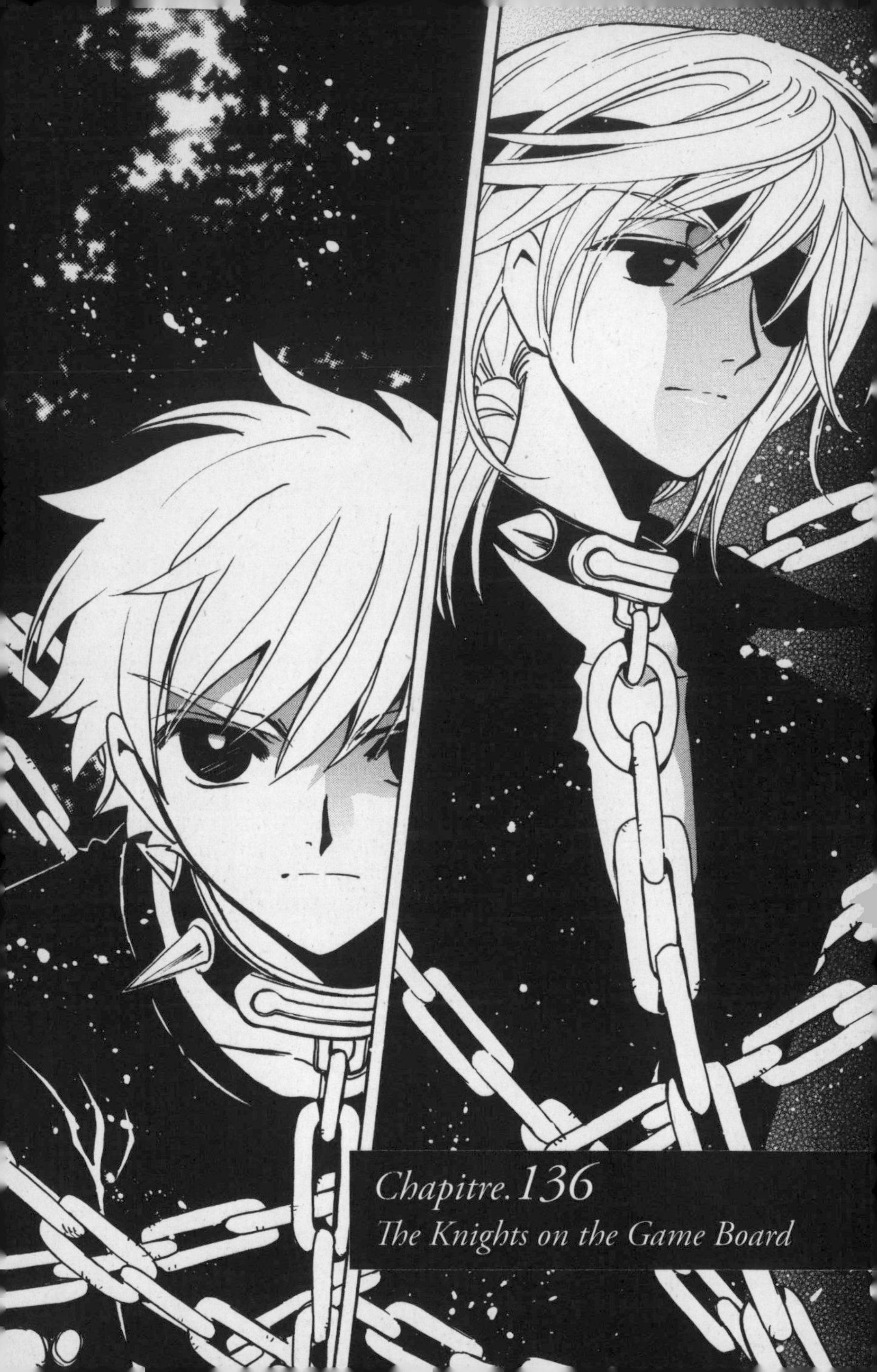
Chapitre. 136
The Knights on the Game Board

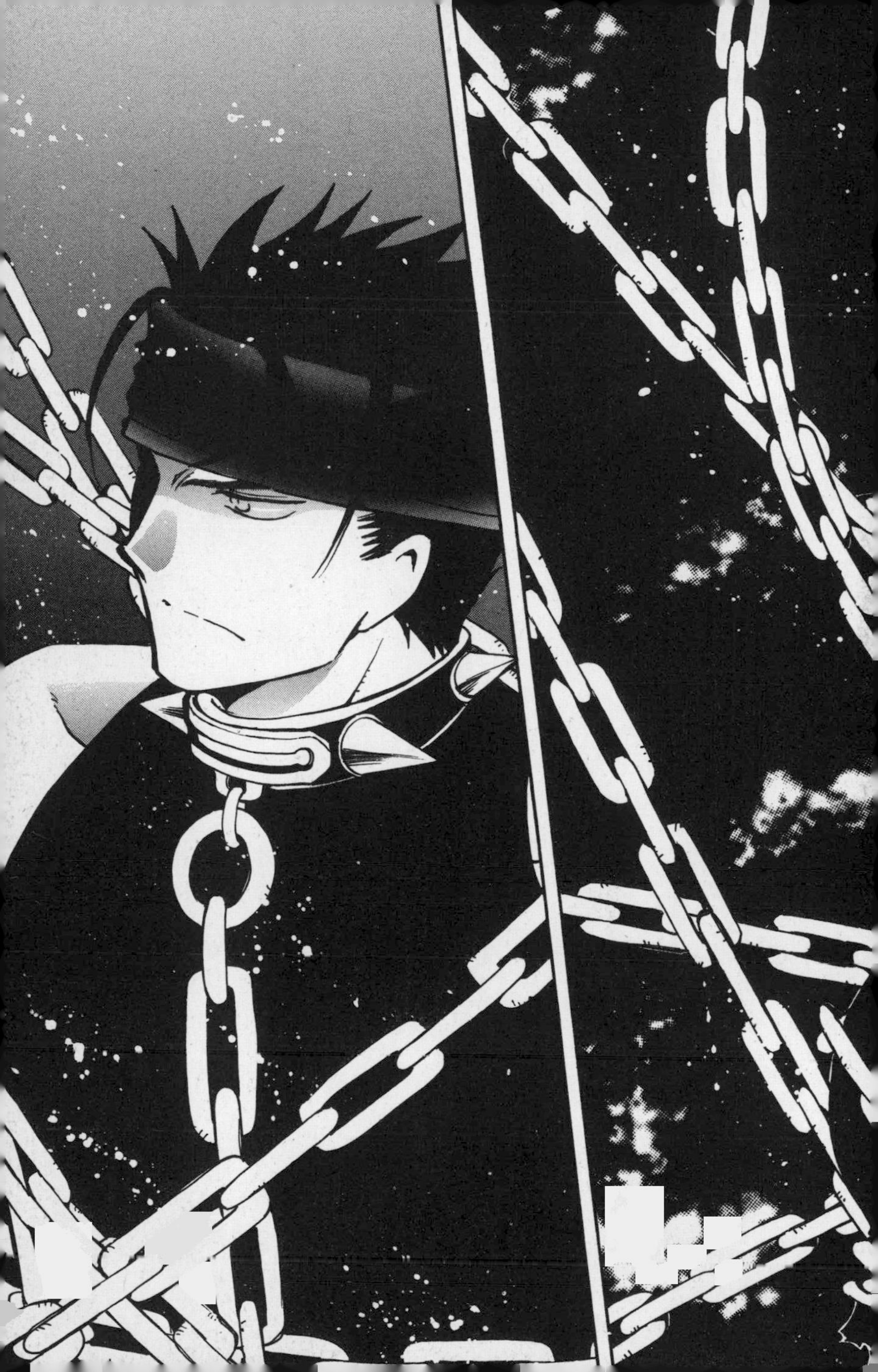

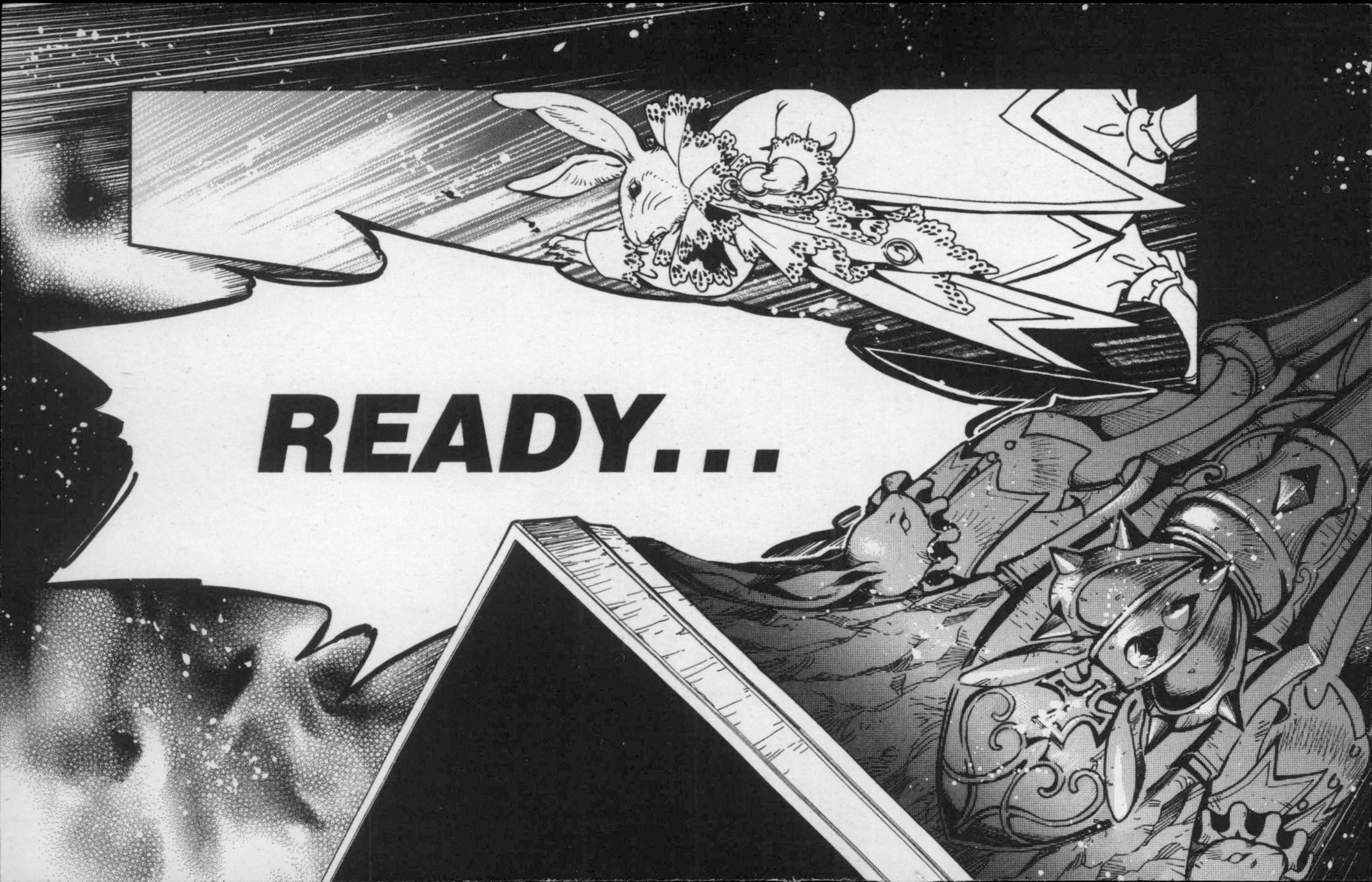
READY...

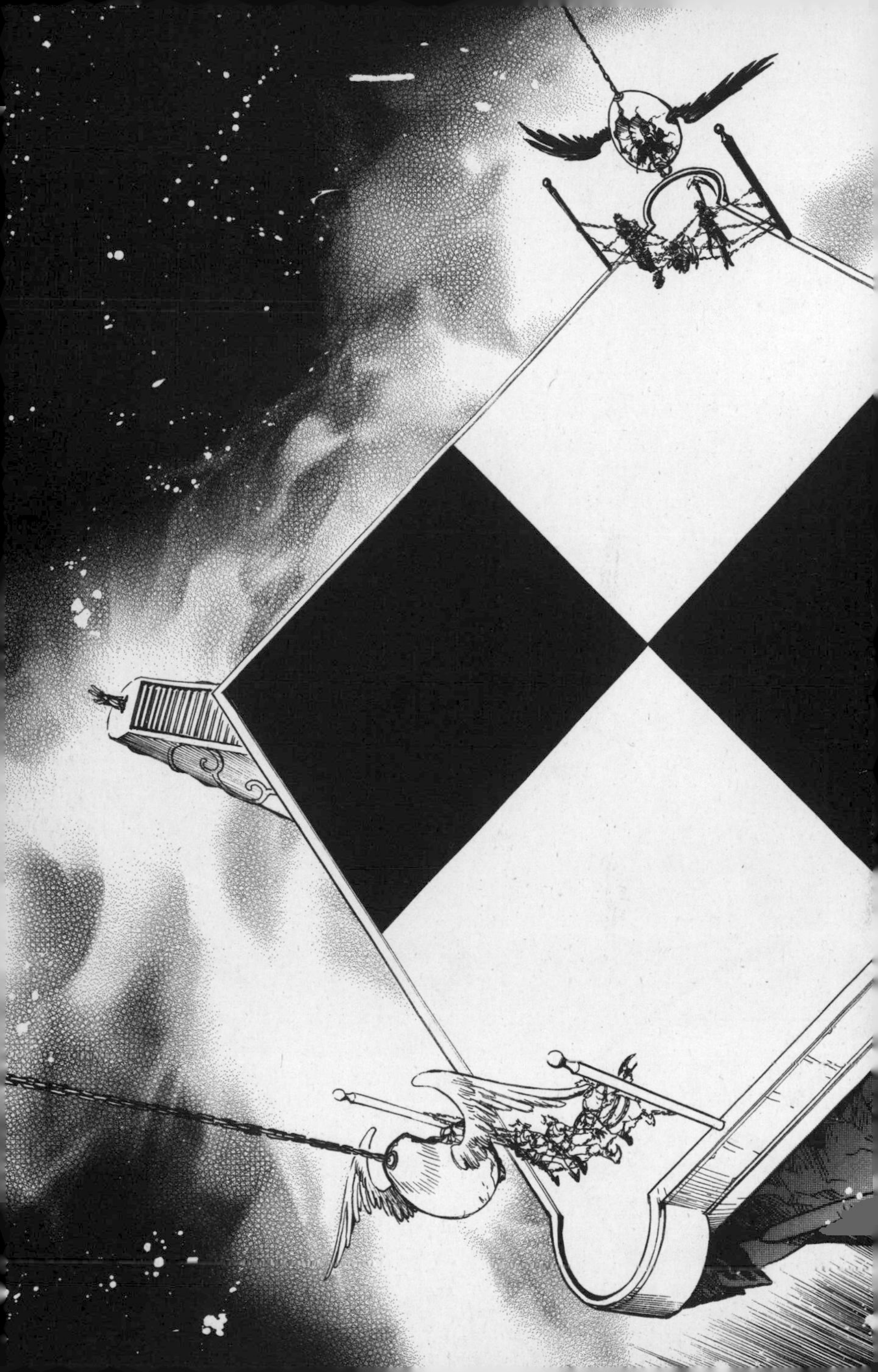

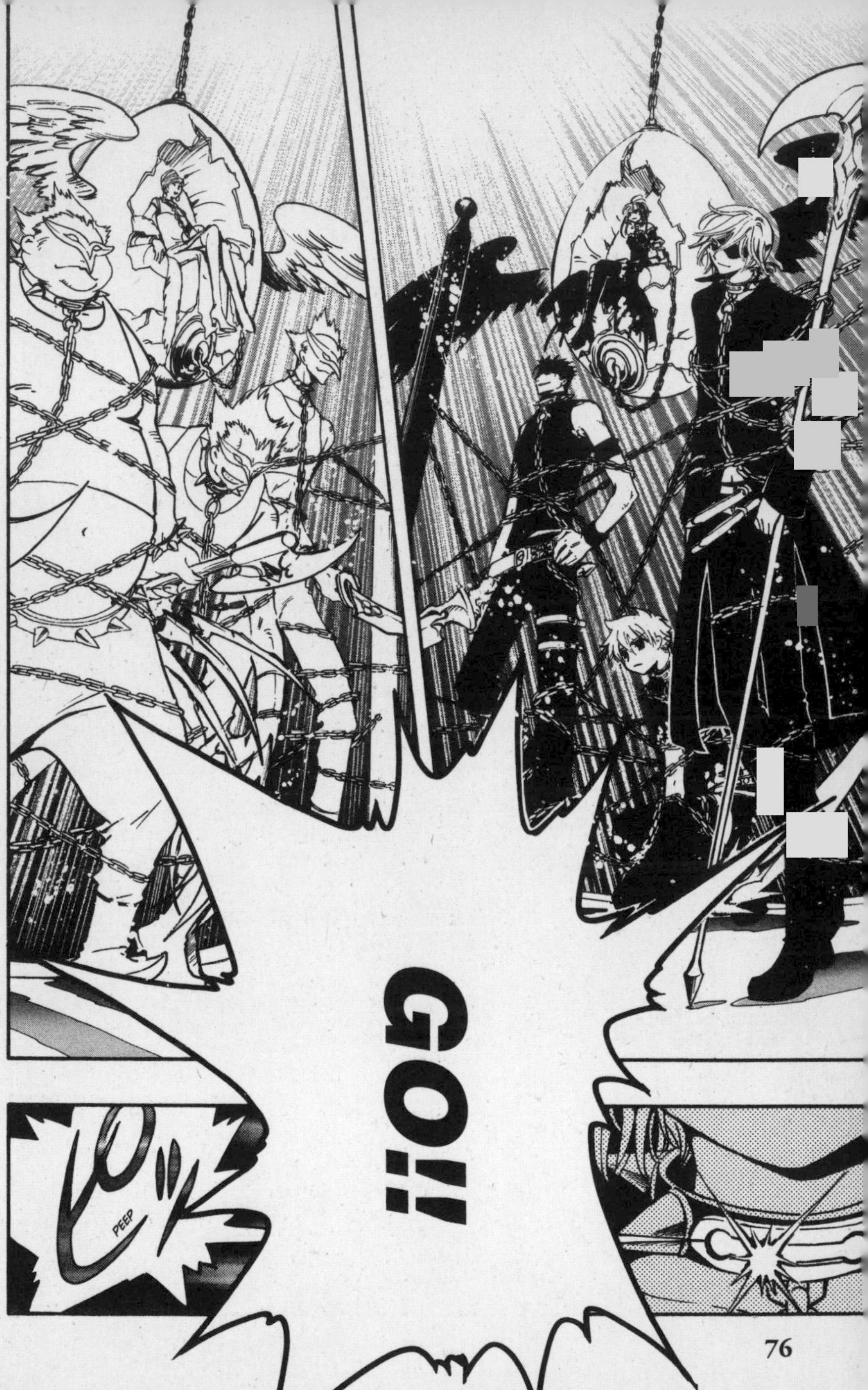
GO!!
PEEP

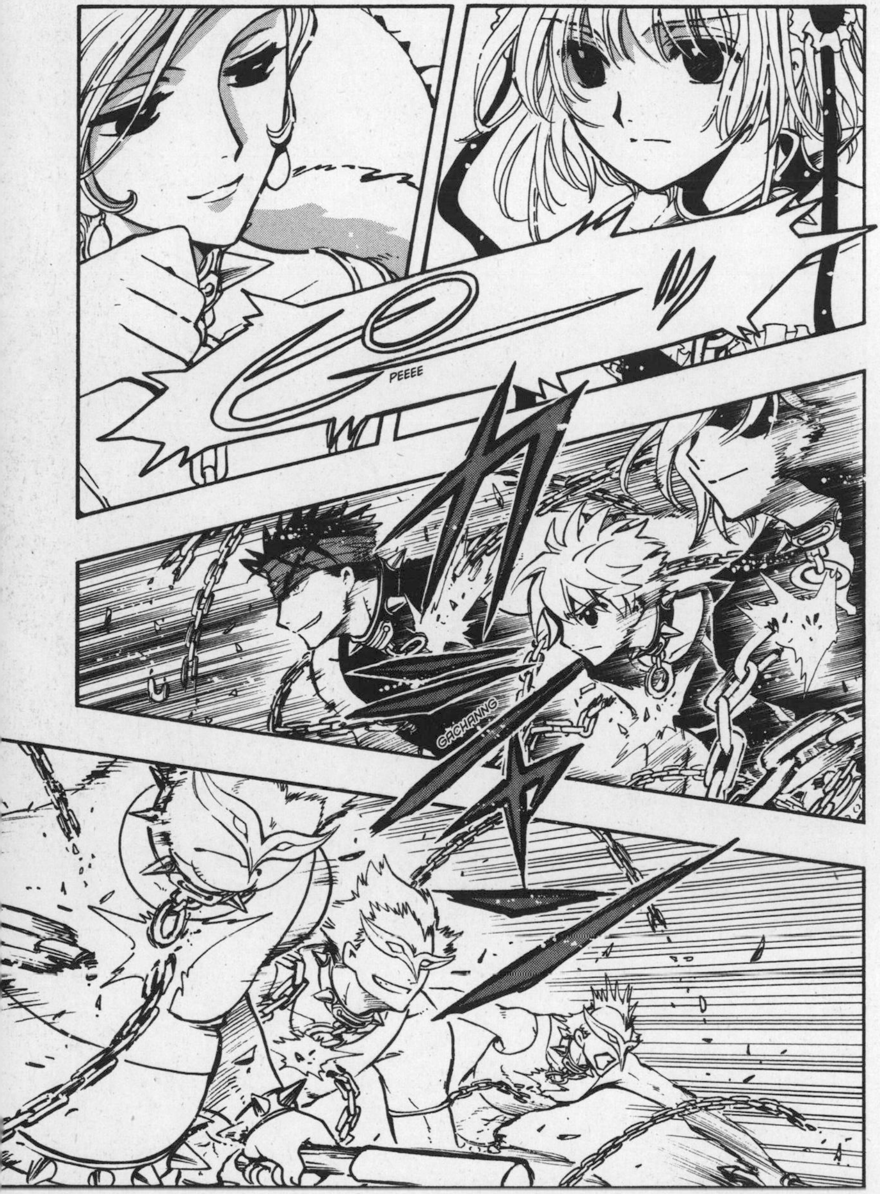
PEEEE
GACHANNG

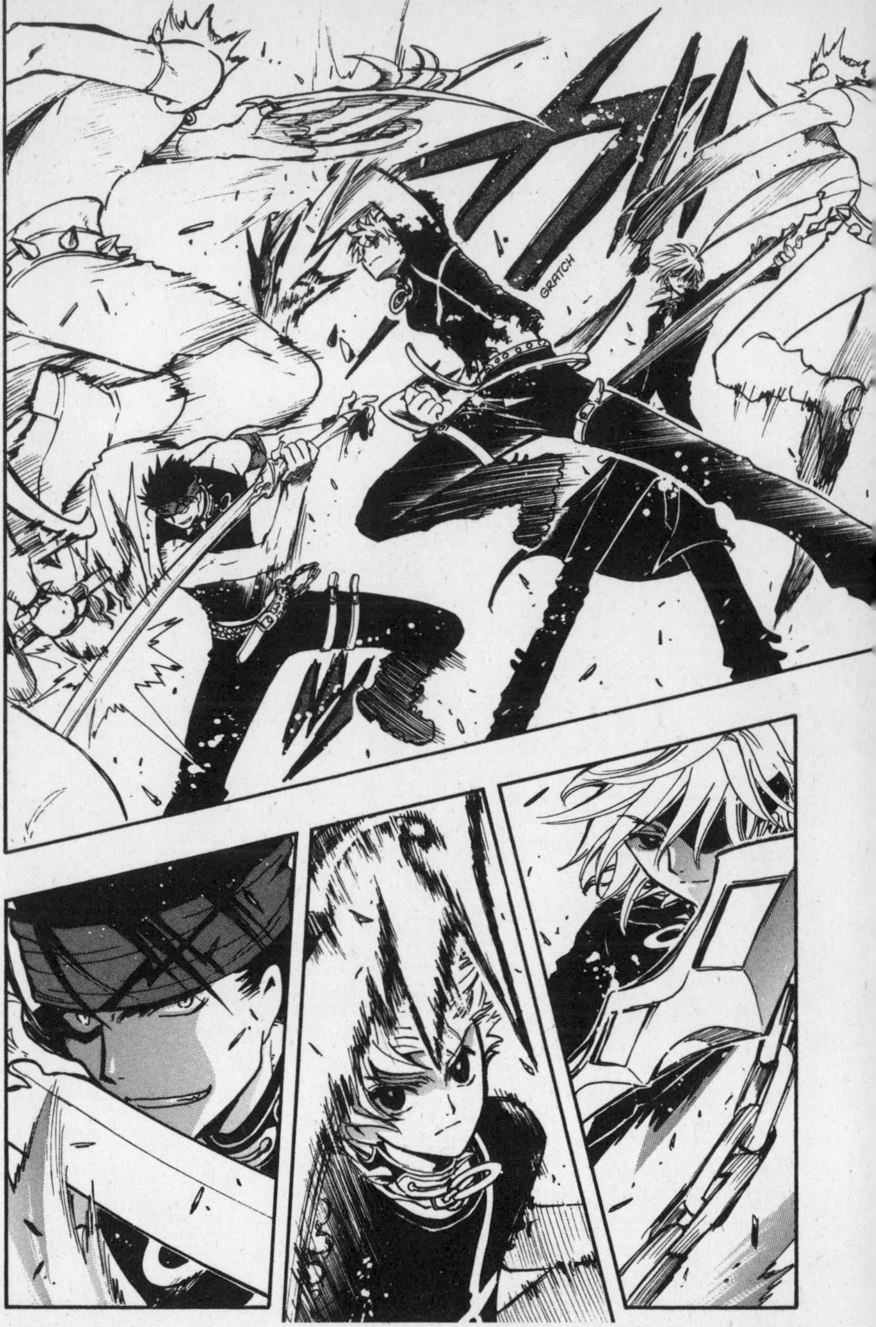
GRATCH

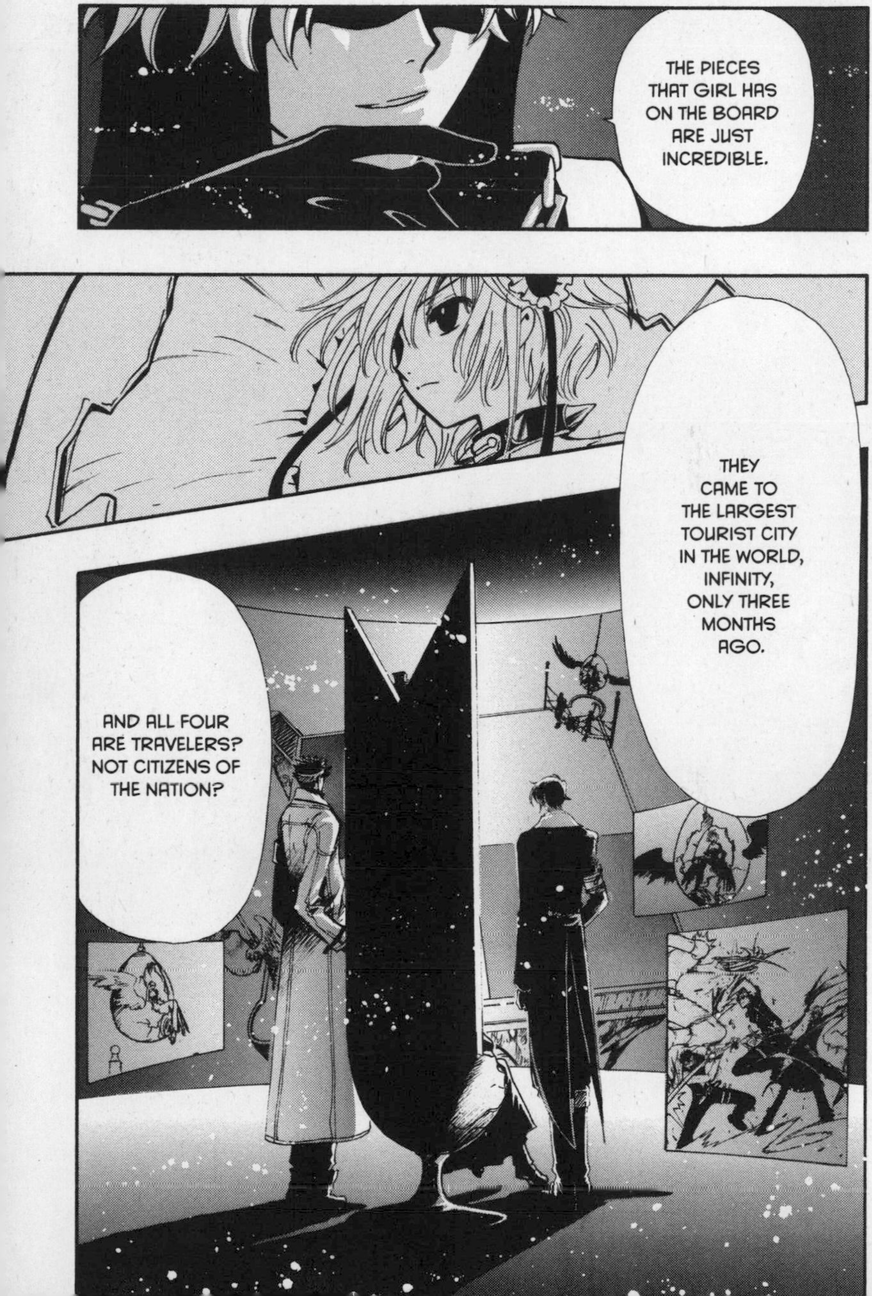
THE PIECES THAT GIRL HAS ON THE BOARD ARE JUST INCREDIBLE.
THEY CAME TO THE LARGEST TOURIST CITY IN THE WORLD, INFINITY, ONLY THREE MONTHS AGO.
AND ALL FOUR ARE TRAVELERS? NOT CITIZENS OF THE NATION?

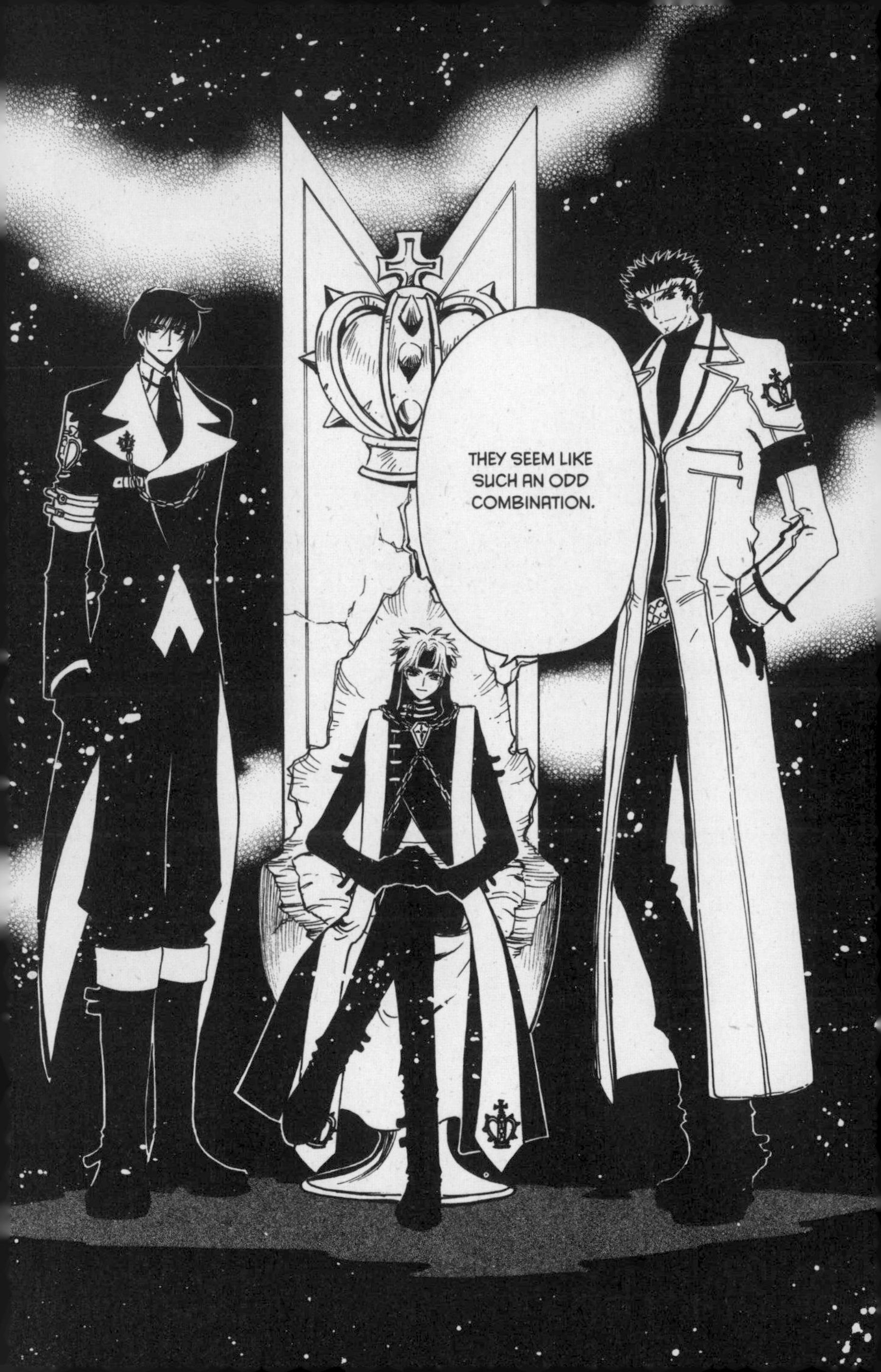
THEY SEEM LIKE SUCH AN ODD COMBINATION.

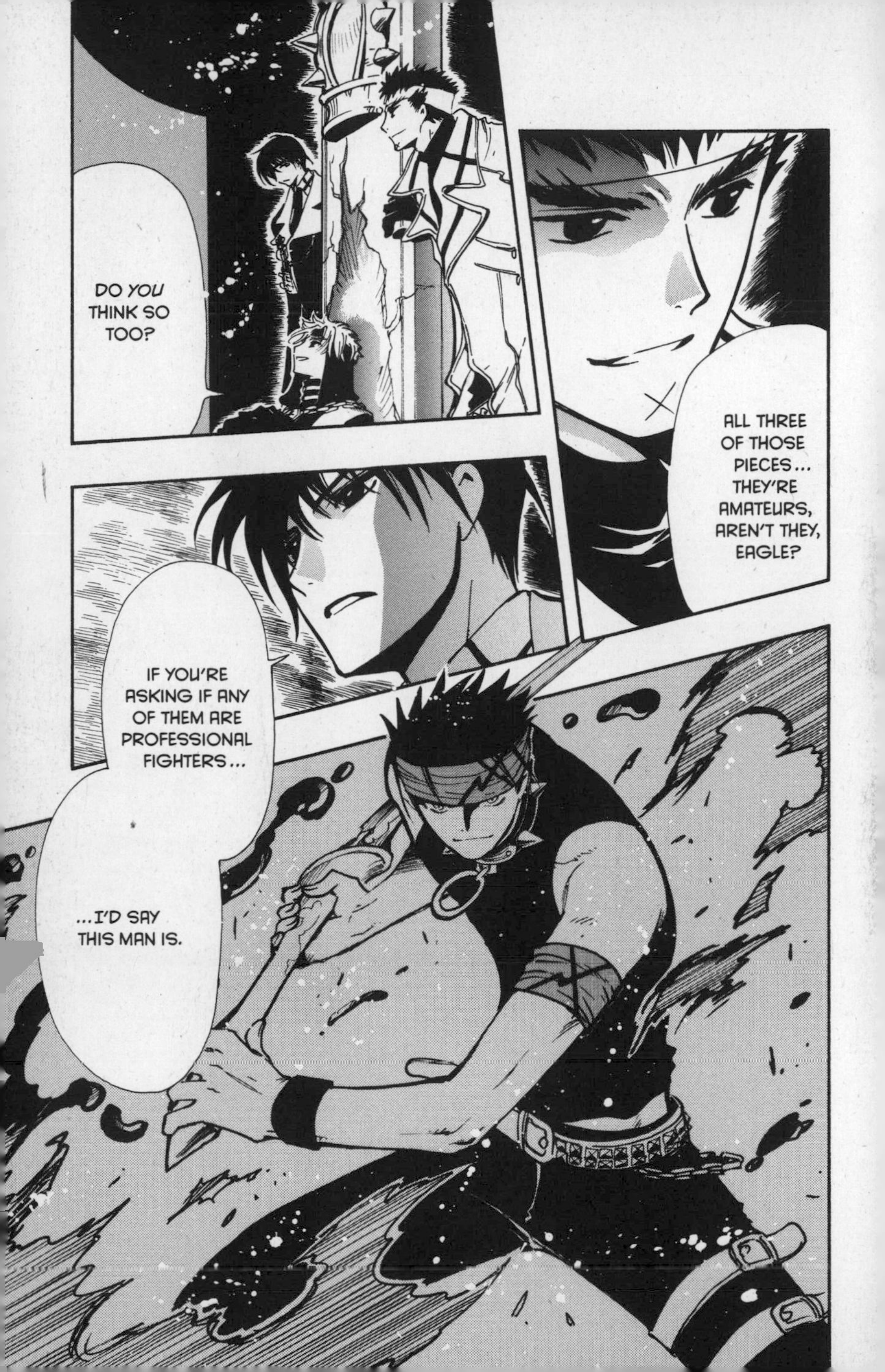
ALL THREE OF THOSE PIECES... THEY'RE AMATEURS, AREN'T THEY, EAGLE?
DO *YOU* THINK SO TOO?
IF YOU'RE ASKING IF ANY OF THEM ARE PROFESSIONAL FIGHTERS...
...I'D SAY THIS MAN IS.

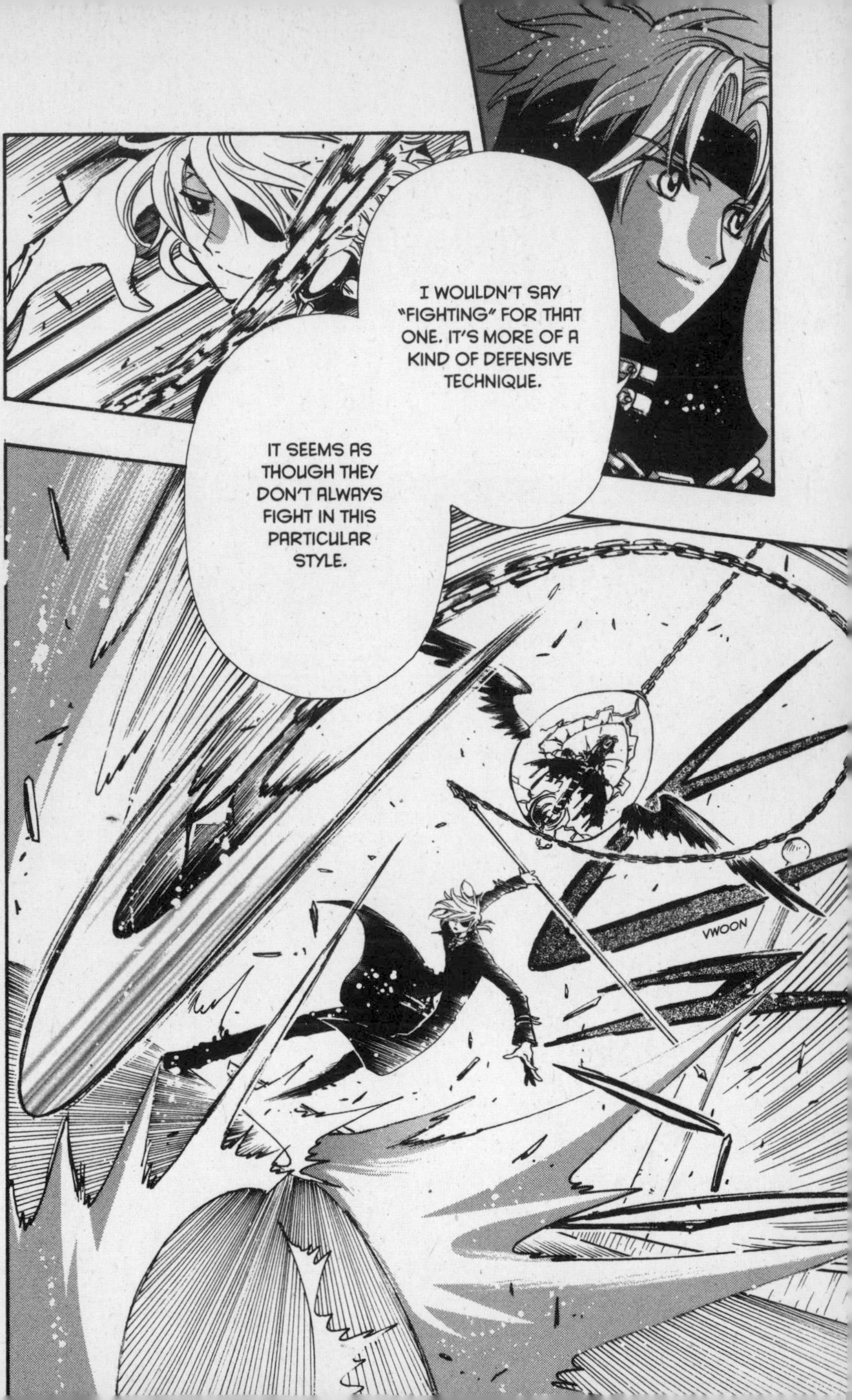
I WOULDN'T SAY "FIGHTING" FOR THAT ONE. IT'S MORE OF A KIND OF DEFENSIVE TECHNIQUE.
IT SEEMS AS THOUGH THEY DON'T ALWAYS FIGHT IN THIS PARTICULAR STYLE.
VWOON

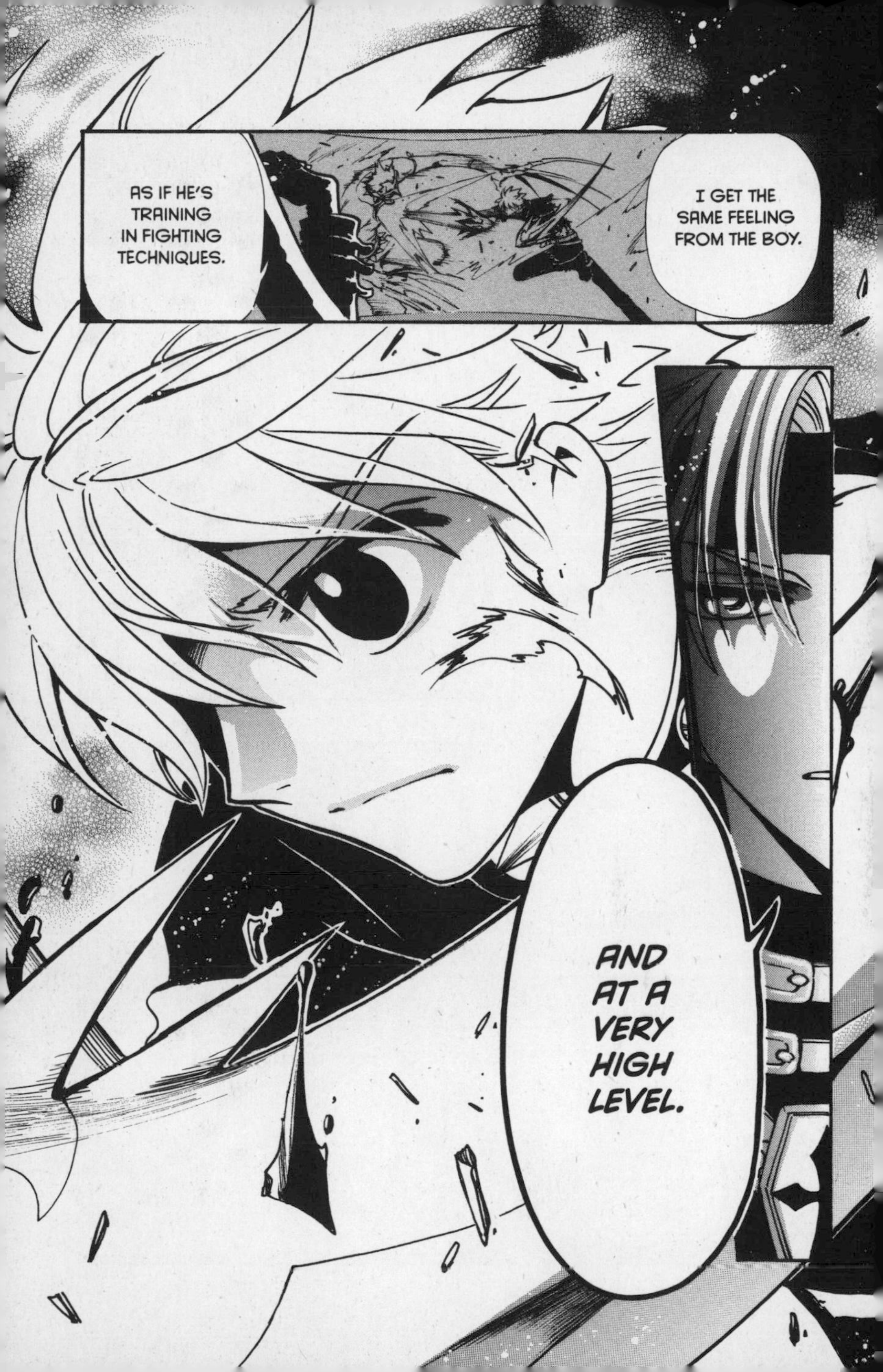
I GET THE SAME FEELING FROM THE BOY.
AS IF HE'S TRAINING IN FIGHTING TECHNIQUES.
AND AT A VERY HIGH LEVEL.

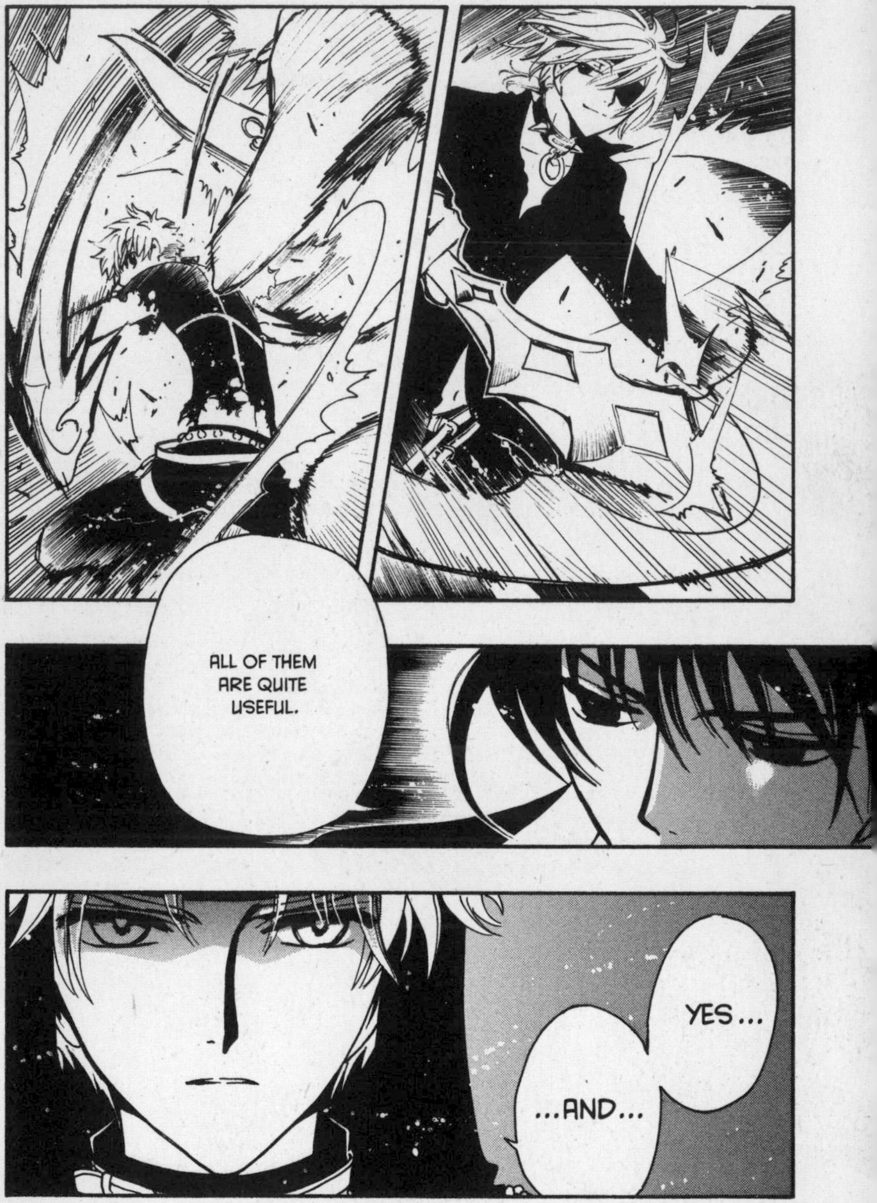
ALL OF THEM ARE QUITE USEFUL.
YES...
...AND...

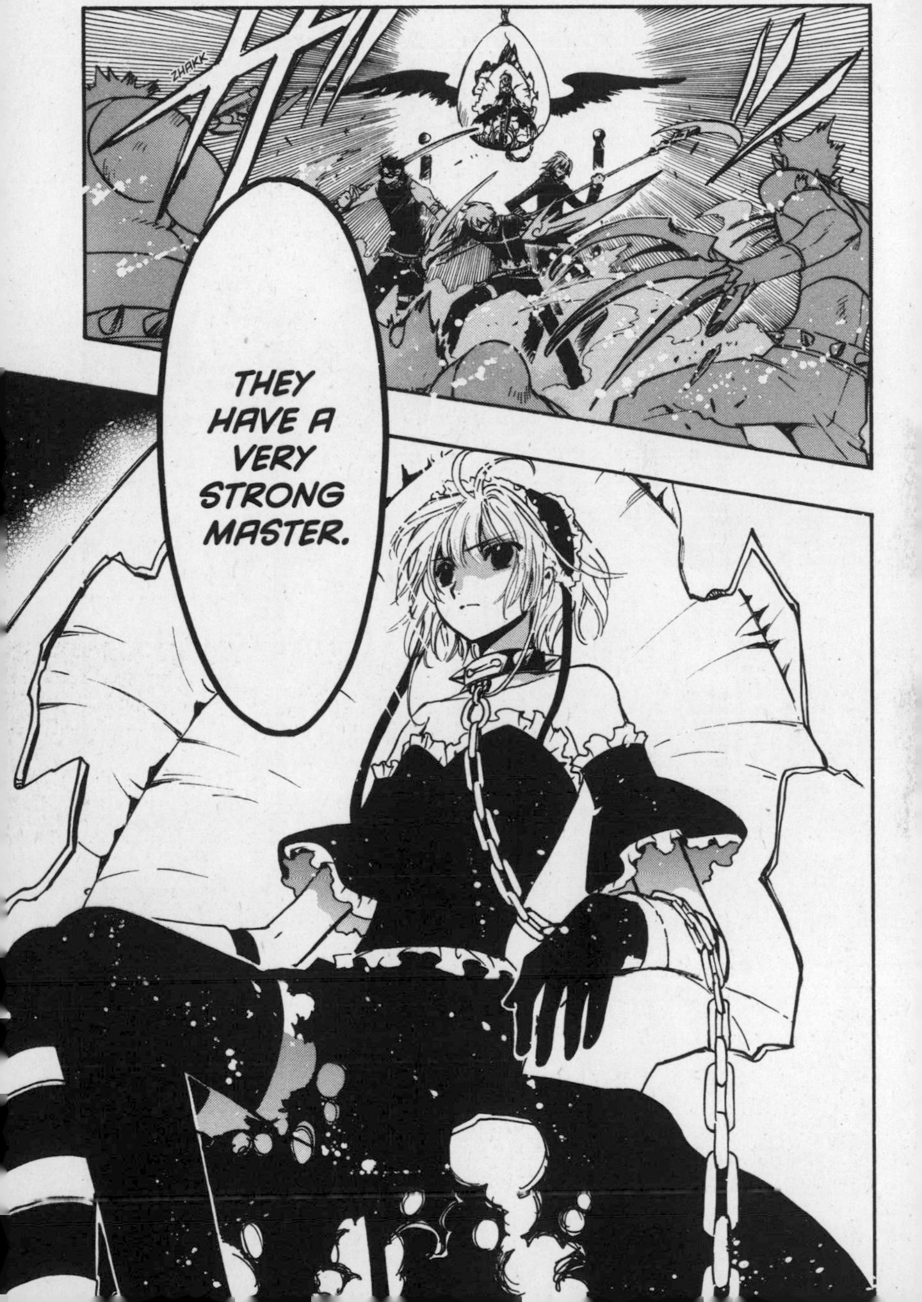
ZHAKK
THEY HAVE A VERY STRONG MASTER.

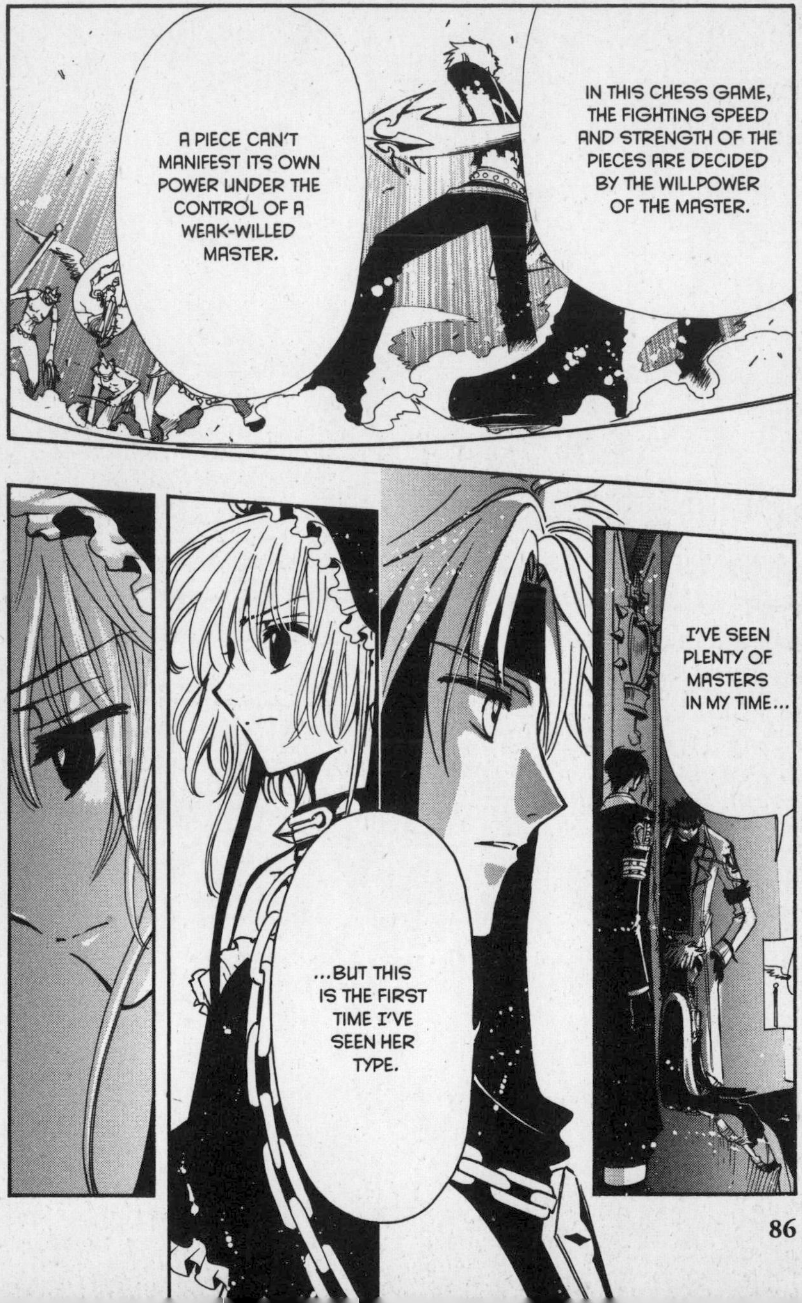
IN THIS CHESS GAME, THE FIGHTING SPEED AND STRENGTH OF THE PIECES ARE DECIDED BY THE WILLPOWER OF THE MASTER.
A PIECE CAN'T MANIFEST ITS OWN POWER UNDER THE CONTROL OF A WEAK-WILLED MASTER.
I'VE SEEN PLENTY OF MASTERS IN MY TIME...
...BUT THIS IS THE FIRST TIME I'VE SEEN HER TYPE.

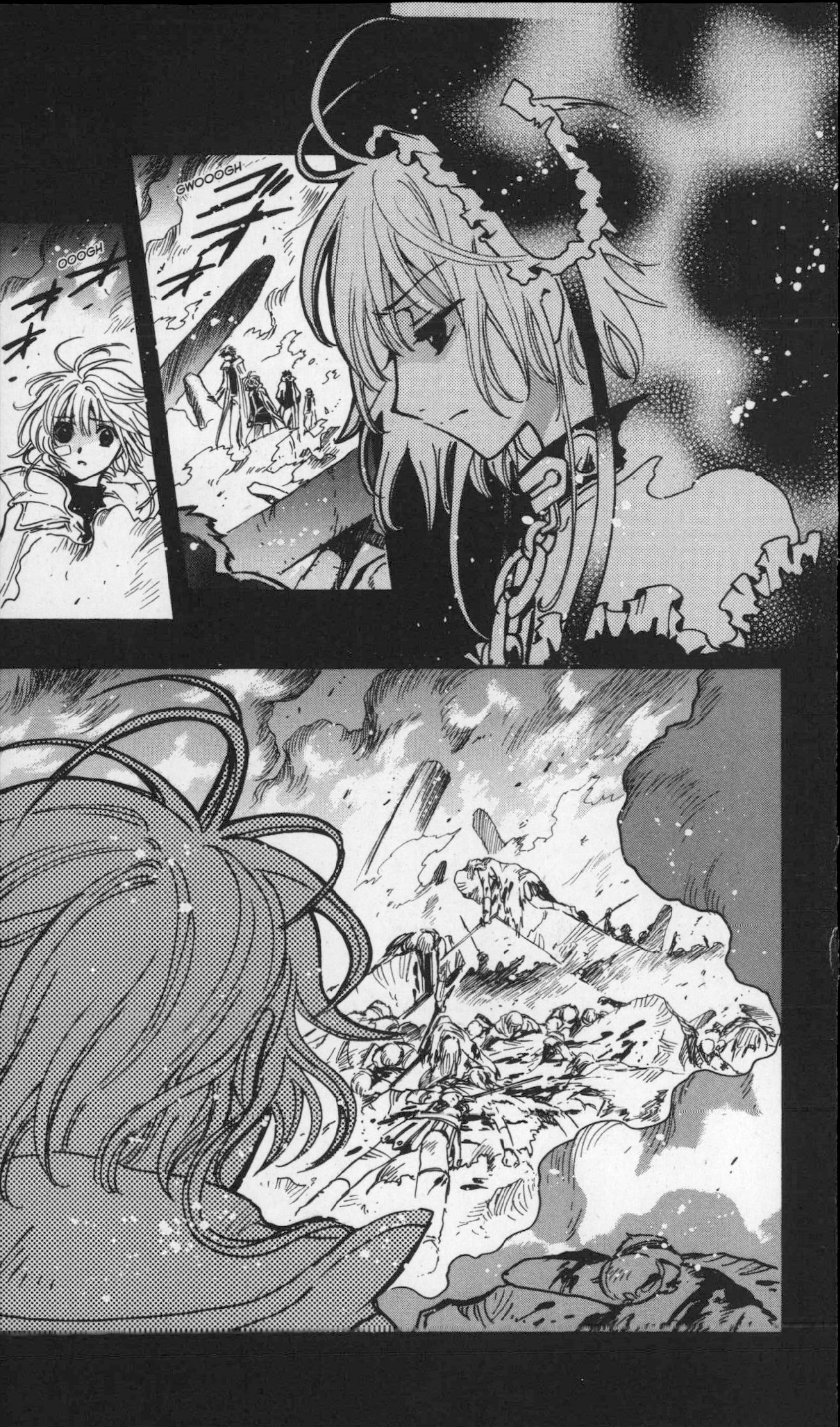
GWOOOGH
ゴオオオ
OOOGH
オオオオ

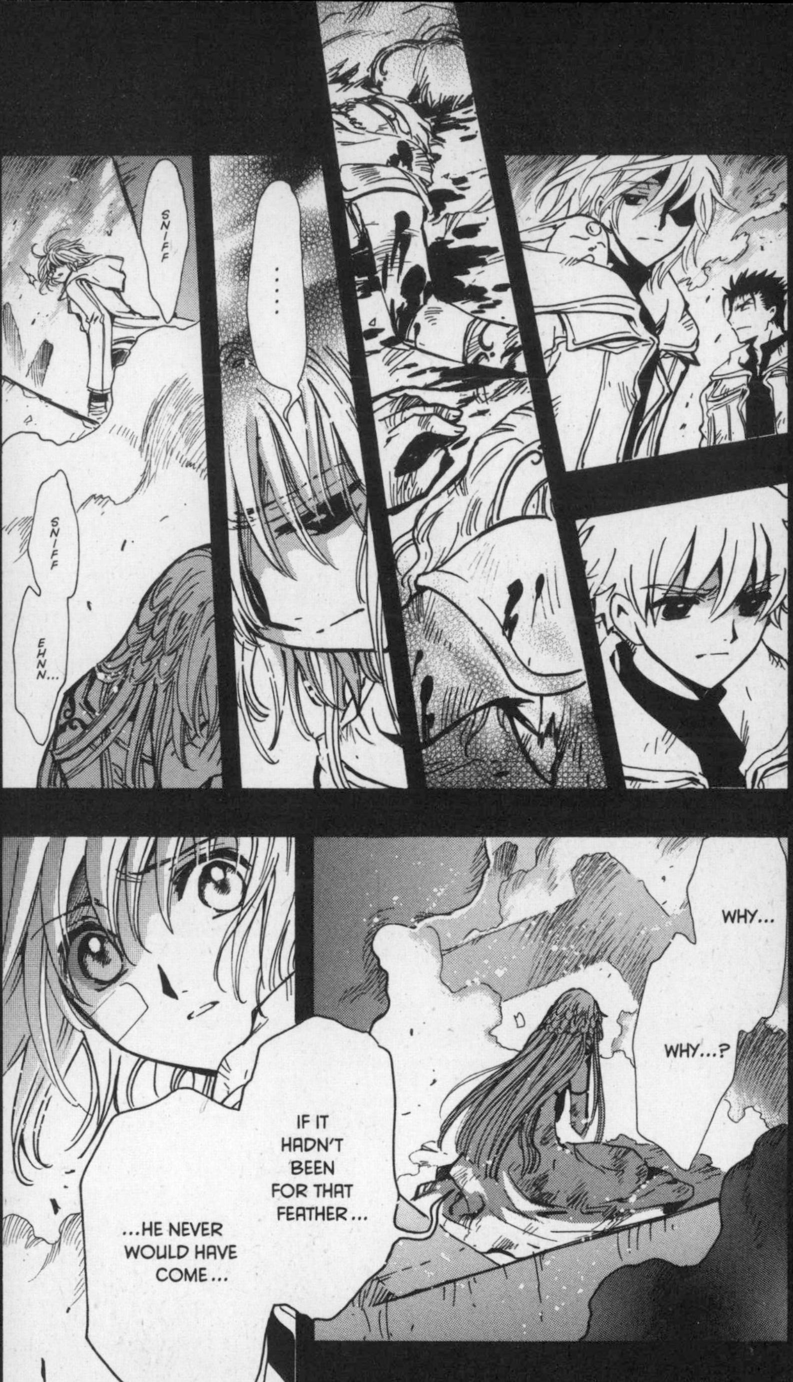
.....
SNIFF
SNIFF
EHNN...
WHY...
WHY...?
IF IT HADN'T BEEN FOR THAT FEATHER...
...HE NEVER WOULD HAVE COME...

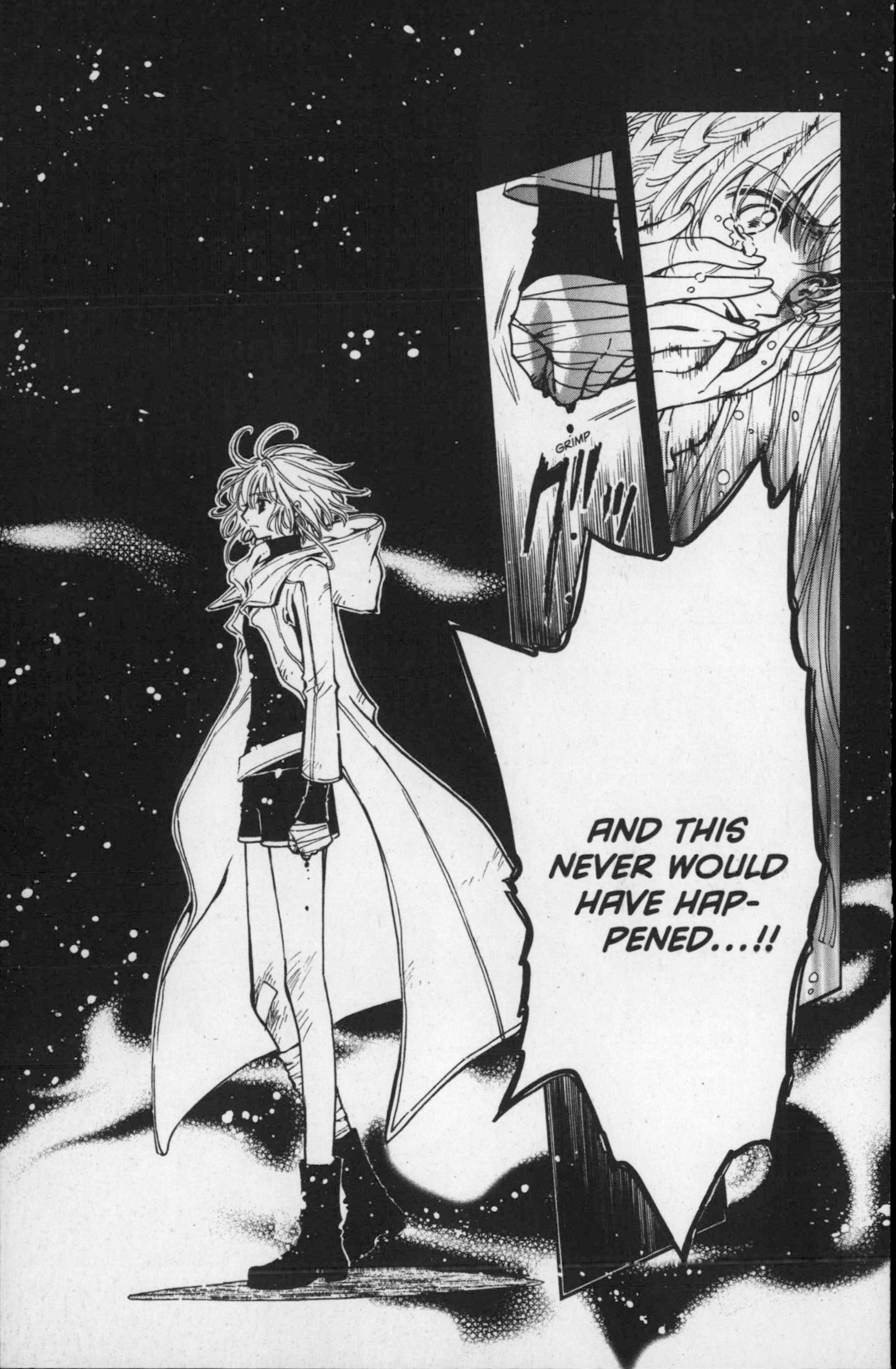
GRIMP
AND THIS NEVER WOULD HAVE HAP-PENED...!!

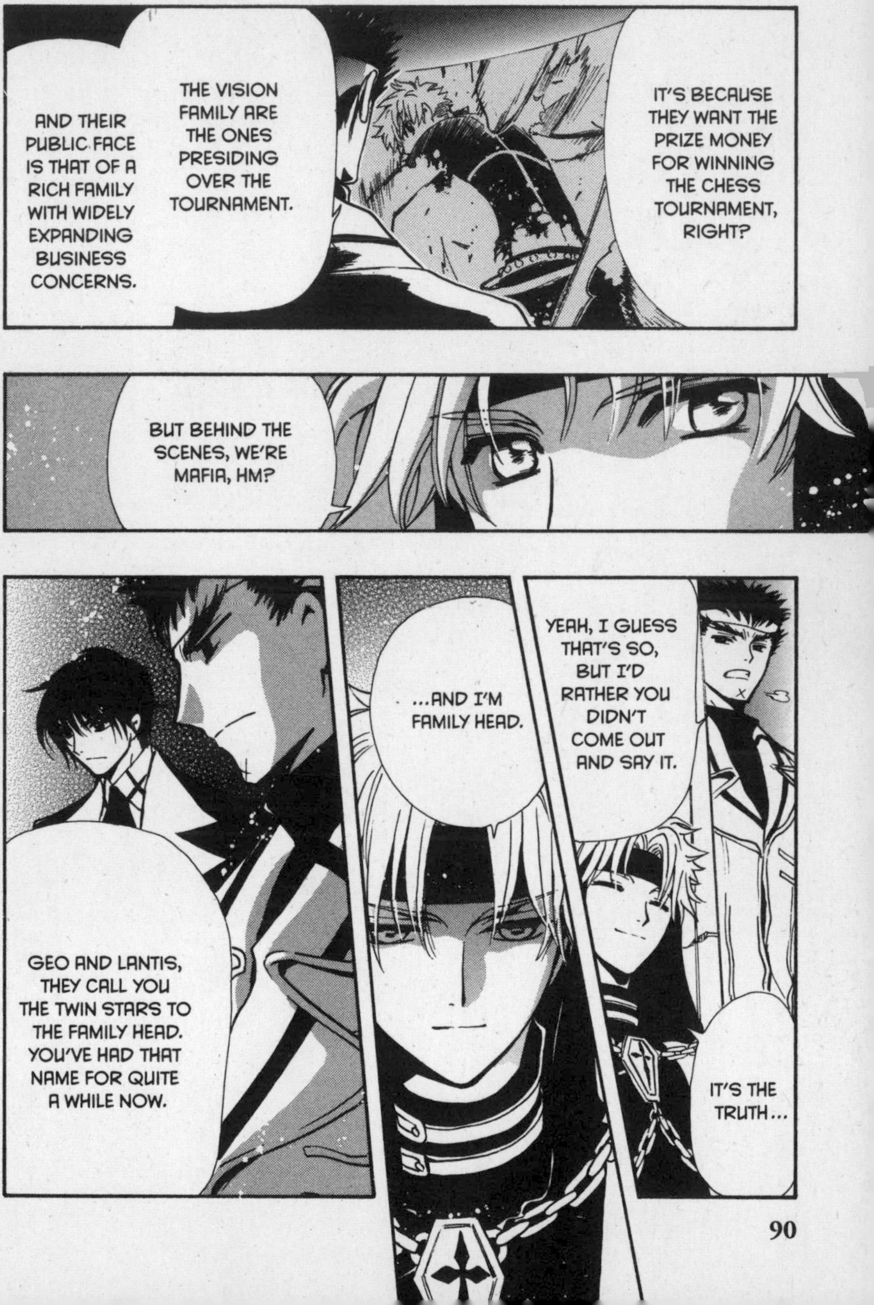
IT'S BECAUSE THEY WANT THE PRIZE MONEY FOR WINNING THE CHESS TOURNAMENT, RIGHT?
THE VISION FAMILY ARE THE ONES PRESIDING OVER THE TOURNAMENT.
AND THEIR PUBLIC FACE IS THAT OF A RICH FAMILY WITH WIDELY EXPANDING BUSINESS CONCERNS.
BUT BEHIND THE SCENES, WE'RE MAFIA, HM?
YEAH, I GUESS THAT'S SO, BUT I'D RATHER YOU DIDN'T COME OUT AND SAY IT.
IT'S THE TRUTH...
...AND I'M FAMILY HEAD.
GEO AND LANTIS, THEY CALL YOU THE TWIN STARS TO THE FAMILY HEAD. YOU'VE HAD THAT NAME FOR QUITE A WHILE NOW.

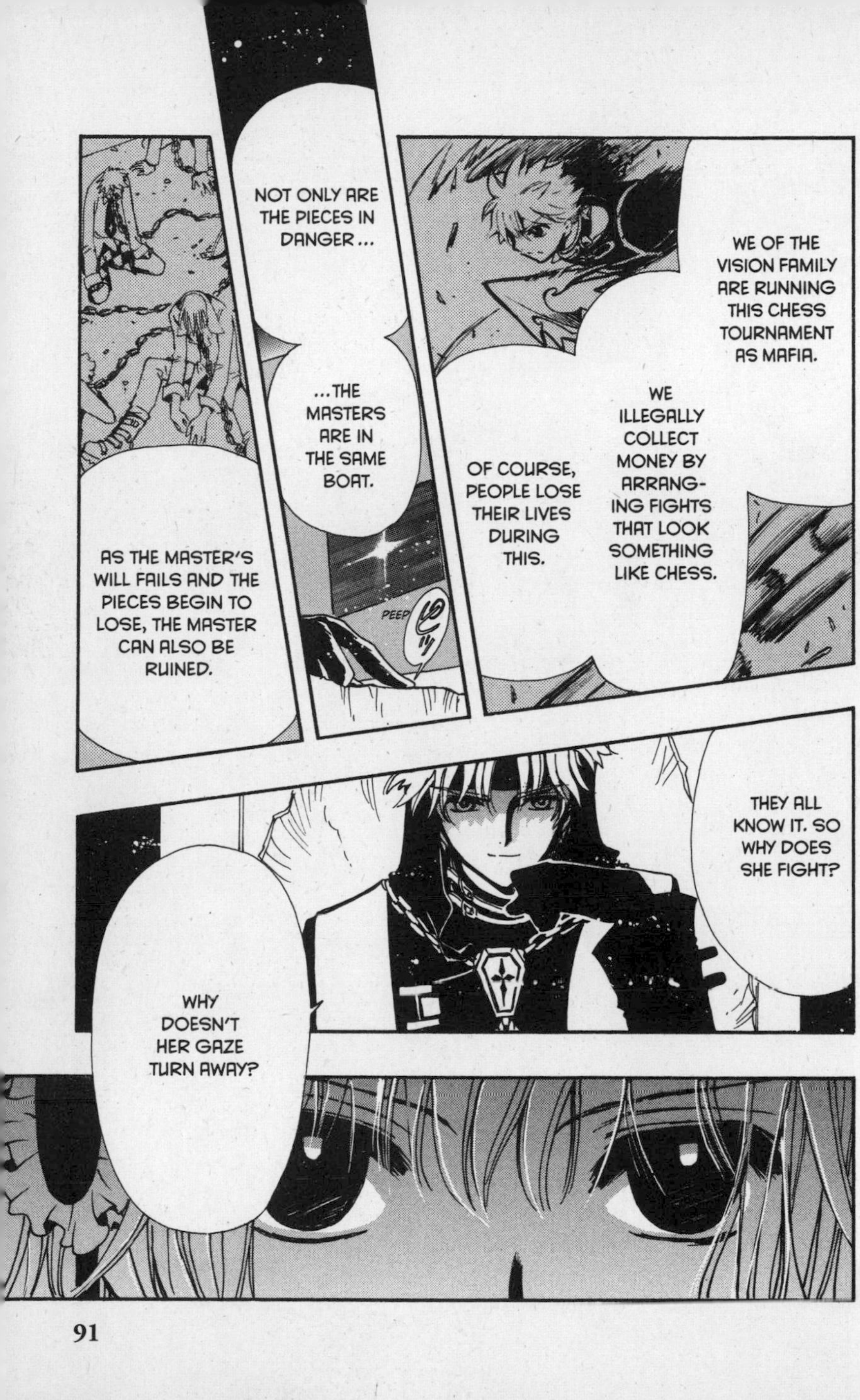
WE OF THE VISION FAMILY ARE RUNNING THIS CHESS TOURNAMENT AS MAFIA.
WE ILLEGALLY COLLECT MONEY BY ARRANG-ING FIGHTS THAT LOOK SOMETHING LIKE CHESS.
OF COURSE, PEOPLE LOSE THEIR LIVES DURING THIS.
NOT ONLY ARE THE PIECES IN DANGER ...
... THE MASTERS ARE IN THE SAME BOAT.
PEEP
AS THE MASTER'S WILL FAILS AND THE PIECES BEGIN TO LOSE, THE MASTER CAN ALSO BE RUINED.
THEY ALL KNOW IT. SO WHY DOES SHE FIGHT?
WHY DOESN'T HER GAZE TURN AWAY?

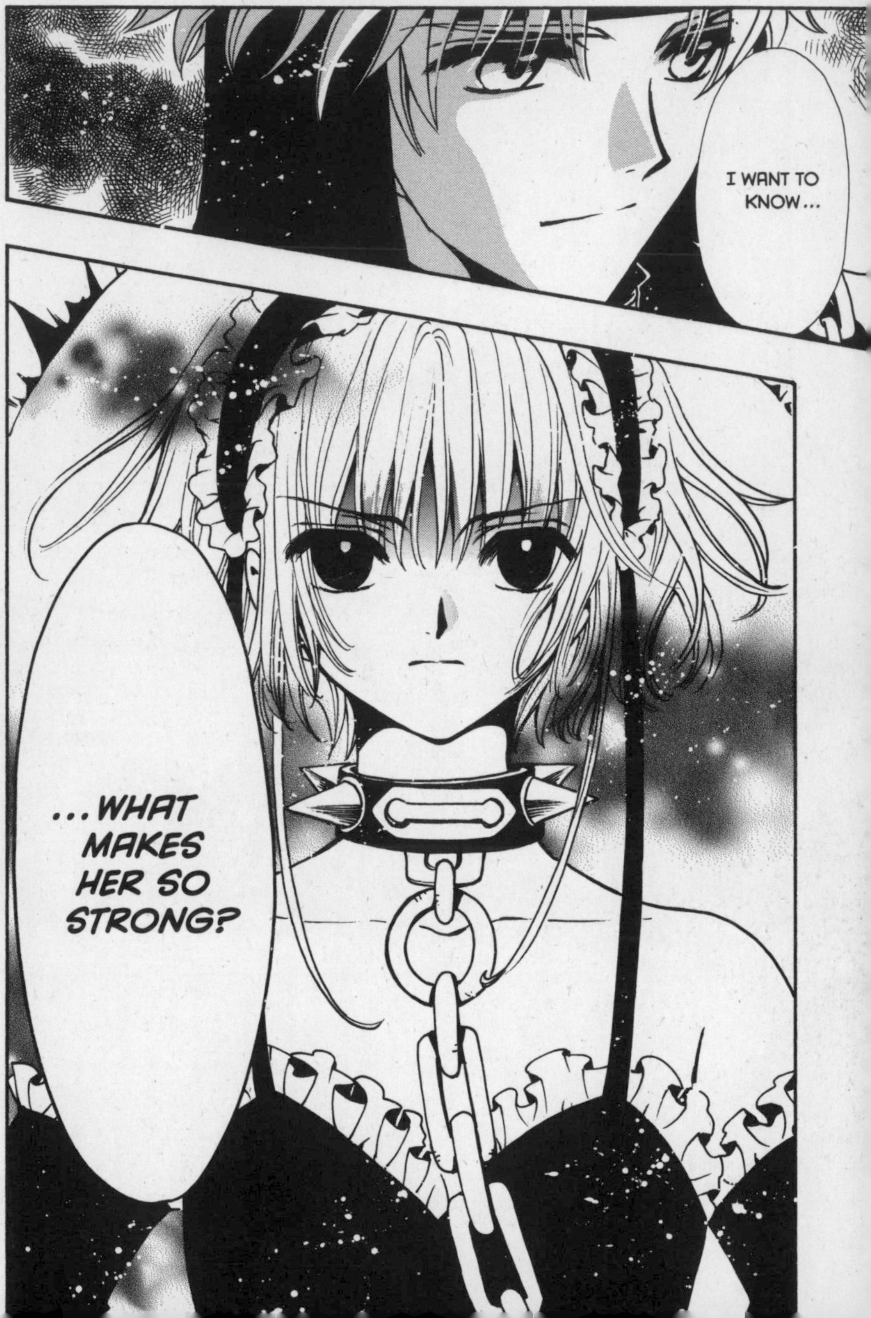
I WANT TO KNOW...
...WHAT MAKES HER SO STRONG?

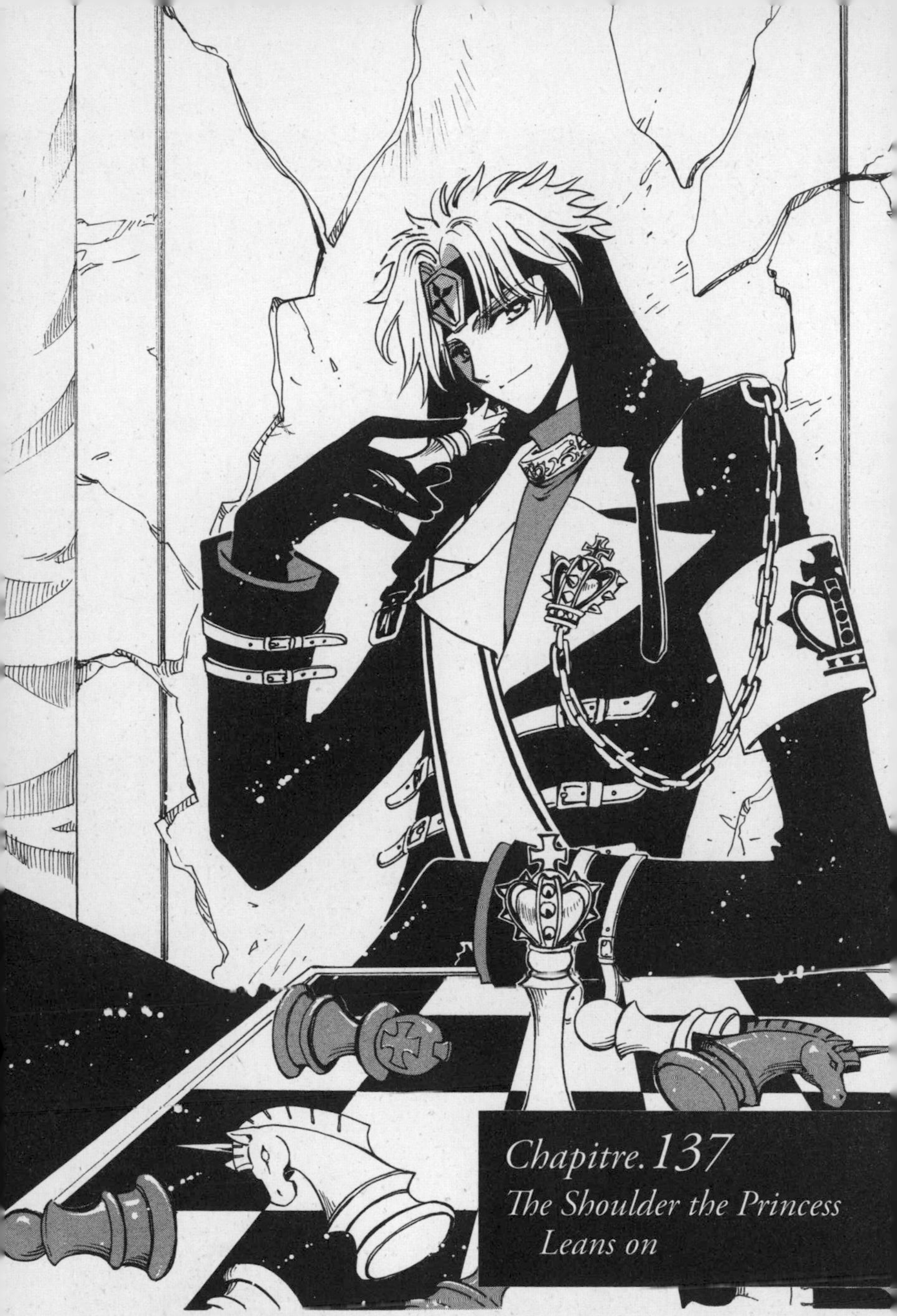
Chapitre. 137
The Shoulder the Princess Leans on

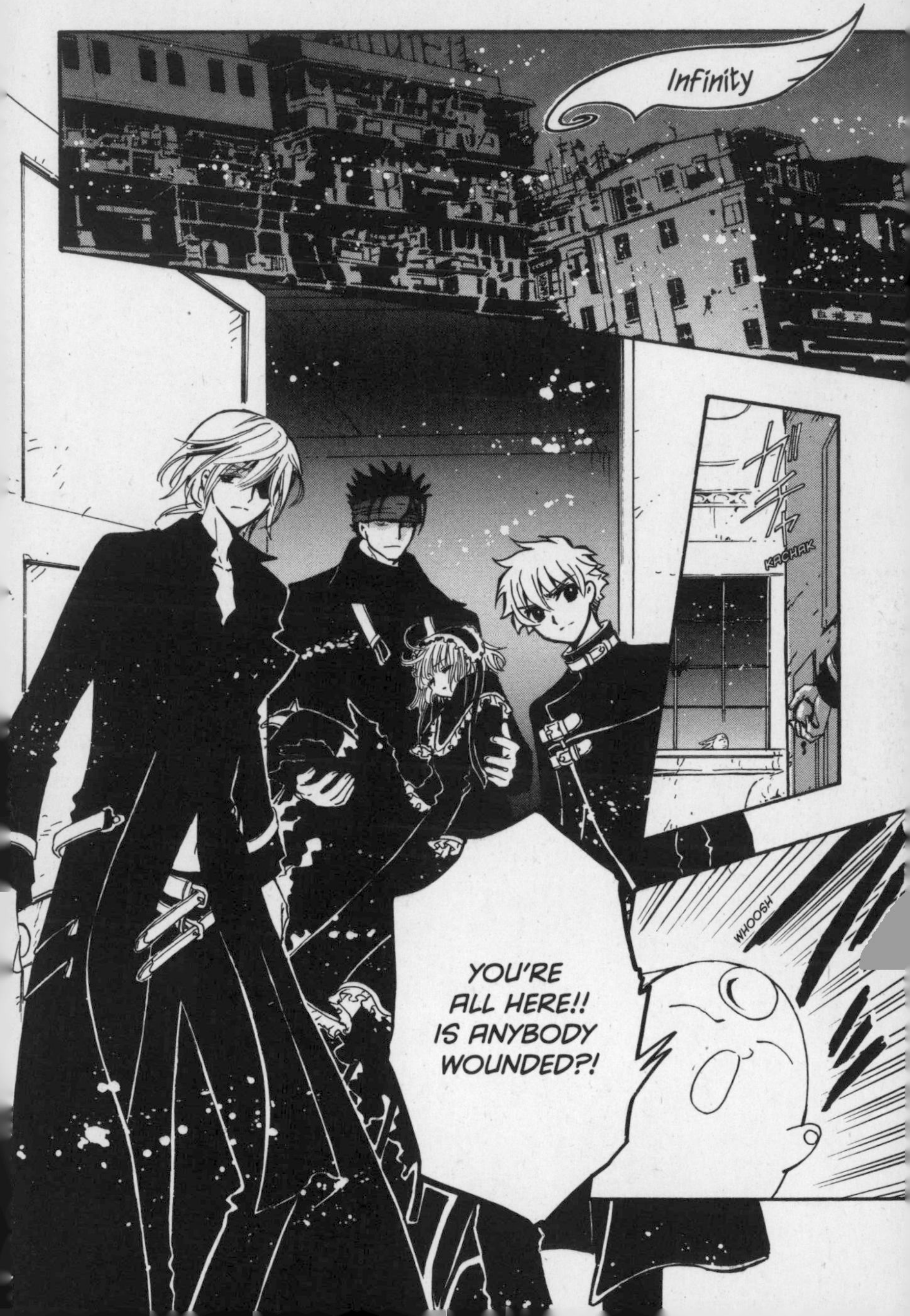
Infinity
KACHAK
WHOOSH
YOU'RE ALL HERE!! IS ANYBODY WOUNDED?!

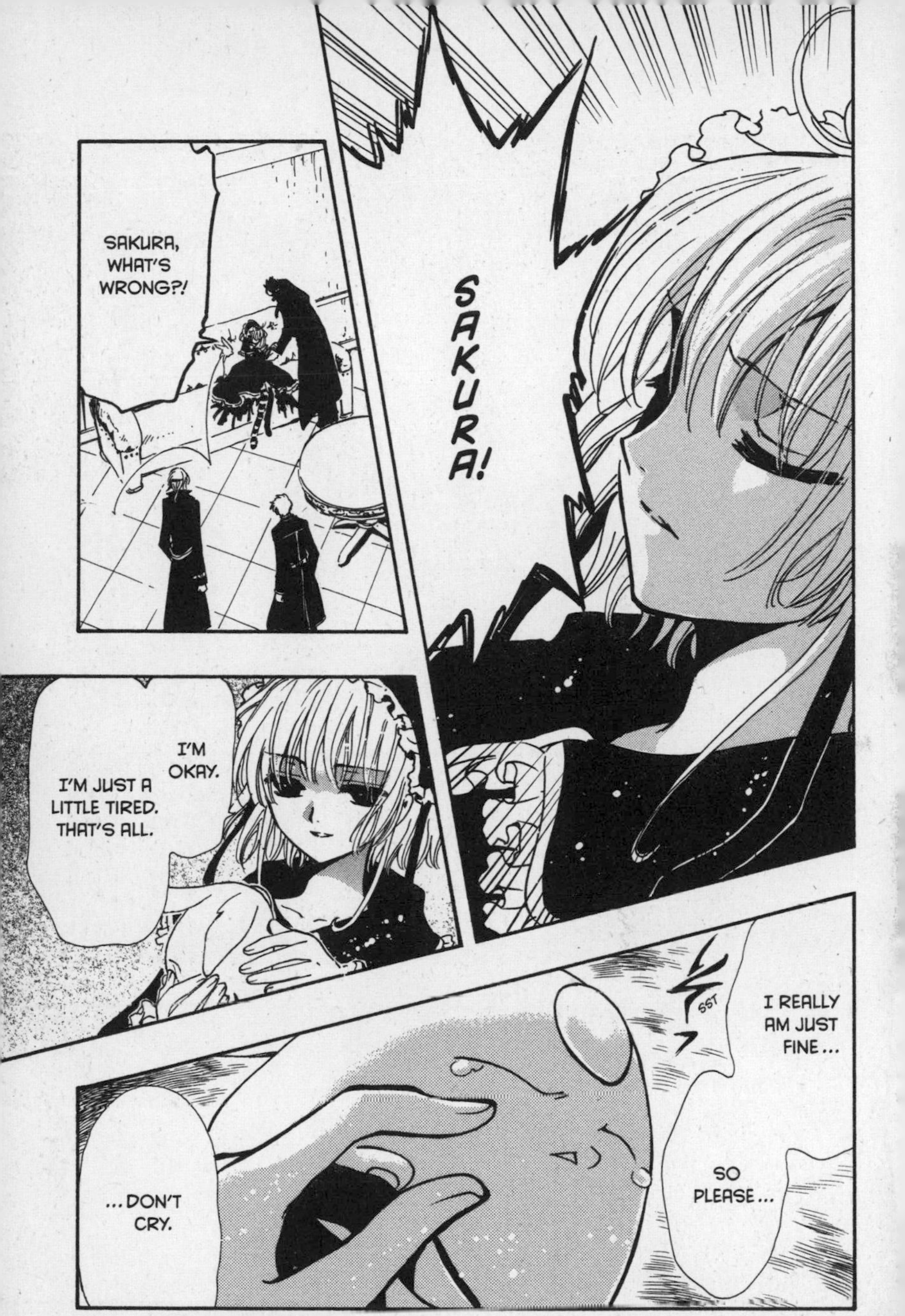
SAKURA!
SAKURA, WHAT'S WRONG?!
I'M OKAY.
I'M JUST A LITTLE TIRED. THAT'S ALL.
SST
I REALLY AM JUST FINE...
SO PLEASE...
...DON'T CRY.

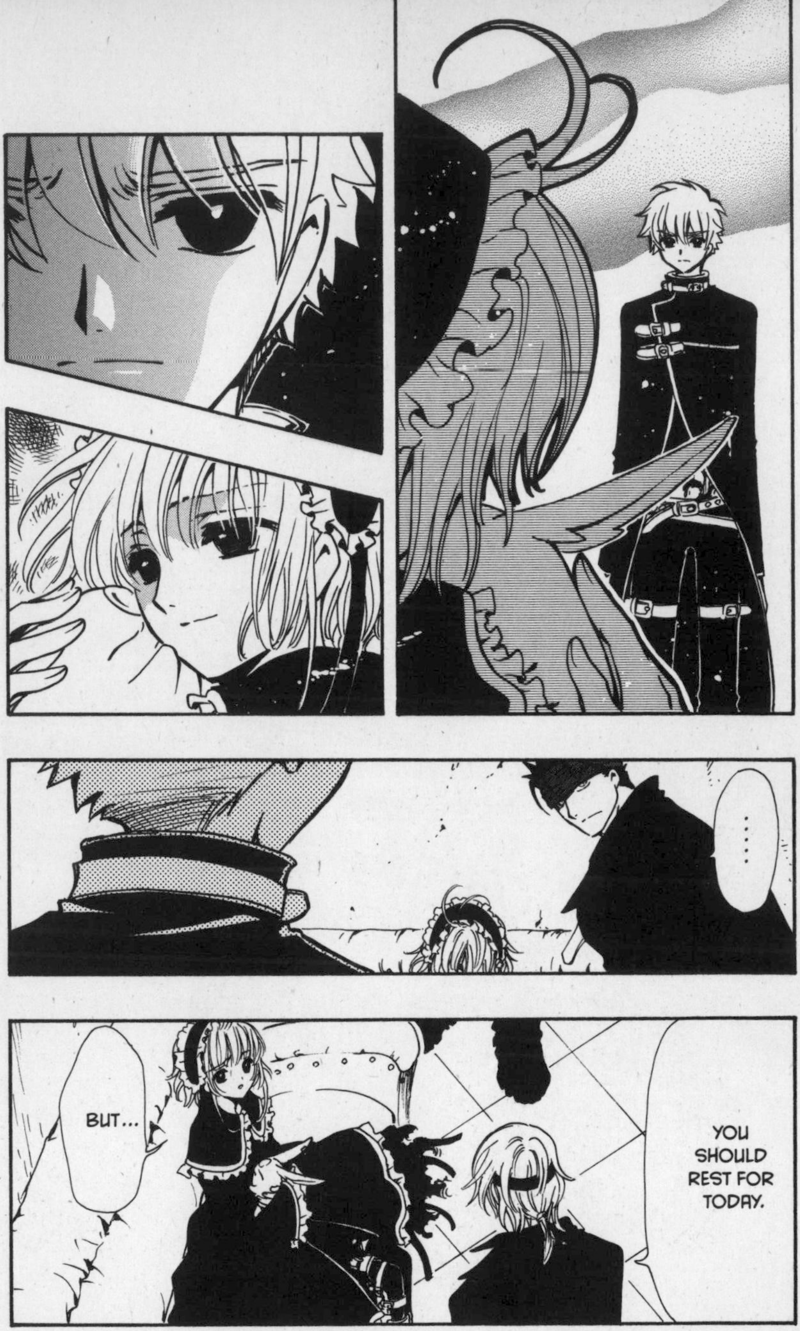
.....
YOU SHOULD REST FOR TODAY.
BUT...

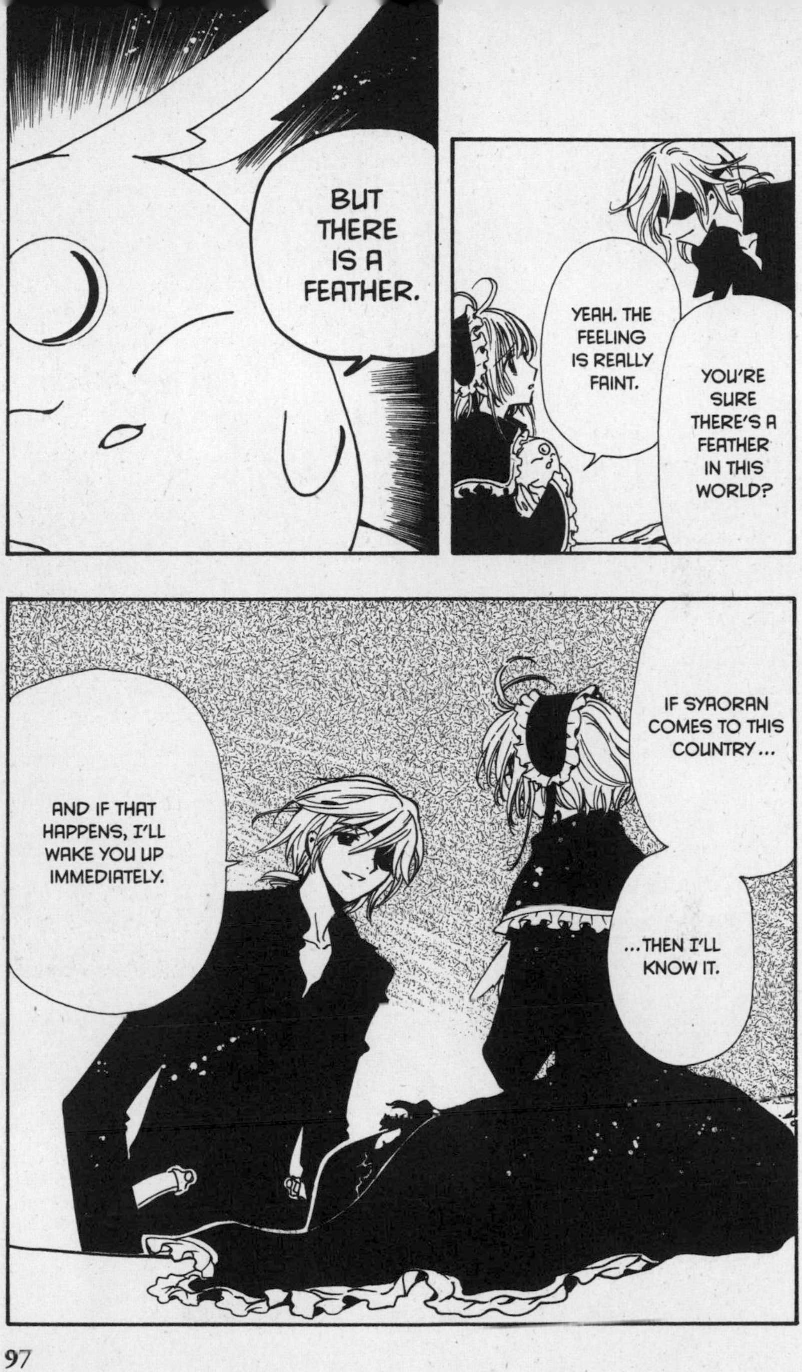
YOU'RE SURE THERE'S A FEATHER IN THIS WORLD?
YEAH. THE FEELING IS REALLY FAINT.
BUT THERE IS A FEATHER.
IF SYAORAN COMES TO THIS COUNTRY...
...THEN I'LL KNOW IT.
AND IF THAT HAPPENS, I'LL WAKE YOU UP IMMEDIATELY.

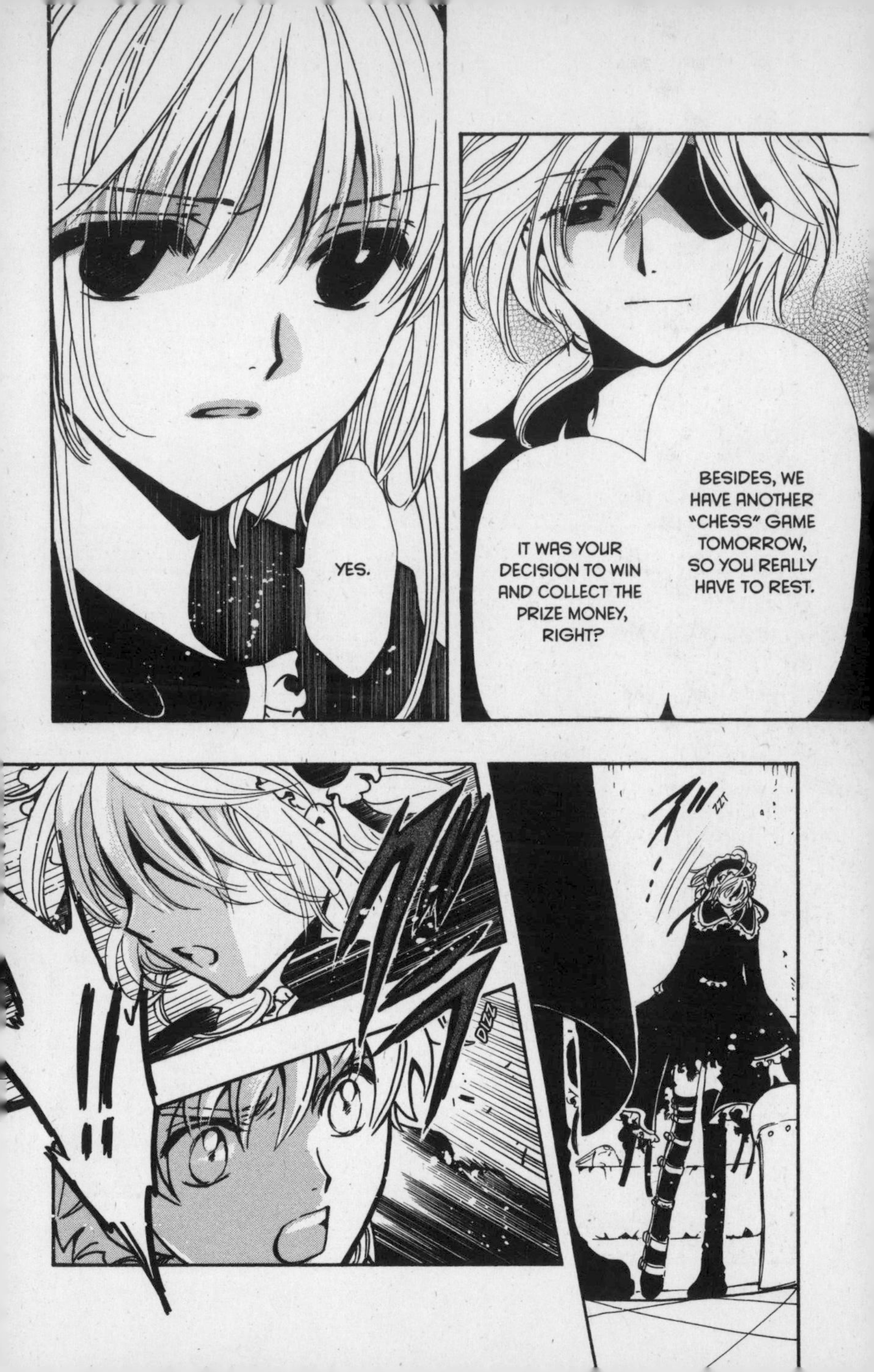
IT WAS YOUR DECISION TO WIN AND COLLECT THE PRIZE MONEY, RIGHT?
BESIDES, WE HAVE ANOTHER "CHESS" GAME TOMORROW, SO YOU REALLY HAVE TO REST.
YES.
ZZT
DIZZ
!!

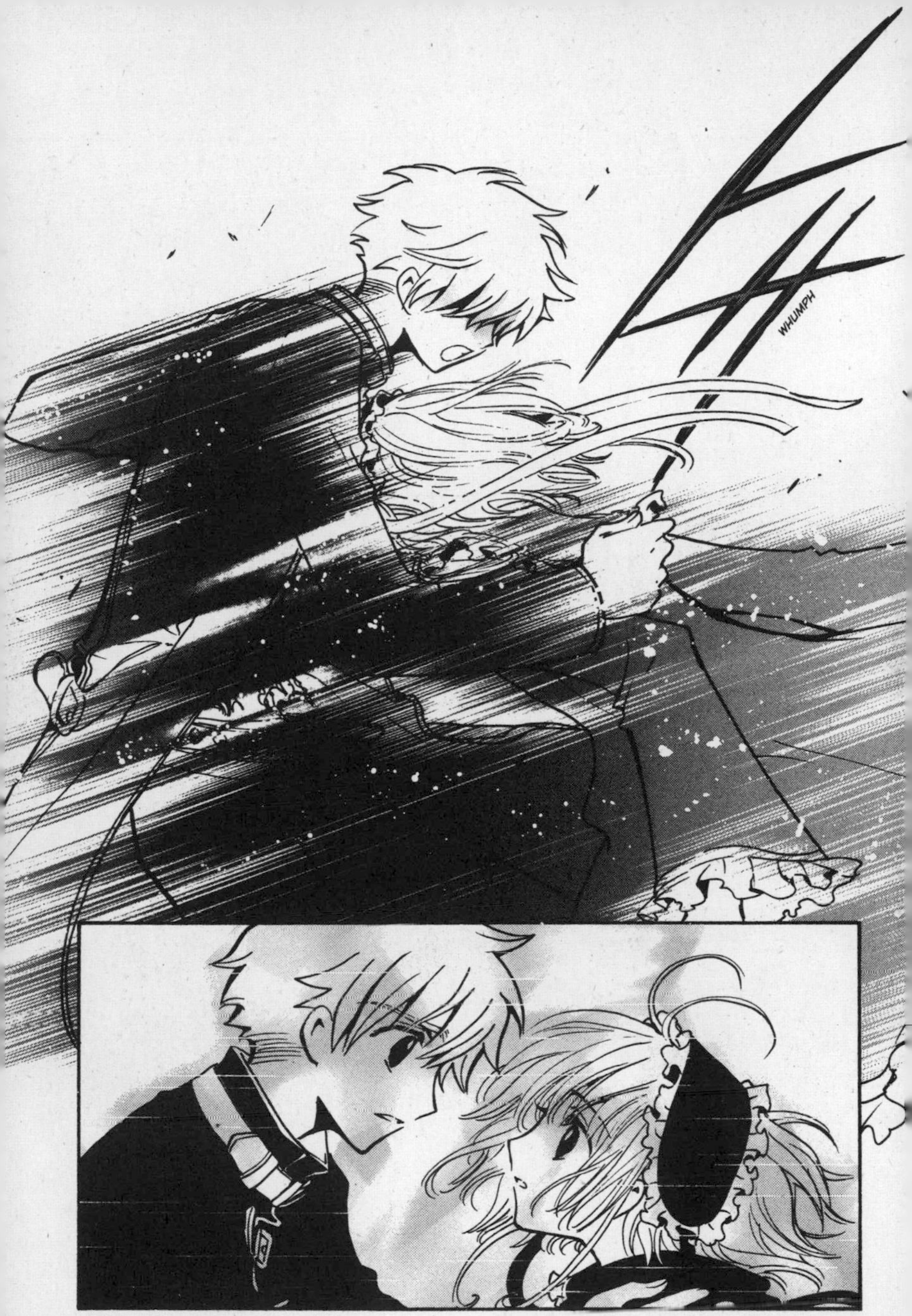
WHUMPH

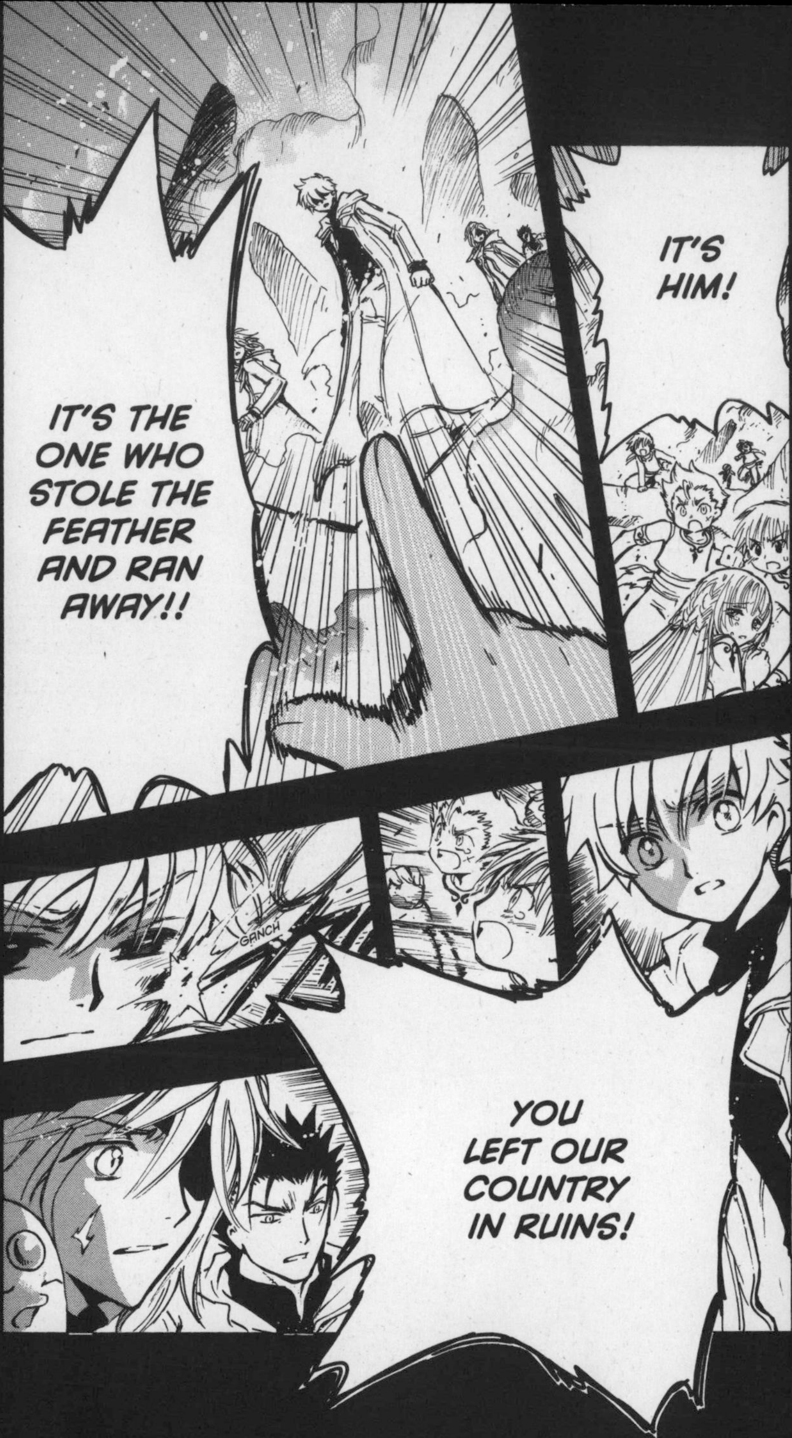
IT'S HIM!
IT'S THE ONE WHO STOLE THE FEATHER AND RAN AWAY!!
GANCH
YOU LEFT OUR COUNTRY IN RUINS!

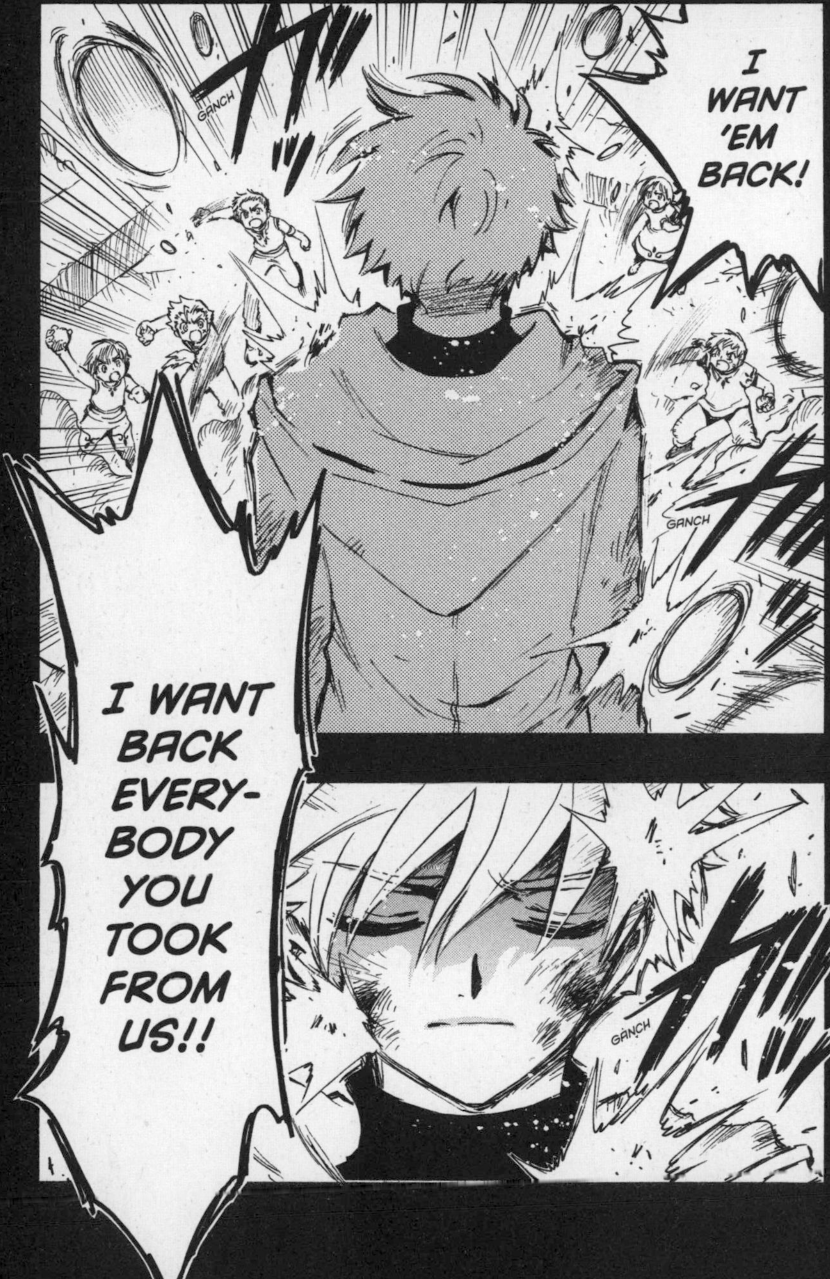
GANCH
I WANT 'EM BACK!
GANCH
I WANT BACK EVERY-BODY YOU TOOK FROM US!!
GANCH

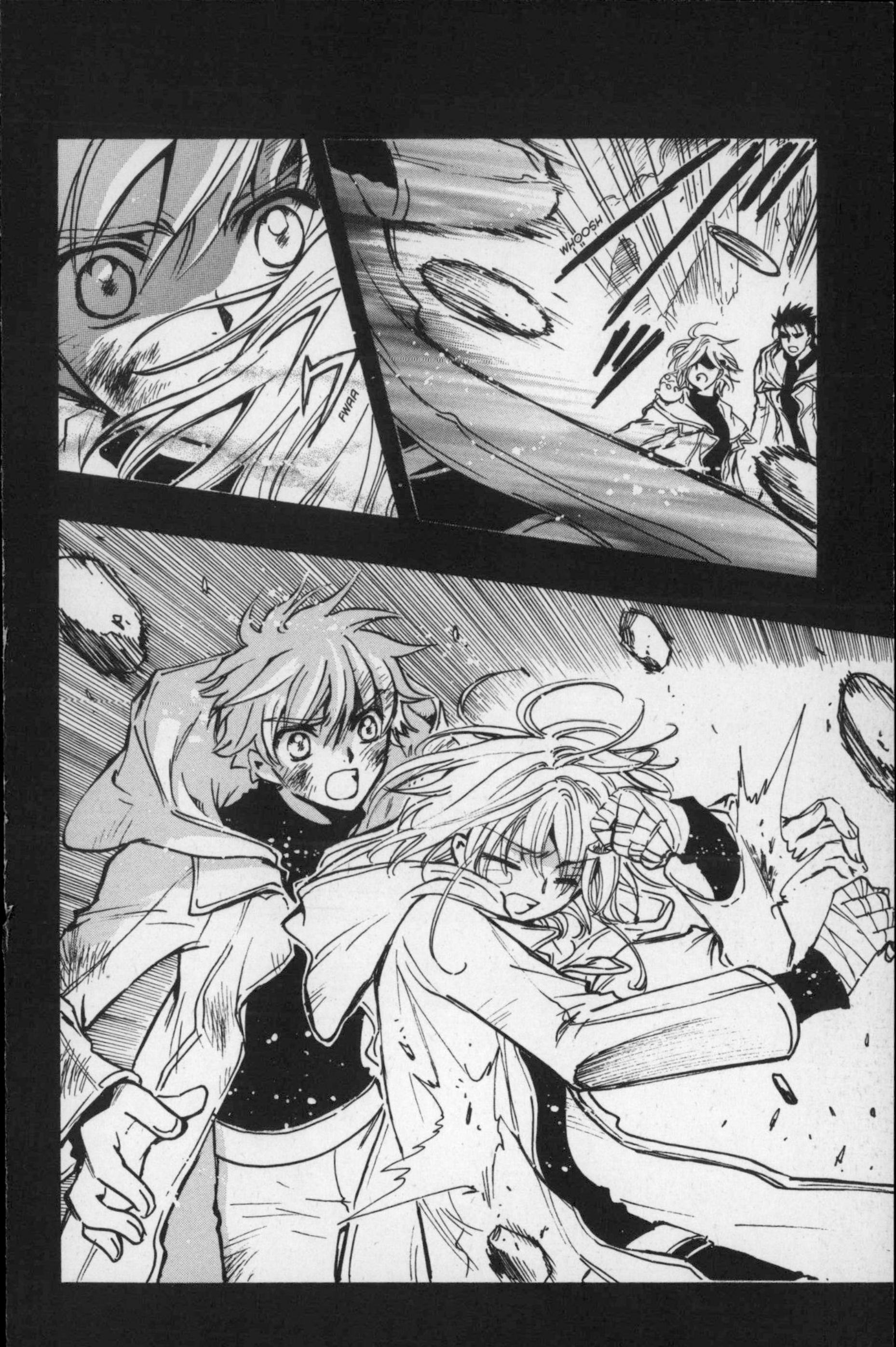
WHOOSH
FWAA

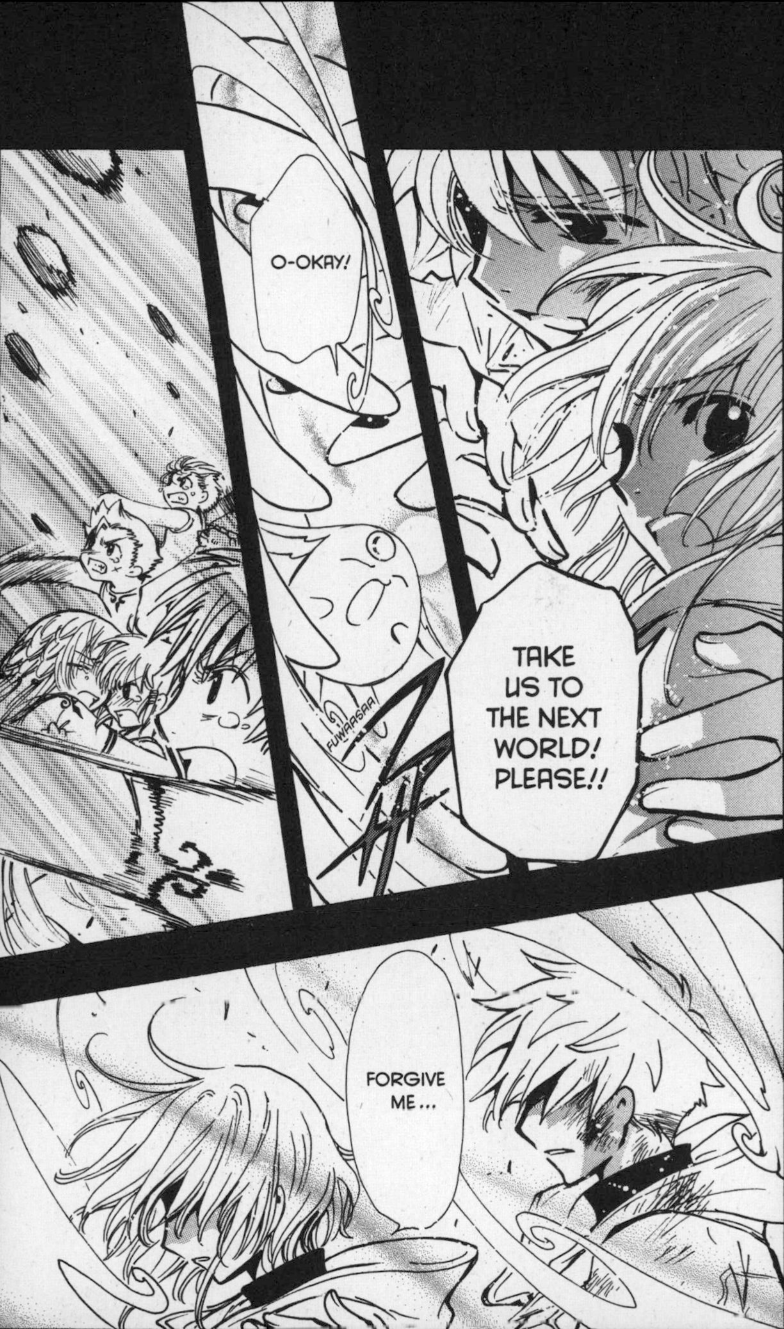
TAKE US TO THE NEXT WORLD! PLEASE!!
O-OKAY!
FUWAASAA
FORGIVE ME...

I'M SORRY...

ALL RIGHT. LET'S GET YOU TO YOUR ROOM.

KACHAK

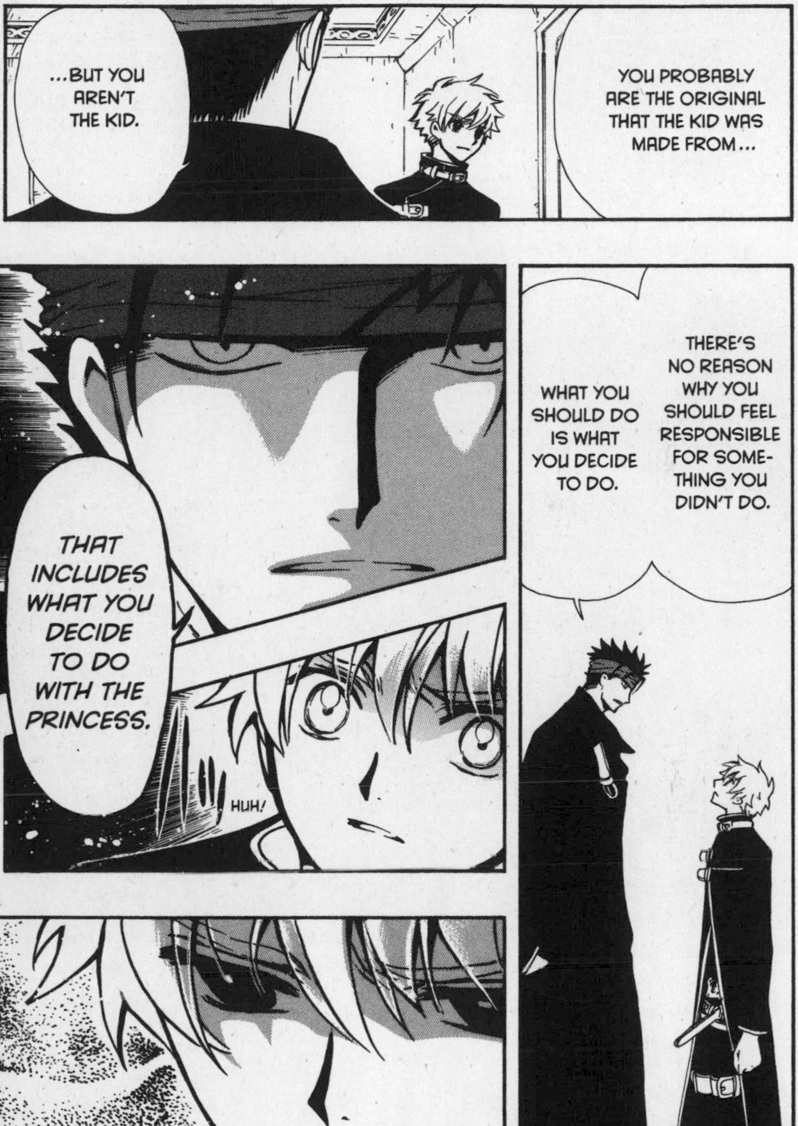
YOU PROBABLY ARE THE ORIGINAL THAT THE KID WAS MADE FROM...
...BUT YOU AREN'T THE KID.
THERE'S NO REASON WHY YOU SHOULD FEEL RESPONSIBLE FOR SOME-THING YOU DIDN'T DO.
WHAT YOU SHOULD DO IS WHAT YOU DECIDE TO DO.
THAT INCLUDES WHAT YOU DECIDE TO DO WITH THE PRINCESS.
HUH!

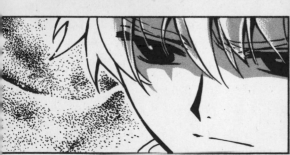

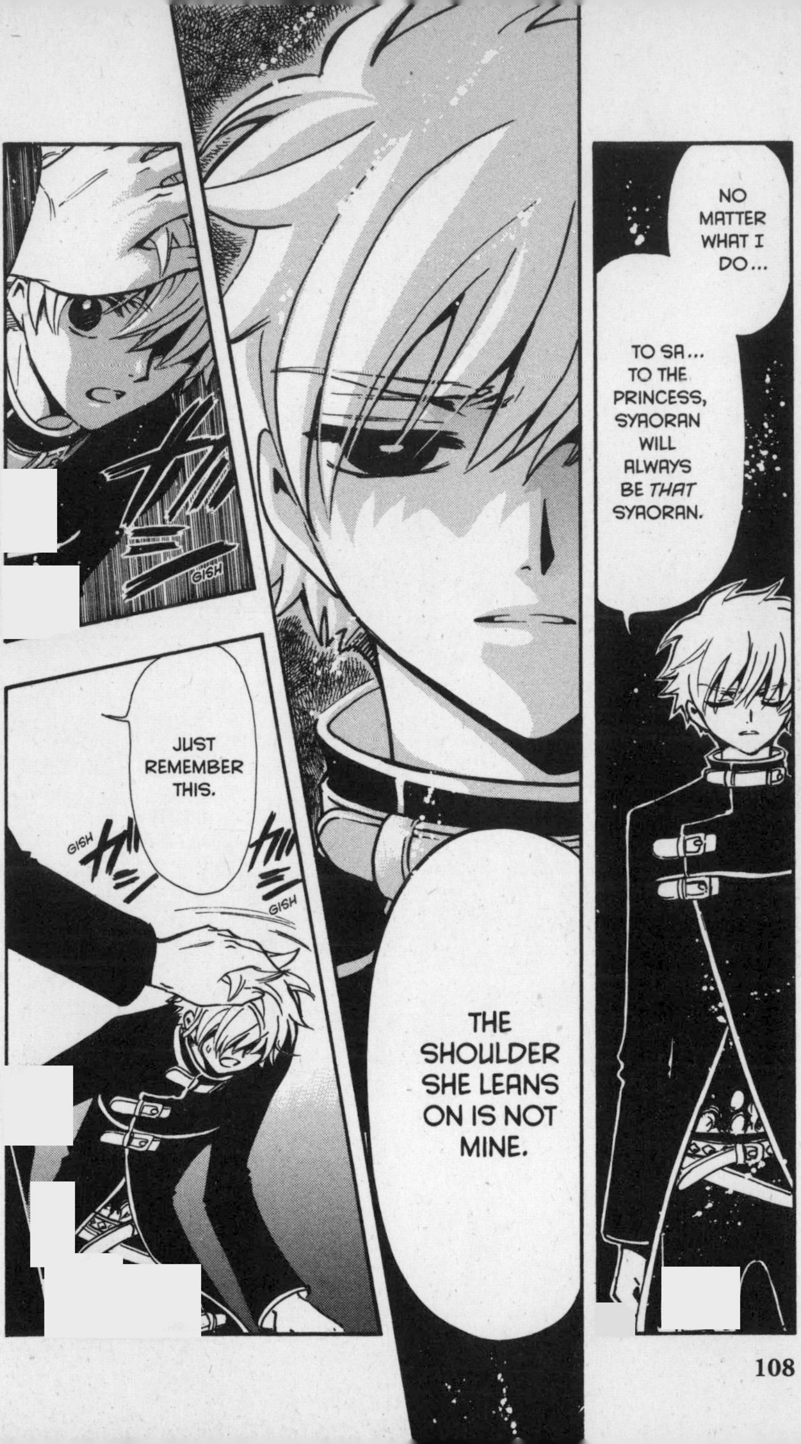
NO MATTER WHAT I DO...
TO SA... TO THE PRINCESS, SYAORAN WILL ALWAYS BE *THAT* SYAORAN.
THE SHOULDER SHE LEANS ON IS NOT MINE.
GISH
JUST REMEMBER THIS.
GISH
GISH

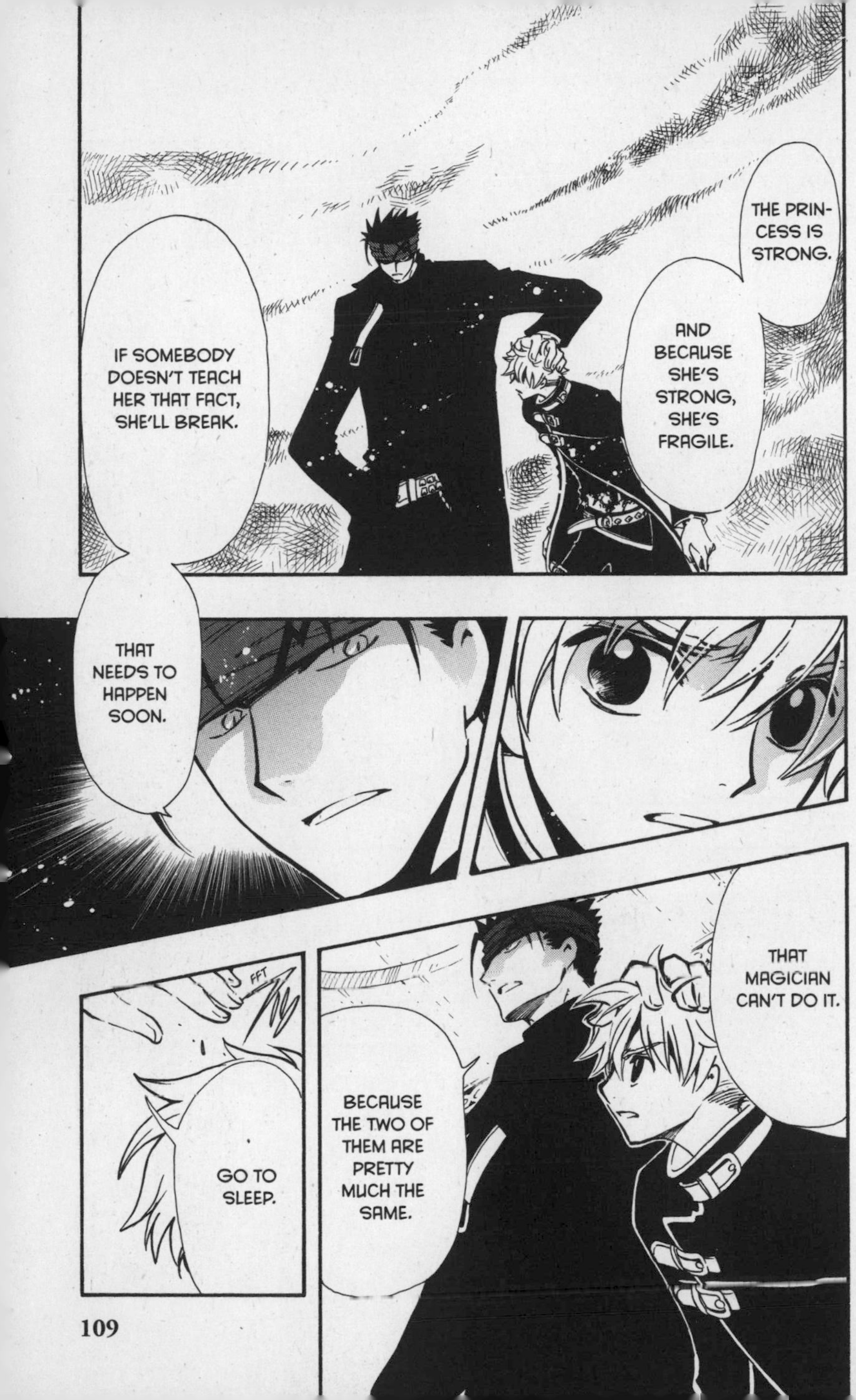
THE PRINCESS IS STRONG.
AND BECAUSE SHE'S STRONG, SHE'S FRAGILE.
IF SOMEBODY DOESN'T TEACH HER THAT FACT, SHE'LL BREAK.
THAT NEEDS TO HAPPEN SOON.
THAT MAGICIAN CAN'T DO IT.
BECAUSE THE TWO OF THEM ARE PRETTY MUCH THE SAME.
FFT
GO TO SLEEP.

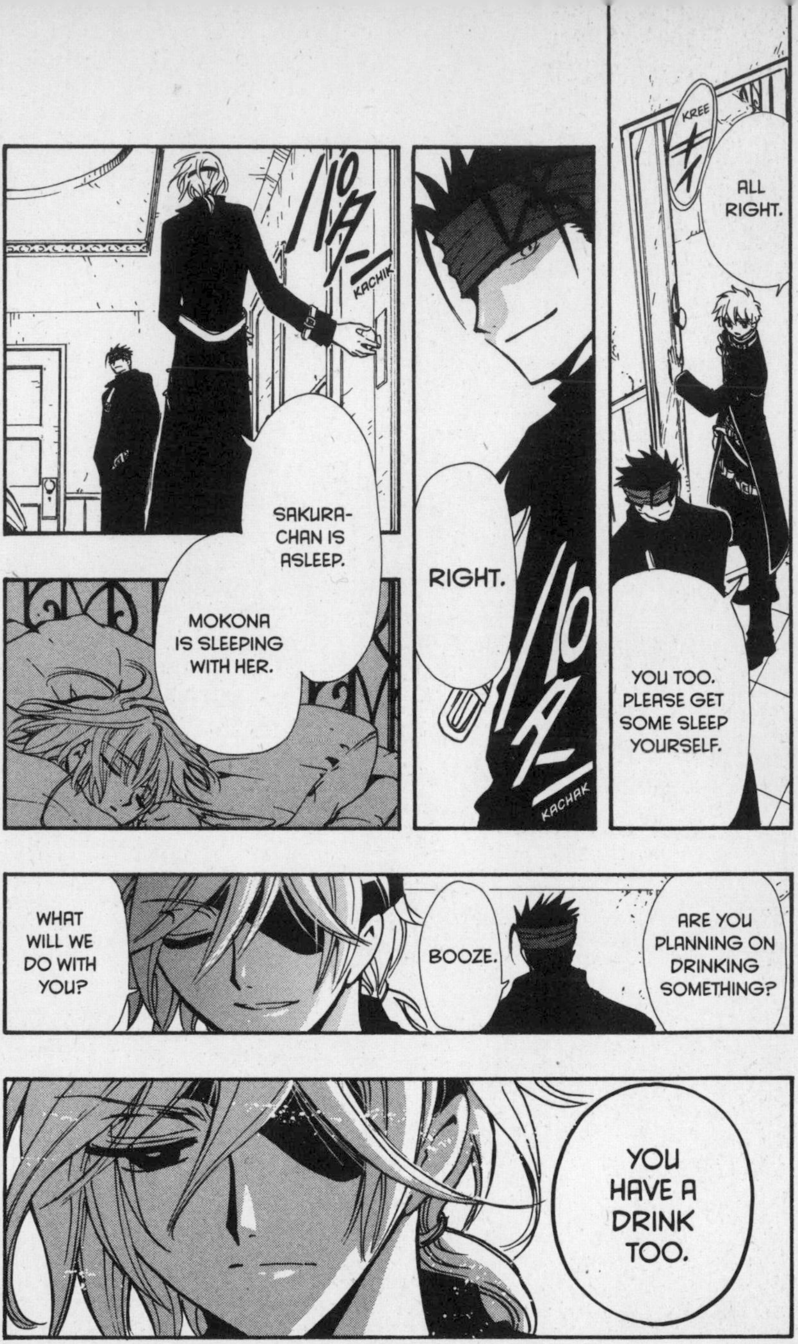
KREE
ALL RIGHT.
YOU TOO. PLEASE GET SOME SLEEP YOURSELF.
RIGHT.
KACHAK
KACHIK
SAKURA-CHAN IS ASLEEP.
MOKONA IS SLEEPING WITH HER.
ARE YOU PLANNING ON DRINKING SOMETHING?
BOOZE.
WHAT WILL WE DO WITH YOU?
YOU HAVE A DRINK TOO.

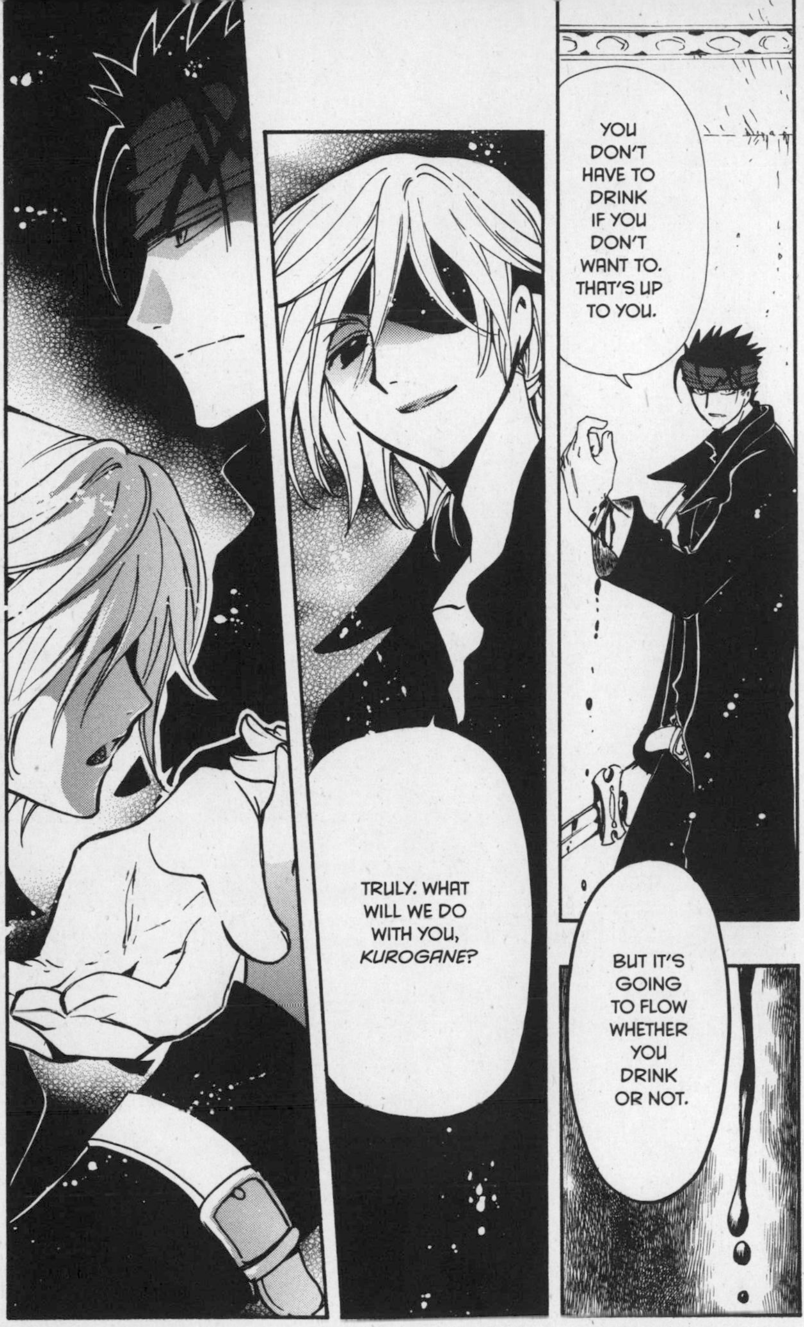
YOU DON'T HAVE TO DRINK IF YOU DON'T WANT TO. THAT'S UP TO YOU.
BUT IT'S GOING TO FLOW WHETHER YOU DRINK OR NOT.
TRULY. WHAT WILL WE DO WITH YOU, *KUROGANE?*

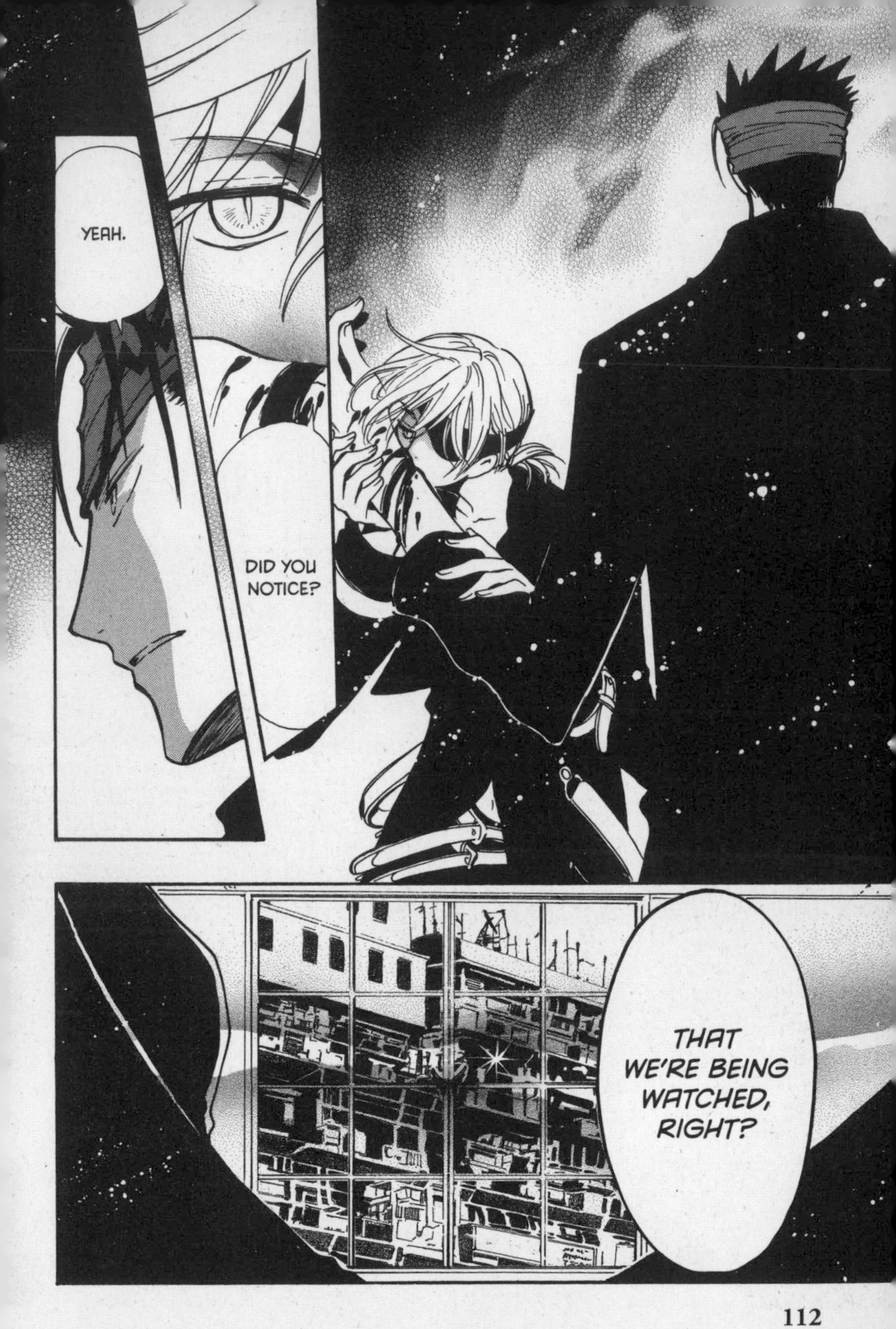
DID YOU NOTICE?
THAT WE'RE BEING WATCHED, RIGHT?
YEAH.

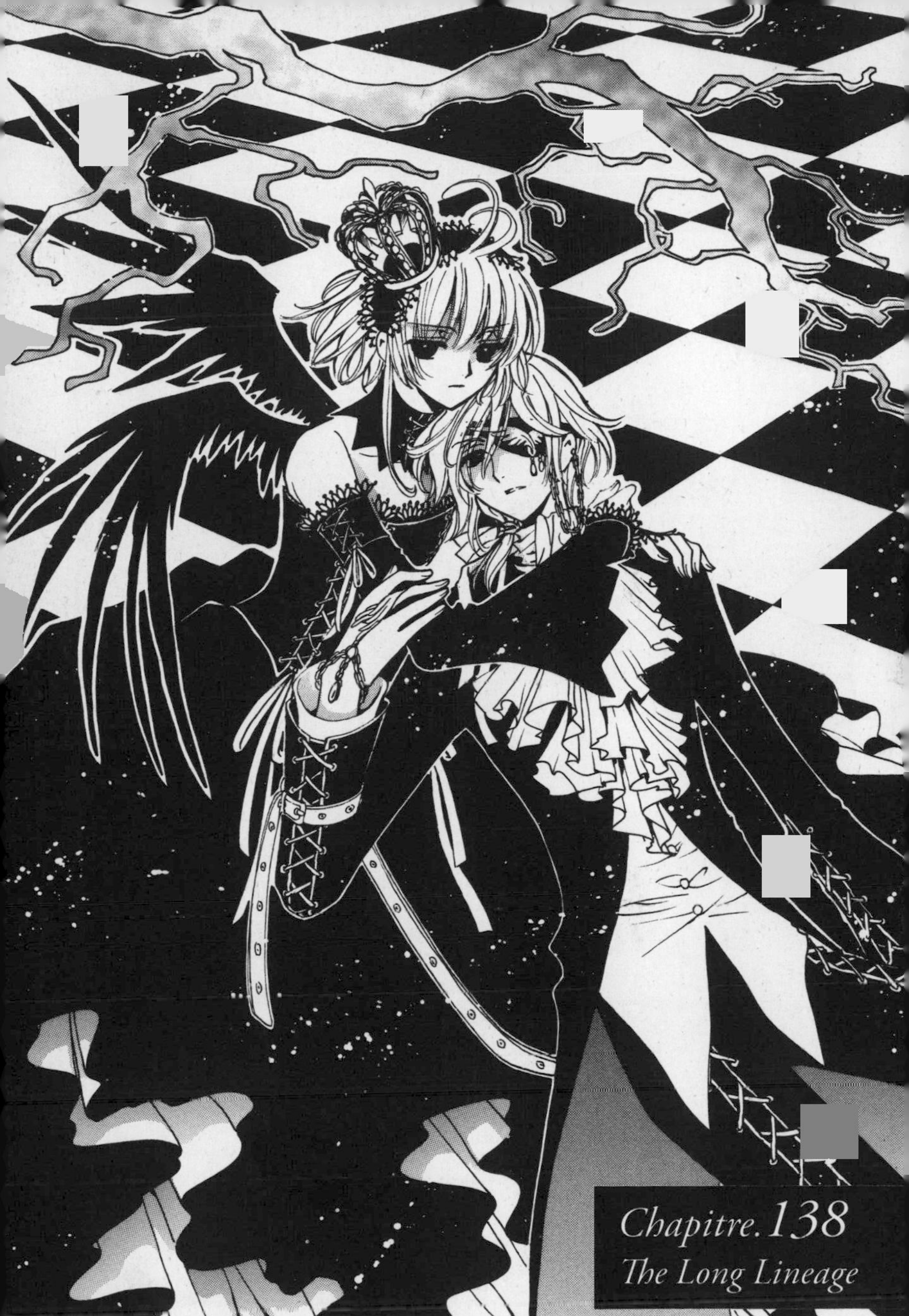
Chapitre. 138
The Long Lineage

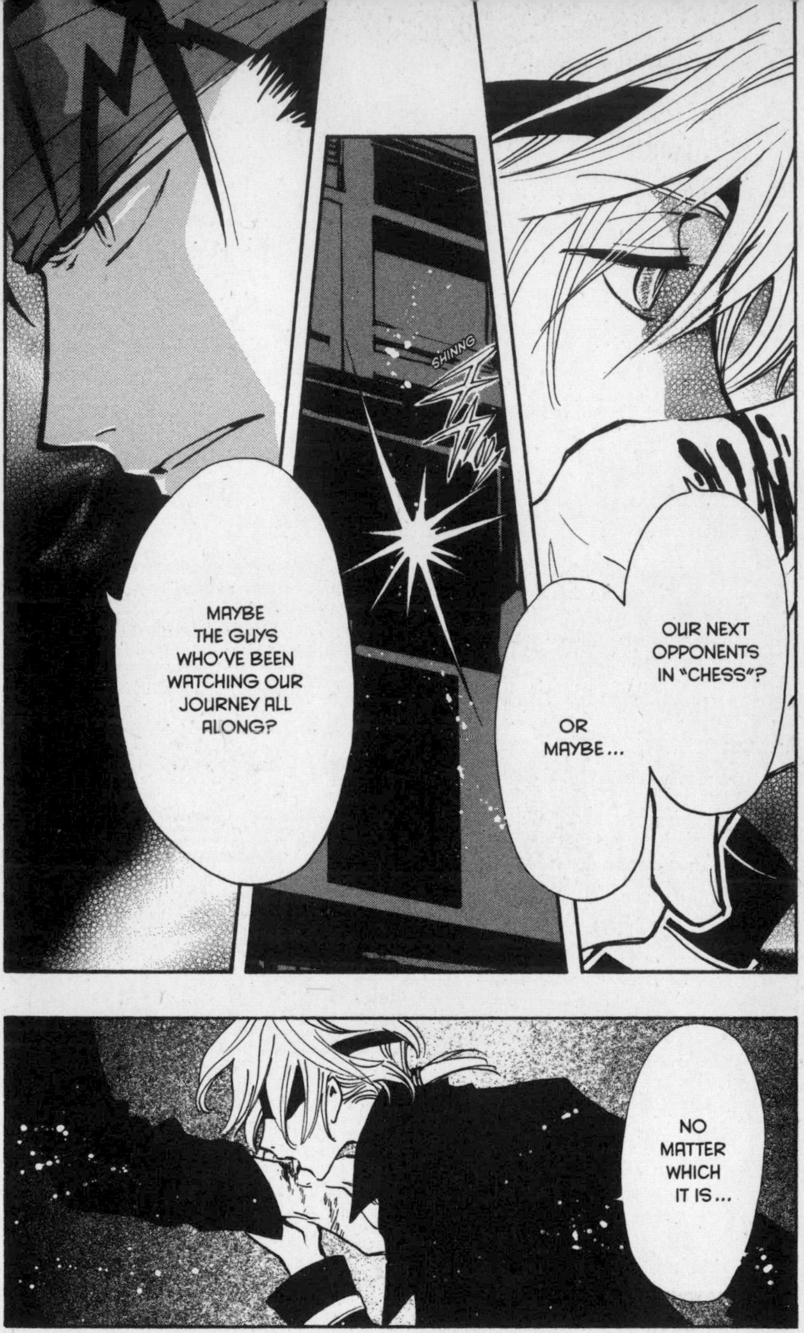
OUR NEXT OPPONENTS IN "CHESS"?
OR MAYBE...
SHINNG
MAYBE THE GUYS WHO'VE BEEN WATCHING OUR JOURNEY ALL ALONG?
NO MATTER WHICH IT IS...

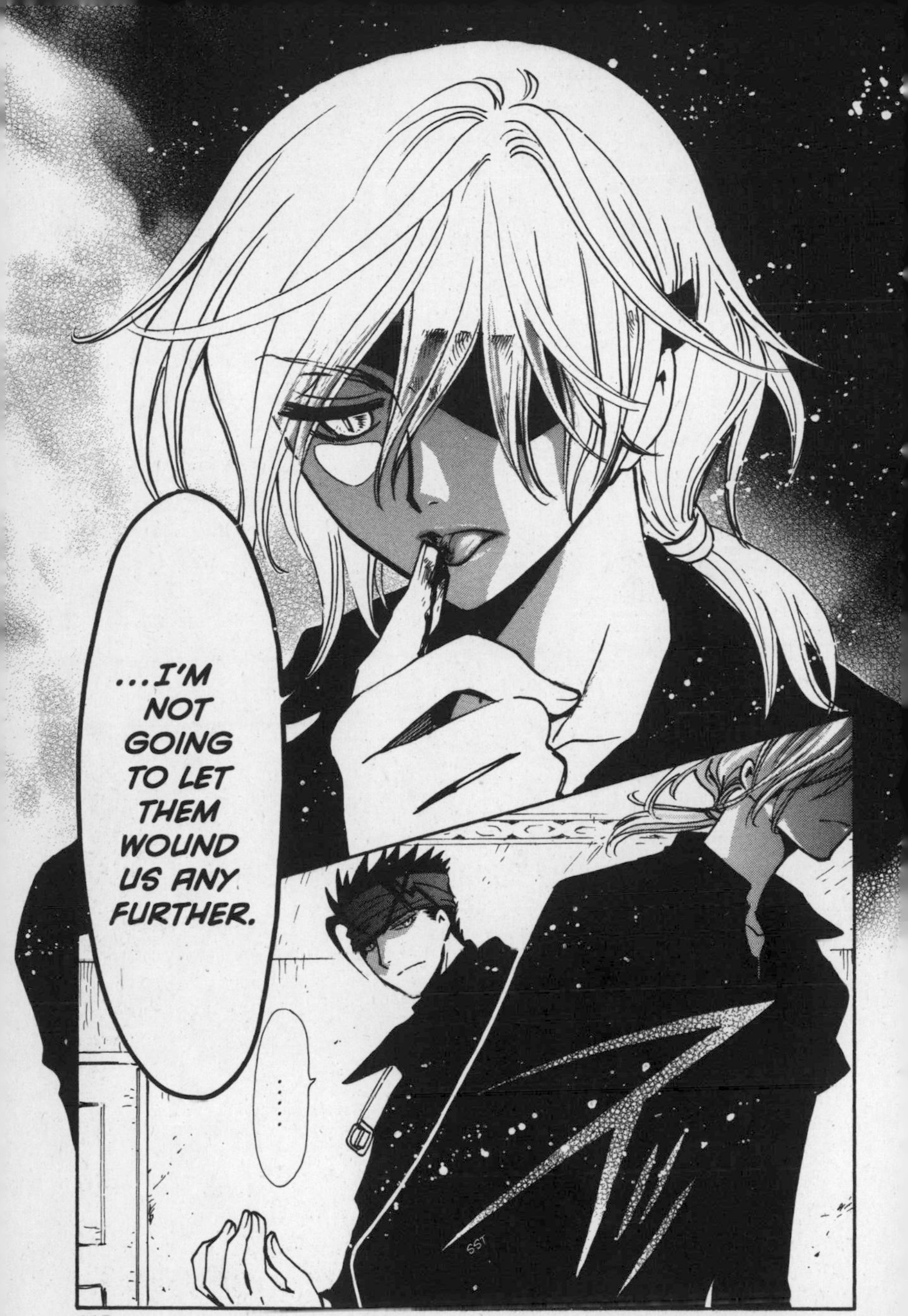
...I'M NOT GOING TO LET THEM WOUND US ANY FURTHER.
......
SST

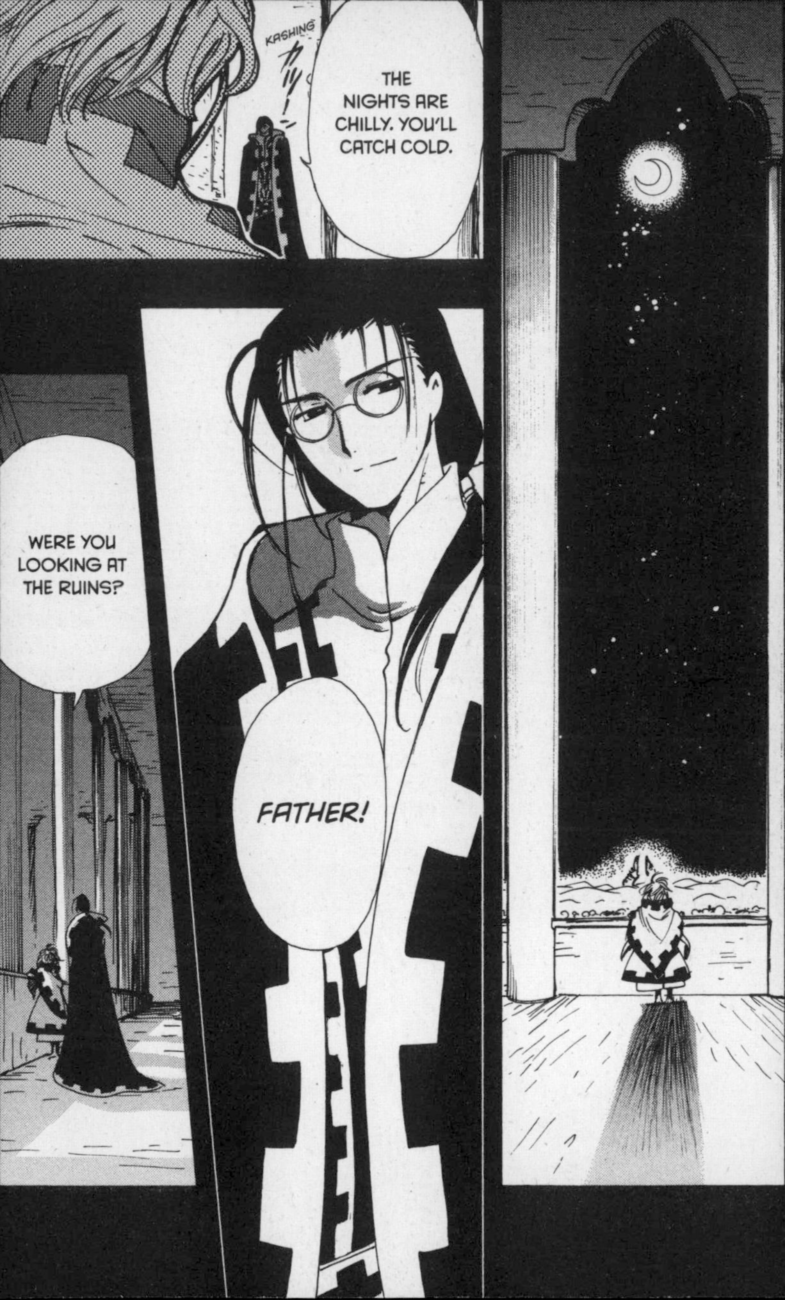
KASHING
THE NIGHTS ARE CHILLY. YOU'LL CATCH COLD.
FATHER!
WERE YOU LOOKING AT THE RUINS?

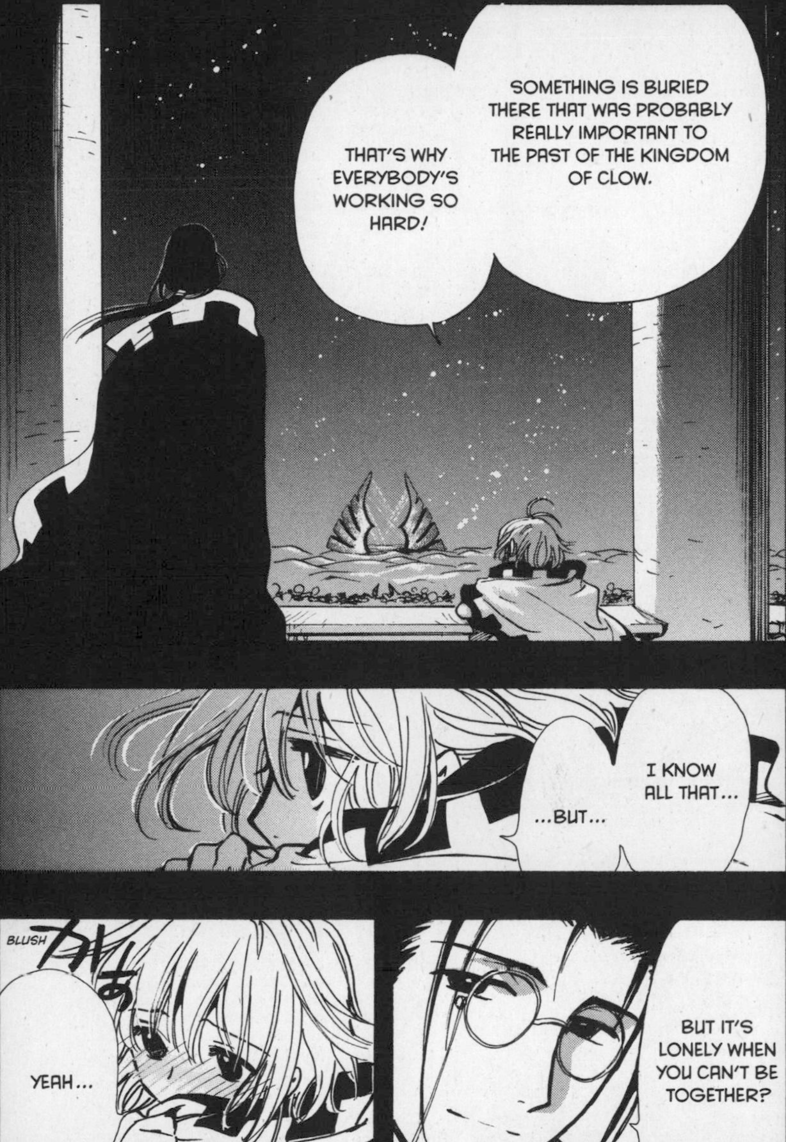
SOMETHING IS BURIED THERE THAT WAS PROBABLY REALLY IMPORTANT TO THE PAST OF THE KINGDOM OF CLOW.
THAT'S WHY EVERYBODY'S WORKING SO HARD!
I KNOW ALL THAT...
...BUT...
BUT IT'S LONELY WHEN YOU CAN'T BE TOGETHER?
BLUSH
YEAH...

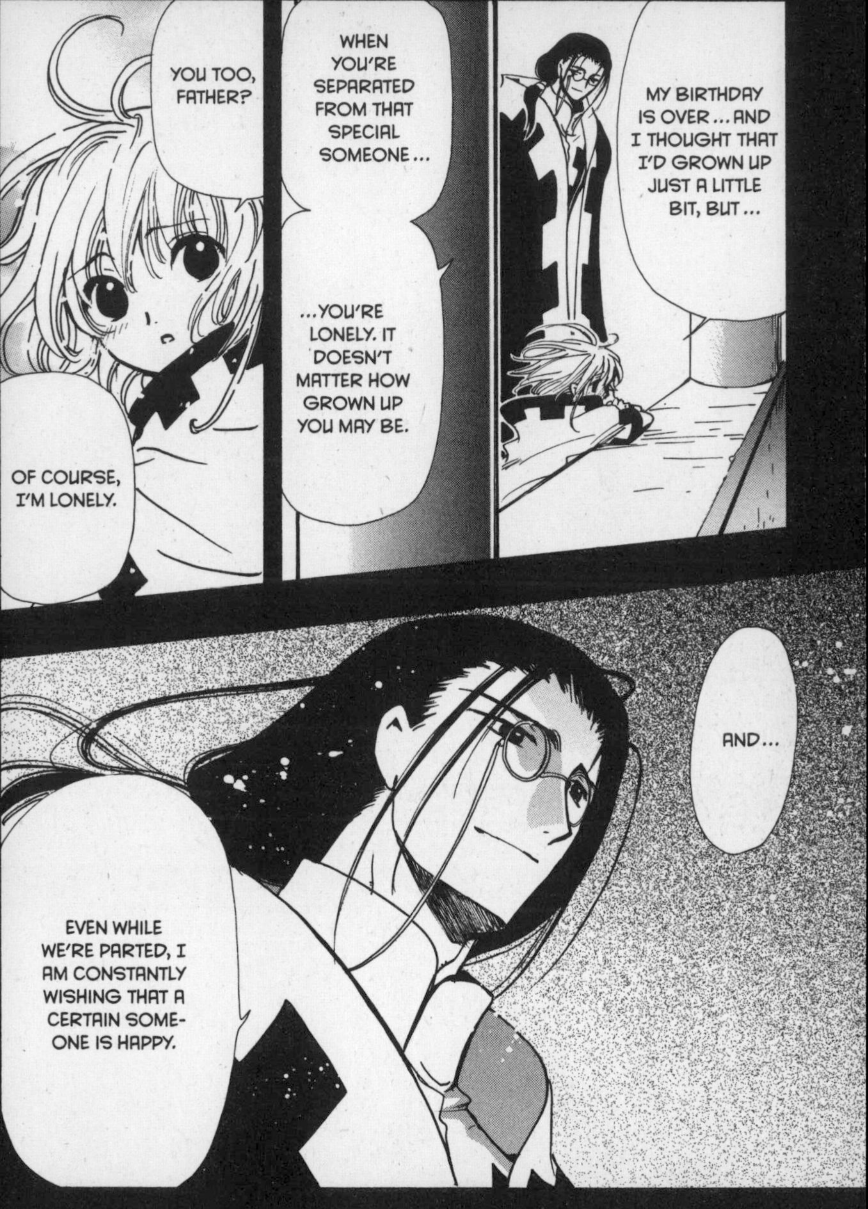
MY BIRTHDAY IS OVER ... AND I THOUGHT THAT I'D GROWN UP JUST A LITTLE BIT, BUT ...
WHEN YOU'RE SEPARATED FROM THAT SPECIAL SOMEONE ...
...YOU'RE LONELY. IT DOESN'T MATTER HOW GROWN UP YOU MAY BE.
YOU TOO, FATHER?
OF COURSE, I'M LONELY.
AND...
EVEN WHILE WE'RE PARTED, I AM CONSTANTLY WISHING THAT A CERTAIN SOME-ONE IS HAPPY.

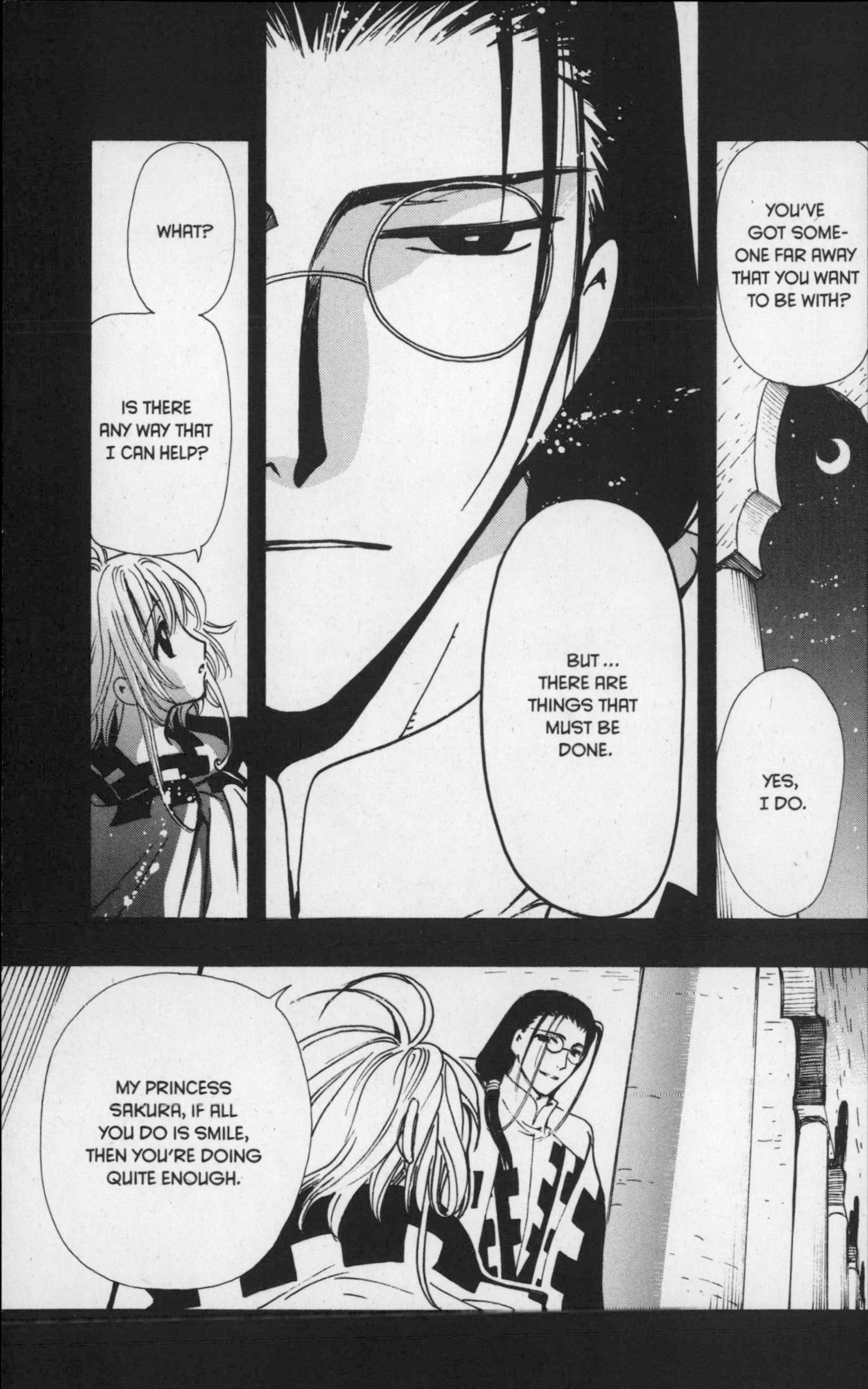
YOU'VE GOT SOME-ONE FAR AWAY THAT YOU WANT TO BE WITH?
YES, I DO.
BUT ... THERE ARE THINGS THAT MUST BE DONE.
WHAT?
IS THERE ANY WAY THAT I CAN HELP?
MY PRINCESS SAKURA, IF ALL YOU DO IS SMILE, THEN YOU'RE DOING QUITE ENOUGH.

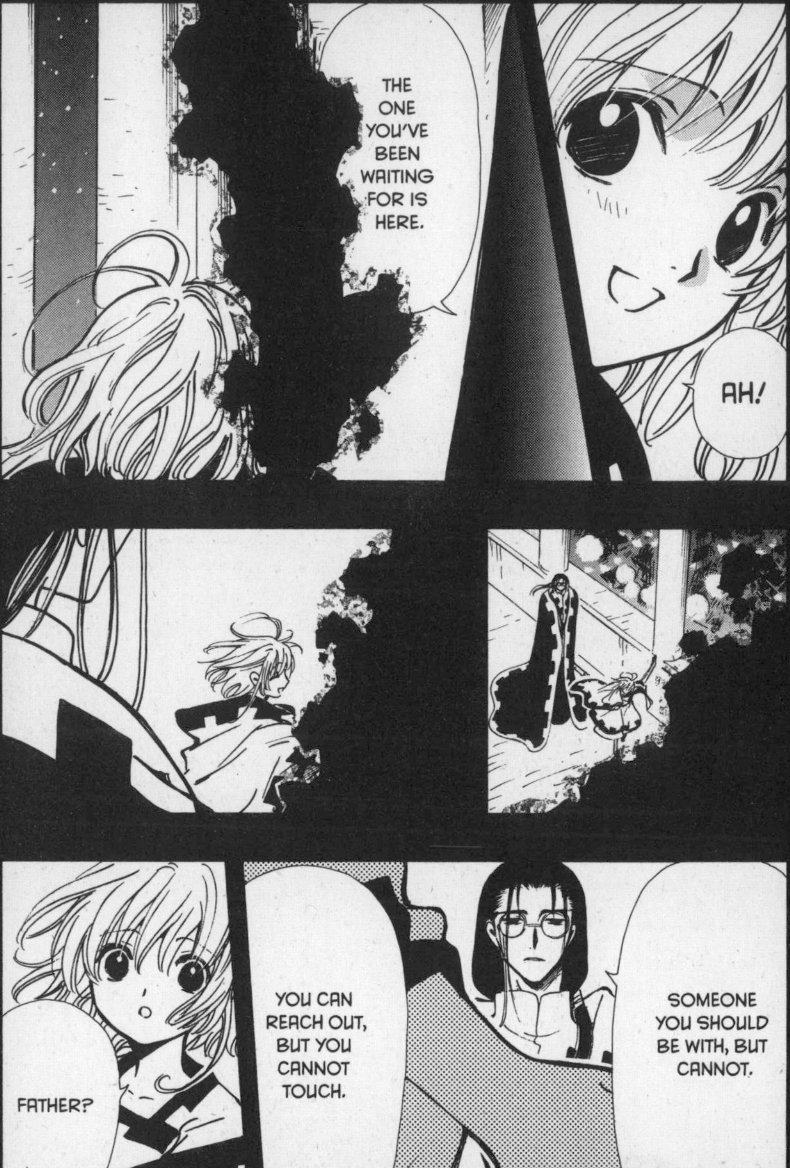
AH!
THE ONE YOU'VE BEEN WAITING FOR IS HERE.
SOMEONE YOU SHOULD BE WITH, BUT CANNOT.
YOU CAN REACH OUT, BUT YOU CANNOT TOUCH.
FATHER?

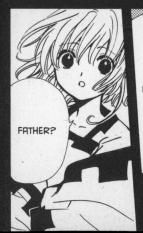

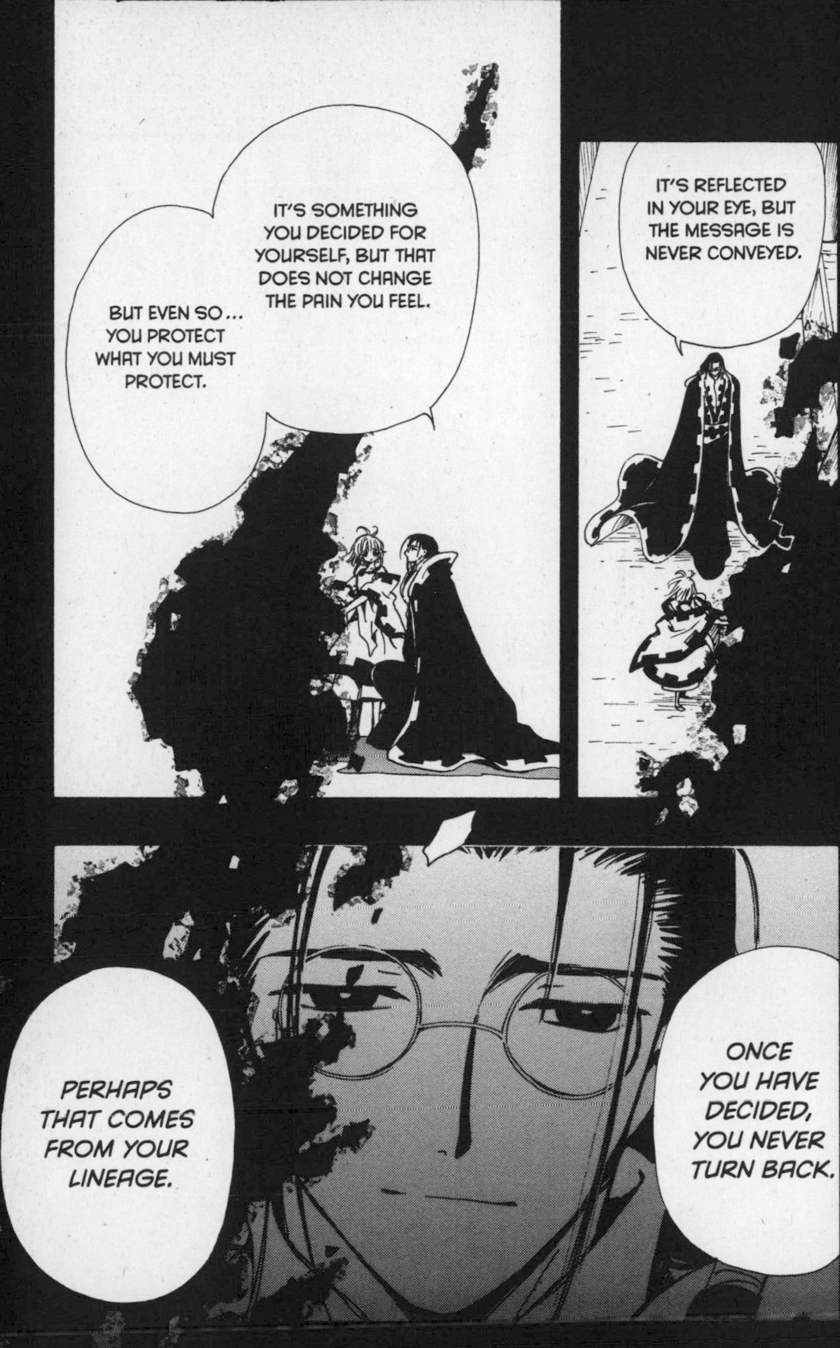
IT'S REFLECTED IN YOUR EYE, BUT THE MESSAGE IS NEVER CONVEYED.
IT'S SOMETHING YOU DECIDED FOR YOURSELF, BUT THAT DOES NOT CHANGE THE PAIN YOU FEEL.
BUT EVEN SO... YOU PROTECT WHAT YOU MUST PROTECT.
ONCE YOU HAVE DECIDED, YOU NEVER TURN BACK.
PERHAPS THAT COMES FROM YOUR LINEAGE.

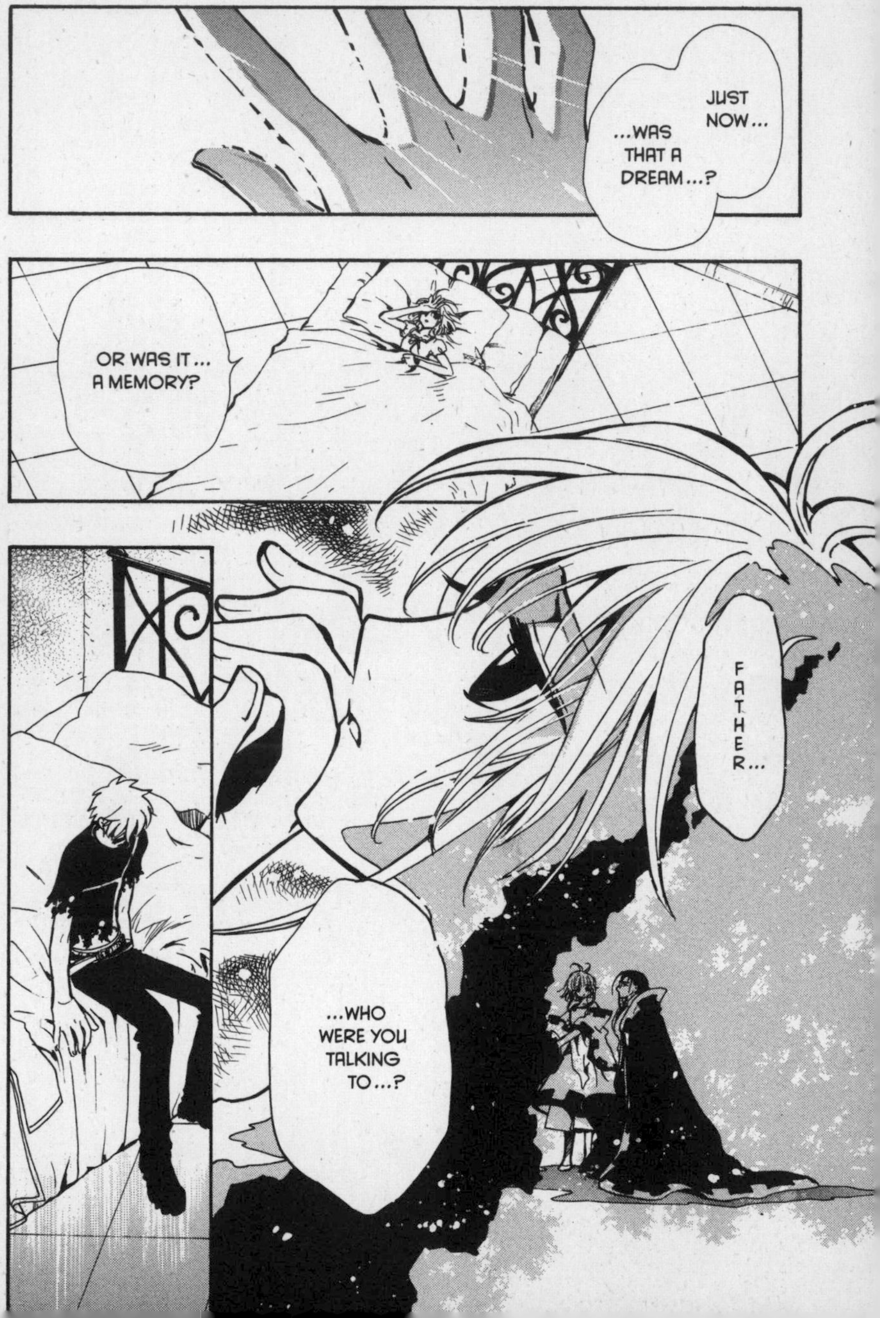
JUST NOW... ...WAS THAT A DREAM...?
OR WAS IT... A MEMORY?
FATHER...
...WHO WERE YOU TALKING TO...?

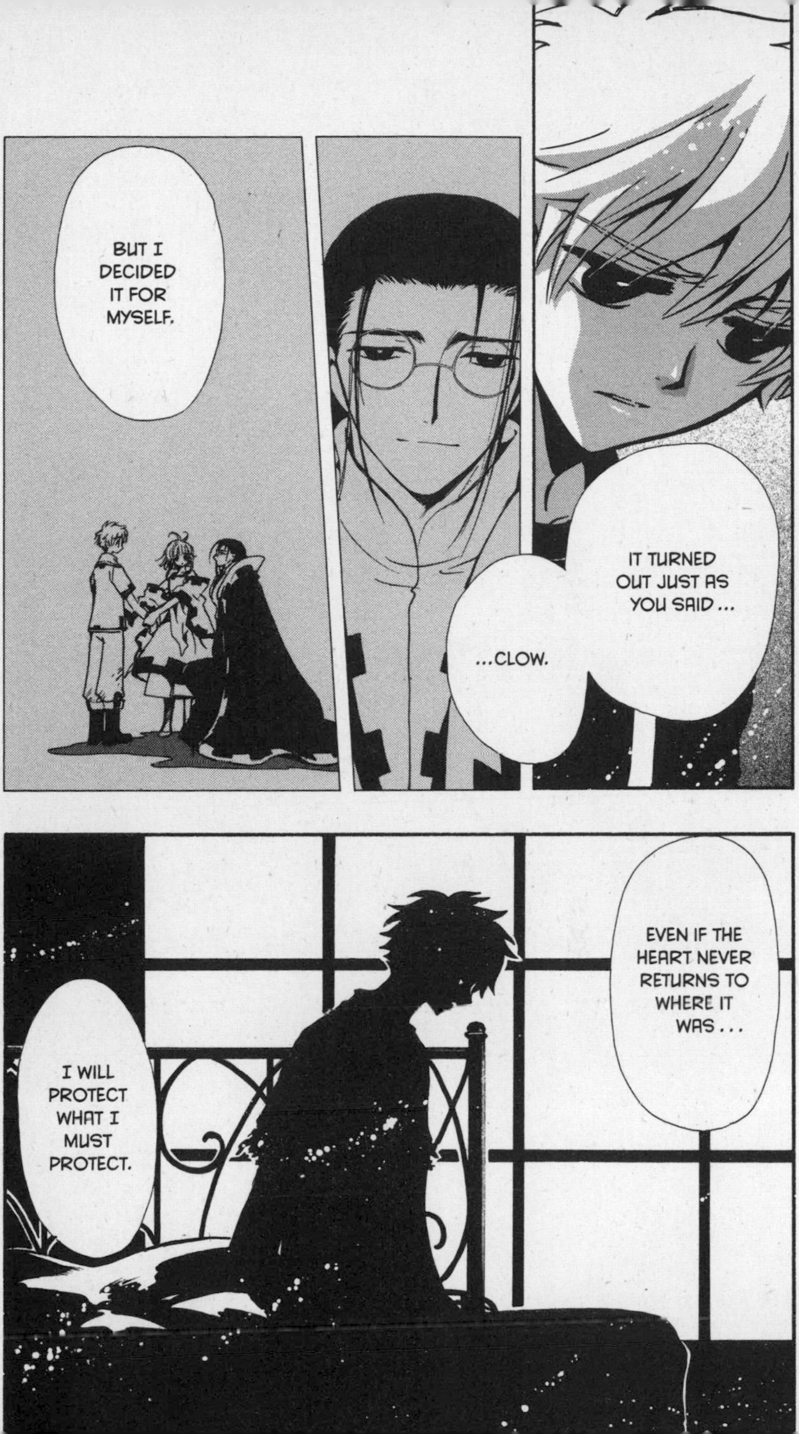
IT TURNED OUT JUST AS YOU SAID...
...CLOW.
BUT I DECIDED IT FOR MYSELF.
EVEN IF THE HEART NEVER RETURNS TO WHERE IT WAS...
I WILL PROTECT WHAT I MUST PROTECT.

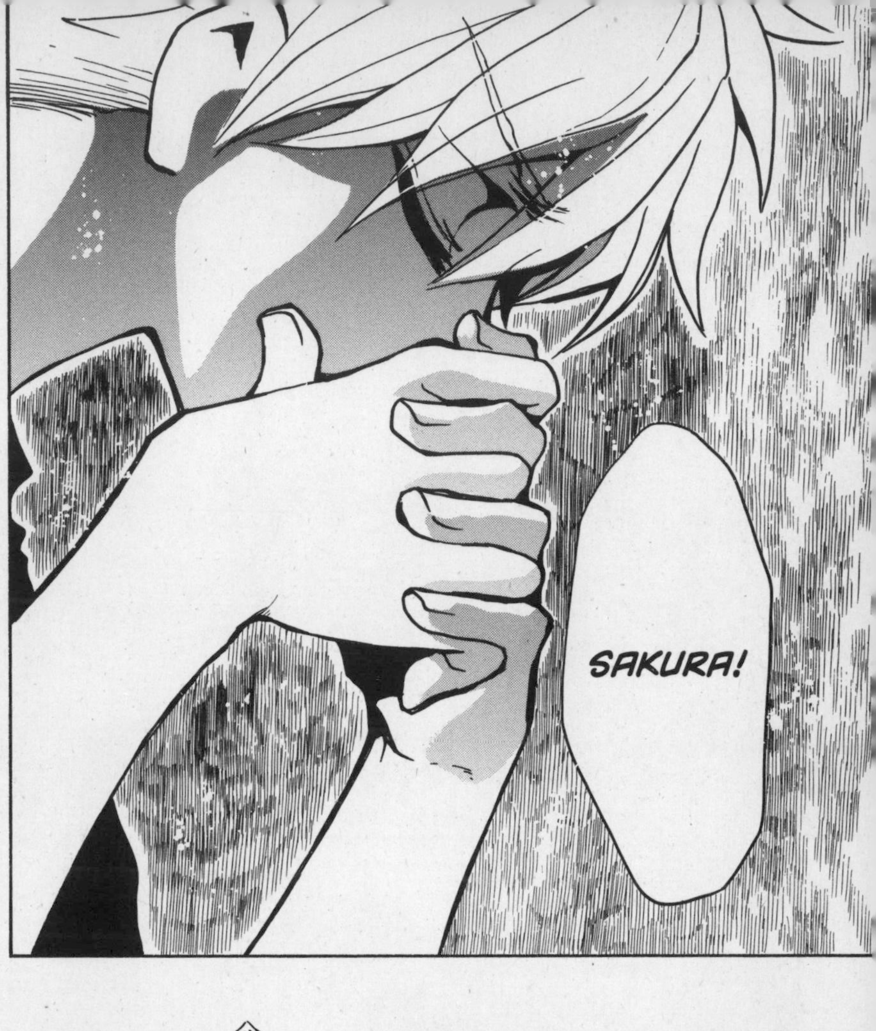
SAKURA!

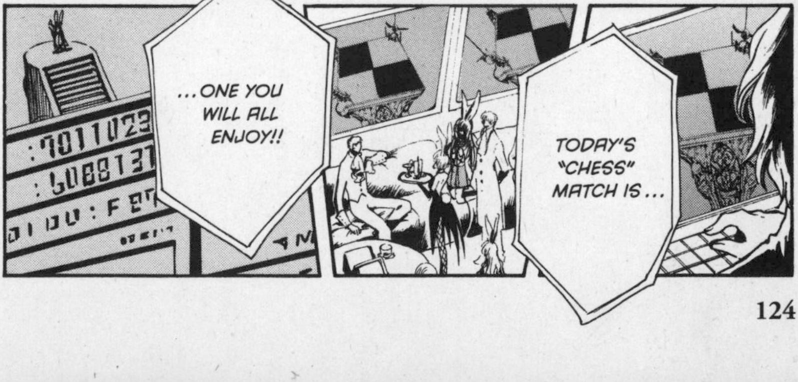
TODAY'S "CHESS" MATCH IS...
...ONE YOU WILL ALL ENJOY!!

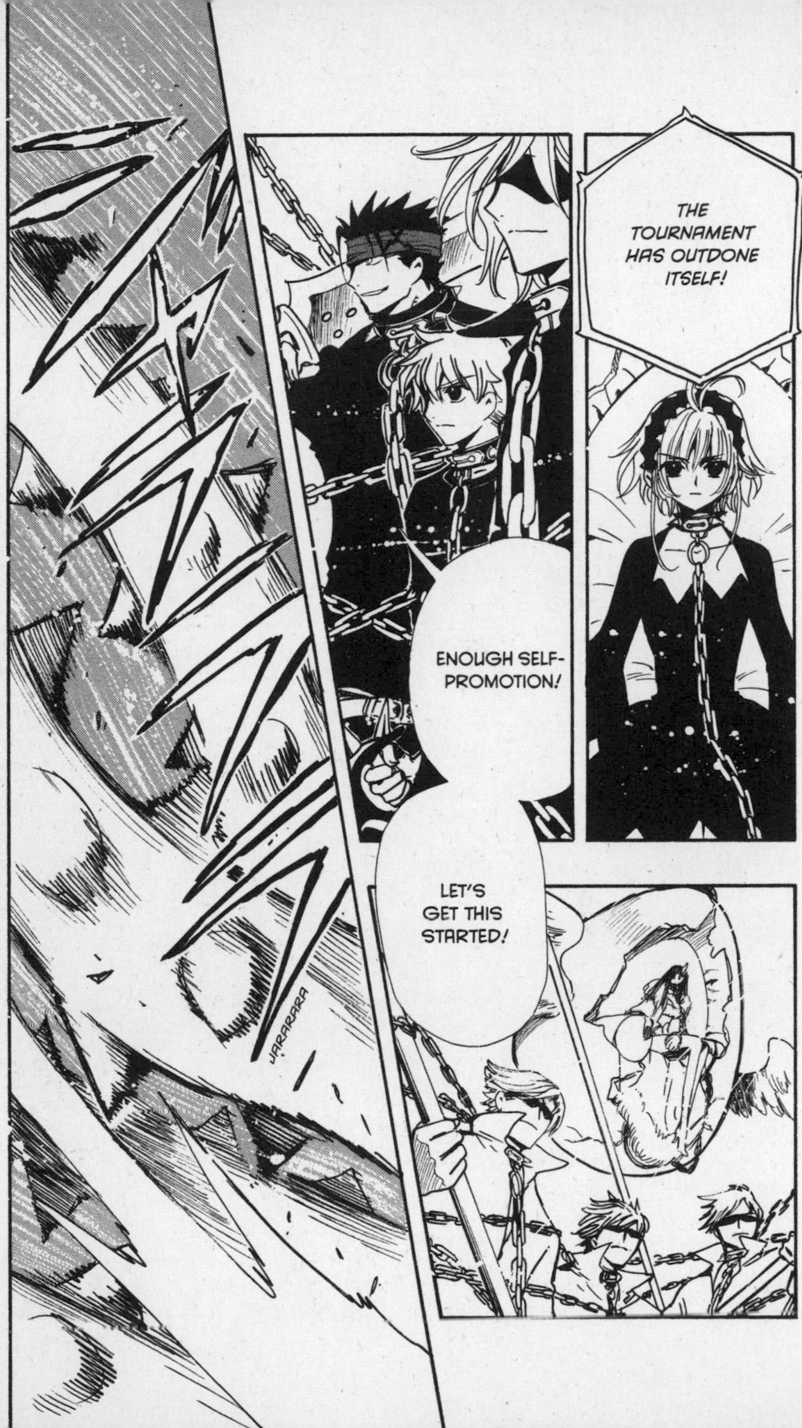
THE TOURNAMENT HAS OUTDONE ITSELF!
ENOUGH SELF-PROMOTION!
LET'S GET THIS STARTED!
JARARARA

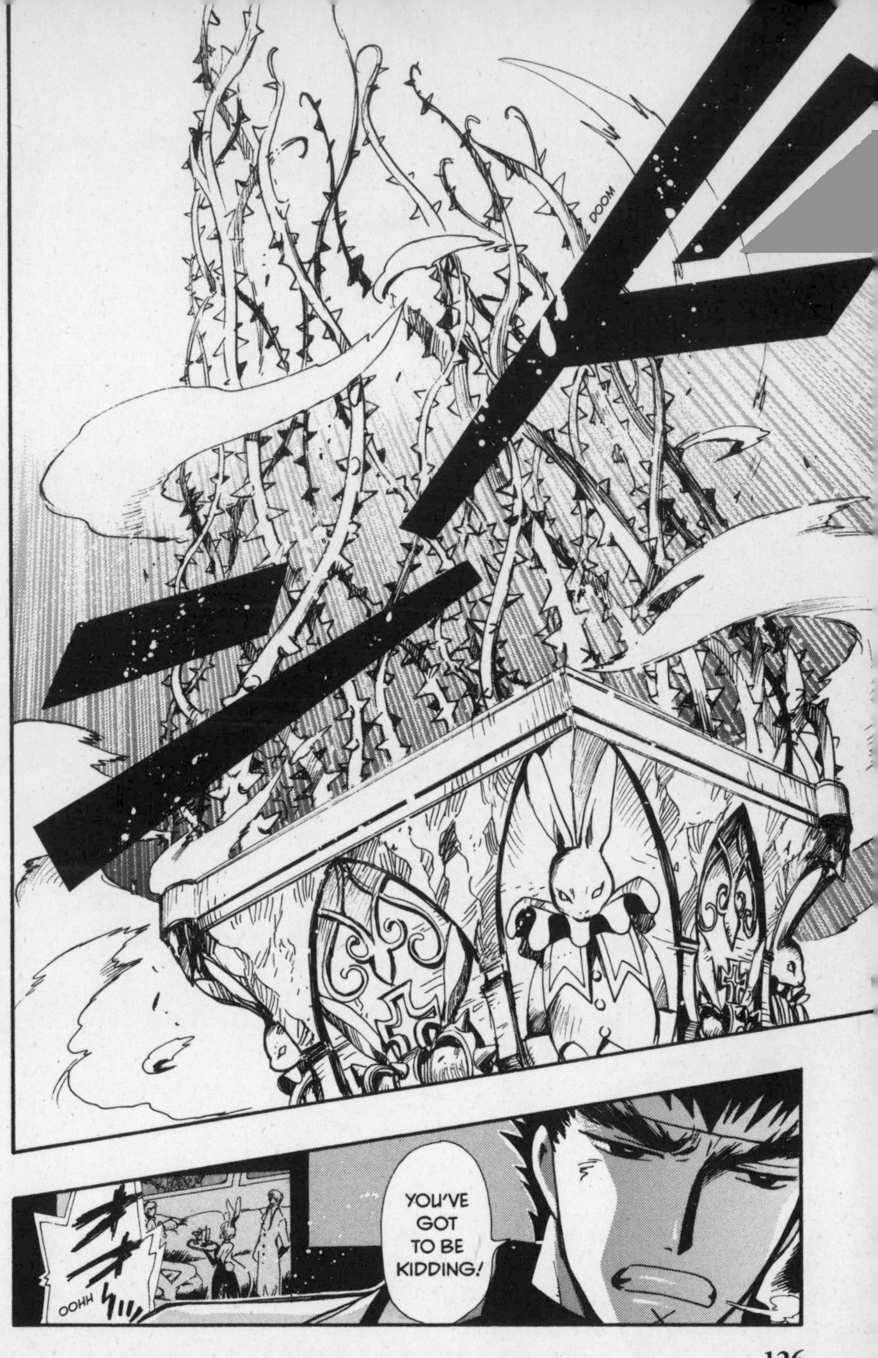
DOOM
YOU'VE GOT TO BE KIDDING!
OOHH

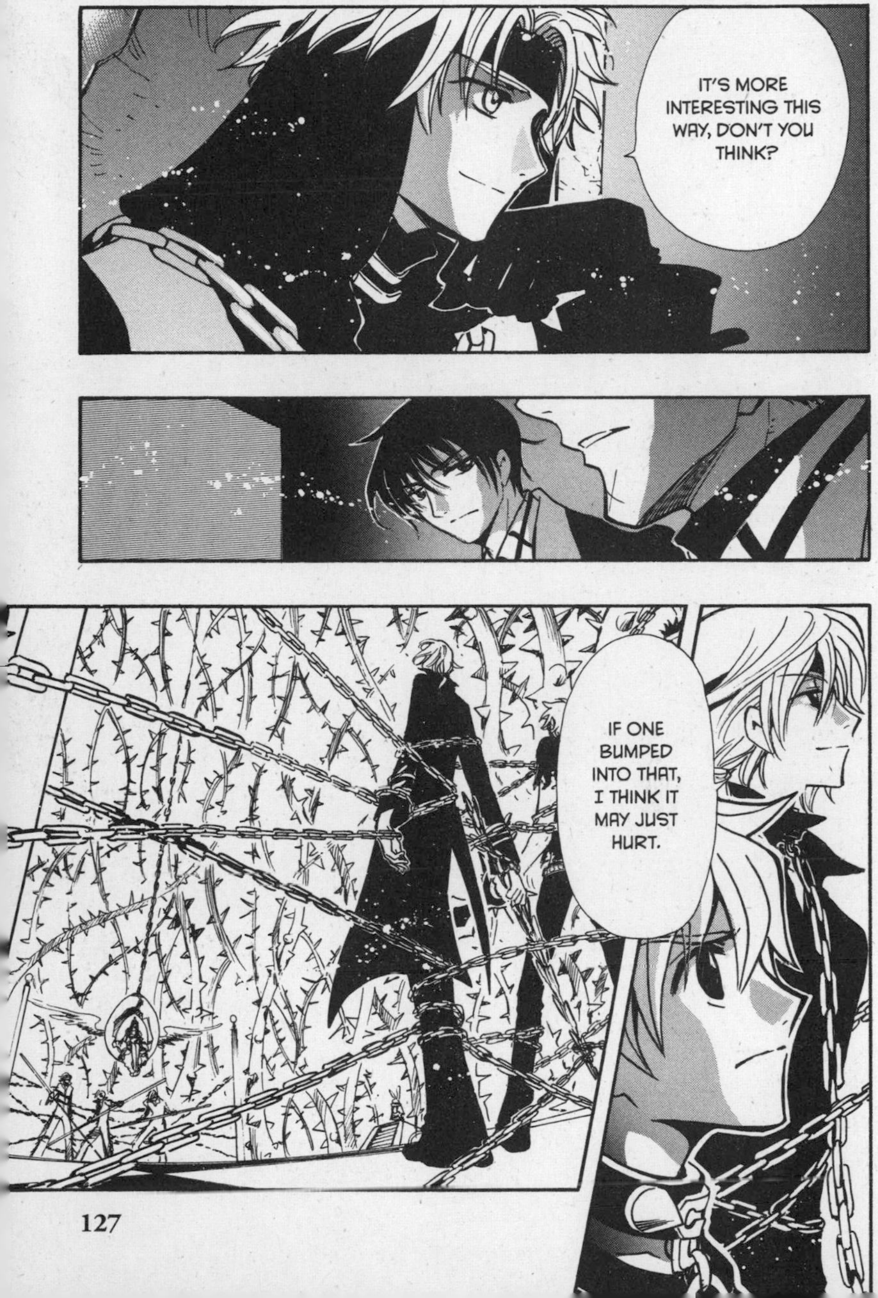
IT'S MORE INTERESTING THIS WAY, DON'T YOU THINK?
IF ONE BUMPED INTO THAT, I THINK IT MAY JUST HURT.

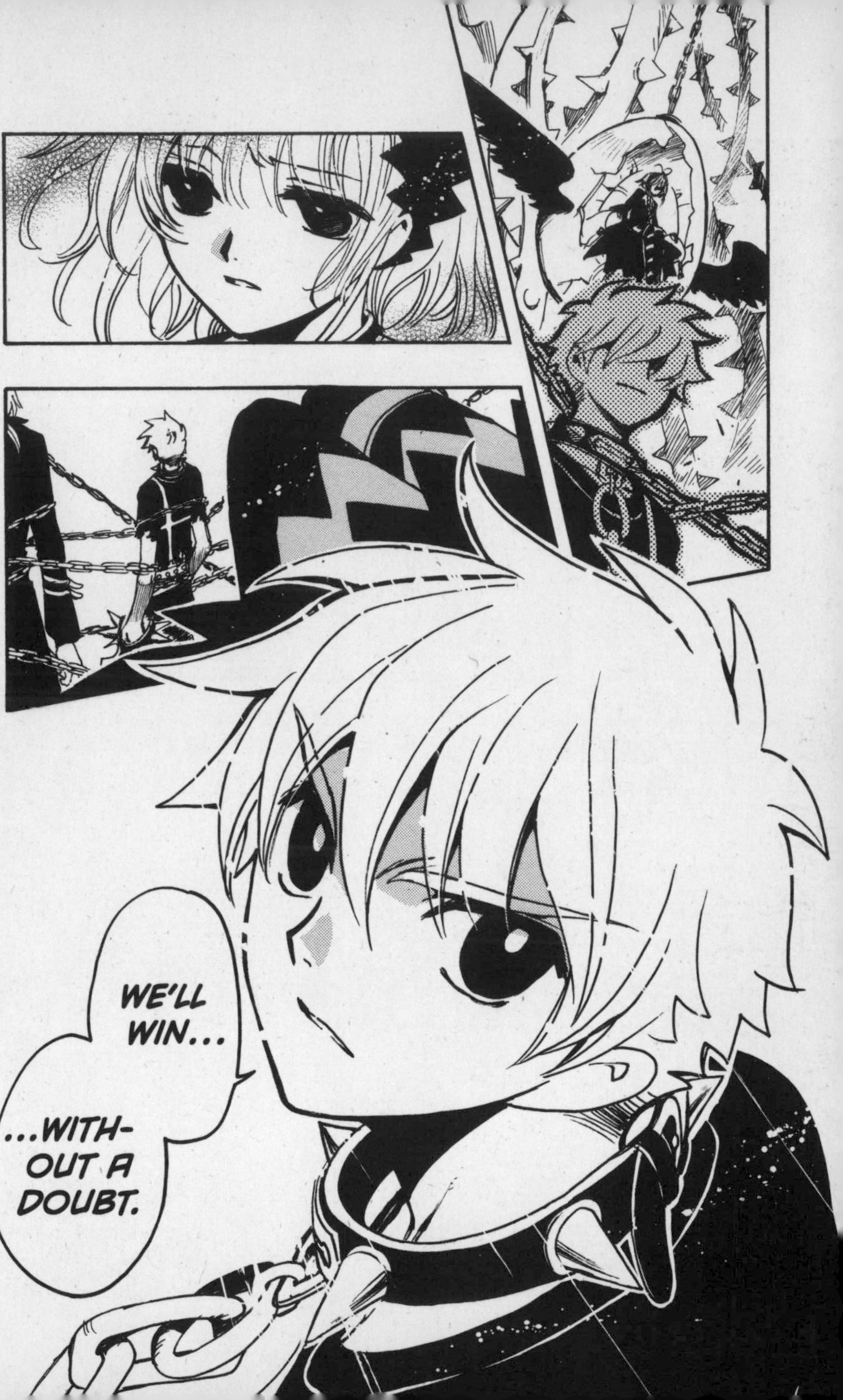
WE'LL WIN...
...WITHOUT A DOUBT.

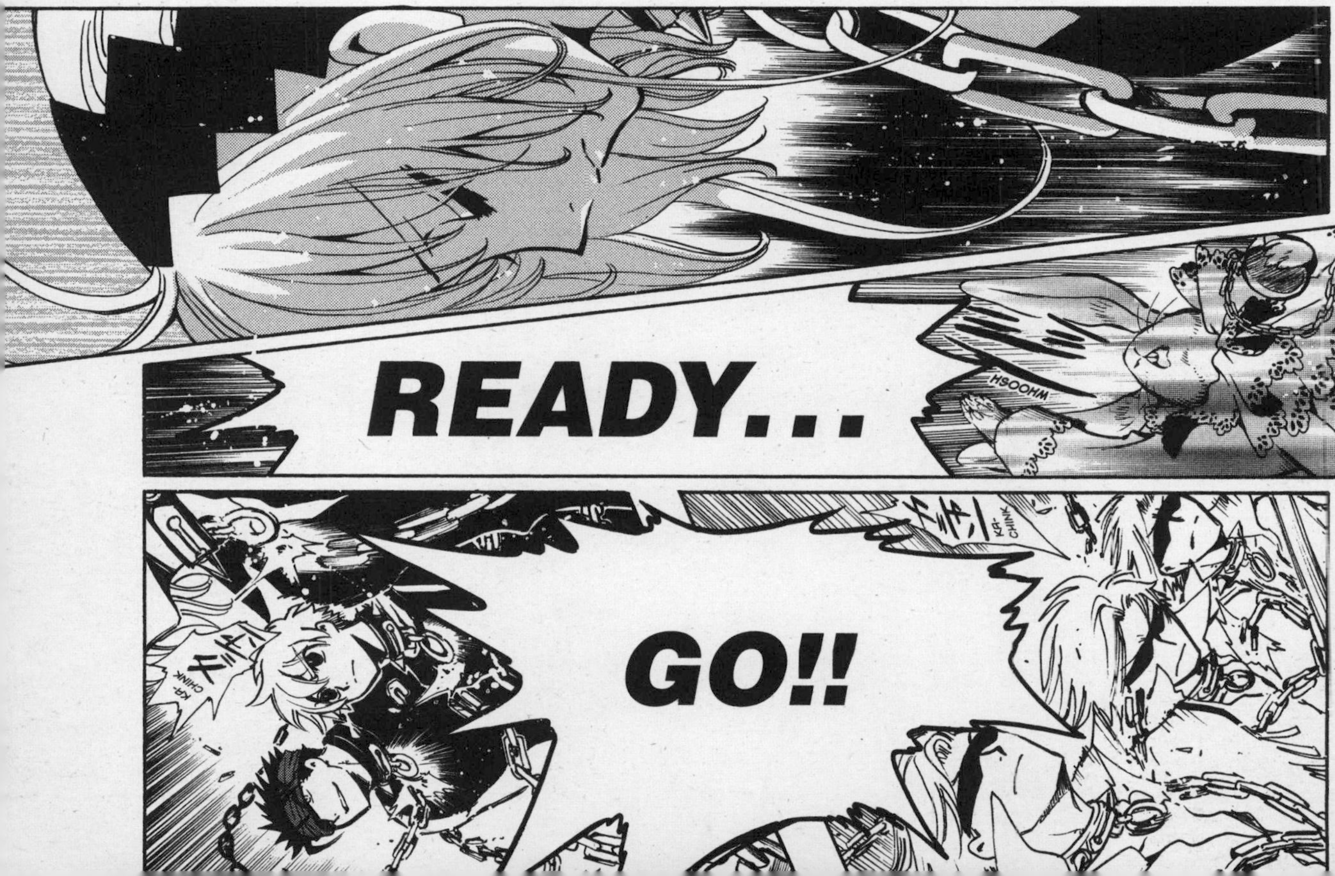
READY...
WHOOSH
KA-CHINK
GO!!
KA-CHINK

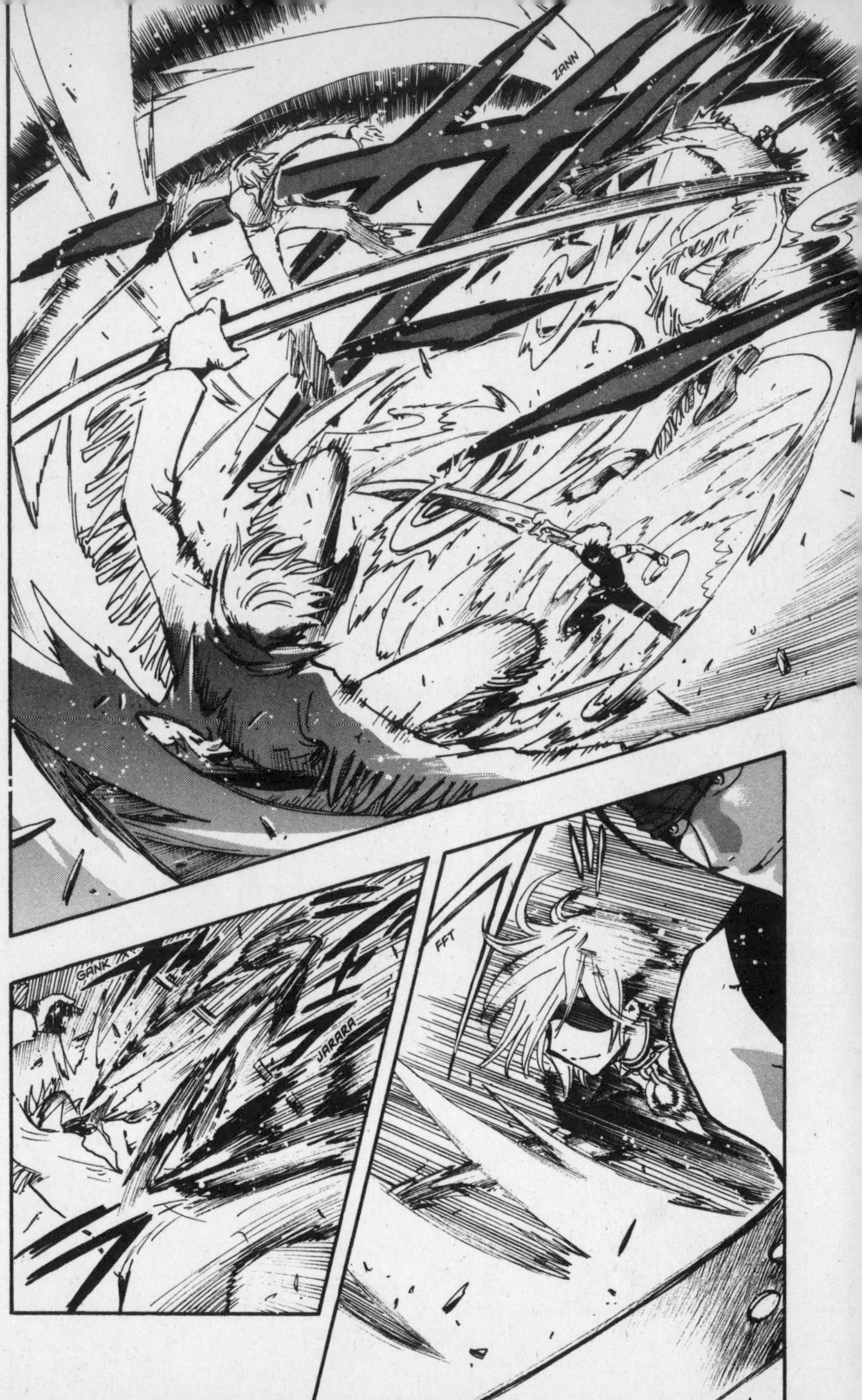
ZANN
FFT
GANK
JARARA

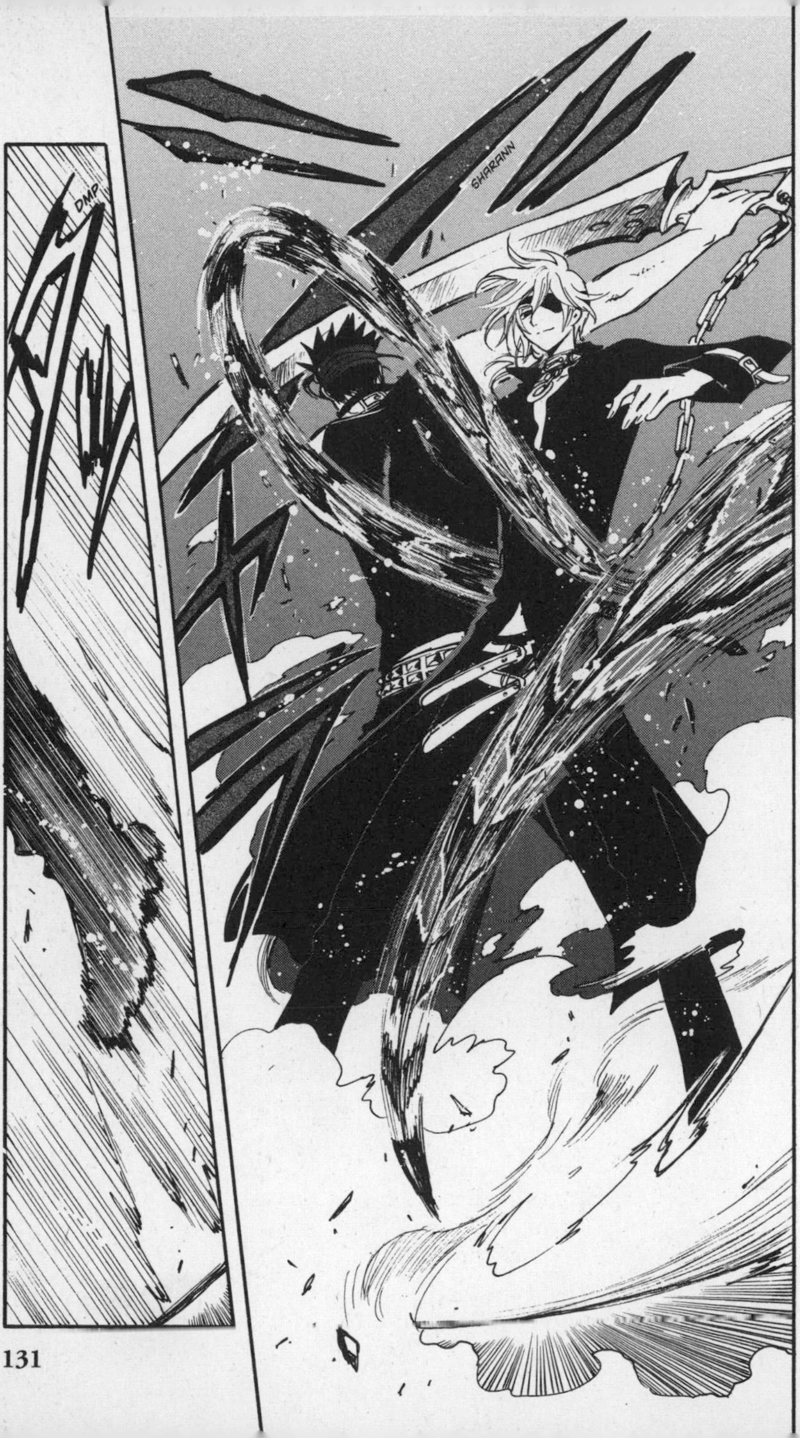
SHARANN
DMP

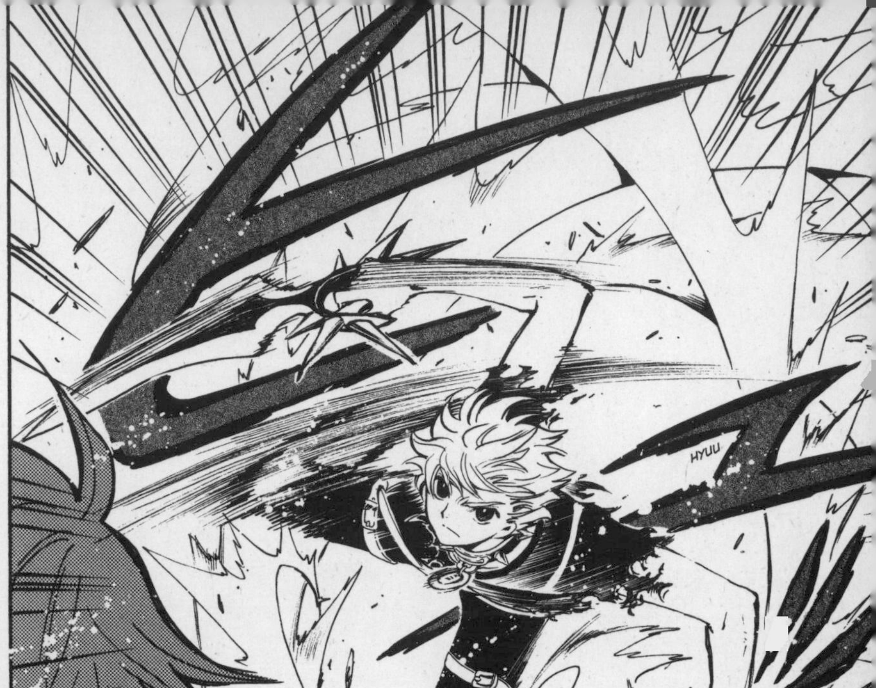
HYUU
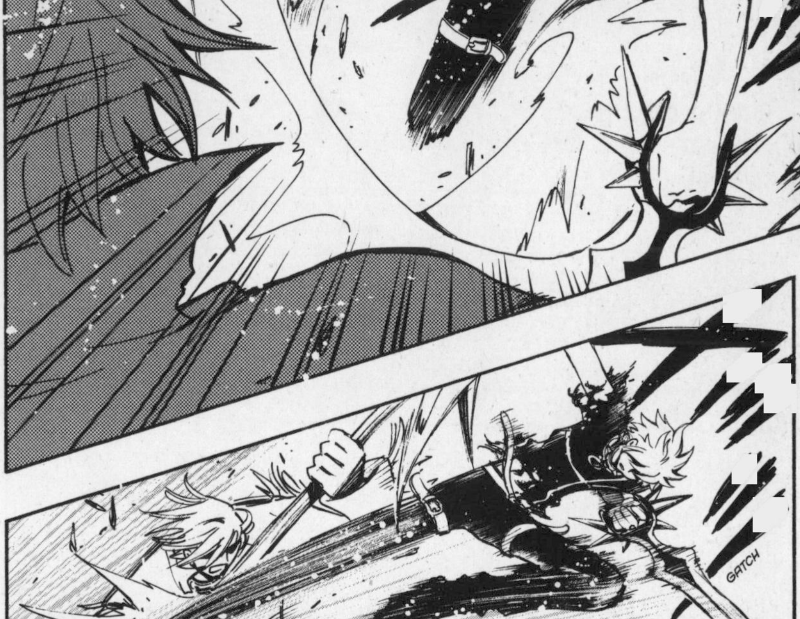
GATCH

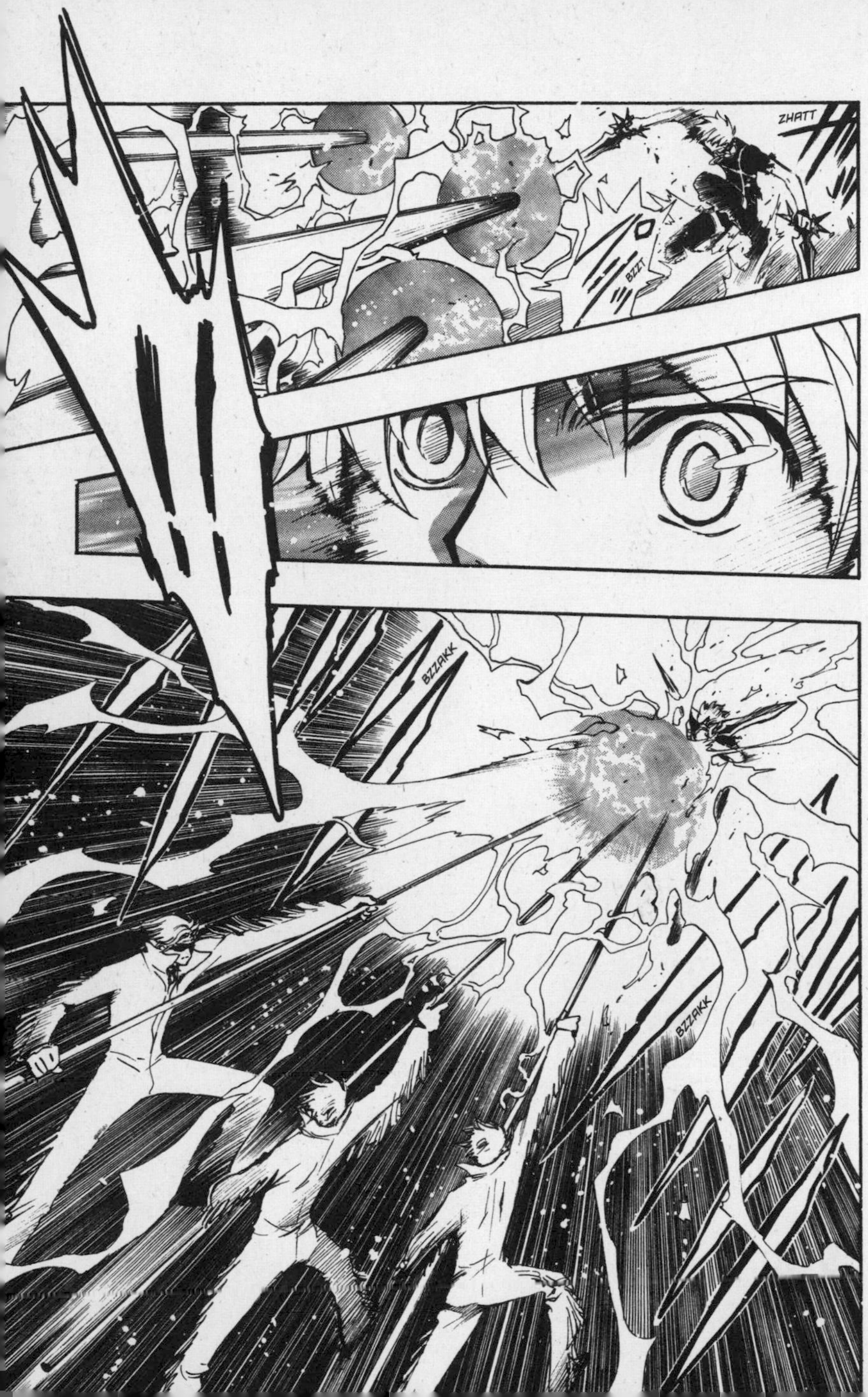
ZHATT
BZZT
BZZAKK
BZZAKK

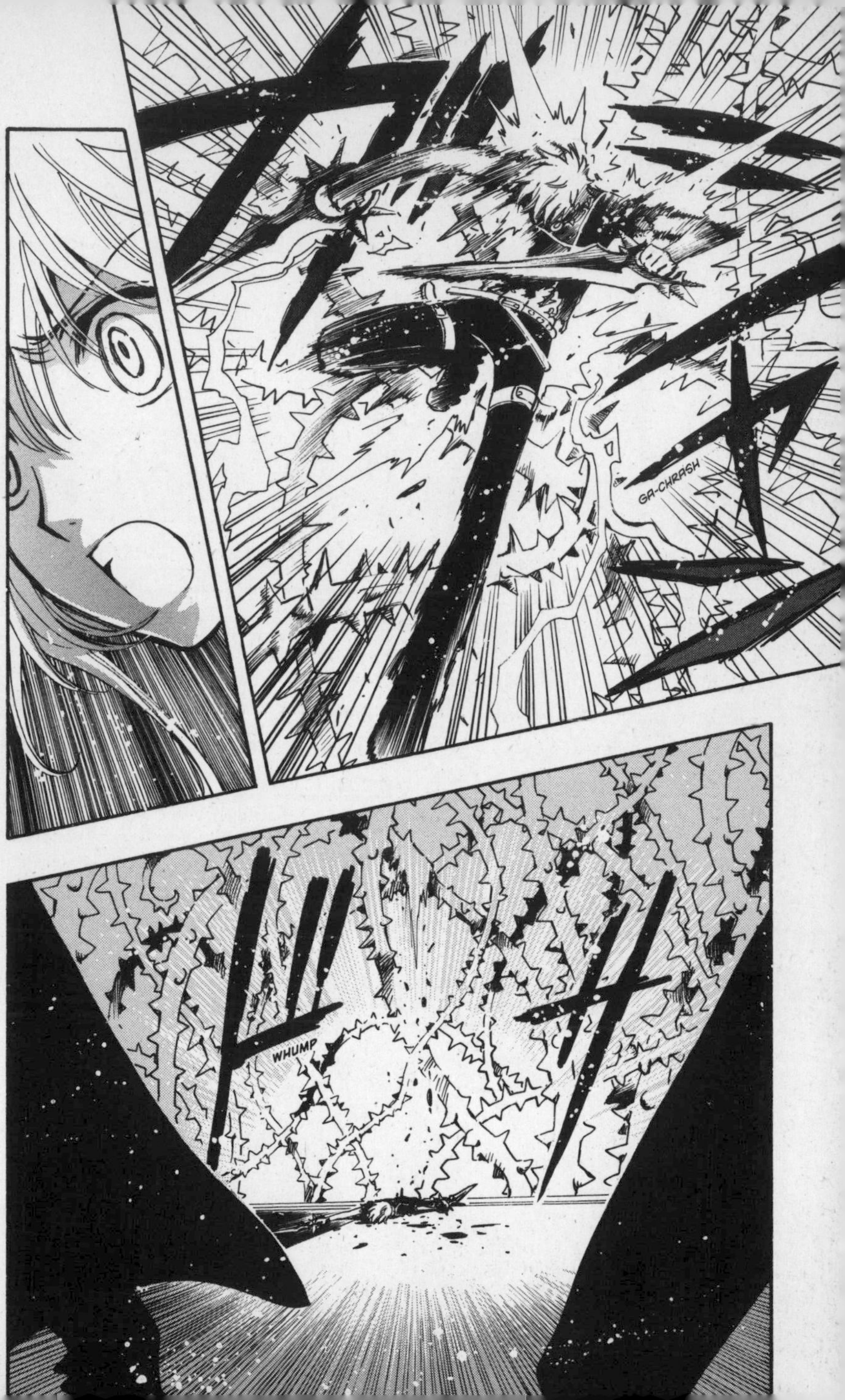
GA-CHRASH
WHUMP

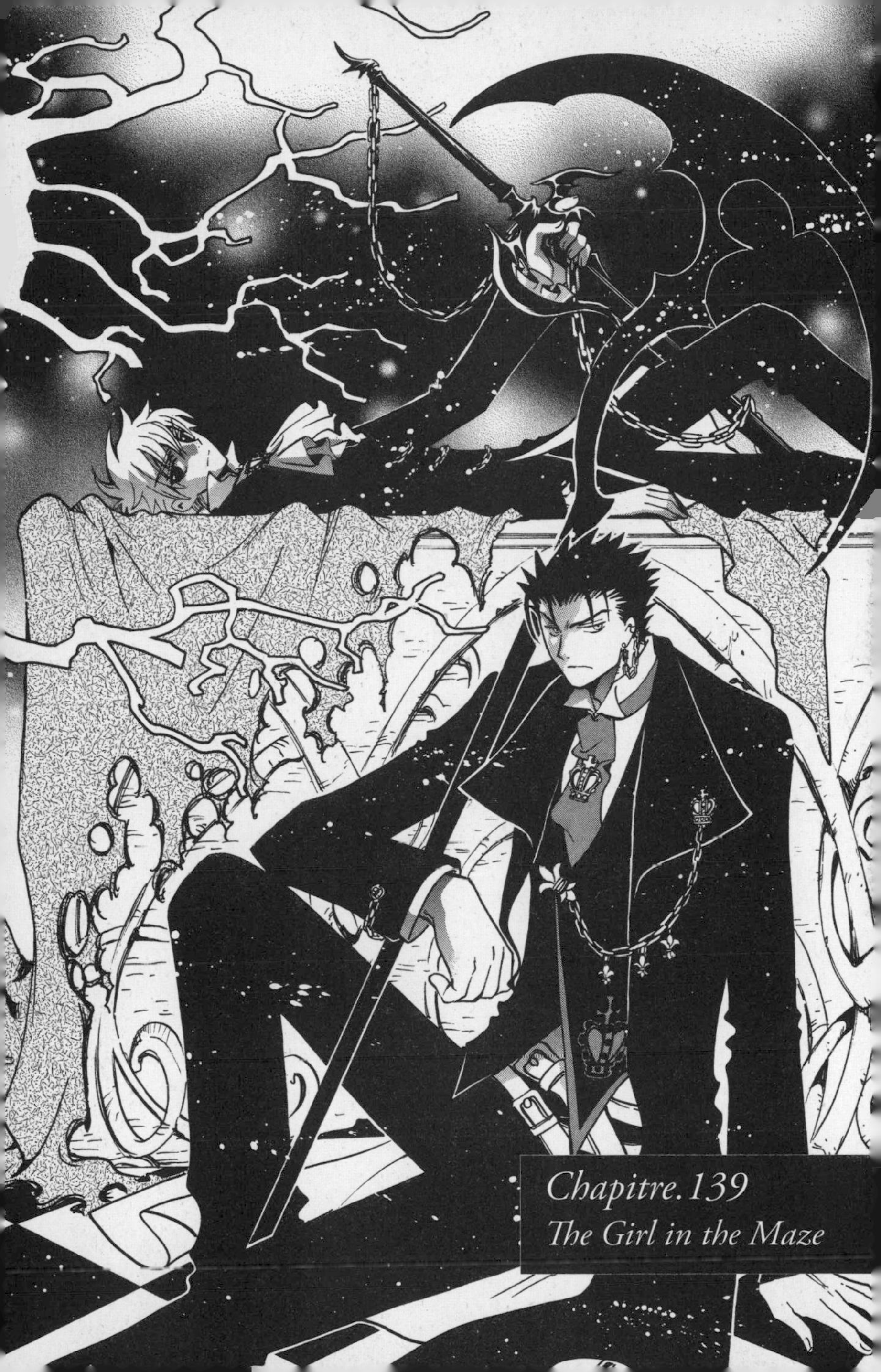
Chapitre. 139
The Girl in the Maze

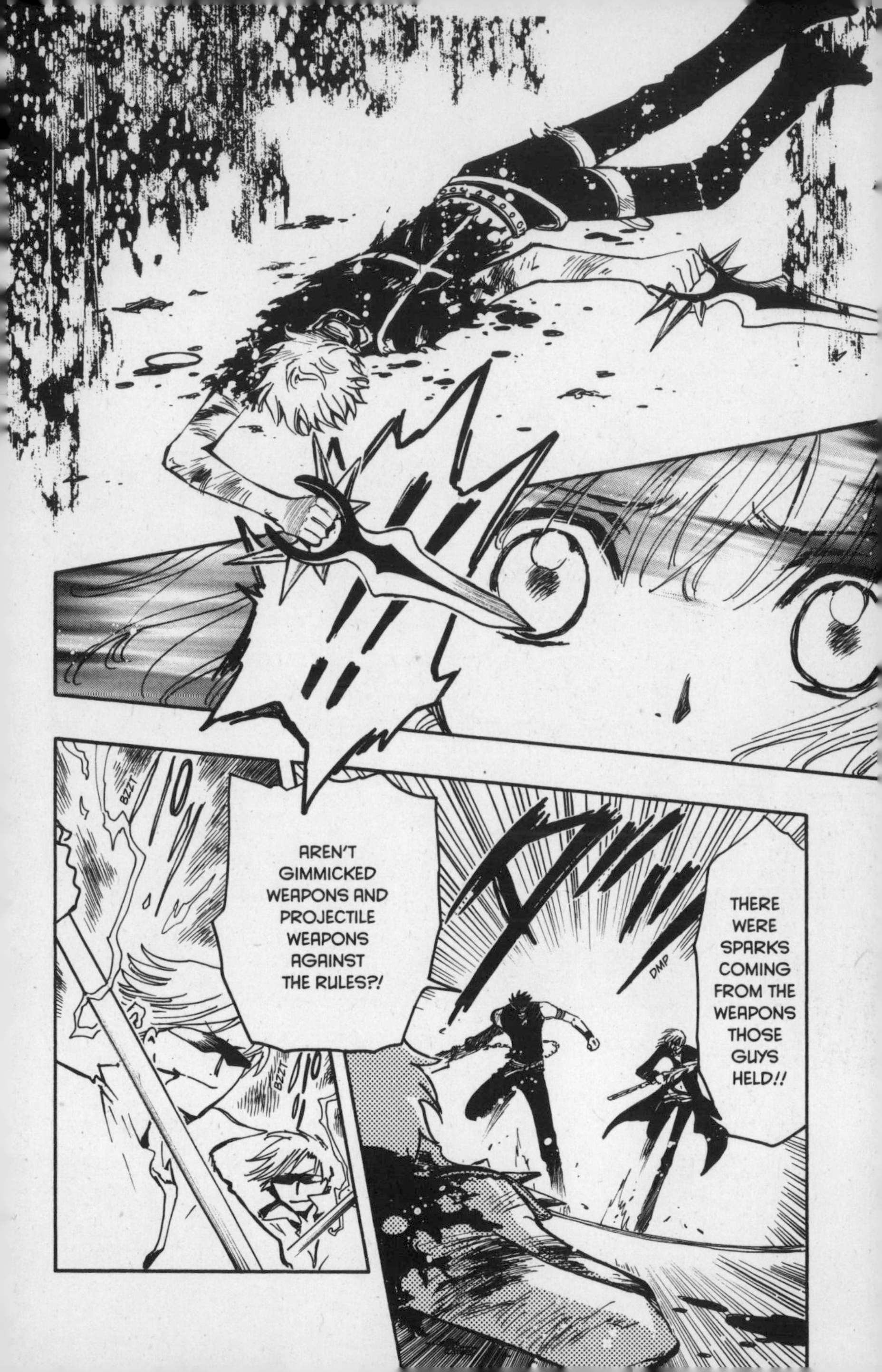
THERE WERE SPARKS COMING FROM THE WEAPONS THOSE GUYS HELD!!
DMP
AREN'T GIMMICKED WEAPONS AND PROJECTILE WEAPONS AGAINST THE RULES?!
BZZT
BZZT

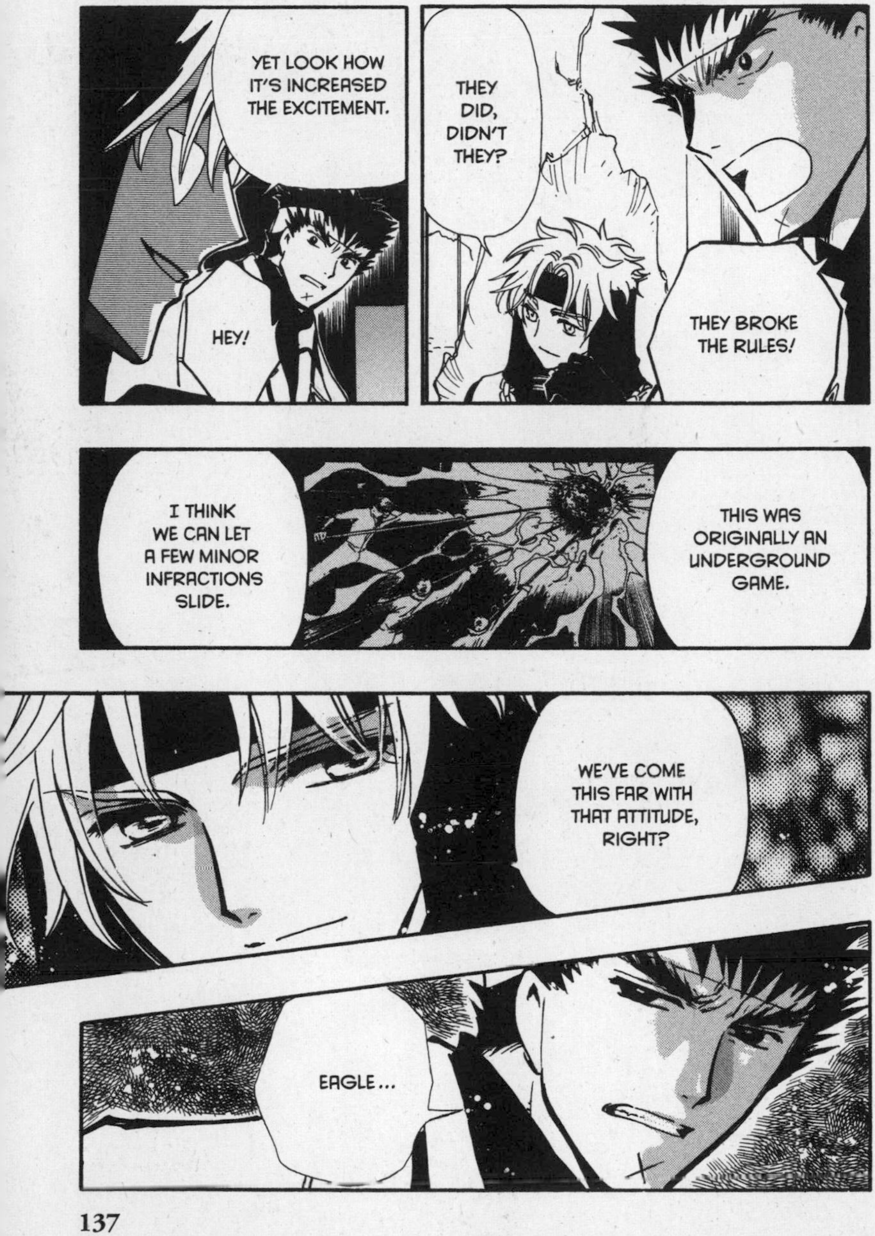
THEY BROKE THE RULES!
THEY DID, DIDN'T THEY?
YET LOOK HOW IT'S INCREASED THE EXCITEMENT.
HEY!
THIS WAS ORIGINALLY AN UNDERGROUND GAME.
I THINK WE CAN LET A FEW MINOR INFRACTIONS SLIDE.
WE'VE COME THIS FAR WITH THAT ATTITUDE, RIGHT?
EAGLE...

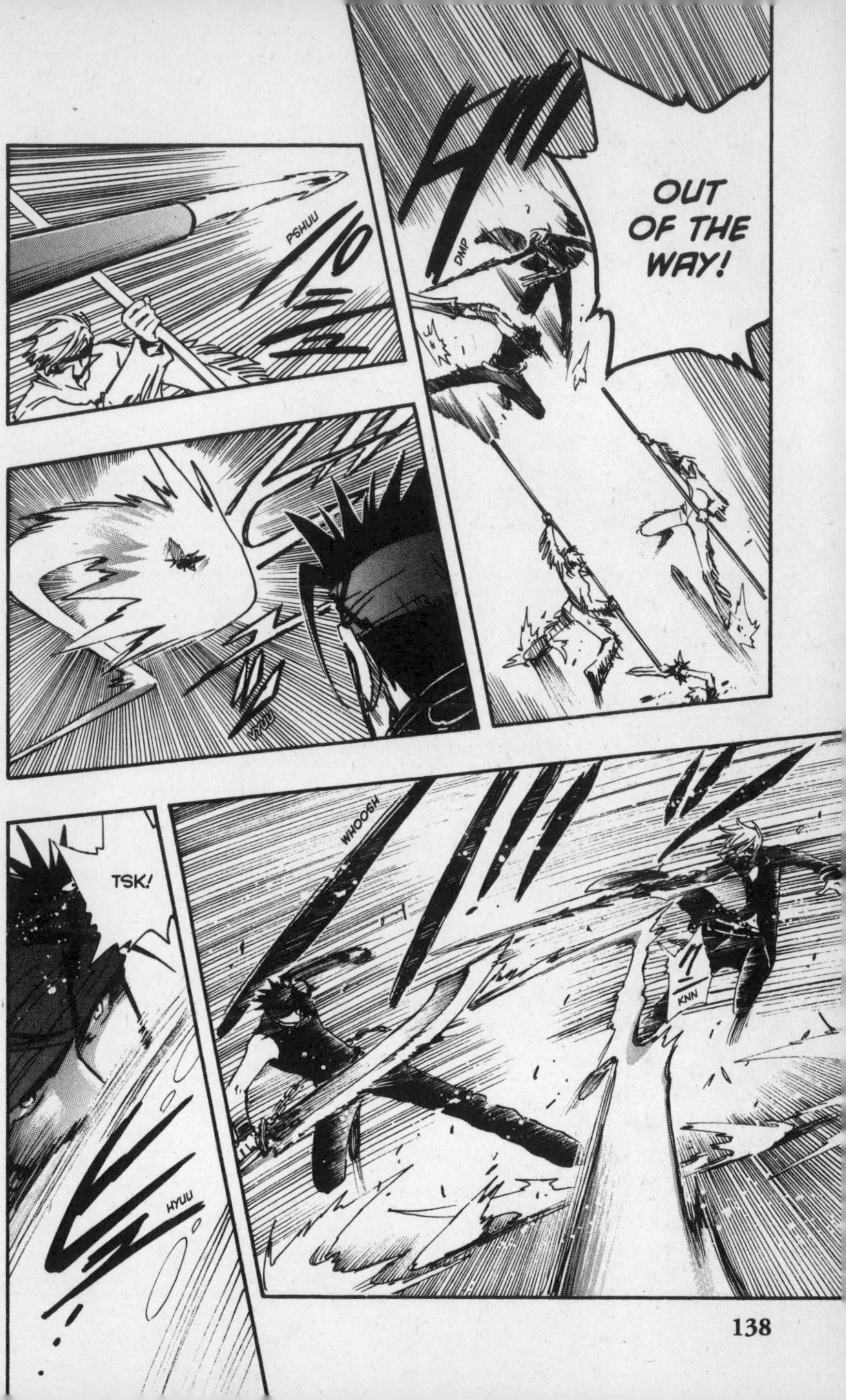
OUT OF THE WAY!
DMP
PSHUU
VYUU
WHOOSH
KNN
TSK!
HYUU

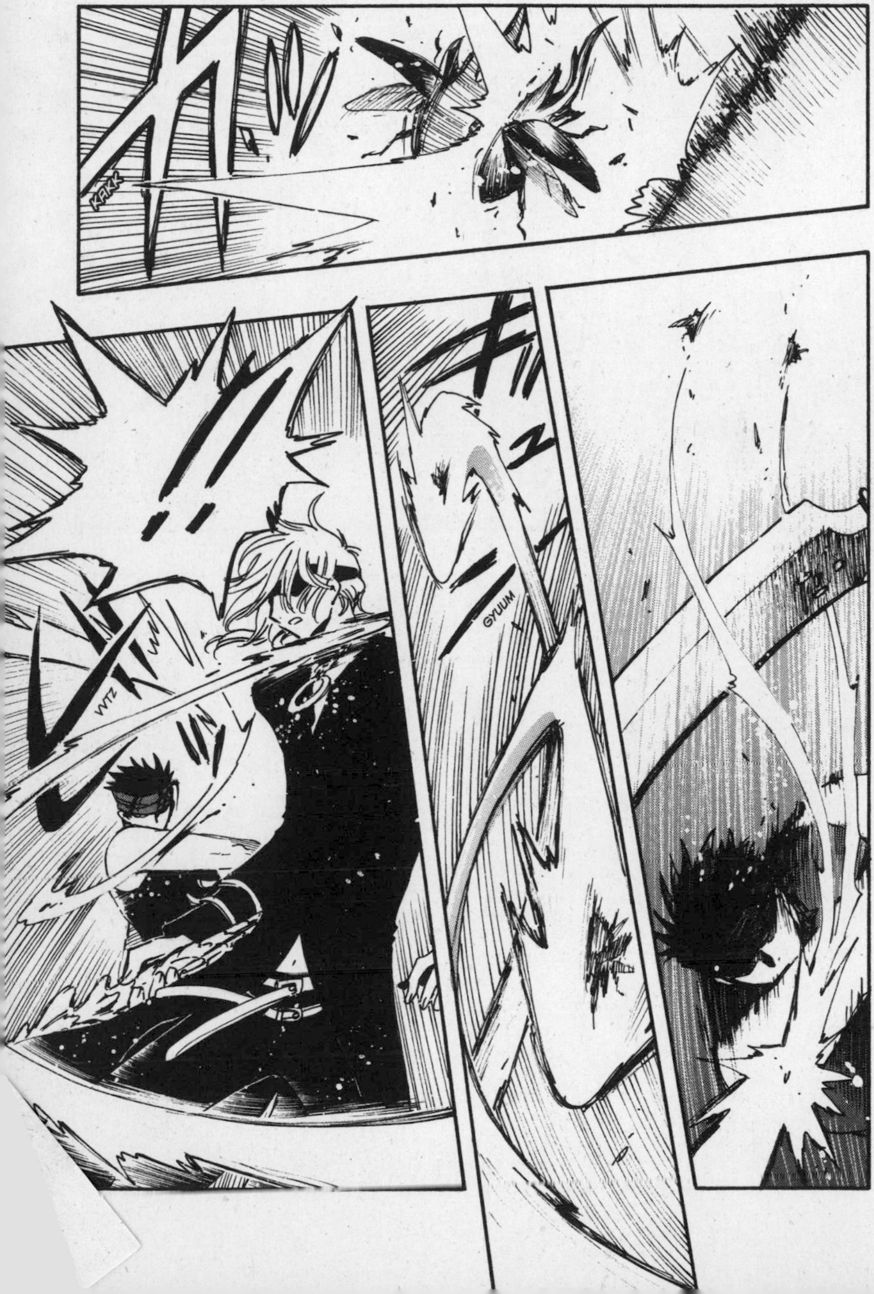
KAKK
GYUUM
VVTZ

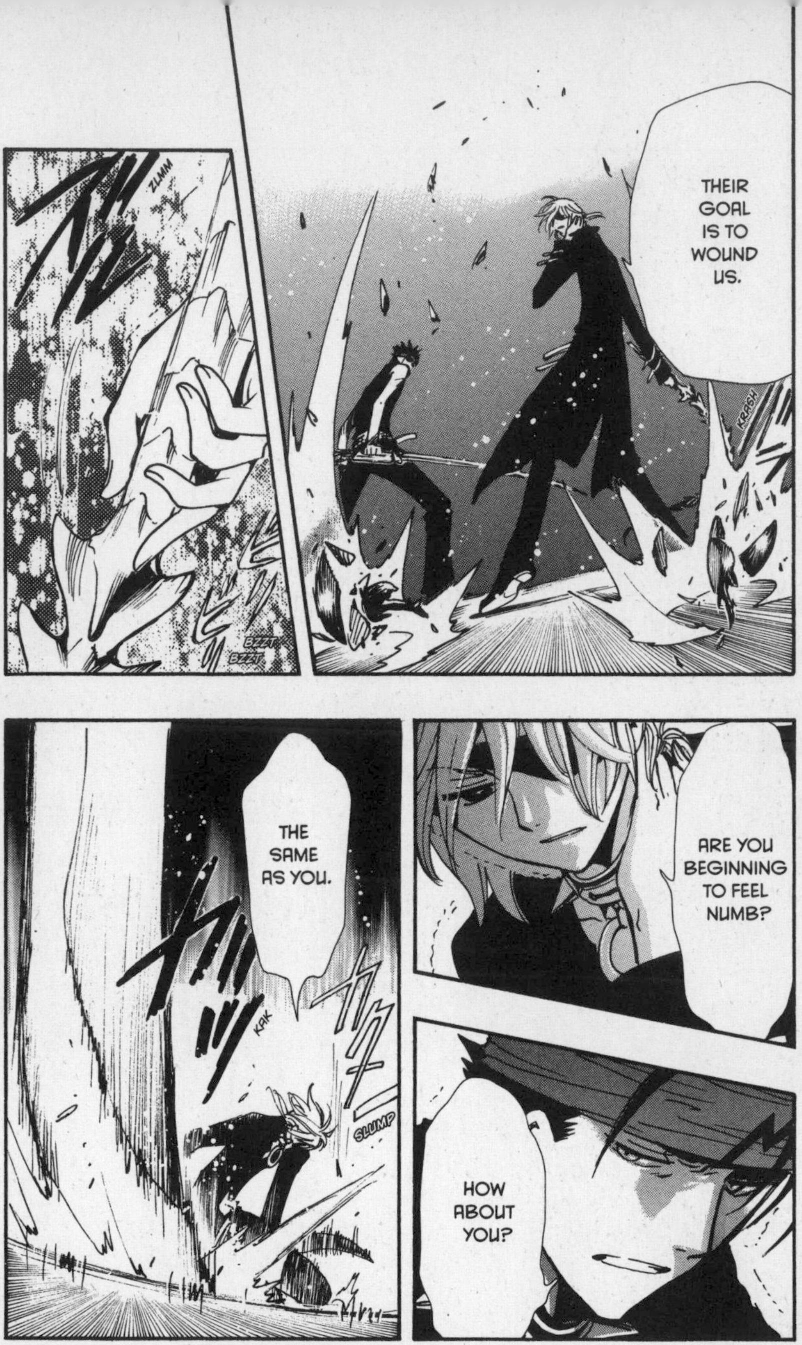
THEIR GOAL IS TO WOUND US.
KRASH
ZLMM
BZZT BZZT
ARE YOU BEGINNING TO FEEL NUMB?
HOW ABOUT YOU?
THE SAME AS YOU.
KAK
SLUMP

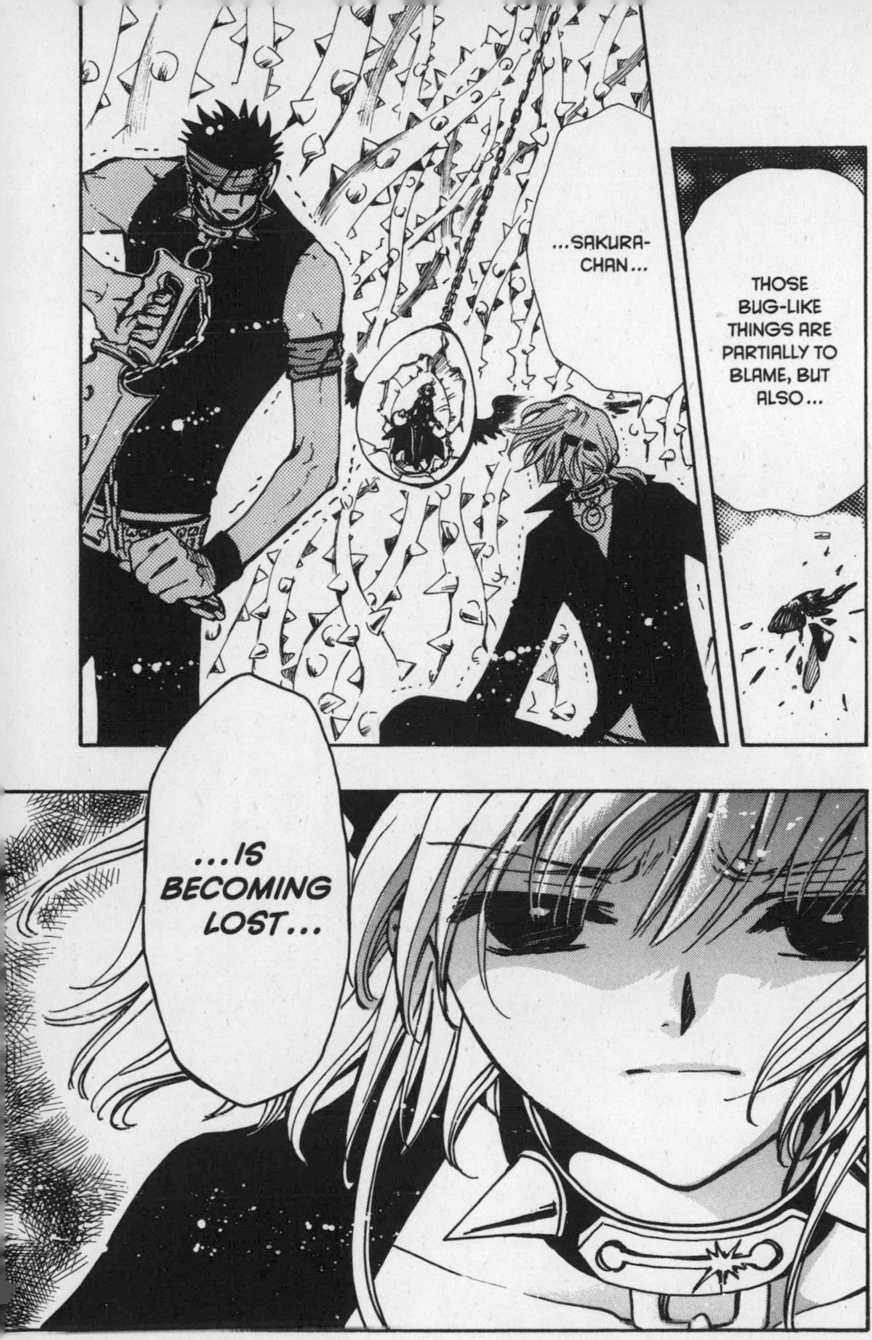
THOSE BUG-LIKE THINGS ARE PARTIALLY TO BLAME, BUT ALSO...
...SAKURA-CHAN...
...IS BECOMING LOST...

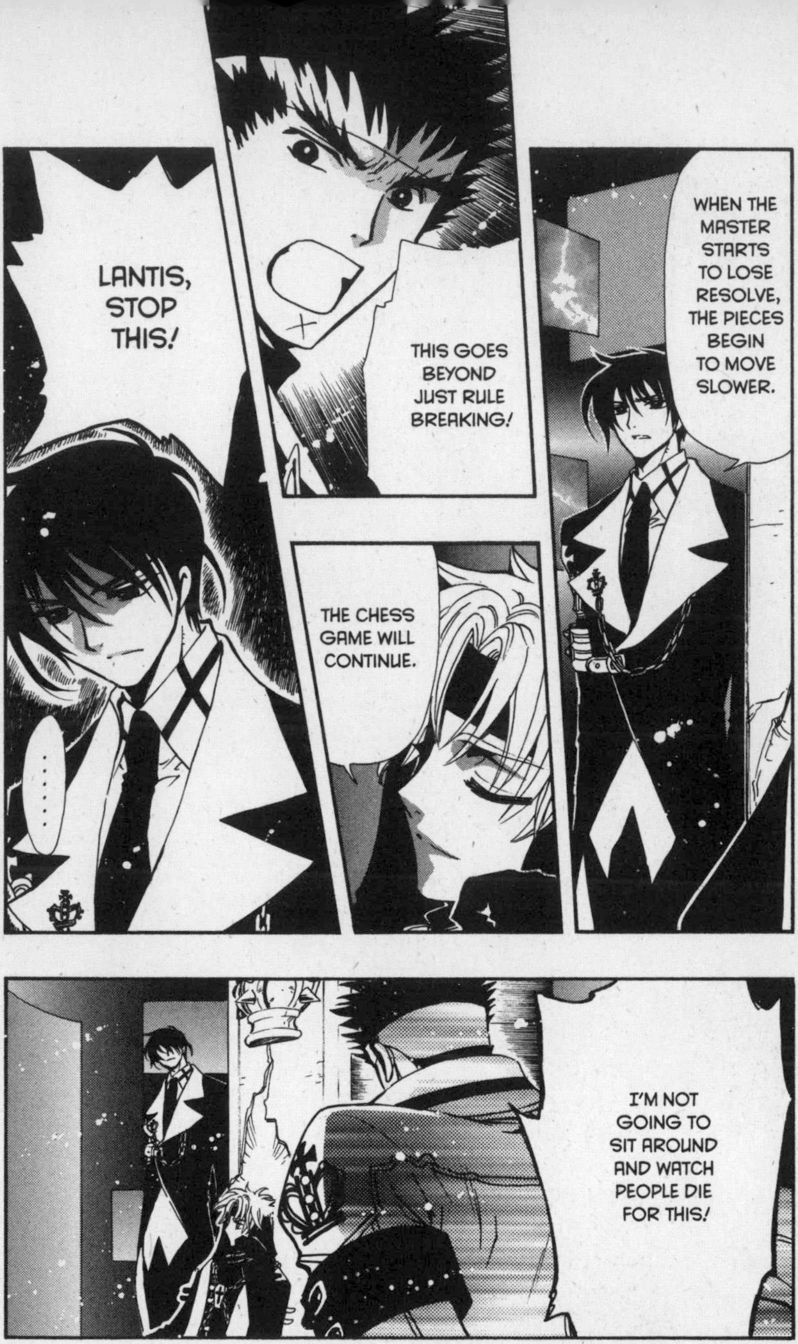
WHEN THE MASTER STARTS TO LOSE RESOLVE, THE PIECES BEGIN TO MOVE SLOWER.
THIS GOES BEYOND JUST RULE BREAKING!
THE CHESS GAME WILL CONTINUE.
LANTIS, STOP THIS!
......
I'M NOT GOING TO SIT AROUND AND WATCH PEOPLE DIE FOR THIS!

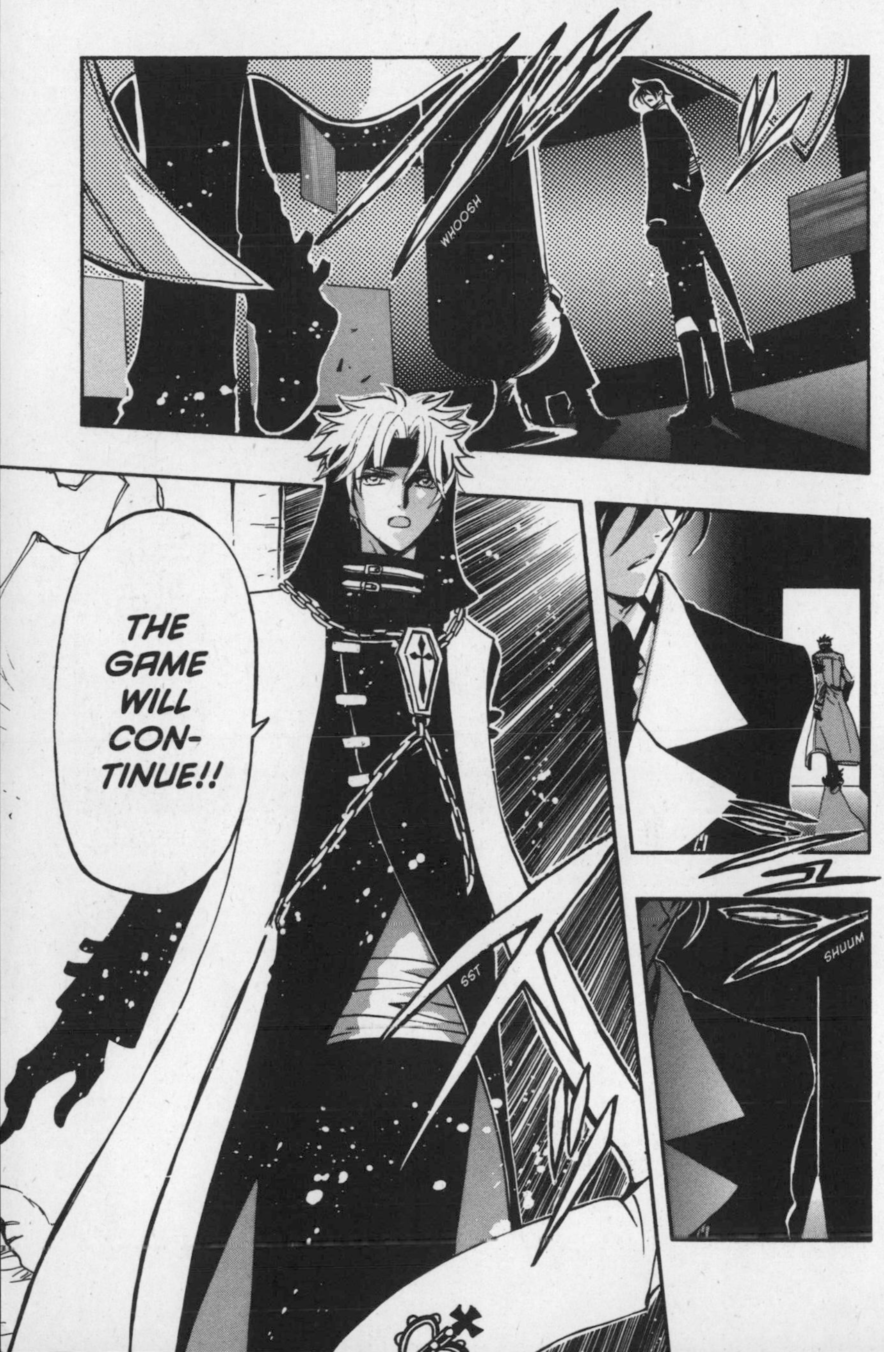
WHOOSH
THE GAME WILL CON- TINUE!!
SST
SHUUM

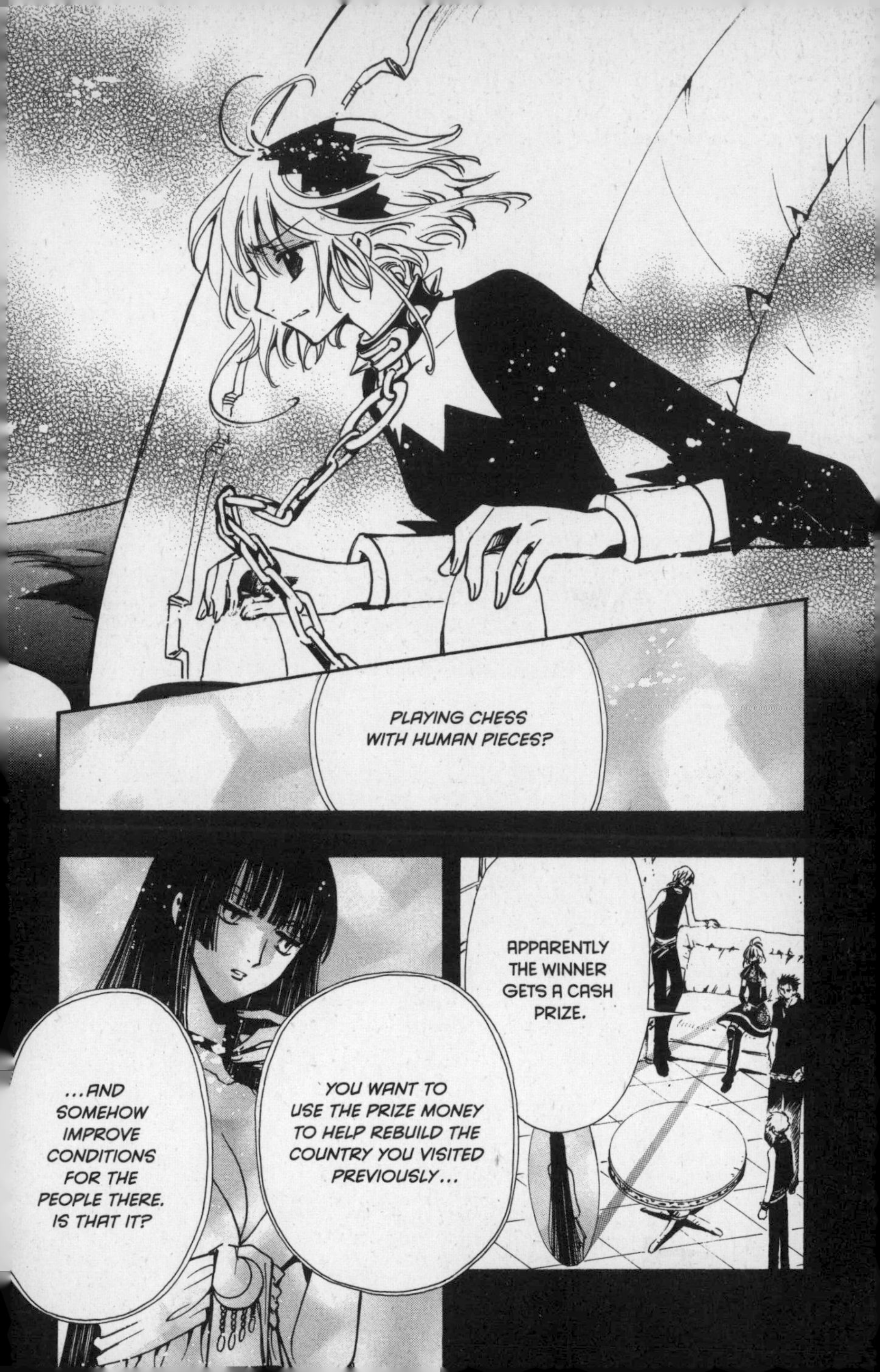
PLAYING CHESS WITH HUMAN PIECES?
APPARENTLY THE WINNER GETS A CASH PRIZE.
YOU WANT TO USE THE PRIZE MONEY TO HELP REBUILD THE COUNTRY YOU VISITED PREVIOUSLY...
...AND SOMEHOW IMPROVE CONDITIONS FOR THE PEOPLE THERE. IS THAT IT?

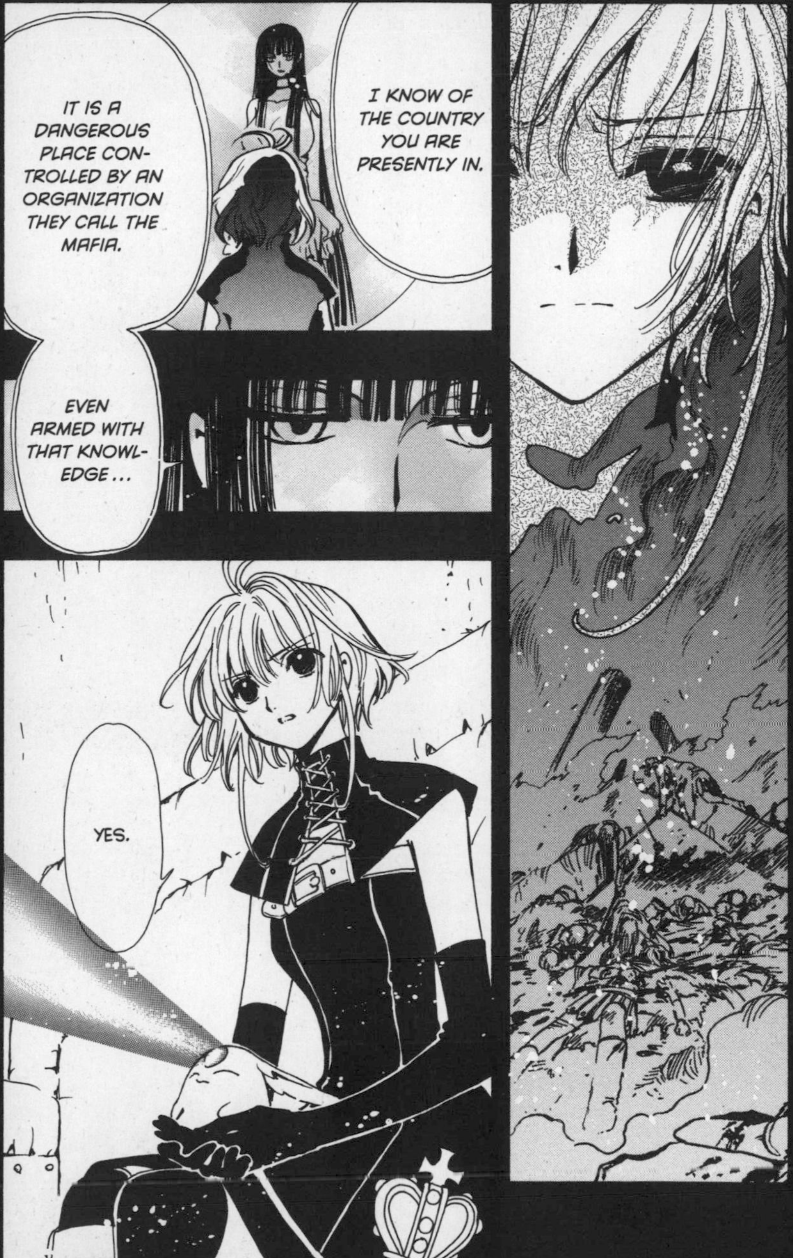
I KNOW OF THE COUNTRY YOU ARE PRESENTLY IN.
IT IS A DANGEROUS PLACE CON-TROLLED BY AN ORGANIZATION THEY CALL THE MAFIA.
EVEN ARMED WITH THAT KNOWL-EDGE ...
YES.

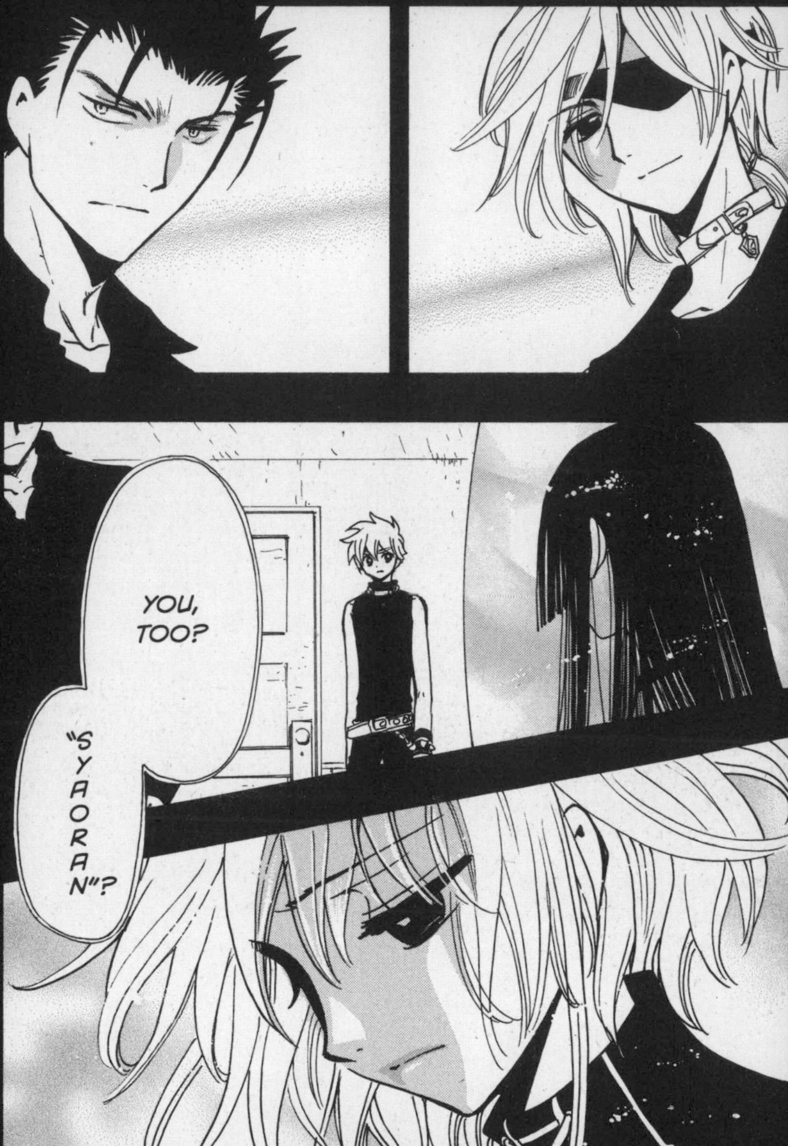
YOU, TOO?
"SYAORAN"?

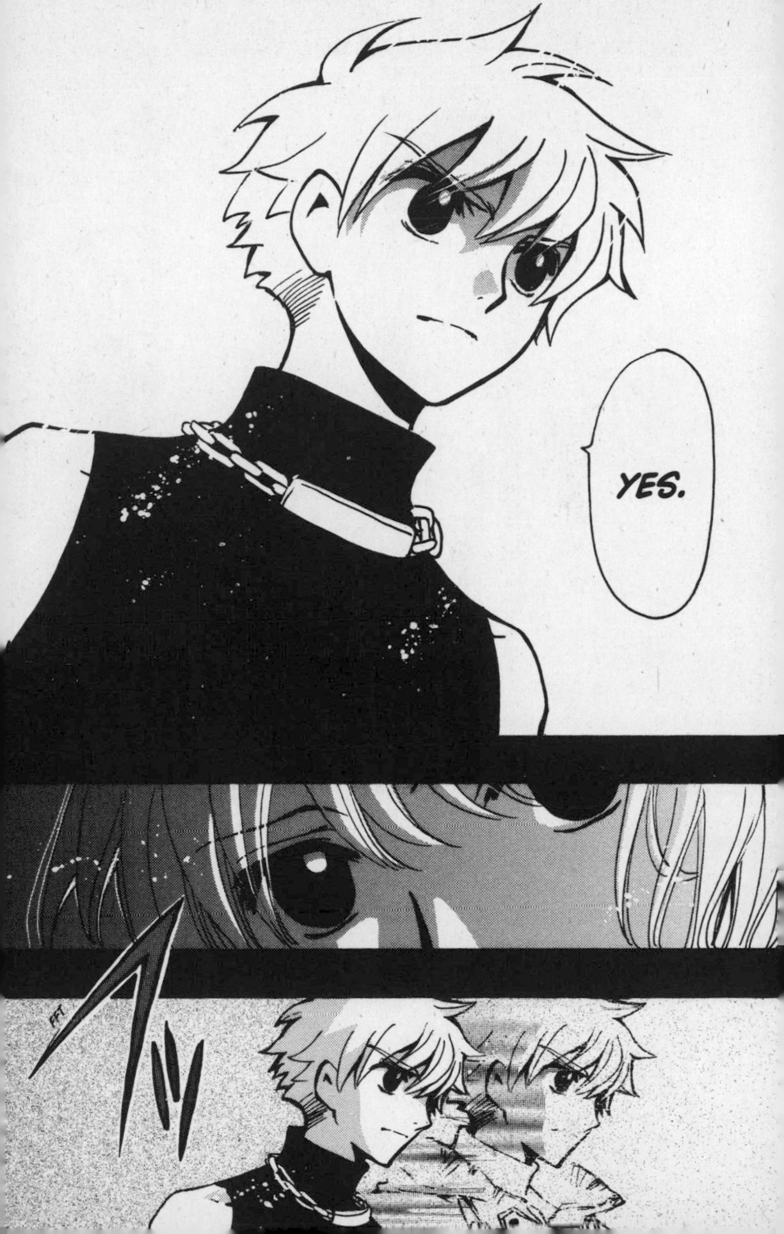
YES.
FFT

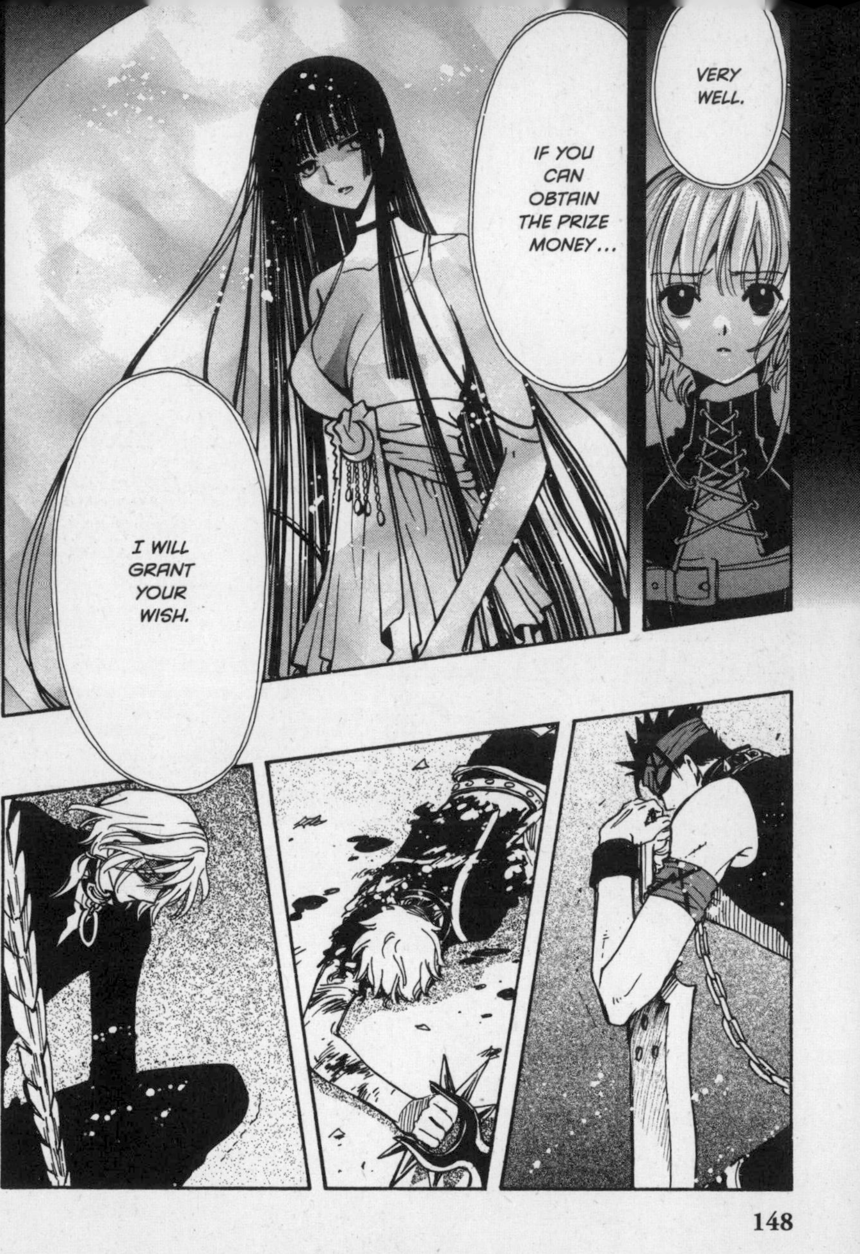
VERY WELL.
IF YOU CAN OBTAIN THE PRIZE MONEY...
I WILL GRANT YOUR WISH.

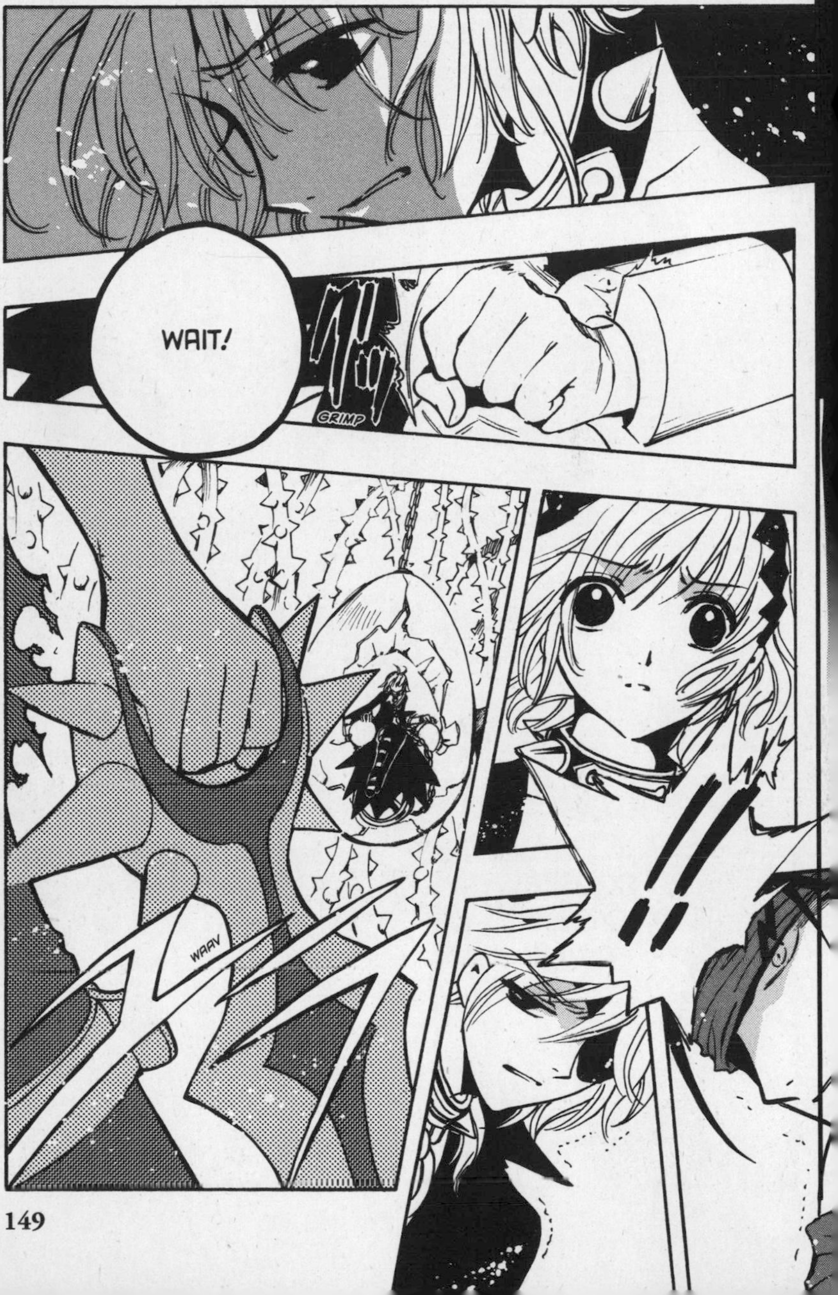
WAIT!
GRIMP
WAAV

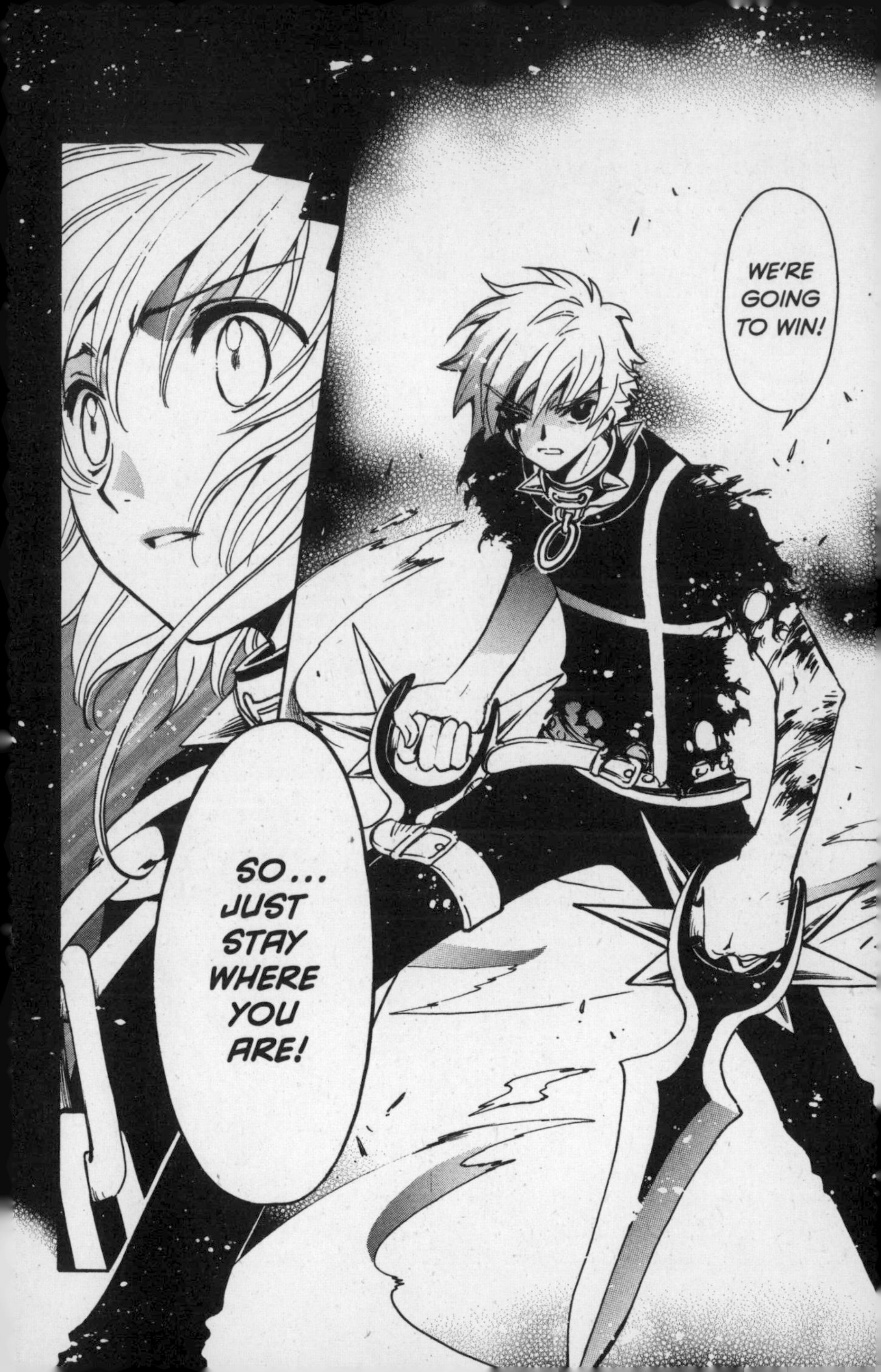
WE'RE GOING TO WIN!
SO... JUST STAY WHERE YOU ARE!

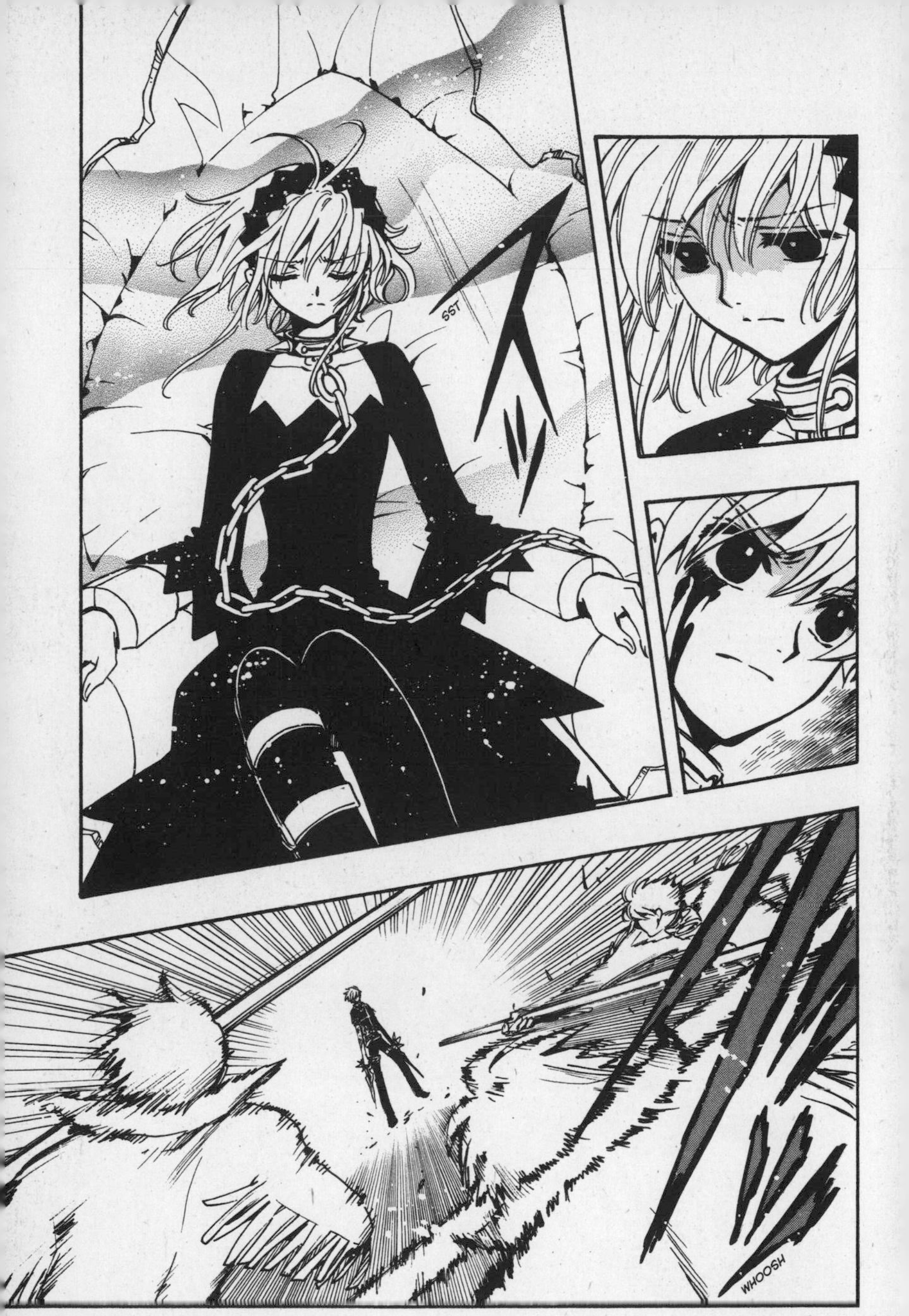
SST
WHOOSH

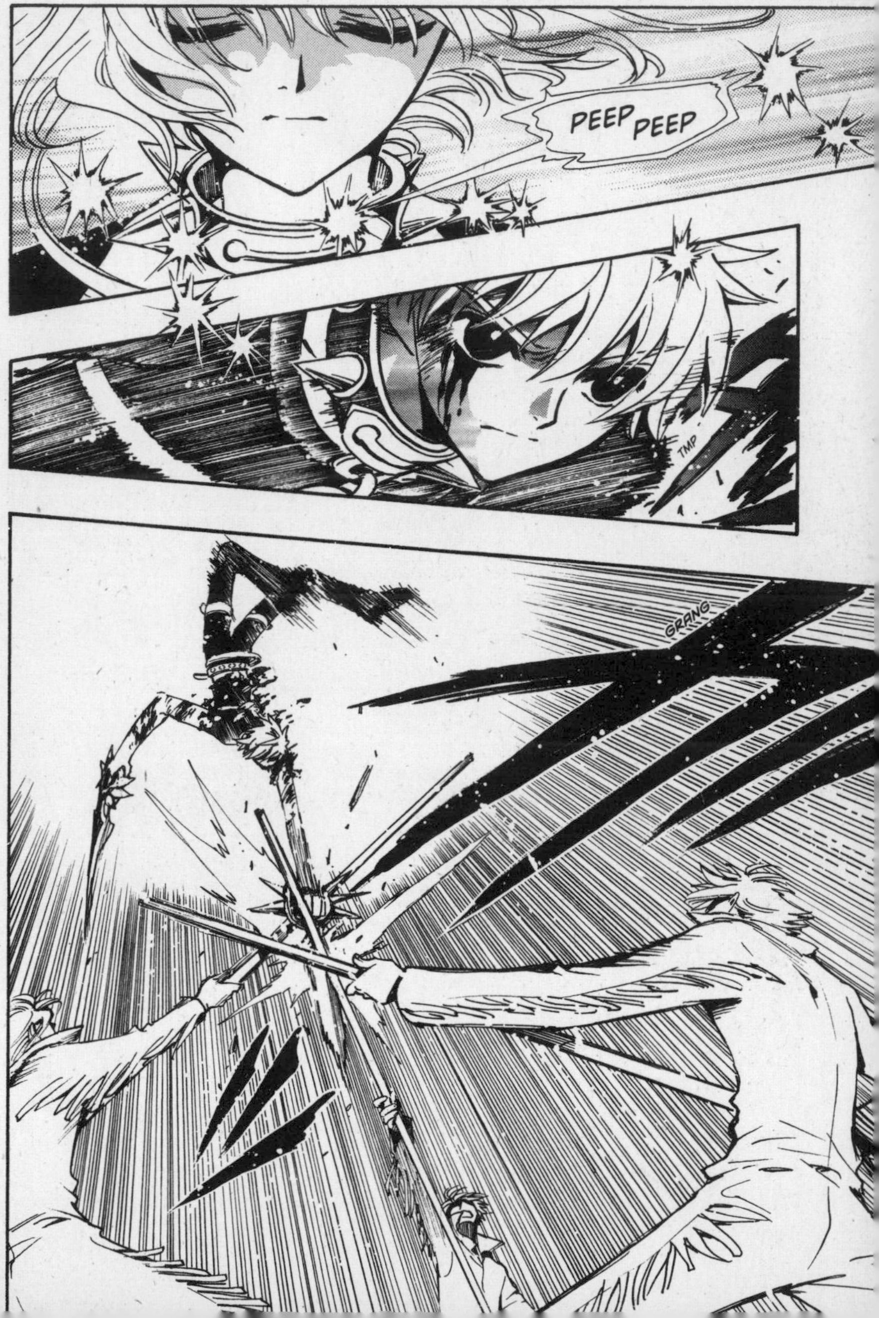
PEEP PEEP
TMP
GRANG

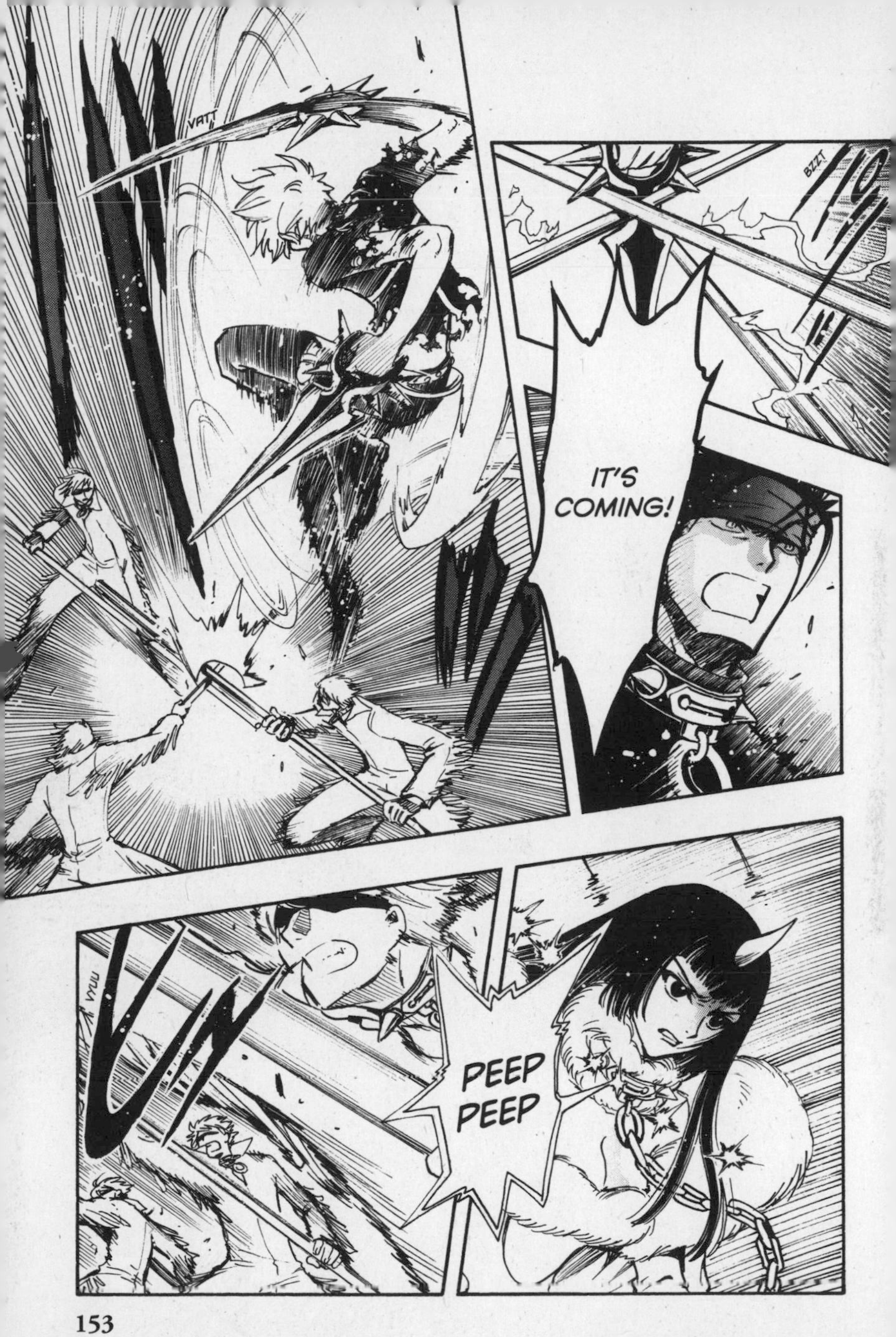
BZZT
IT'S COMING!
VATT
PEEP PEEP
VYUU

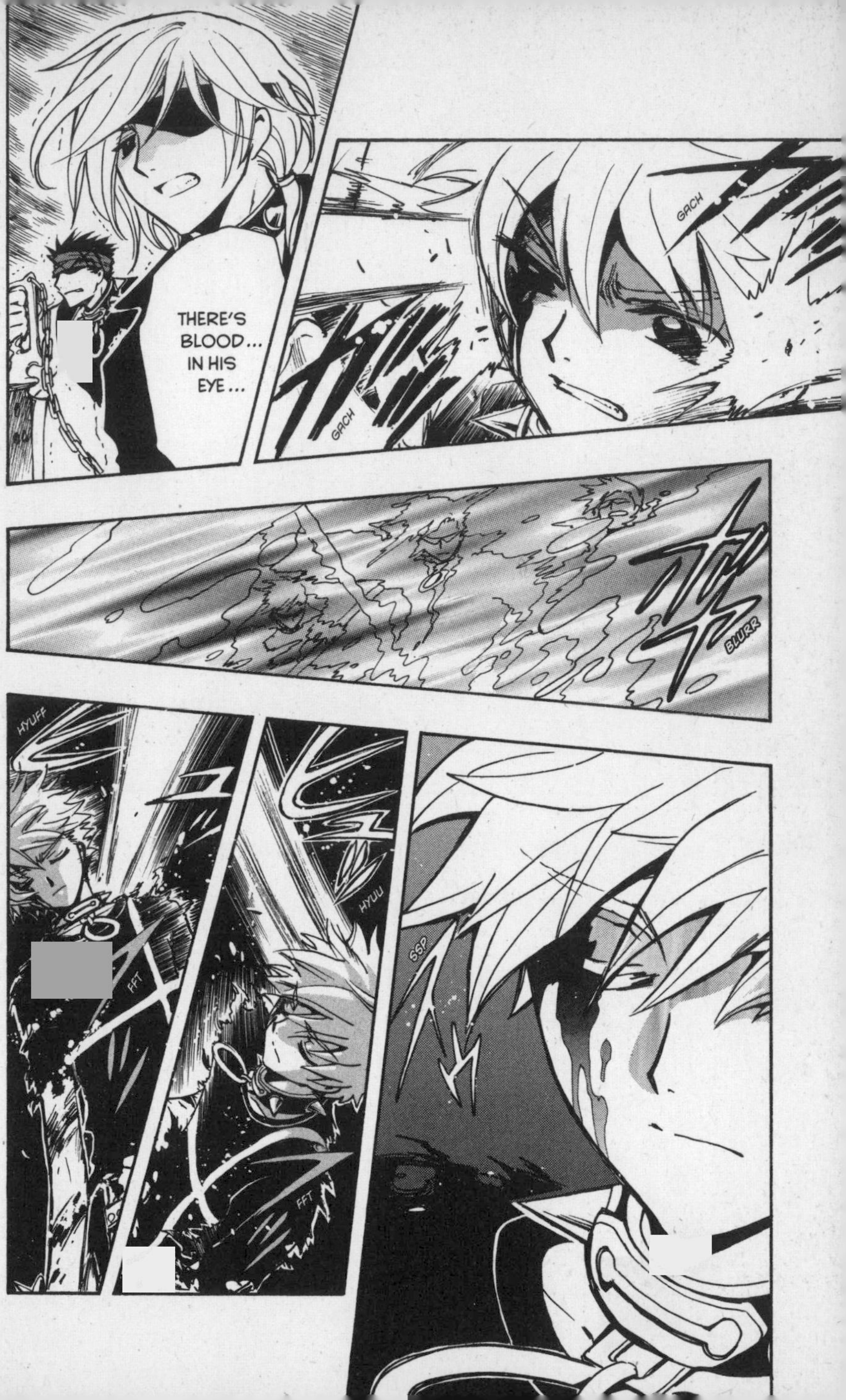
GACH
GACH
THERE'S BLOOD... IN HIS EYE...
BLURR
SSP
HYUU
FFT
HYUFF
FFT

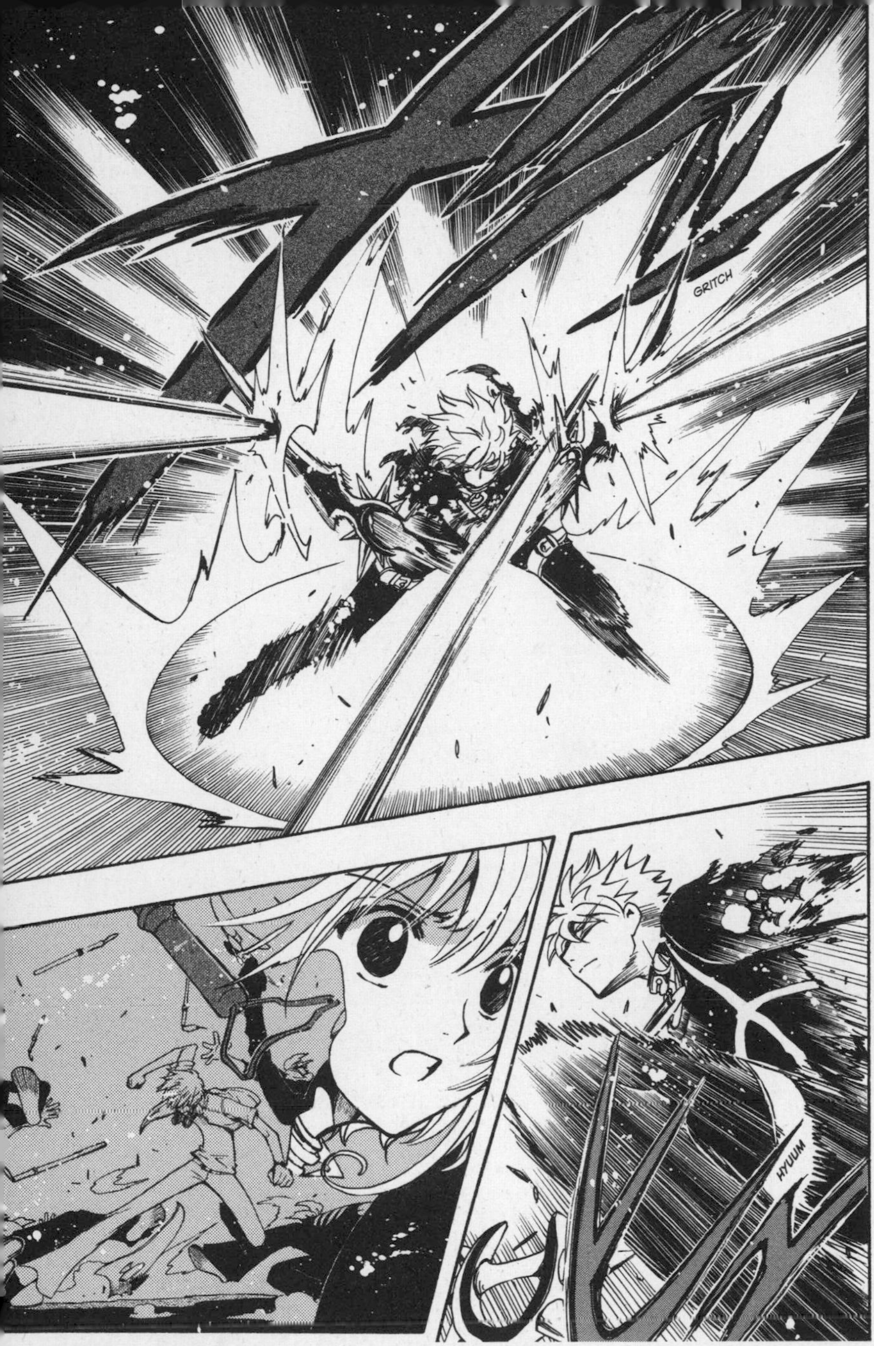
GRITCH
HYUUM

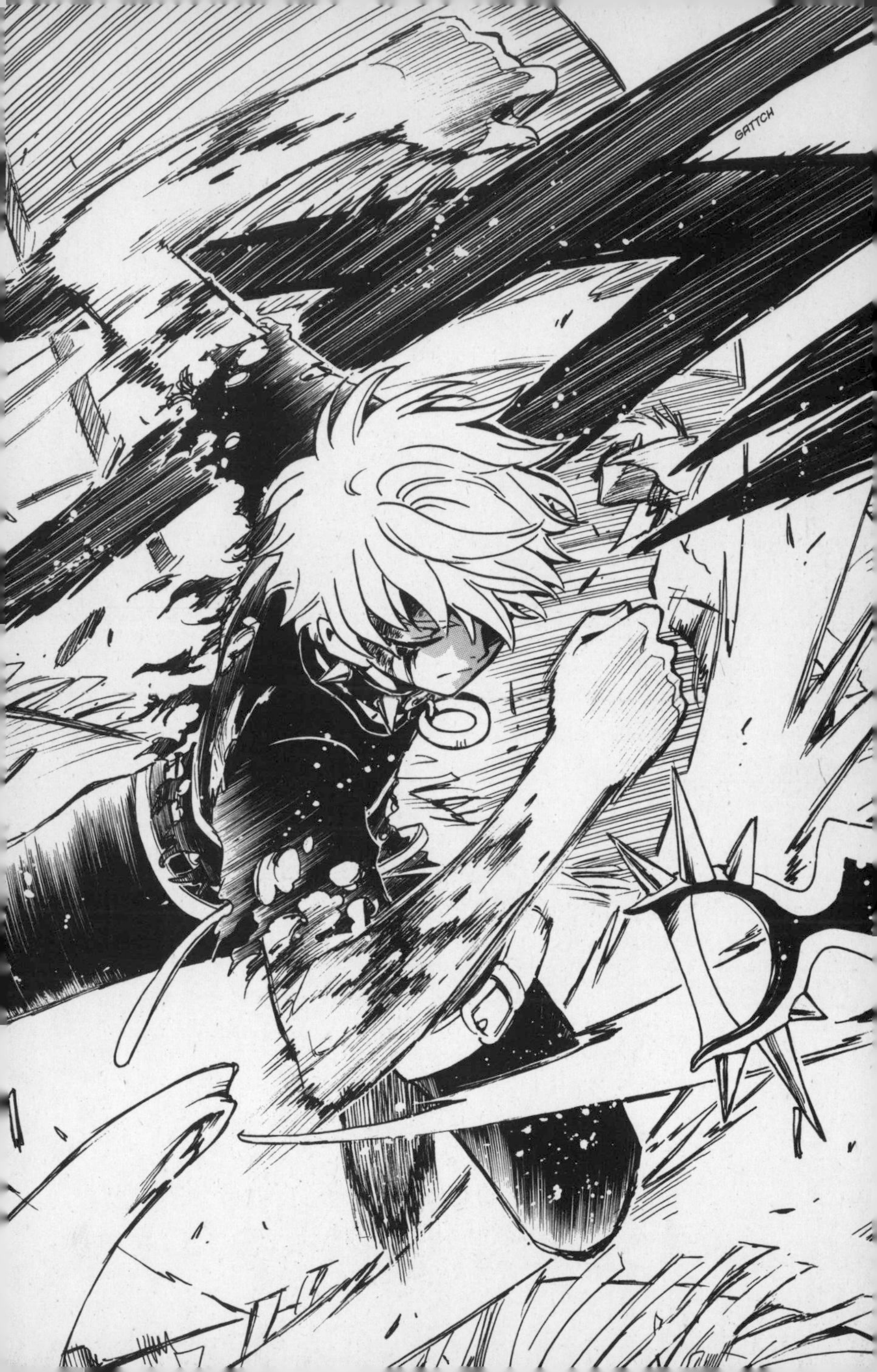
GATTCH

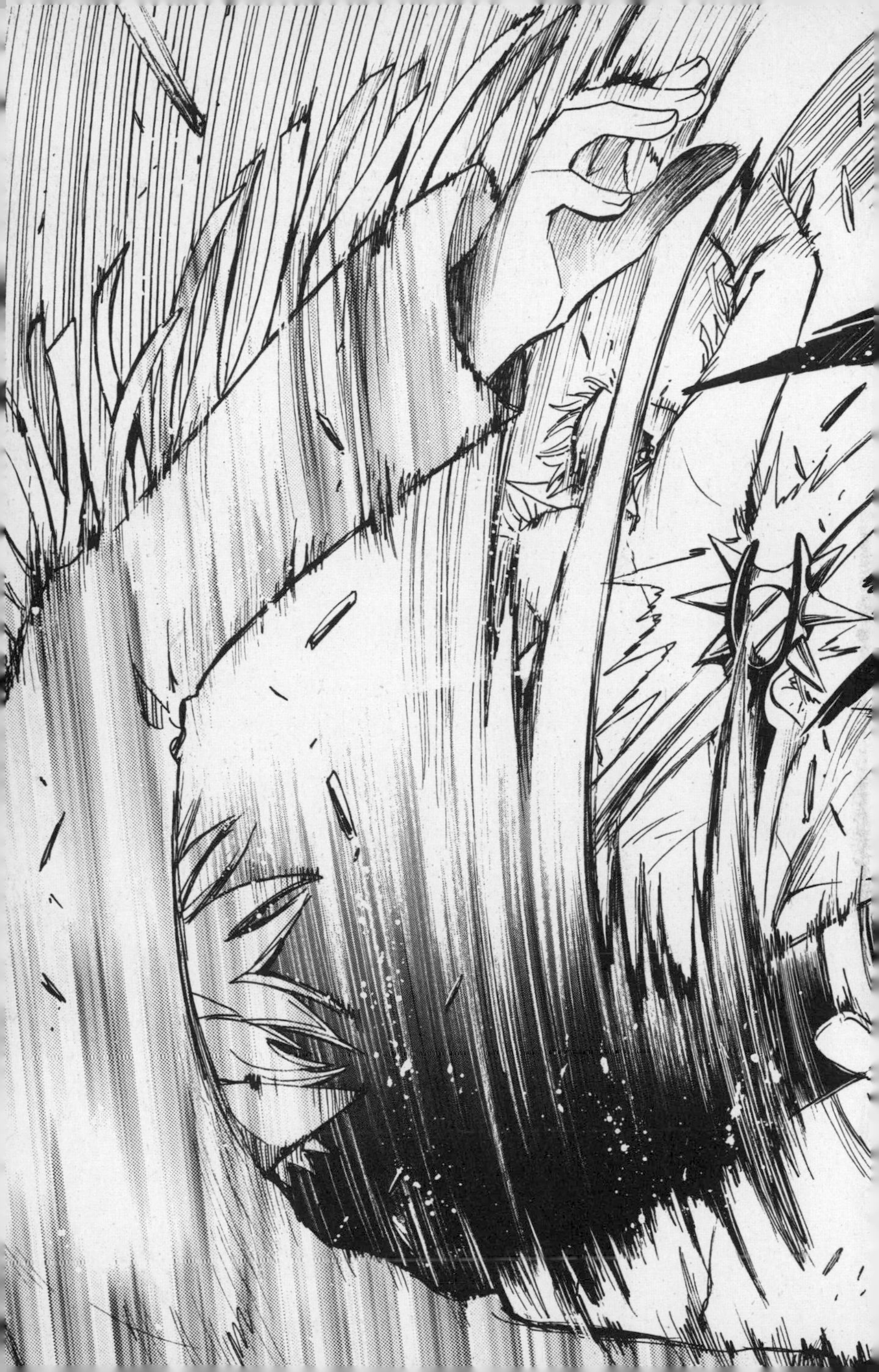

ツバサ
RESERVoir CHRoNiCLE

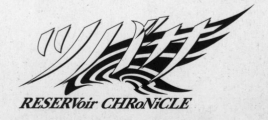

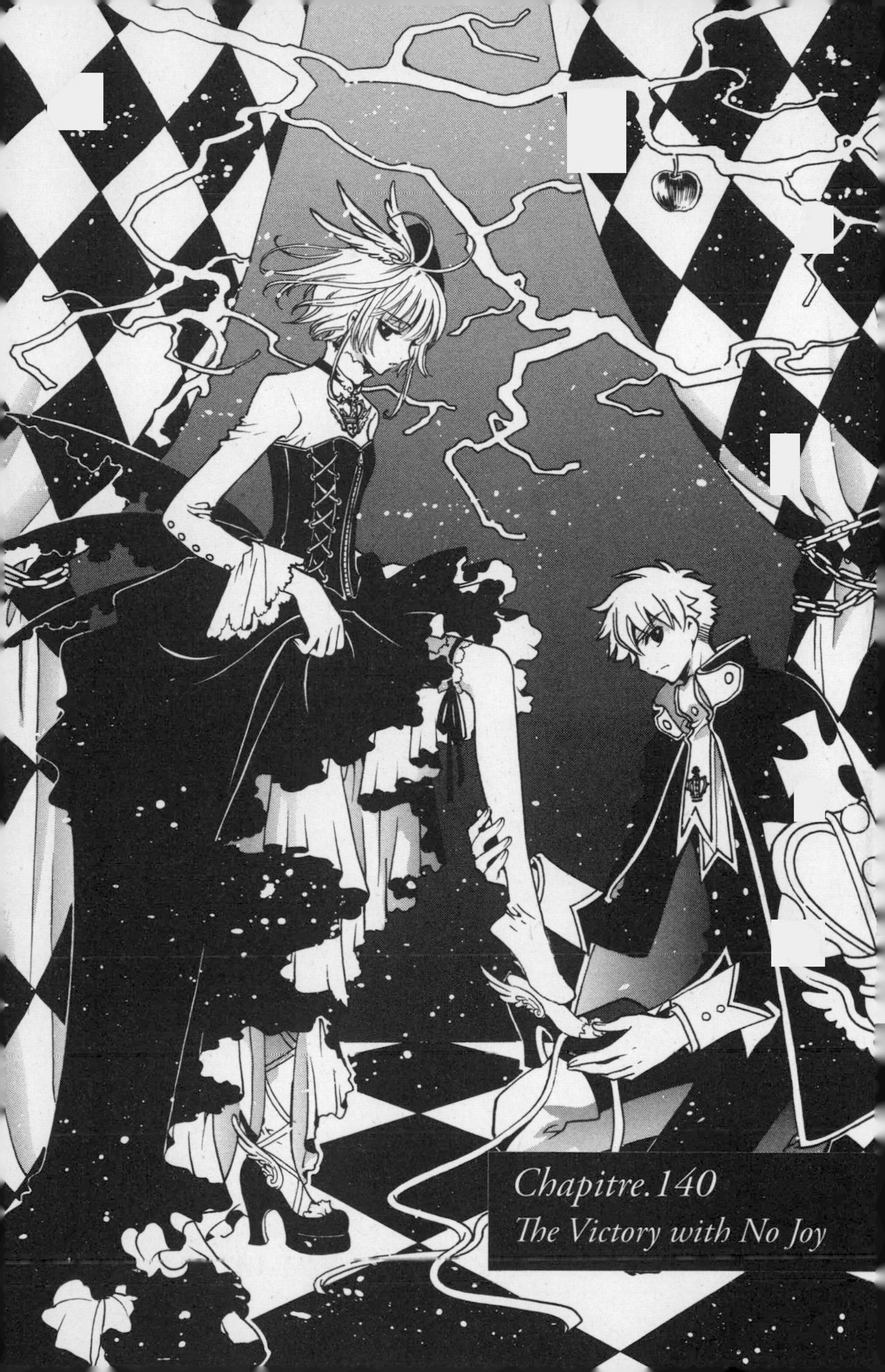
Chapitre.140
The Victory with No Joy

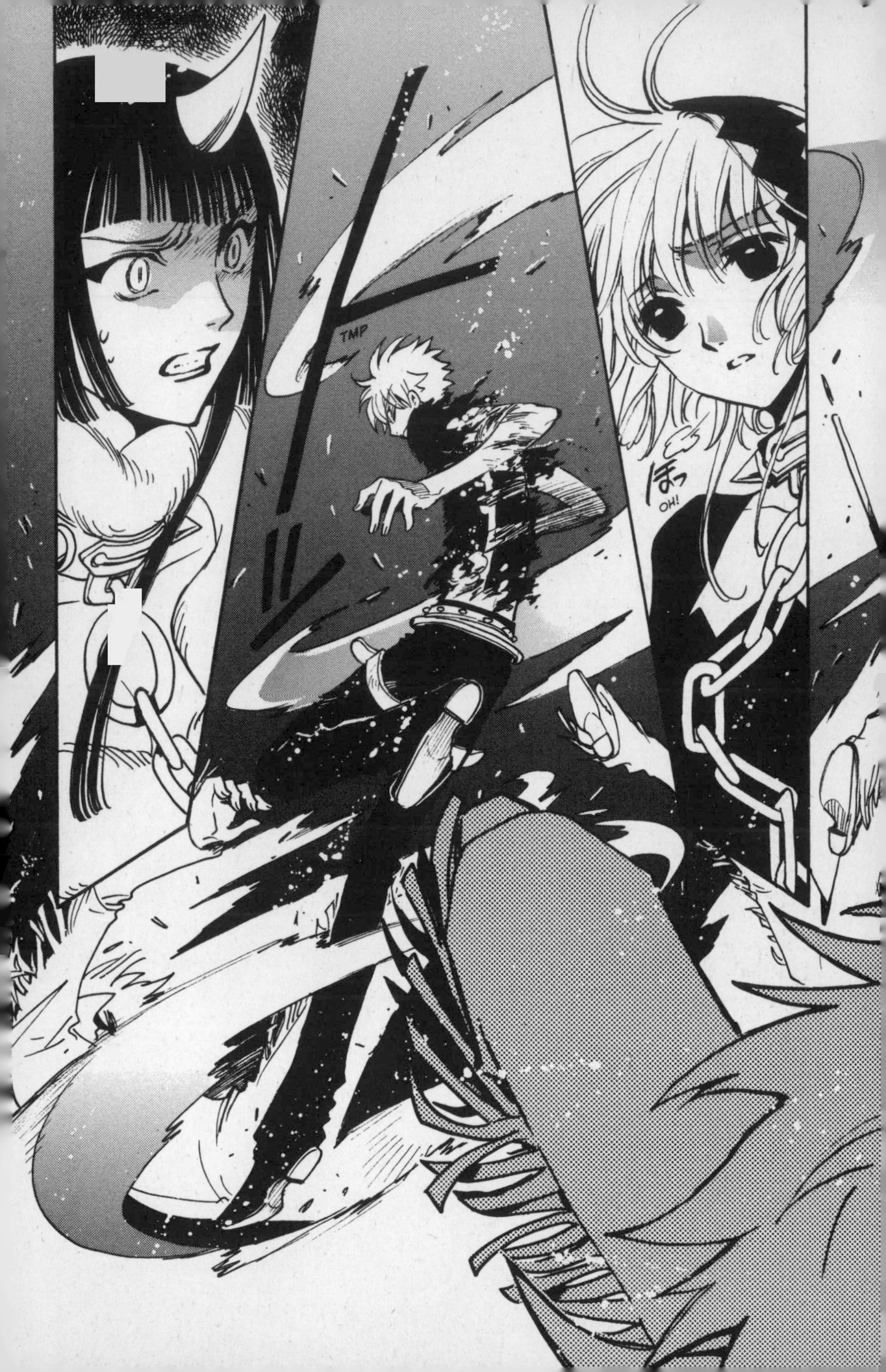
ほっ
OH!
TMP

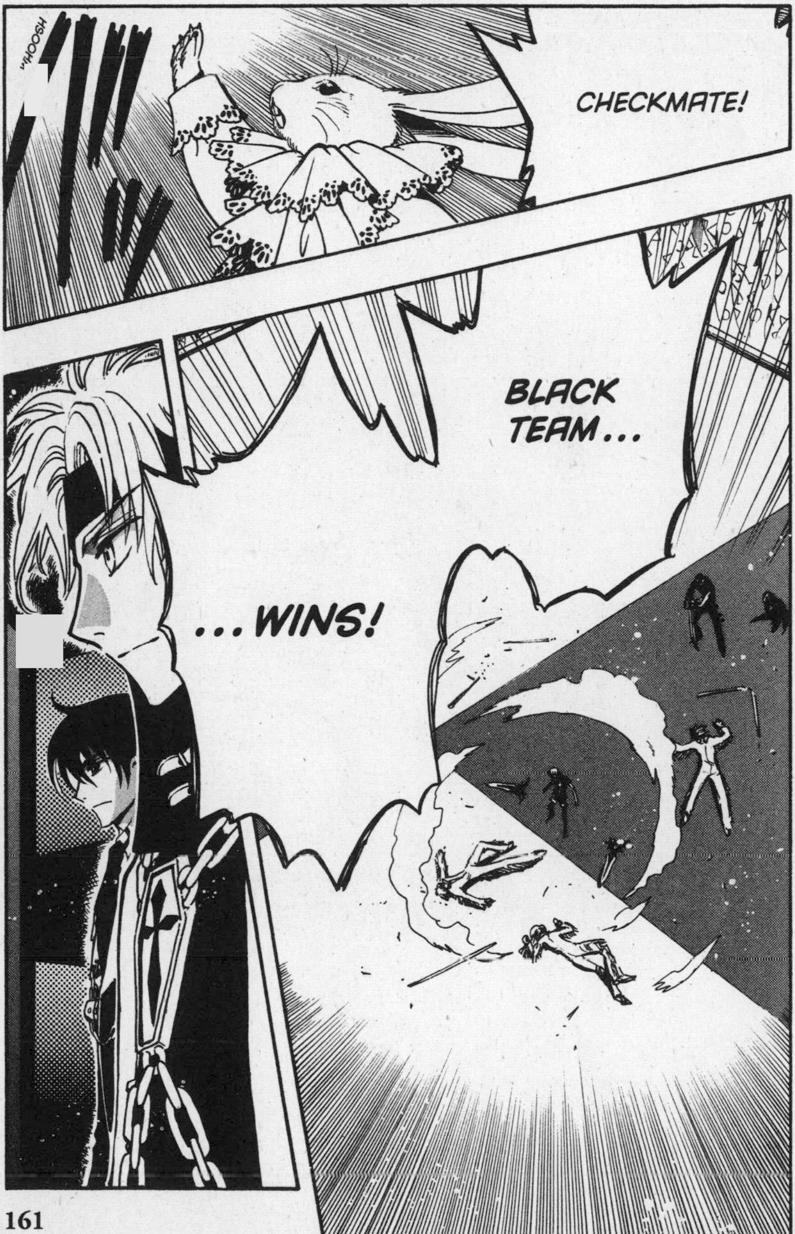
WHOOSH
CHECKMATE!
BLACK TEAM...
...WINS!

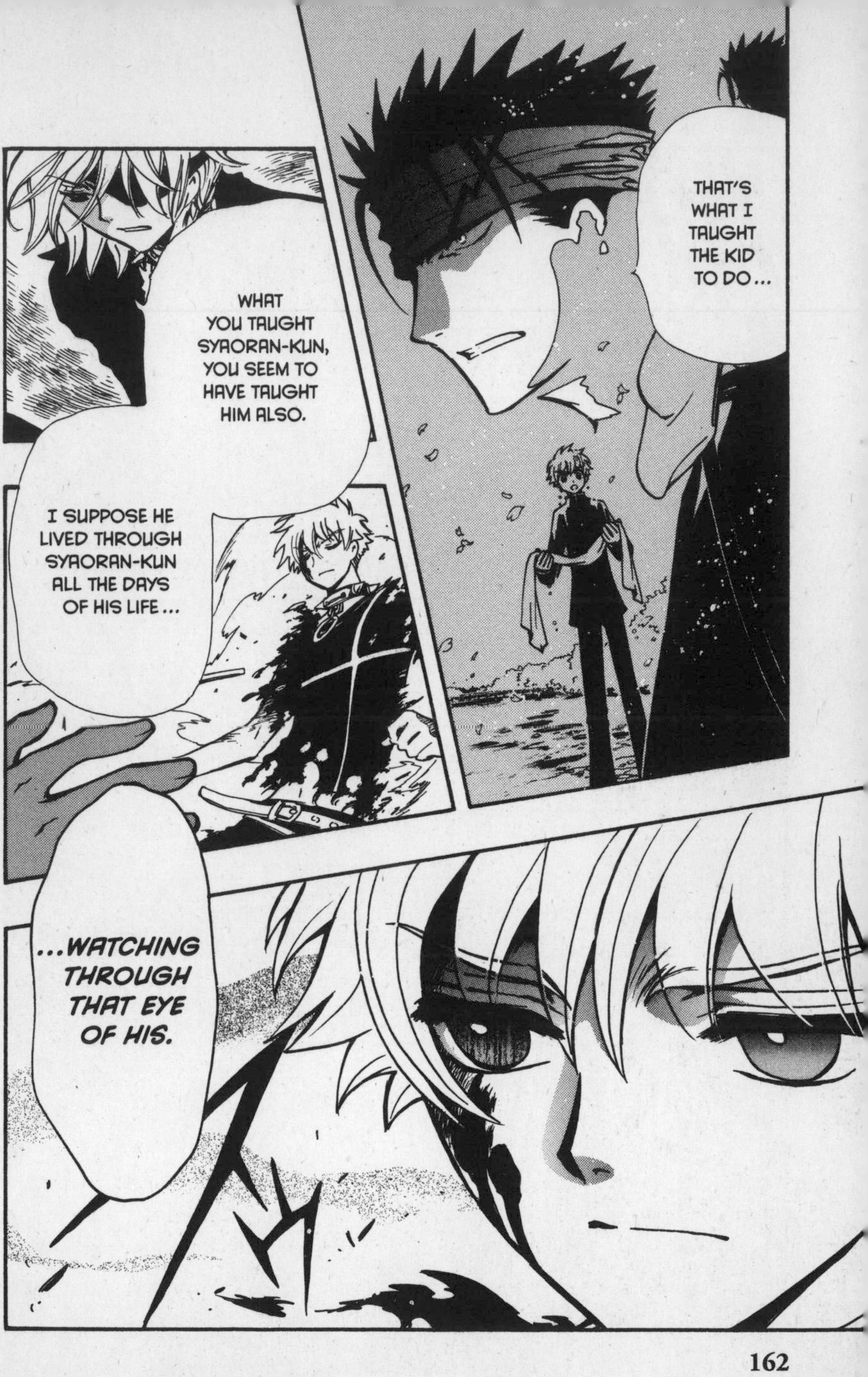
THAT'S WHAT I TAUGHT THE KID TO DO...
WHAT YOU TAUGHT SYAORAN-KUN, YOU SEEM TO HAVE TAUGHT HIM ALSO.
I SUPPOSE HE LIVED THROUGH SYAORAN-KUN ALL THE DAYS OF HIS LIFE...
...WATCHING THROUGH THAT EYE OF HIS.

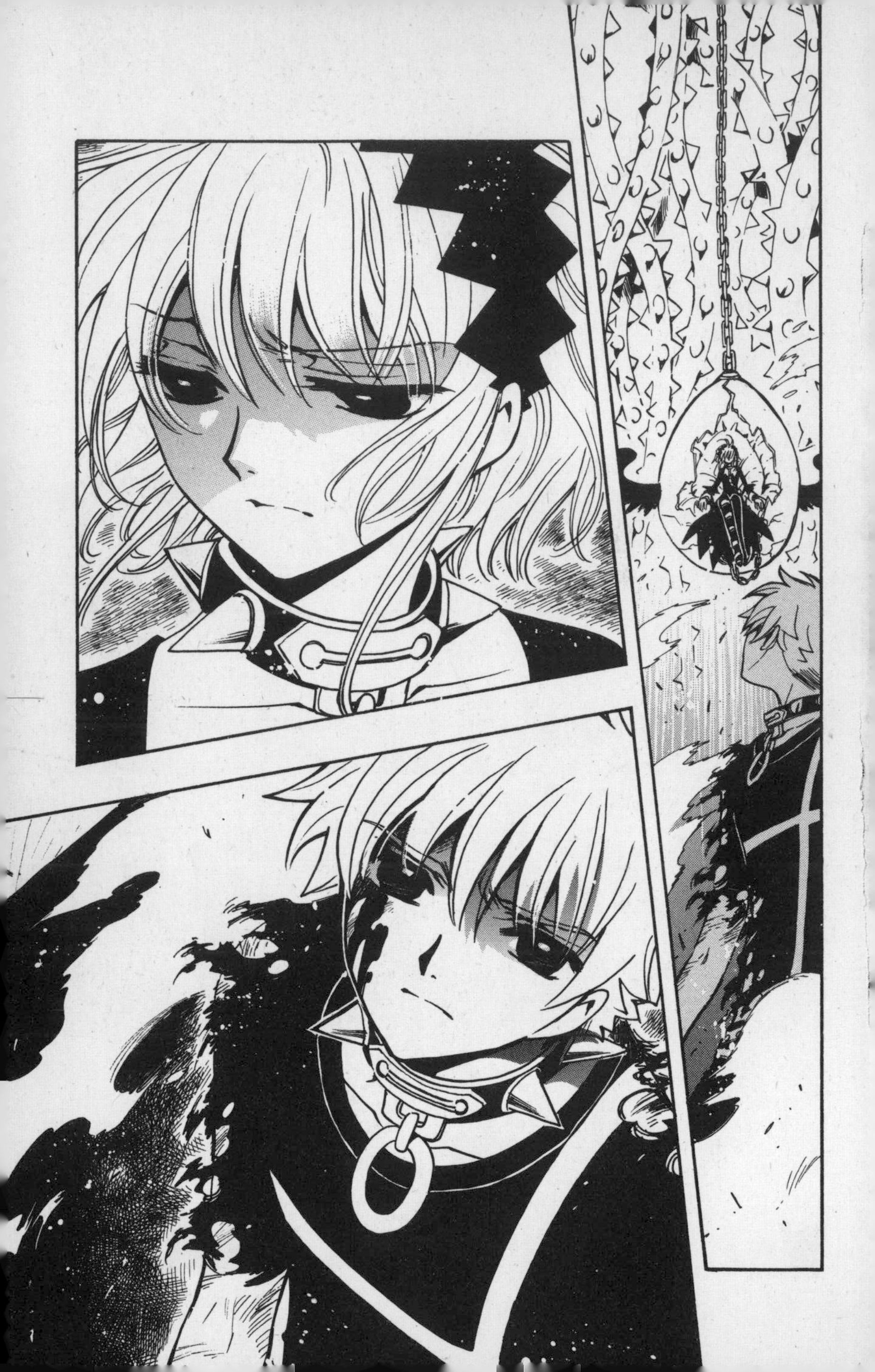

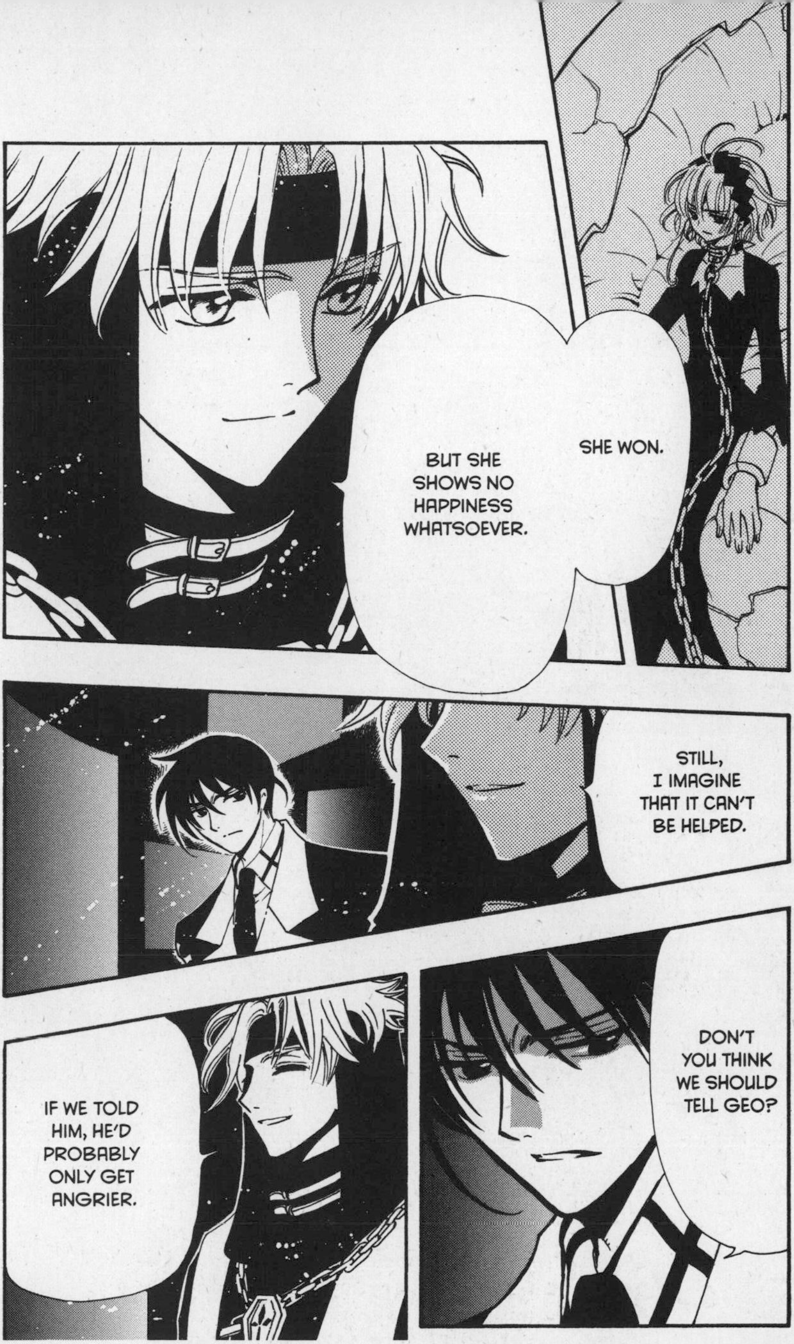
SHE WON.
BUT SHE SHOWS NO HAPPINESS WHATSOEVER.
STILL, I IMAGINE THAT IT CAN'T BE HELPED.
DON'T YOU THINK WE SHOULD TELL GEO?
IF WE TOLD HIM, HE'D PROBABLY ONLY GET ANGRIER.

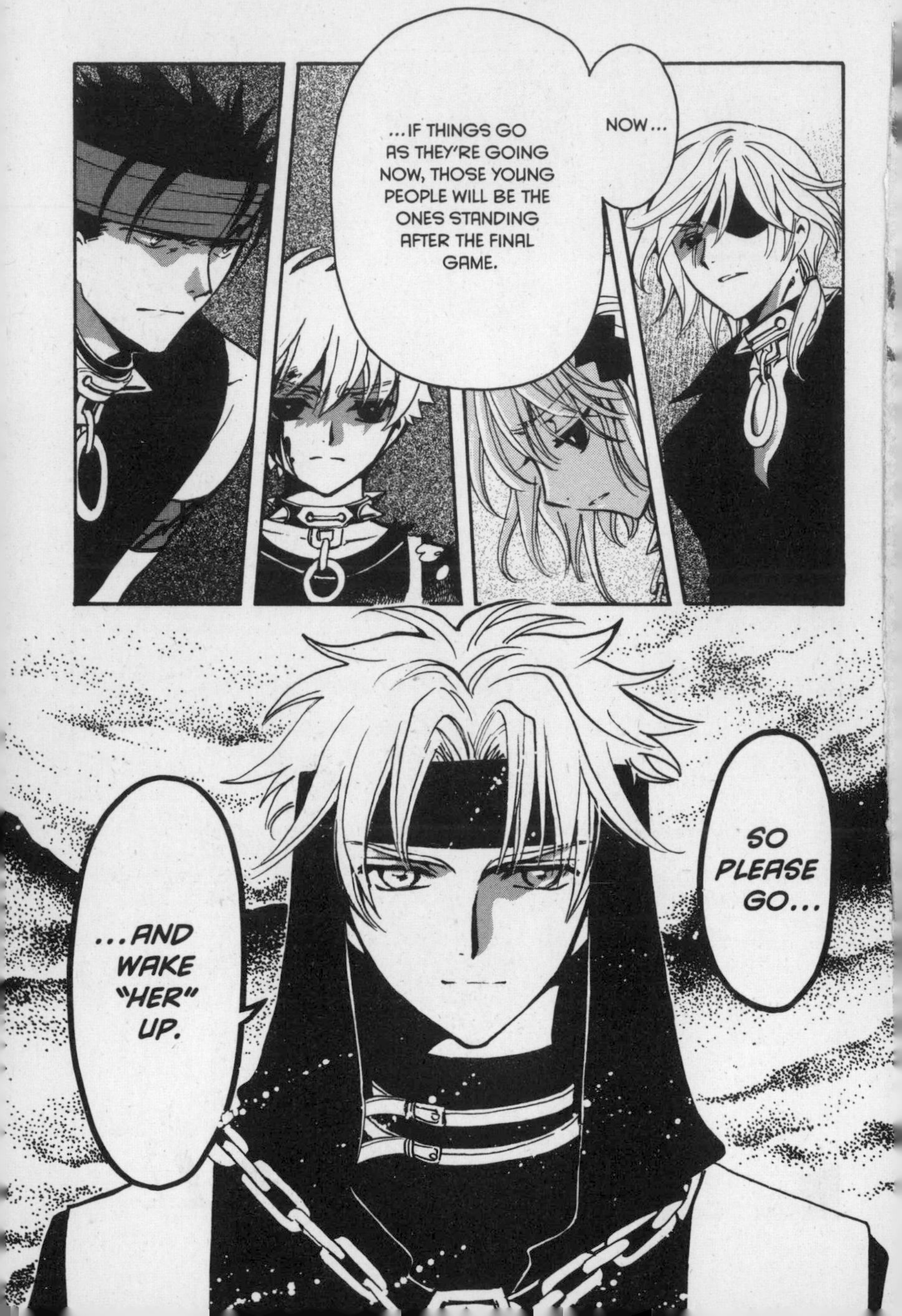
NOW...
...IF THINGS GO AS THEY'RE GOING NOW, THOSE YOUNG PEOPLE WILL BE THE ONES STANDING AFTER THE FINAL GAME.
SO PLEASE GO...
...AND WAKE "HER" UP.

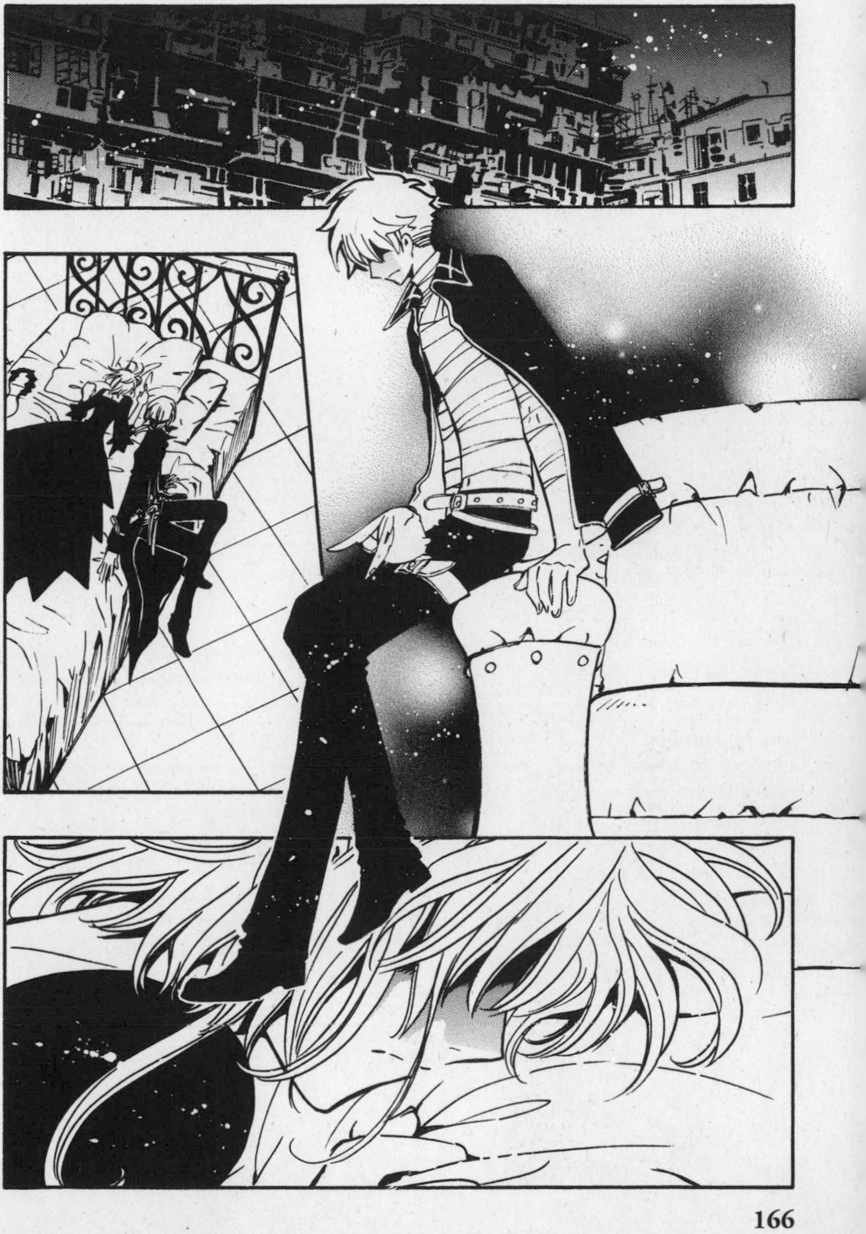

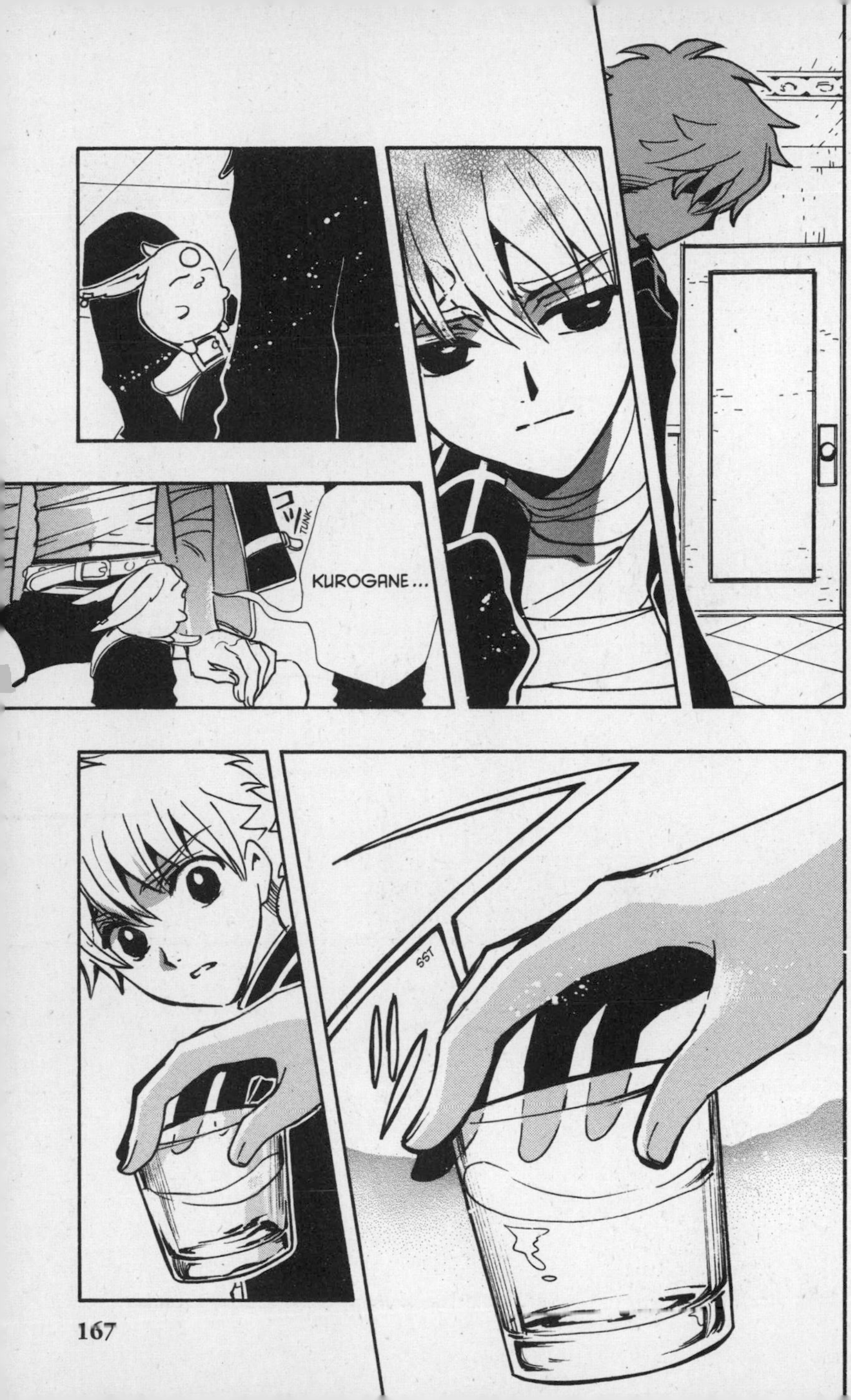

コッ
TUNK
KUROGANE...
SST

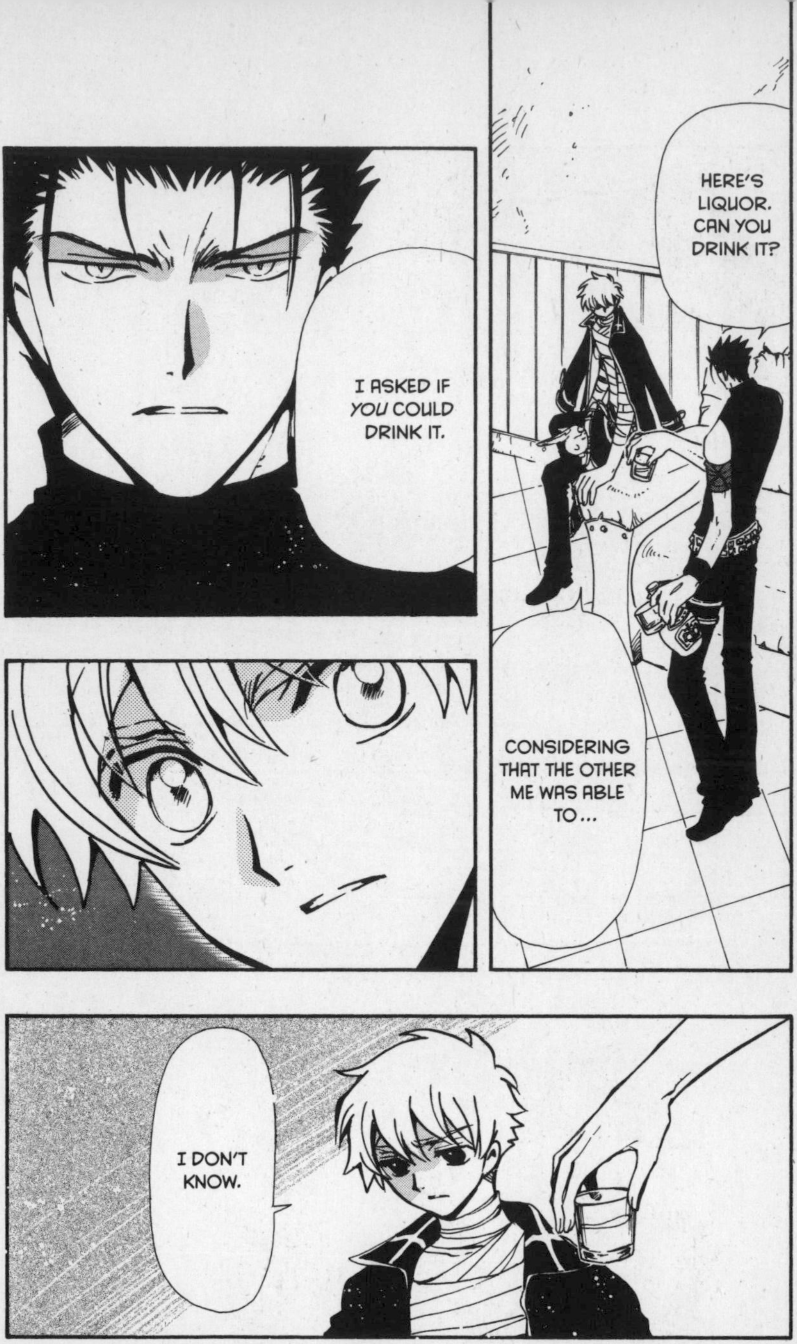
HERE'S LIQUOR. CAN YOU DRINK IT?
CONSIDERING THAT THE OTHER ME WAS ABLE TO...
I ASKED IF *YOU* COULD DRINK IT.
I DON'T KNOW.

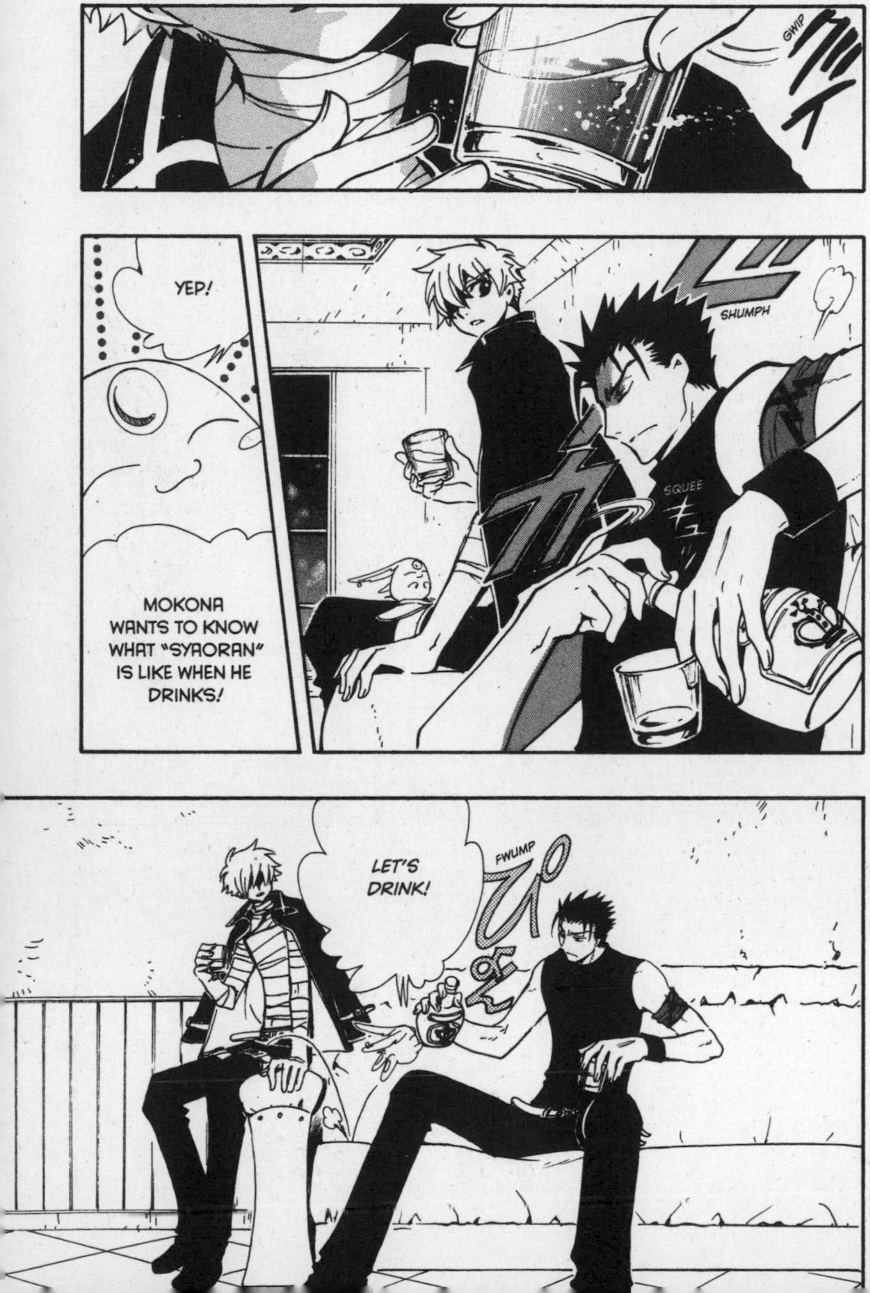
GWIP
SHUMPH
SQUEE
YEP!
MOKONA WANTS TO KNOW WHAT "SYAORAN" IS LIKE WHEN HE DRINKS!
FWUMP
LET'S DRINK!

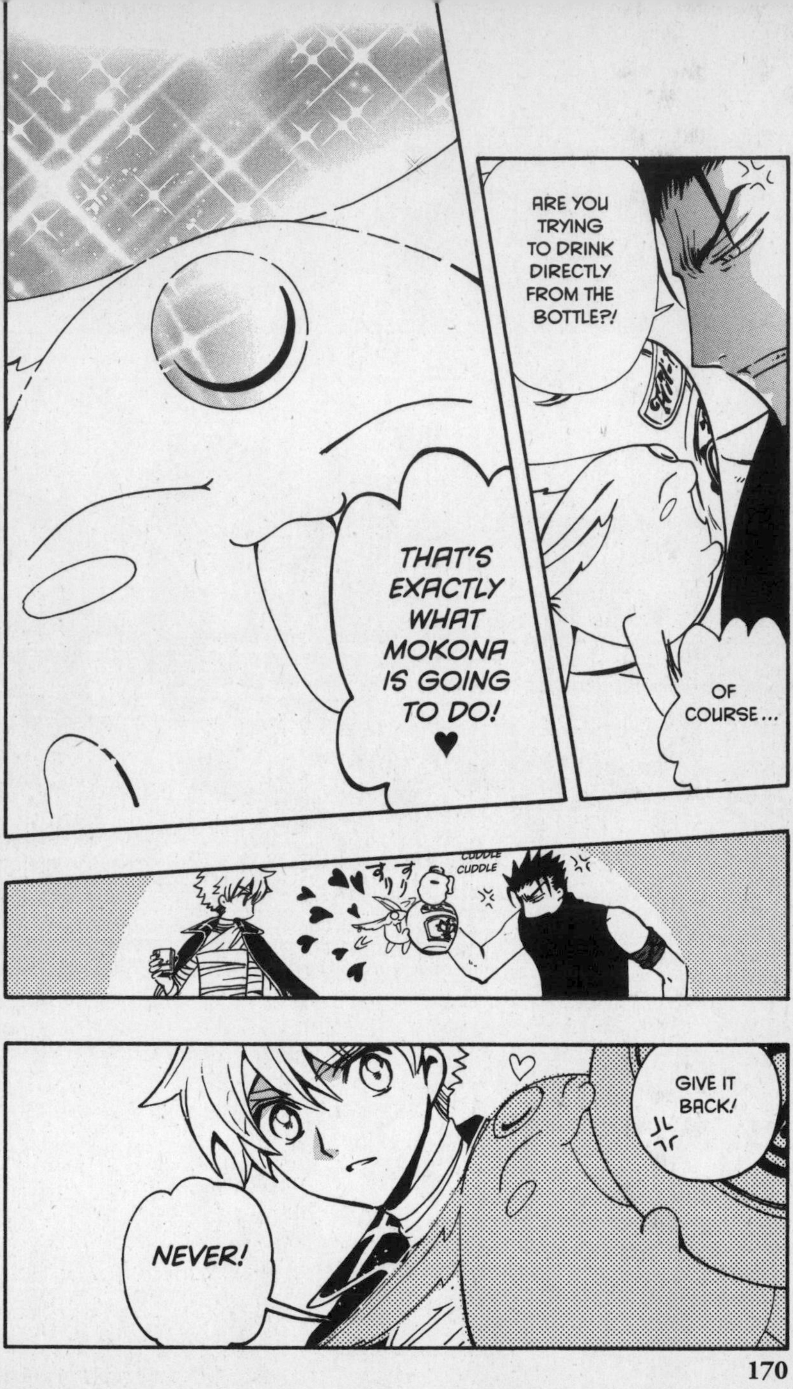
ARE YOU TRYING TO DRINK DIRECTLY FROM THE BOTTLE?!
OF COURSE...
THAT'S EXACTLY WHAT MOKONA IS GOING TO DO! ♥
CUDDLE CUDDLE
GIVE IT BACK!
NEVER!

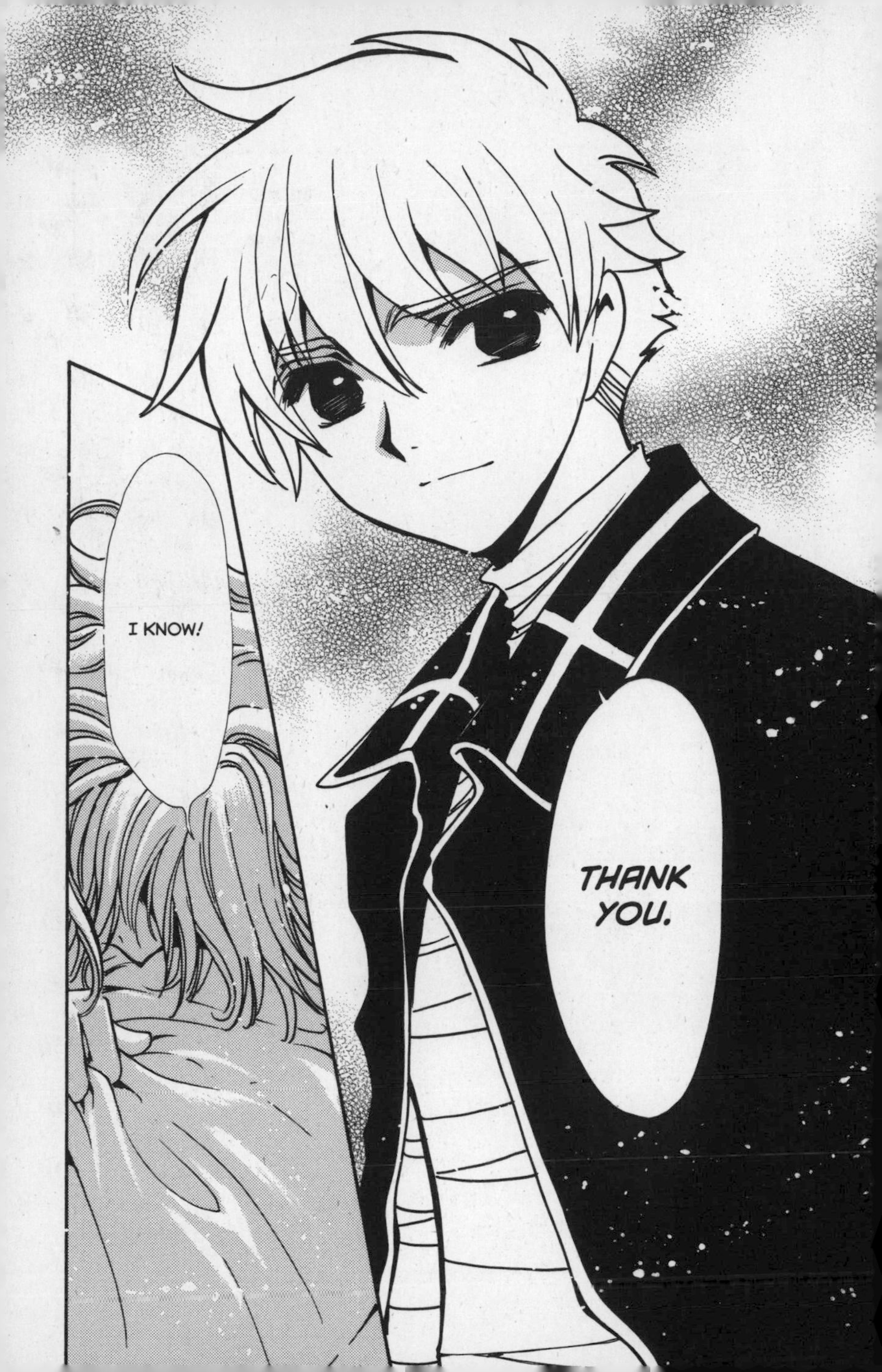
THANK YOU.
I KNOW!

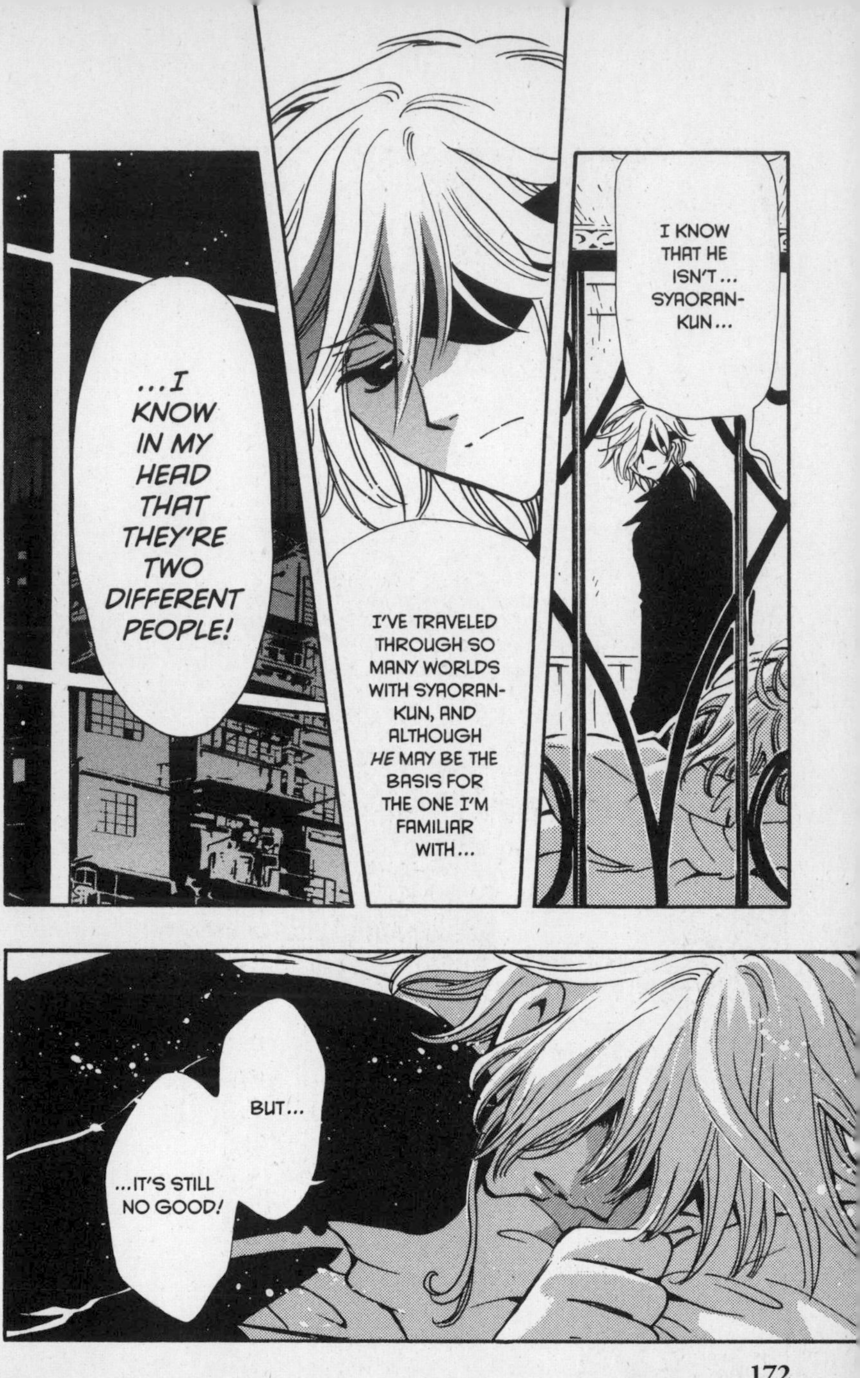
I KNOW THAT HE ISN'T... SYAORAN-KUN...
I'VE TRAVELED THROUGH SO MANY WORLDS WITH SYAORAN-KUN, AND ALTHOUGH *HE* MAY BE THE BASIS FOR THE ONE I'M FAMILIAR WITH...
...I KNOW IN MY HEAD THAT THEY'RE TWO DIFFERENT PEOPLE!
BUT...
...IT'S STILL NO GOOD!

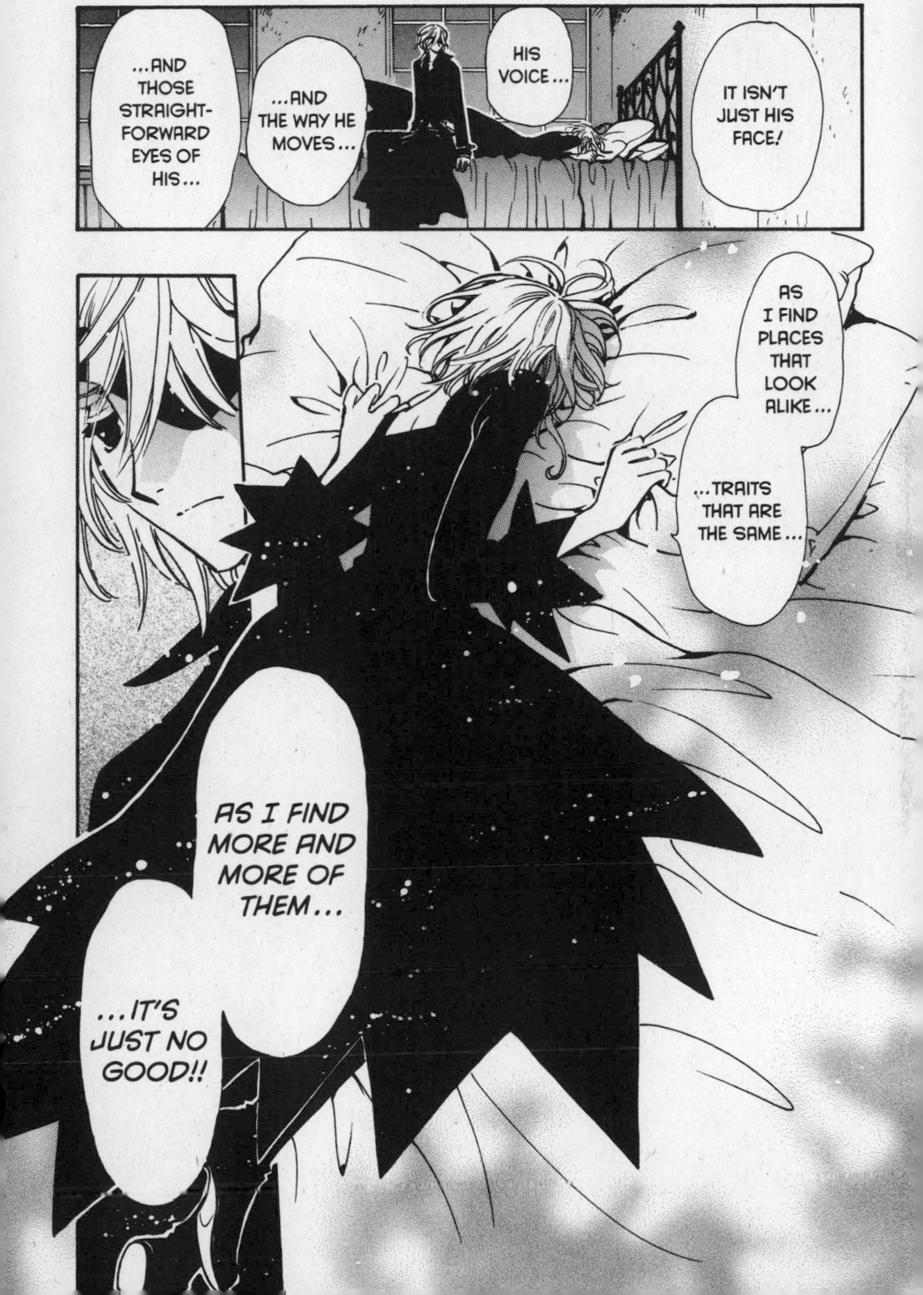
IT ISN'T JUST HIS FACE!
HIS VOICE...
...AND THE WAY HE MOVES...
...AND THOSE STRAIGHT-FORWARD EYES OF HIS...
AS I FIND PLACES THAT LOOK ALIKE...
...TRAITS THAT ARE THE SAME...
AS I FIND MORE AND MORE OF THEM...
...IT'S JUST NO GOOD!!

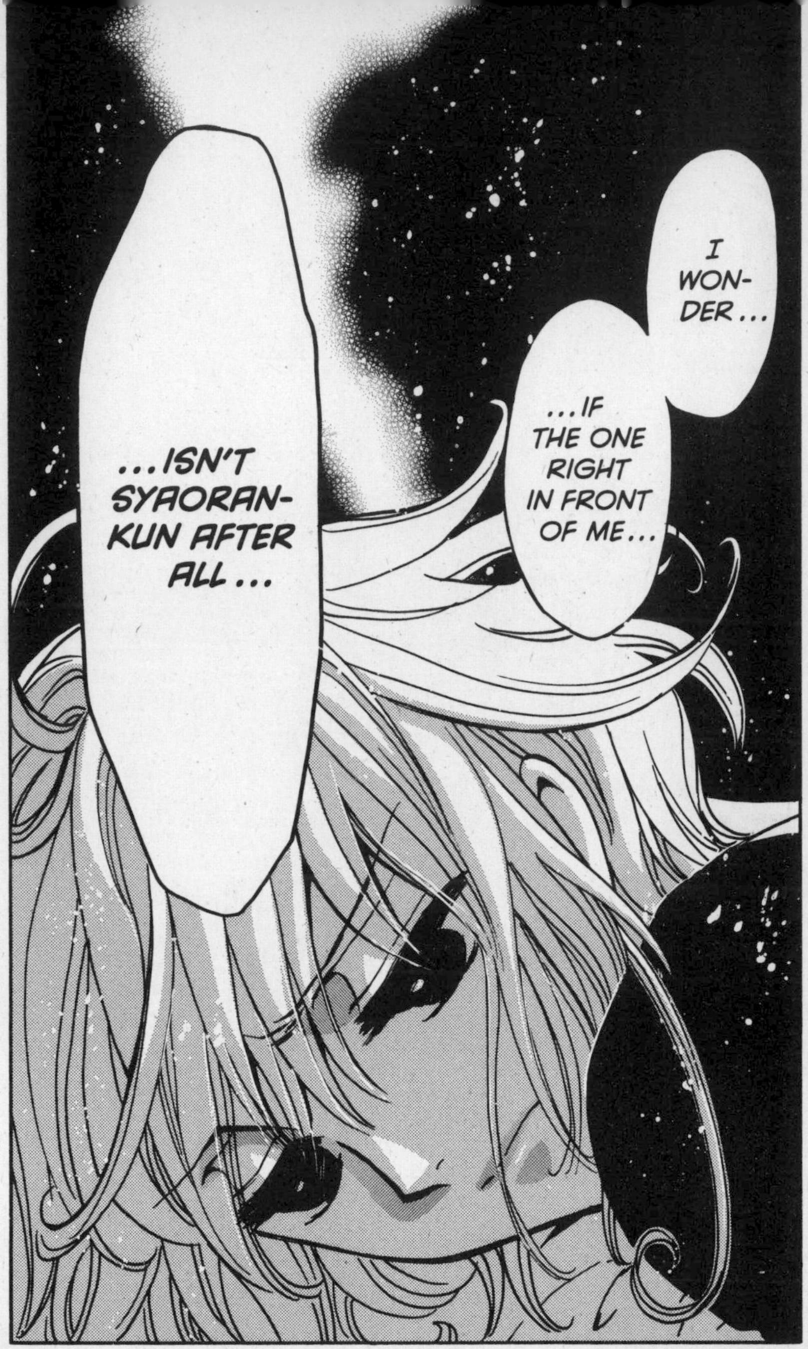
I WONDER...
...IF THE ONE RIGHT IN FRONT OF ME...
...ISN'T SYAORAN-KUN AFTER ALL...

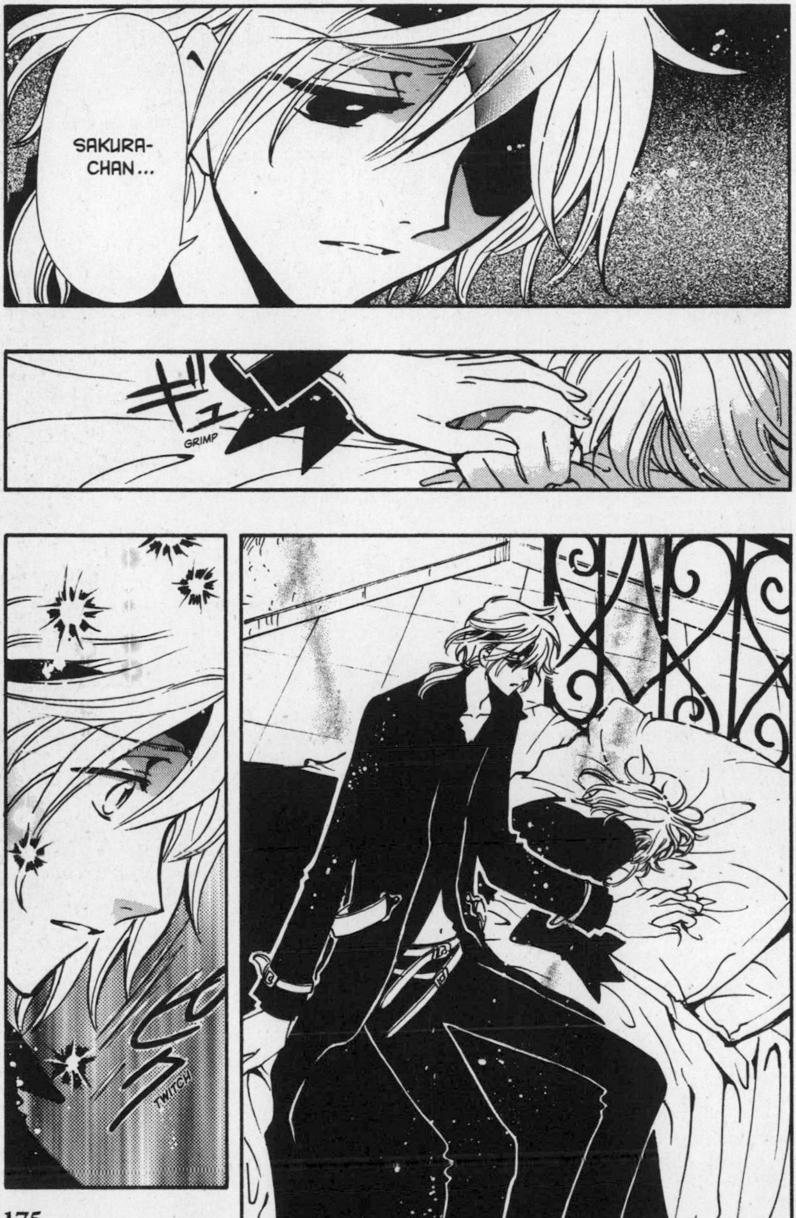
SAKURA-
CHAN...
ギュ
GRIMP
TWITCH

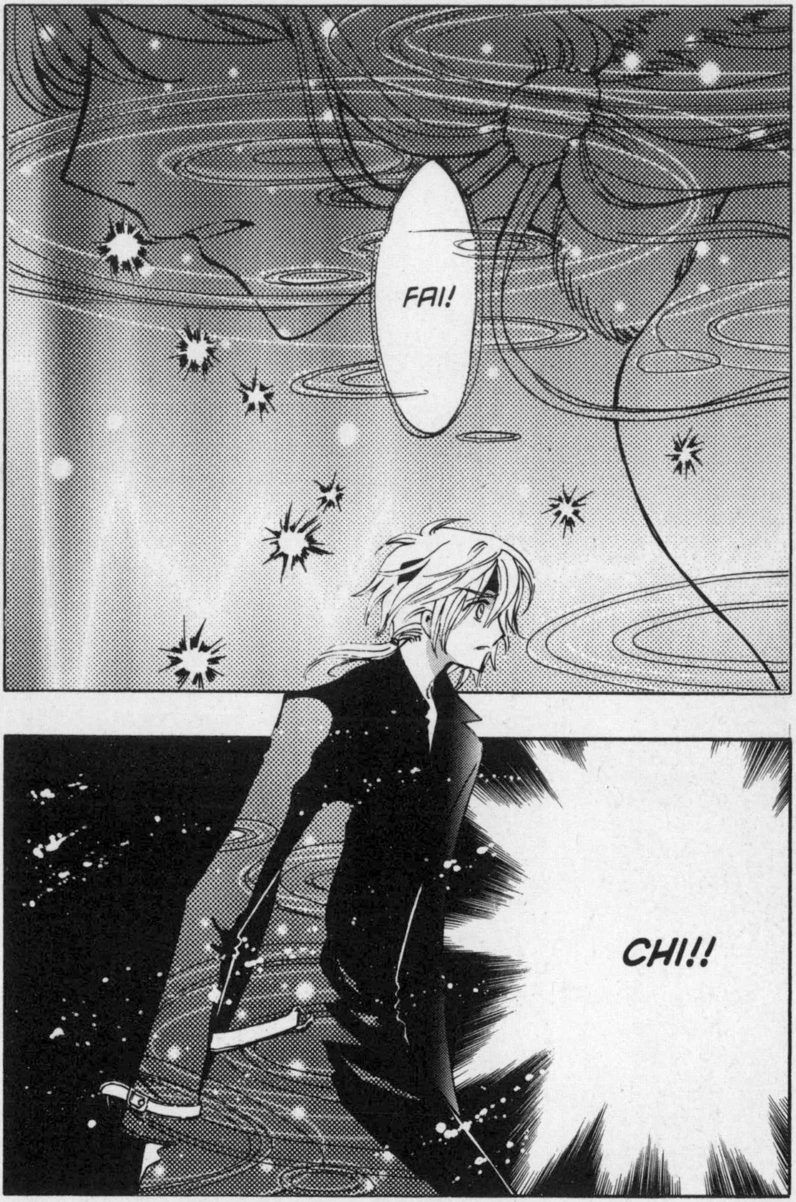
FAI!
CHI!!

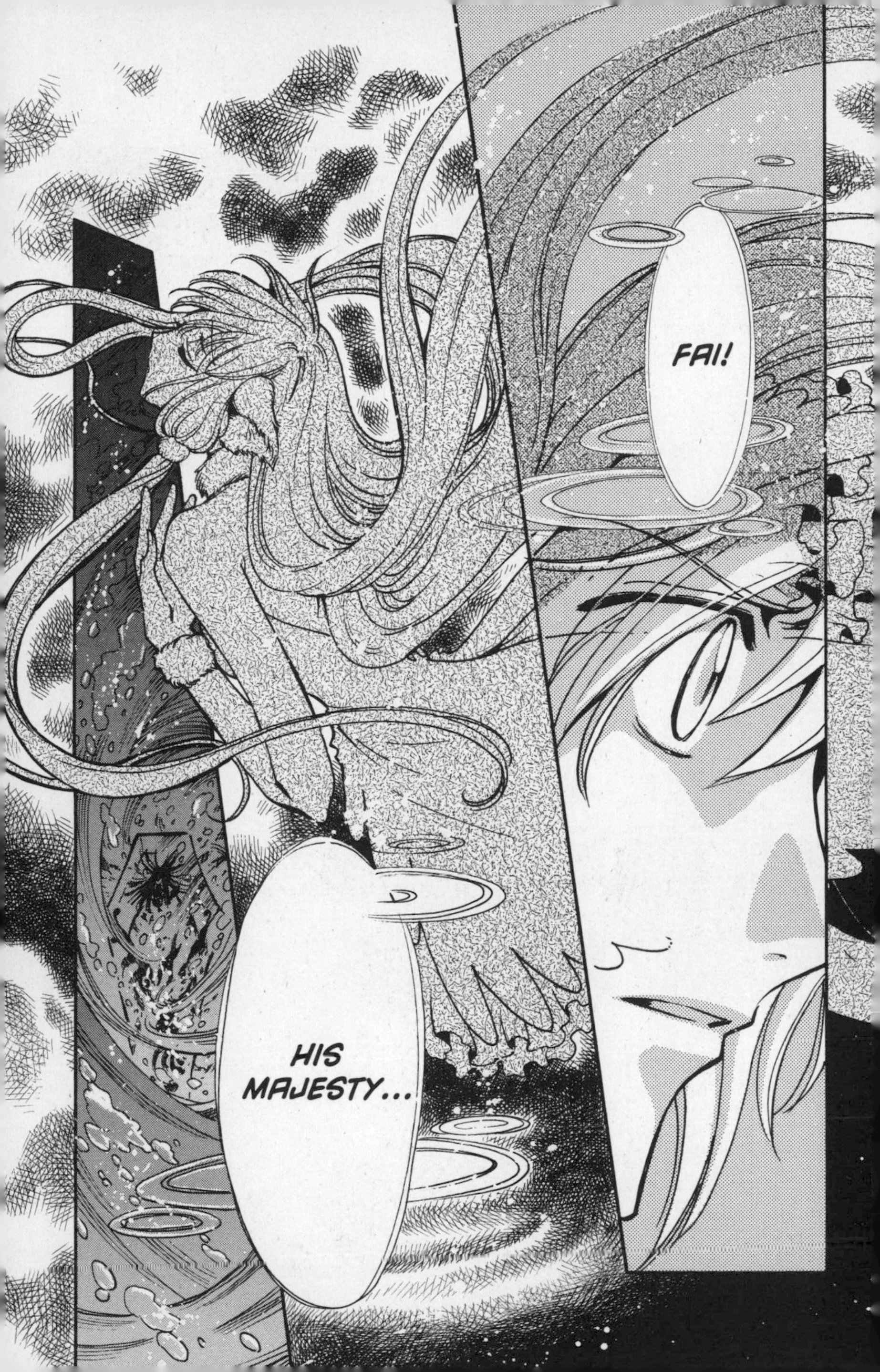
FAI!
HIS MAJESTY...

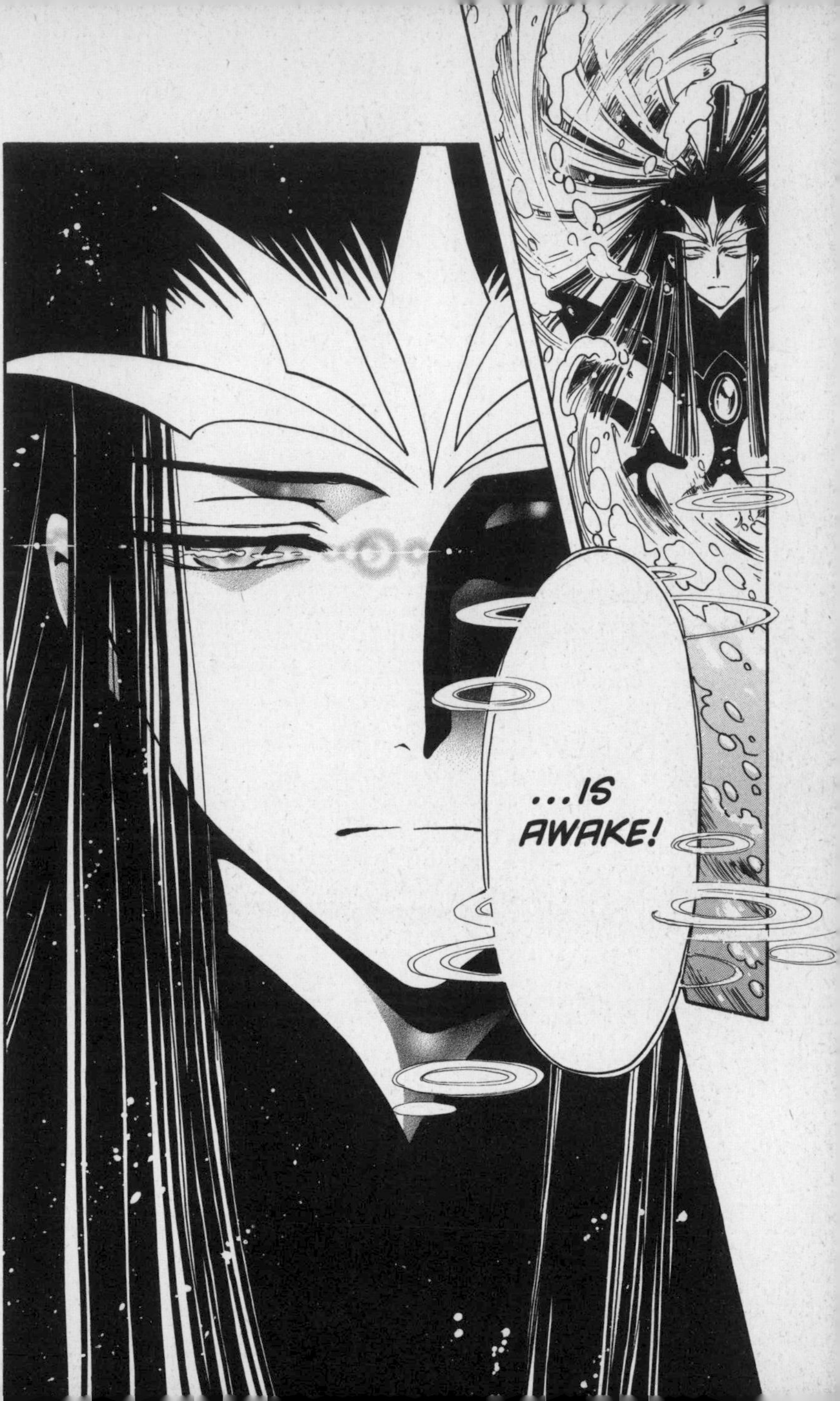
...IS AWAKE!

To Be Continued

About the Creators

CLAMP is a group of four women who have become the most popular manga artists in America—Ageha Ohkawa, Mokona, Satsuki Igarashi, and Tsubaki Nekoi. They started out as *doujinshi* (fan comics) creators, but their skill and craft brought them to the attention of publishers very quickly. Their first work from a major publisher was *RG Veda*, but their first mass success was with *Magic Knight Rayearth*. From there, they went on to write many series, including Cardcaptor Sakura and Chobits, two of the most popular manga in the United States. Like many Japanese manga artists, they prefer to avoid the spotlight, and little is known about them personally.

CLAMP is currently publishing three series in Japan: Tsubasa and xxxHOLiC with Kodansha and Gohou Drug with Kadokawa.

Translation Notes

Japanese is a tricky language for most Westerners, and translation is often more art than science. For your edification and reading pleasure, here are notes on some of the places where we could have gone in a different direction in our translation of the work or where a Japanese cultural reference is used.

BECAUSE EVERYTHING IS HITSUZEN.

Hitsuzen, page 25

Those who are reading Tsubasa without reading the cross-over book xxxHOLiC might have forgotten that *hitsuzen* is a word meaning a foreordained, unchangeable, necessary destiny. Yûko's favorite line of dialog in xxxHOLiC is, "There is no such thing as coincidence in this world. The only thing is hitsuzen."

Vi la princia, page 37

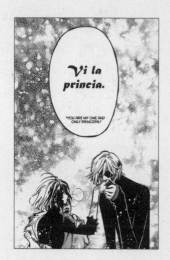

Vi la princia.
"YOU ARE MY ONE AND ONLY PRINCESS."

In the Japanese version, the Japanese language translation of Fai's statement was the larger of the two. "Vi la princia," was *katakana* subtitles (*furigana*) next to the Japanese. I used my best judgment with regard to transliterating sounds that the *katakana* can't handle (such as the distinction between "L"s and "R"s). And I asked the letterer to make Fai's sounds (rather than his meaning) the larger element in the word balloon. There may have been a better way to handle the situation, but it seemed best at the time I was translating it.

If I can protect you, I'd like to, page 44

This is one of those Japanese sentences where I have to cringe while translating it. The sentence is subjectless and objectless, leaving just verbs. A direct translation would be "Can protect, then want to protect." Obviously the subject is "I," and the situation makes it pretty obvious that the object (the one to be protected) is Sakura. But CLAMP chooses their words with care, and it's not outside the realm of possibility that what the original Syaoran wants to protect is not Sakura herself, but some aspect of her . . . such as her destiny. (Doesn't that sound CLAMP-like?) Still, to make the sentence as vague as the original would have made a rather dramatic declaration laughable, so I added subject and object to the line. (I may weep over this decision around volume 21 or so, but that's what I get for translating a series by terrific authors while it's still being serialized.)

IN THIS CHESS GAME, THE FIGHTING SPEED AND STRENGTH OF THE PIECES ARE DECIDED BY THE WILLPOWER OF THE MASTER.

Chess, page 86

No, it doesn't look much like the chess that we know, but there was no term substitution in the translation. Eagle called it chess (in *katakana* spelling), and that's the word used in the translation.

Infinity, page 94

Most of the worlds that start with the words, "The Country of" in the English translation have the *kanji* pronounced *koku* (which means country/nation) in their Japanese names. Exceptions still usually have *koku* in their names, but it is a part of a larger word that includes the *kanji* for *koku*. For example, in the case of the Hanshin Republic, the Japanese word *kyôwakoku* when taken as a whole means "republic" even though the final *kanji* when taken alone would mean "country." However, the world Infinity is unusual in that there is no *koku* connected to the word. Written on the feather was nothing more than the English word written in *katakana* letters, Infinity.

Infinity

Drinking from the bottle, page 170

When a group are drinking together in Japan, it is considered rude to drink directly from the bottle. Drinks are normally poured into glasses, and one's glass is subsequently kept full by the other drinkers. (Similarly, one should be aware of the emptiness of others' glasses in one's party, and be ready to refill them when daylight can be seen between the rim and the liquor line of the glass.) When one wants to stop drinking, one must either forcefully protect one's cup from neighbors trying to refill it, or use the less aggressive tactic of leaving one's cup full. Kurogane is known to drink from the bottle, but he doesn't do it in a group situation. Mokona, as mentioned in the translation notes for volume 9, either doesn't know about manners or doesn't care.

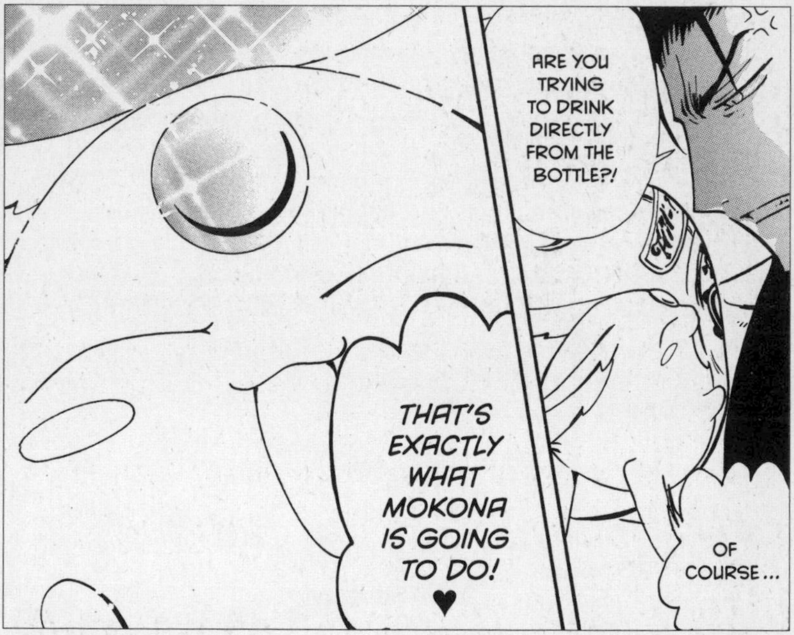
ARE YOU TRYING TO DRINK DIRECTLY FROM THE BOTTLE?!
OF COURSE...
THAT'S EXACTLY WHAT MOKONA IS GOING TO DO! ♥

TOMARE!

[STOP!]

You're going the wrong way!

Manga is a completely different type of reading experience.

To start at the *beginning*, go to the *end*!

That's right! Authentic manga is read the traditional Japanese way—from right to left. Exactly the *opposite* of how American books are read. It's easy to follow: Just go to the other end of the book, and read each page—and each panel—from right side to left side, starting at the top right. Now you're experiencing manga as it was meant to be!